They Call Me CO

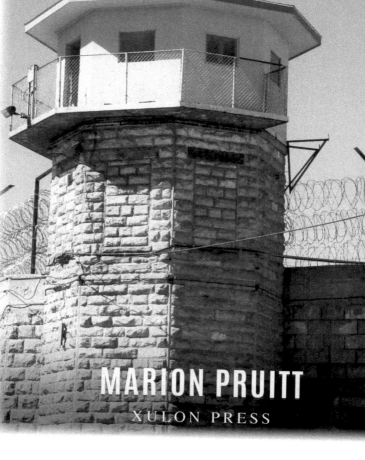

THEY
CALL ME CO

MARION PRUITT

XULON PRESS

Xulon Press
2301 Lucien Way #415
Maitland, FL 32751
407.339.4217
www.xulonpress.com

Scripture quotations taken from the American Standard Version
(ASV)–*public domain.*

Edited by Xulon Press.

Printed in the United States of America.

ISBN-13: 978-1-5456-3124-9

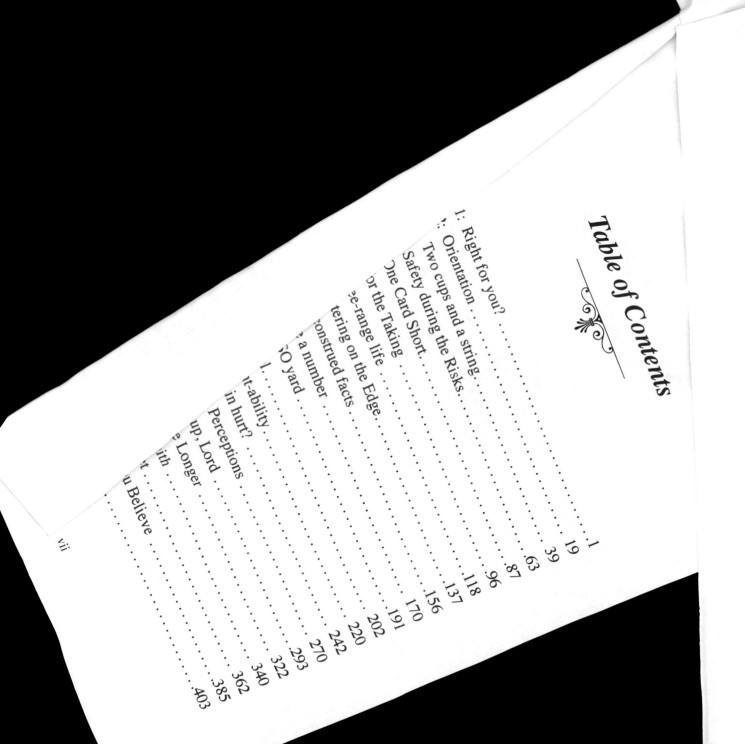

Table of Contents

I dedicated all name changes to facilitate my story to be told
confidential of all prison location and persons
especially to:
Auntie Marge and Uncle Howie (Ofc. Howard Pruitt, Chicago
including the helpful support of thanks to
Heidi Lowe and Monica Velasco
in His glory!

CHAPTER 1

Right for you?

*T*he finest citizens had been considered by the State Department of Corrections, who were cherry-picked among the Peace Officers in law enforcement that distinguished the police cousins apart of the general public. It was the academy selected for the Correctional Officer, where I received the badge for the enclosed community in prison.

It was the day I saw five of the aspiring cadets, gathering just inside the front lobby door. They waited all primped up in their uniforms, facing their fifth week of training. I longed to hope for the best in the maximum lockdown of my unit, when I was held aside.

I could've worked the floor with the rest of my team. The Worker's Compensation physician reassigned light duty, but it was my injury. Just like anyone else, I ignored my physical boundaries. Facing retirement's tenure became the weak link, as I hid the pain obvious among the inmates. My foot tendon tear was good enough to work somewhere else, or whether I was needed at all.

I was the extra, as the up-and-coming officers arrived. I gawked! I froze! My life-time events rushed through my mind, when I was no longer in charge. I could've relaxed, lowering my guard, when I stood inside the bullet protected glass for a closer look.

The budding officers were still in training at the academy, when I realized that training was never going to be over. They collectively dropped off their clear backpacks on the counter before they moved through the scanner. Everything should've been just fine, except for the camera's lenses that couldn't detect the back of CO (Correctional Officer) Gordon's 'gatekeeper' post. I kept an eye out of the searches they owned, who understood the protocols, but their contents were spilled upside down onto the table, as if nothing was sacred. Surely, they were trustworthy who stood aside, but they felt violated. Their belongings were intentionally mistreated that felt too painful, since some things just couldn't put a stop to that.

They grew more indignant on their faces, infuriated by the way their personal property had been cruelly handled, but it was all valid. I couldn't ignore their pursed lips, but there was no reason to be offended. They were just being messed with (them). It was just a game, which was nothing too serious, since it wasn't my place... like before. I learned how to detach from anything personal, but I didn't belong which wasn't my place for the easy way out. "It's alright, don't worry. Just let them look" I thought and shrugged it to myself, as I let them experience it for themselves. The cadets were meticulously scrutinized, who collect his disheveled goods aside for the next one at a time.

CO Gordon barked: "Wait at the bench," as the tempers sucked up by his firm finger that pointed toward a room to the next area. CO Gordon's demeanor was dry and cold, almost robotic, while they obediently hobbled away to regroup again. They barely carried all of their things in their stocking feet for their newly arch-support shoes to be laced back up with a slight smile who felt wonderful all over again.

"They're so young." I murmured through a subtle head-shake, who I hoped that they were the fast-learners within ear shot of my fellow officer nearby.

I dedicated all name changes to facilitate my story to be told
confidential of all prison location and persons
especially to:
Auntie Marge and Uncle Howie (Ofc. Howard Pruitt, Chicago PD)
including the helpful support of thanks to
Heidi Lowe and Monica Velasco
in His glory!

Table of Contents

CHAPTER 1

Right for you?

*T*he finest citizens had been considered by the State Department of Corrections, who were cherry-picked among the Peace Officers in law enforcement that distinguished the police cousins apart of the general public. It was the academy selected for the Correctional Officer, where I received the badge for the enclosed community in prison.

It was the day I saw five of the aspiring cadets, gathering just inside the front lobby door. They waited all primped up in their uniforms, facing their fifth week of training. I longed to hope for the best in the maximum lockdown of my unit, when I was held aside.

I could've worked the floor with the rest of my team. The Worker's Compensation physician reassigned light duty, but it was my injury. Just like anyone else, I ignored my physical boundaries. Facing retirement's tenure became the weak link, as I hid the pain obvious among the inmates. My foot tendon tear was good enough to work somewhere else, or whether I was needed at all.

I was the extra, as the up-and-coming officers arrived. I gawked! I froze! My life-time events rushed through my mind, when I was no longer in charge. I could've relaxed, lowering my guard, when I stood inside the bullet protected glass for a closer look.

The budding officers were still in training at the academy, when I realized that training was never going to be over. They collectively dropped off their clear backpacks on the counter before they moved through the scanner. Everything should've been just fine, except for the camera's lenses that couldn't detect the back of CO (Correctional Officer) Gordon's 'gatekeeper' post. I kept an eye out of the searches they owned, who understood the protocols, but their contents were spilled upside down onto the table, as if nothing was sacred. Surely, they were trustworthy who stood aside, but they felt violated. Their belongings were intentionally mistreated that felt too painful, since some things just couldn't put a stop to that.

They grew more indignant on their faces, infuriated by the way their personal property had been cruelly handled, but it was all valid. I couldn't ignore their pursed lips, but there was no reason to be offended. They were just being messed with (them). It was just a game, which was nothing too serious, since it wasn't my place... like before. I learned how to detach from anything personal, but I didn't belong which wasn't my place for the easy way out. "It's alright, don't worry. Just let them look" I thought and shrugged it to myself, as I let them experience it for themselves. The cadets were meticulously scrutinized, who collect his disheveled goods aside for the next one at a time.

CO Gordon barked: "Wait at the bench," as the tempers sucked up by his firm finger that pointed toward a room to the next area. CO Gordon's demeanor was dry and cold, almost robotic, while they obediently hobbled away to regroup again. They barely carried all of their things in their stocking feet for their newly arch-support shoes to be laced back up with a slight smile who felt wonderful all over again.

"They're so young." I murmured through a subtle head-shake, who I hoped that they were the fast-learners within ear shot of my fellow officer nearby.

I ran the same post in the Main Control room during the grave-yard shift by myself, except I crowded in with an extra body on the day shift. Its full 360 view of windows that also inundated the entire wall above the camera screens, where I perched safely from anyone else. I operated the prison's communication equipment that cluttered its counters for everything returned back in order from the prior shifts. I adjusted easily to pitch in automatically, but it was quite differently in comparison throughout the feast or famine nights.

Sick time had been accrued on the books, but none of that could have been collected enough to recuperate at home. At least I didn't lose my job, step down, or fired, when Ibuprofen couldn't cut it. I slugged an orthopedic boot during work, but it was expected for an extra partner, since someone always got injured with someone else, and it was just my turn.

I didn't think it could've been me, as if I was invincible to tolerate anything, but I was wrong. Blind obedience affected every order, but I wasn't alone. How foolishly we became a bit too over-confident, until we were comfortably broken in, or inevitably worn down one injury after another, where 'the extra' sat out in the Main Control. The OHN (Occupational Health Nurse) monitored our progress to heal, and many of us sucked it up to deny that weakening and vulnerable hint that demanded no-inmate contact to recover. The OHN fought my side that trumped my protection, until I was cleared to return on the job. My welfare had been negotiated by the Worker's Compensation Department to be retained within the career. I sheepishly admitted, or overstepped my limits, but we all pushed it to the maximum efforts. "You could've been injured anywhere," coined that final excuse that wore down DOC's unmet budget against FMLA sick-time. Either way, I stayed on.

"This place is turning into a god-damned fish bowl." Officer Hansen grumbled under his breathe, when the cadets paraded through in a weekly basis. He reached over me, scooping up the ID cards from the sliding trap drawer that logged into their name entries.

"Ready?" CO James' powering voice carried all throughout the lobby, who seemed to magically appear in perfect timing, as CO Hansen buzzed him in from the Administration Department. I'd forgotten about the door that was never used on the graves, which the office bustled in the daytime shift, when the cadets almost tripped over each other in attention.

CO Hansen flew their IDs into the trap drawer to the other side of my room, as he tapped the computer touch screen with one smooth maneuver with each cue to urged them along. The solid security door held behind The Special Management Unit, respectfully called 'the Lockdown'. Officer James mindless illustrate each ID, promising them right back from another sliding drawer, but it was their first decision to be collected... inside, to process: first things first. Normally the sound of each locking mechanism would've been welcomed by any other push into the prison from the lobby, until each cadet might've been tempted to make a complete 180 slam behind that door, who stared. There was an obvious hesitation, before their eyes darted back and forth for each other's support, or whether they'd survive the first half way toward graduation's parting ways of their career options' elsewhere.

"Don't forget to pick up your ID cards," CO James repeated his memorized tour without a thought, while the cadets complied inside, nonetheless.

"I hope the hell they don't put them all on my unit," CO Hansen bumped into my chair, where I ducked from his computer's touch screen for the next door of the sally port.

The five cadets shuffled together than the normal strides, which was timed by the automatic magnet locks, until they ran after that unmistakable pin drop... trapped!

"Ha! They look like they're gonna piss themselves!" CO Hansen laughed. I laughed too, but not for the same reason. I couldn't believe how flippantly CO Hanson made fun of their expense, which could've planted the fear of God in a good jerk of truth… once before.

The academy coached and prepared them, who were cloaked within their uniforms, when I was also about to face the harsh truth. How many different ways experienced the same messages? They all got that surprise, shock, or each awakening ounce of strength arrived together at the beginning, when I saw how they split, whether their fragile pact had a bond at all.

At first the cadets followed in unison. They were all glued together, believed to be the elite. They were 'the shit', except CO Hansen knew who operated the controls. One entering gate had to be closed before the other end buzzed, planned a bit prematurely, who were embarrassed for himself. They abandoned their classmates who sprinted, trying to make it, which was a little too late… of another lesson! CO Hansen took what little joy he filled in his seat, as I swatted the back of his shoulder.

"Shame on you!" I scowled. The cadets were in a startling panic, and CO James casually flagged at CO Gordon for its lock release again.

My post allowed enough time to process their conjured fun that wasn't funny to me. I still remembered how it affected every lie of forgiveness against the childish games throughout my life. Their enjoyment grew tired, realizing of what deserves more than a slap on the wrist. CO James also behaved a bit too cocky, showing off, or playing down the dares, as if it could've been me. I'd shrugged, tried to move forward, but I carried every hit to spare my loved ones. I had to hide the pain and recovered later, while I refused the option to give in… or quit and walk away.

How many recruits had been pressed against the edge with every test, which continued through the week? Any one of them could've made it an about-face right and never seen again. And, who was going to plea forgiveness that couldn't fill of the rosters or deny the harm? CO James just let it roll, as if nothing happened.

The cadets became all the more anxious throughout the tour. The dead-man's perimeter walked toward the depth core of prison, as CO James pointed at one thing after another element of courage that became normal over the years.

The daunting walk approached their ominously grey structure that also wrenched in my gut, as I watched how they clung closely behind CO James who had nothing more than his mercies. He hardly made eye contact. He seemed to mechanically point out DOC's security devices, as their nervous caution forced even closer together, when the cells kicked up a living example of the perfect criminals.

Wing two just went off, simultaneously banging at anything available in the roaring noise that elevated beyond its safe decibels. Its slamming was deafening, shouting who were also wolf-like howling at the top of their voices, when CO James just spoke louder as if it was okay to focus on his voice, alone. The inmates were retaliating that spilled outside their walls, regardlessly demanded anything (or nothing at all), but the cadets were impossible to read their lead.

In a lot of times, the inmates were merely causing a nuisance, but I wasn't always there to check out the disruptions for the other officers' posts. The COs grew too nerve-wracking, as if they cried "wolf" a few too many times, like when their portable cell-phone was taken away to be recharged who quieted down for an answer.

I stared back at the cadets, who were swallowed inside the prison by the lone cadet's nudge who stood below the warning signs boldly spelled out that captivated the high voltage hum. There always seems to have that one, who rose his head slowly to the top of the coiled razor wire that barely balanced and clearly swung... or a wave. It might've thumbed its distance threat, or mocking his attention at the fence edge near the fall, when I returned to my work at Main Control.

"I heard that our complex got seventeen from the academy this month." I mentioned the news about the other units that would only guess how many came through, but CO Hansen didn't want to hear anything more than a numbers' game. How many applicants didn't matter who filled the academy classes, where we were always short-handed with our lockdowns coming in as they left all too soon.

I went right back to the piles of key sets and hand-held radios that were dumped in the heaps on the countertop, and I pitched in. I didn't have to be told to update the inventory, which was a given. The key sets were restored by the specific cabinets wide opened, as I double checked the abandoned hooks and missing equipment slots of the more tedious tasks from my partner's hands. Multitasking lived ADHD in the whelm of my world, while CO Hansen seemed to shut down to focus with another officer's work alongside of him.

The officers had been sorted out from their versatile posts all around, while I'd fought against its redundancy to be prepared for the next staffing, while the daily rosters swapped the officers throughout the other units, where I remained connected of each one in view throughout the prisons.

However, there was another picture behind the scenes. The global budgets wield its own sense of power, where DOC also monitored business that didn't satisfy its pay during the depressed economy. Private firms had been cut back. Heads of households were robbed from their work titles that downsized to meet the financial needs, until DOC tantalized their openings (or last resorts). Roadside bill-boards and the parking lot fliers advertised its work in the prisons, when the academy swelled with every graduating class more than ever before, but the turnover rate strained its training expense.

Too many officers tried, who walked quietly away. They shook their heads, who quit. They'd left as soon as another recruit barely survived, until it was the time when I stood in line, and I jumped in with both feet. Anyone else's job could've fed the family to be carried over temporarily, except I came in for the career.

DOC adjusted the budget with our safety equipment, which included the private contractors to wear the state-issued duty belt to carry pepper spray, two-way radios, and the PPE (personal protection equipment) kits, regardless of the trained officers. The security staff additionally supplied a stab vest and face shield during the two-tier housing pods. If it didn't make us any more cumbersome, it made us all the more aware of the increased risk as the numbers continued to roll backwards.

Furthermore, the post orders reworded into policy by softening its severity on paper, while the staff assaults made it appear more attractive, which also redesigned a step-down program for the inmates with a promise toward rehabilitation that rested on the shoulders of everyone's responsibility.

But, ah recidivism. That was the ugliest word, where nobody cared to hear about that. The inmates were reinstated, who were just as quickly revolved through the inmates, who packed the prisons full, instead of the officers who were headed out... one way only. The lack of rehabilitation weighed the blame. Failures stressed its ratio imbalances, when DOC bled out the financing and staff toward a regrouping halt.

"Did I tell you that I put in my request to transfer out of the lockdowns?" I timed any chance to say in between the roaring cycles of the air conditioners that were mounted right above our roof.

"Sure, why not?" CO Hansen did nothing to invite an ongoing conversation. "What unit did you put in for?" He had to ask, worried of another ping-of-pain by another lost team player. I applied for the move out of the lockdowns where the violent inmates were also moved to be relocated from their isolated cells. They graduated to a lower level and free-range yard, who once distinguished the inmates between the two lockdown units of our complex. They were segregated which specified mentally damaged inmates between both kind of risks, but I preferred to leave the details in another book about the lockdowns, altogether.

"Hamilton Unit." I eventually answered, as I adjusted our slow responses and emotional energy, during our separate corners that demanded a zero percent chance of errors. "I visited the Warden's office yesterday." I knew I had to leave behind the grueling stairs. "I'm next in line." I hinted to offer him the hope to leave too, but he turned an eye toward me as if I was a traitor.

"Why the hell would you want to work with those perverts?" He asked, showing no desire to support me.

"An inmate is an inmate." I said, while he shook his head at me in disbelief.

"Did you ever take the time to read some of those escape fliers? Do you have any clue who're capable of?" He ranted, trying to build up against my fellow officer... held against me.

"No, and I make it a point **not** to." I threw it right back at him, resenting his decision over me, regardless of my transfer from the lockdowns for another set problems. I already knew about the sex crimes, where they were protected in Hamilton Unit. They had to have been difficult to manage the women among the inmates, while I worked without prejudice of any other unit. "Sin is sin." I growled under my breath, as if it was the final word, but he just got started.

"Don't tell me you're a 'hug-a-thug'?" CO Hansen taunted by egging me on, but I didn't react his insults to take me on.

He had been employed by DOC for as long as I had been there to create their own style on the job, but anyone could've grown all the more cynical. A lot of the COs couldn't justify the respect of any SO, where the other prisoned inmates were fired up against the SO's worse crime. The convicted inmates earned their lowest low. They were the most disgusting level of crime, in comparison to any other crimes. The SOs were calculating predators who destroyed the most innocent or vulnerable 'pickin's', but their insatiable desires still prowled throughout their lives, where I chose to float among them. What other officers would sign up for that?

"Look, they're coming back!" I nudged CO Hansen to press the button coming back, since he cut out the ol' shenanigans by our new policies.

"They just went in for their bullshit pep talk (with the Captain)." CO Hansen relented, knowing how he had to change. "Who the hell do you think is going to be training?" He questioned out loud, wondering if any of them would complete the rest of the week, or whether they'd continue to see any of them again.

"We don't have that sink-or-swim mentality anymore." I realized underneath my breath. "Remember what it was like at briefing?" I saved it for later, once the white noise rumble stopped between the cycles. "We'd freak out during their assigned posts," I rambled on. "Someone always said something like: 'I never worked that post before.' And then, we got something like: 'well, you won't be able to say that again after today.'" I started to lighten it up, laughing off the trial-by-fire orders, some time ago. "Don't you remember how it was when you first started?" But I should've kept it to myself. He was irritated, and finally blew.

"It doesn't matter. You and I . . .well," CO Hansen paced, although he was unable to walk much more than a turned around, back and forth in place. He paused, needing a moment who practically stuttered uncontrollably, when he daggered right at me eye to eye. I was cornered and couldn't get away. I cringed to brace for more, as he came too closely in my face! "We're old school!" He planted a moment of truth to put it out there as clearly as possible. "This is a whole new generation coming in." His hands waved in the air with a feminine sort of gesture, dramatized a sweeter and touchy-feel using every bit to drive it home.

I took it. I heard what he said. It wasn't about anything wrong for a rebuttal or a comeback. I understood. CO Hansen and I weren't raised that way anymore.

We came from the baby-booming era. It was a dog-eat-dog world, back then. We fought our way up the ladder, or we gratefully landed to appreciate any common-labor work available. It was the time when governmental aid was too proudly frowned upon, while the elite went on to college by the prized few entrepreneurs to etch the future.

My dad had my advice that "you will either get ahead by using your head or by your back," as I'd heard it all coming back. People, like CO Hansen and I, fought among the greatest numbers for its foundation. We were the youngest adults overwhelming the work-forces. The magical age at eighteen, when we were dubbed: mature. Ready or not, it was time to be sent out for a living who flooded in all at once. There were three times the amount of the jobs of the prior generation, where I made it into the 'foot in the door' base. I started out low, as I strived every next pay rate higher, but I had to change over the years, adjusting out of the industrial age and into the computers, until my career faced its final stage toward retirement.

"I guess." I was almost apologetic. What could I say? I grew up strong-willed and a bit rebellious. I was determined all the more, as if I sprinted toward the final race. The new 'reward-not-punish' mentality replaced the 'tough-love' parenting styles of the past, when the political parties penetrated the penal pendulum swung toward the left.

The Department of Corrections was respectfully called the Department of Change within the whispers among the security staff. We recited our oath to dutifully serve and protect once we came out of the academy, until we understood the evolutionary process that also swept us up in a constant flux. A stifling weight wore a heavi-ness during the following briefs every day. Shockwaves riveted through every prison that was reevaluate to accommodate the risks, while I swore the oath to provide the better humanitarian lifestyle… of the law.

The inmates complained against any trivial claim, until another petition was tabled in the courts. I dismissed the lawsuits that came up of any other issue that would never end! But then, they were heard. They cried for better treatment, as if the inmates had nothing but time on their hands, until something actually stuck.

They won, and it fell in my lap and all the way down the nation-wide dominos. Their legalized pleas faced against their inhumane treatments and conditions that affected the whole penal system, whether it was successful or not.

Recently the Federal and State courts pressed the action to be remedied from the inmate's psychological damages who'd been impaired of solitary confinement. They were kept alive, but sur-viving in an eight by ten-foot room within their twenty-three'ish hours a day was suddenly deemed unhealthy.

Clumsy or not, our most violent criminals promptly were imple-mented in the pilot program, according to the court orders, but no one could've seen it coming. Another amendment forced the laws to evolve, when policy changed toward the opposite side. Suddenly, solitary cells had to make their accommodations to require some quality time to socialize face to face with their fellow inmates, when nothing was hardly routine any more. It could have been wrong, but we had no choice. The liberals, colleges, or any given culture of society indoctrinated the law.

The inmates affected the way they'd resigned to accept their sentences over the years, of how many received the original incar-ceration to be changed. Their comfort level relied on its protection beyond the concrete and iron walls, when they had more than two inmates allowed together in their rec pens outside of their cells.

Many of the inmates even awaited their executions. They lived contently during their complete detachment over the years, as if psychologically damages weren't already impaired before incarcer-ation (?). They were wrong to rely on the false sense of security that became an earth grounding shift, like a time warp or skip forward generational change, then or now, but change was always fearful, as we'd adapt all together.

The most unruly inmates counted on them to serve out their sentences, who trusted the rock-hard walls to believe the worse possible decisions in the lockdowns, when even the hardened criminals began to shutter. It was a free for all, when they verbally acted out to one another that should never had said, as if words could never hurt, or forget. They couldn't take it back a little too late by mere words. I felt the teasing, insults, and provoked challenges of my loved ones, while the inmates' feared the hardened grudges that couldn't be undone either. Who'd believe their excuses, which were coated in forgiveness? But, didn't I have a lifetime of forgiveness and second chances, too?

They talked trash who harbored their long memories, who were just as deeply hurt and offended. They imagined and reenacted it all out in the minds, until there was an actual opportunity. Was their mental status on trial, or whether something else had been conceived on the table? The young bucks and new CO recruits couldn't have known, except the inmates worried about the chance to even the score... for the first times.

Single-cells (apparently) suffered among the most nasty and cunning men, when the inmates started to sweat it. It was time to be escorted outside, and for the first time, a deep breath filled their lungs that seemed refreshing.

The emergency iron doors used a little W-40 that finally pried open when DOC's posted the early responders of the seasoned officers up front. The sacrificial lambs were set aside to watch, who were still learning in probation for a cleansed and slow exhale, instead. The finest and well-seasoned officers were prepared, suited up like a proactive referee, as if Early Spring training season was over for the real game in play, when the court's mandate was put in play.

It didn't take too long, when every inmate finished their reviews. The proposal was discussed, who cordially nodded with the in-house counselors. It seemed unbelievable, but my team braced shoulder to shoulder, according to the highest ranks.

All of the inmates smiled through the motions, as if no one cared to hesitate by the first one who jumped up like it was a new sense of freedom. DOC's efforts couldn't possibly have overseen it all, but I knew they'd merely obey to 'make nice', like when my ma was more important to 'save face'. One thing promised one thing, the fingers crossed behind their backs, and DOC and ma darted 'that look' with the most urgent and final words to do the same things. The warnings fit in pure obedience, as if ma had unexpected company to behave, or all hell would let it fly 'or else'. How could I argue against it, and didn't anyone else already know the risks?

Thousands of dollars spent on the newly built pens readily created the high chain fences, poles, concrete, and razor wire that ate up the dead man's area. One by one inmate had been agreed to a little one-on-one basketball hoop exercise, or an iron picnic table was bolted into cement on the other end for the first chosen pair. Naturally the inmates were enthusiastic to denounce their resentments over the years, and everybody was happy.

Behind the scenes, every officer rehearsed its new routines. Some additional updates tweaked the Urgent Command System and its potential problems, while our lessons remembered: "Don't trust the inmate. They are opportunists with long memories", from the academy, as the chain-smokers multiplied alongside the walls of the courtyard. Pleasant conversations ceased, where I worried for my fellow officers.

It was my turn to be held aside during my light duty assignment of Main Control, since I heard those late-night arguments between the inmates on the graves. The war of the words was a common thing, who had nothing holding back or out of reach in the isolated cells of the lockdown. They acted like if they were shadow boxing, wildly venting a bit too colorful to 'get it all out' with every security check, alone. It was if they were painlessly raised above it, who had to know it was going to be saved 'one day'.

A few hours satisfied the counsel's agreements, but I couldn't buy it. It was not about to erase their deeply seated wrath against each other, whose problems were bound to 'bite in the ass'. I even wondered if I was just crazy against my choice career, but no words had to offer the same loved-one's, as if their hands were washed who knew it was never undone. I had to keep it to myself, while I kept my nose down from affecting anyone else, too.

Was I brave? Was I a hero, masochistic, or was I blatantly stupid for another job somewhere else? I could understand CO Hansen as the time went by, still lugging my orthotic boot around to heal, as I sheltered another injury inside. Was I coincidently pulled aside to abandon all of the rest, who pitched in to fill my place instead? I was cooped up in Main Control with another partner after another, but not me? Was he sulky, mad, or jealous instead of my place? Was I being blamed, because I hurt myself? I was nothing special. Someone else was about to get hurt, when the real question was "which one", and "how badly".

The COs were familiar with the padlocks at the gates behind every detail. The two inmates had been led, and the cuffs were removed inside the pen, simultaneously. That was as good as it could've been. It was social time. It was required... with a whispering prayer.

The inmates massaged their ankles and wrists who dawdled along, but it didn't need much more than the first few minutes, when the officers were out of sight. One inmate unleashed onto the other. Their rage was determined to even the score, when he was finally satisfied, accomplished, and finally settled... inmate style.

My fellow officers frantically swarmed in the back fighting-pen. One inmate was unrecognizable, while the other inmate sat and waited to be rehoused to his isolated cell inside. Wounded inmates could've been there to break up the fight, but the first officers on the scene didn't expect to find that in the Health Unit. Bumped bruises or the occasional stitches should've been enough, but an enraged inmate was unstoppable... like the results of a known snitch. It was called street justice, and for them, it was fair.

Escalated inmate assaults were overwhelming, as if they squeezed in every blow behind empty promises... after the fact. Misplaced trust was its consequences, but the mistakes rippled out all directions. How many inmates were left, returning, or coming in? And, how many officers made the decision to detach or assimilate?

Officer Cortez put his own safety aside, although he was contaminated to his knees. CPR pushed with his deepest chest thrusts, who tapped the shoulders to take over, but hope against hope was no use. The facial bones were crushed, unable to apply his PPE as his eye sockets moved up and down with each compression. There was no blood left to pump anymore, but that wasn't his call. "You're not medical" was how it was explained. "Do not diagnose or assume anything." CO Cortez was exhausted over a corpse, while the other inmate waited out the remaining social time at the picnic table, vindicated and unscathed.

Main Control resounded with every aspect of the murder's crime. My fellow officers rushed with every radio throughout the prison who reiterate back each order, while I managed to preserve the monitoring cuts that couldn't possibly explain the emotional or financial damages left behind.

The day shift officers ran a tight schedule, who'd been stretched out so thin. They knew the guidance and instructions of how many escorts had been walked along aside of their shackles, according to the routines throughout that unit every day. Each inmate assumed his hands-on escort, fully restrained like the back of my hand, until the program was newly redesigned. Change (or improvements) needed a second look. An interruption put a stop to dissect every plan in review.

I was one of those officers who returned to work regularly, but nothing was ever assumed the same. My duties obeyed, ordered, and resumed any job as needed, but my background was no differently, where I'd belonged in a career choice… to improve.

A therapist once explained my fears, "knowing about the tigers lurking over my shoulders". I was on high alert, watched, and prepared for the kill. Although the life and death stakes remained in prison, I could foresee the 'tigers' at home, too. My defenses were well established to be embedded in stone; except there I had a team who had my back with the courage where I belonged.

"You guys work too fast on this shift." I picked up where I left off with CO Hansen, about the transfer away for the SO yard. "Don't you worry about the inmates out of their cells so often?" I chatted mindlessly. "Those inmates are bound to catch-on to see how they'd overcome someone." But I looked over to my partner, when he was shutting down, staring into space.

Officer Hansen was a young man in his late forties, about six-feet-tall and well over 200 pounds. He was in the prime of his life, with a wife and family. He was well-grounded of the skills he needed to perform the duties demanded of him… and yet, there was an undoubted sense of fear in his eyes. I dropped the subject, but the opposite was clear. I had nothing left for a lone residence in an apartment, instead of anything else to lose.

D I lost count of the number of officers who committed suicides, dismissed, or they'd been resorted from the crimes under protective custody for the rest of their sentences. "It takes a special kind of person to do the work of a CO," since I remembered every opportunity. "This job is not for everyone." The academy offered any applicant to leave any time, while I stayed on.

"That place is going to change you." My mother warned, using every trick in the book to keep me from leaving 'the family', as if I was rejecting her personally, but I had my own reasons. I wanted to give it that one last chance. I maxed out the ladder when I discovered employment in a maximum-security state prison with another direction of the career. "That's no place for a lady." My mother was relentless, even questioning whether I had 'turned butch' that didn't matter. I had to go! There was something I needed... in prison.

CHAPTER 2

Orientation

*N*o was happy the day I took my first day on the job. I didn't think about the other prison assignments just before Graduation Day's commencement, when I shined in the finest attire. The orders began when I arrived orientation week, which it just happened to be the most harsh placement with my lockdown unit.

I thought I came through every step. I dawned my badge over my chest, but I wasn't hardly prepared for that. Something was wrong, but the problem was up to me to figure it out myself, scrambling in my mind: "When mama's not happy, ain't nobody happy." Well, DOC wasn't happy... through the entire unit!

Someone didn't return a set of keys. The Main Control inventory was checked and rechecked, and still, it couldn't materialize. It wasn't logged out or briefly borrowed back in, but even DOC offered amnesty. A wish and a prayer couldn't have been returned, when that key set was in the wrong hands!

My fellow officers were split up in groups to be searched of every inch and crevice throughout the unit. An unending search scanned underneath the dirt with a metal detector, while the inmates and cells were shaken down. Nothing! Officers were privately interrogated, when everyone was also patted down next to their vehicles by the SST (Special Security Team) flagged over in and out of work before Traffic Control's clearance. Searches went through the flashlights and mirrors, but nothing was found.

Finally, the decision was made for the locksmiths to be outsourced, when the State budget didn't plan its expense against our second lowest paid officers of the nation. The key set was not going to be returned, anymore. It didn't matter about any form of punish that couldn't compare with the financial expense of its recalibrated locks, too. We were going to pay by all who expected the consequences. We were bound to suffer, and there was nothing we could do, but it was the way it was.

Expediency was paramount, but overtime was not offered to cushion the additional efforts. The already stressing demands on the job were forced to work twice as hard. Except for the innocent inmates who were clearly spared to be maintained throughout the daily routines, I'd been thrown in and pooled along where I was expected to step up the pace.

Every minute was already scheduled to stand, but I had no comparison to include all of that much more than I imagined. I jumped up once my name popped up on the roster. A snapped finger picked out a female partner with me, and I obeyed. I should've felt quite blessed, relieved to identify more closely with another woman, but I was already sized up in return. She kept her head down, hardly spoken a word, or any form of small-talk that came in a brazen attitude, instead. But, what did I do? It couldn't have been about her! It had to be about the added load. I couldn't have explained it out of anything else.

I didn't know its routine, history, or reputation. I was a blank screen, while she consciously pursed her lips and bit her tongue, as I then tried to overcompensate by showing her respect. Clearly, I had a long way to go before I could measure up, but the day didn't have any other 'F' word. I amped up the efforts, as I took on the challenge of forgiveness with another excuse to be satisfied. How could I help, or hinder? The recalibrated key sets were ready with the locksmiths, who were also anxious to be emptied with the cell pods.

"Cuff up," demanded from my direction, as if the gun had been fired off to begin the race. I took a glance to imitate my partner for the upper tier escorts. Training was over when I took each one down, but that didn't cover everything at the academy. My Folger's key was enough to understand that in the front of Inmate Johnson's cell. A million times covered over the years, but the first time alone meant everything I needed to know before I couldn't fool anyone. The fear of a dog (or inmate) could sense 'fish', which was just as easily... either way.

I put on that professional and confident face, but inside I cringed, afraid anyone would detect anything close to be called a fish, although I truly was one! I swallowed hard and wouldn't dare let it out, until I was called the 'stinking fish' by the dirtiest name... of my secret. Its most vulgar language uttered through my childhood that remained its affect. Name calling spew the most disgusting titles, when I couldn't bear to tolerate it. I might as well had been defined next to my picture, imagining the worse sweltering stench. I might as well die, buried, burned, or considered to be rotted for fertilizer, but "for heaven's sakes... get it out of here!" The thought etched on my mind, forever. I hated name calling, but especially how I feared *that* name to my bones. "You might as well push up daisies," who'd wish I was as good as dead! I recited my bed-night prayer: "If I should die before I wake...", gave up a long time ago. I broke into bitter sobs, as if nothing was left of my value to recover, after every distorted scar to my soul.

Self-banishment had become an automatic reaction to run, as if I was ridden out of sight to spare the rest. I struggled. I wanted to believe above it, as I continued to disprove my worth on the job, when I'd left off back home. The academy covered our most susceptible or weakened areas about safety and protection, when I work alone, just like I had a partner on the first orientation day, as if I couldn't have been more disoriented. I should've been covered against any possible threat, which I pushed all the further away to avoid it.

I figured out once I applied a little muscle when the tightened hinges finally opened the trap door in front of my first cell, as if it didn't show on the outside, but an inmate saw the first few seconds didn't miss a thing. I backpaddle its first impression. I reached down every bit of courage, anticipating an inmate to grab or stab me through a shank, when I must've step backwards, but he'd already turned his back around for the cuffs.

Inmate Johnson's hands were palms up, shown through the trap door, when he stretched his wrists out a little further, but he was enormous! For just a second, I might've grabbed my balance at the upper tier rail, and damned near peed my pants.

"Move it!" CO Sanders hollered up at me. The cuffing exercises practiced alongside my fellow cadets in class, but they weren't near his size. Inmate Johnson waited patiently, right there next to me, instead. "You put 'em on backwards, and I'm not taking them off for you." CO Sanders hurried me along, but what if I put them on too tight? It would pinch his skin. I could set him off with another set of leggings needed, but she was already gone.

"I don't think they're going to fit." I murmured under my breath, half hoping my partner would've helped me, half hoping I'd deal it on my own.

"They'll fit ma'am," spoke from a low but soft, guttural tone. "They'll be tight ma'am, but don't worry. I'm used to it." He urged ahead.

His hands were rough and dry in the typical desert, while mine were wet and clammy. I scooped the opened cuffs from below the wrists, seating each cuff in place, as Inmate Johnson forced his wrists with a slight twist before I curled each bracelet with a click. He seemed to make it easy for me, but even that was unnerving. I had to look away for the control operator's permission, but "Where are you?" My mind screamed when no one was there. Inmate Johnson's wore the cuffs inside, when I instinctually slammed the trap door closed, as if that was safer.

"Leave the trap opened!" Her shrilling voice was already back for the next inmate, when I hadn't done the first one yet. "That's how the control officer can tell how many cells are empty," as I jammed down the lump in my throat. I wanted to run away and never come back, as if any barking hint was way over my head. How many other things would I miss?

I'd pulled out the secure pin left dangling, but any inmate could've manually pushed it opened. I turned my back of my mammoth sized inmate, who should've pressed the buttons behind the glass control room. I felt like a sitting duck, waiting with my arm raised for its cue, but there was no response. I leaned over the guard rail and waved my arm up and down to get his attention. And finally, the grinding gears pressed that button to open the cell door. My knees weakened, buckling beneath me. The grinding gears finally stopped to be completely opened for him, as he shuffled backwards from the cell in his stocking feet that were shoved into his state issued flip flops, where he waited sideways to face the wall, but then he just stood there!

"I need to escort you to south visitation," I said, but my feeble hands didn't really grip onto any control. I couldn't possibly manage anything against his overly developed triceps, but the academy couldn't possibly cover that either.

"Raise your arm again ma'am." An inmate redirected me. "They need to close the door before we can start walking." Inmate Johnson knew more than I did, but he spoke so quietly. He hushed it near my ear from the rest of the pod. If I couldn't make it, if I crumbled underneath the pressure, my family would've loved to watch me crawl back home, but even that was still too important to me. I hesitated when I trusted an inmate, instead of my partner, guide, or loved ones.

I kept my strong arm kept free, which maintained the hand's-on procedures, but I wasn't barely alone... among inmates. There were two emptied cells, indicating two opened trap doors of the ground floor, but I also noticed how CO Sanders was twice as efficient. Nonetheless, I had Inmate Johnson outside of his housing cell in strange territory, who could've easily been overcome with no officer support to speak of.

The dusted control room windows were barely visible that reflected right back at me. Its glass barriers couldn't wrap around anything to believe, until I faced the end of my career during the daylight shift inside Main Control, where the backyard sunlight also screened ma's premonitions through her farmhouse window barely visible inside.

Did my co-workers watch to see what I was made of? Did my OJT and partner put me through the tests? Or, was I the entertainment from ma's kitchen window, who were coached for my reaction? Their bullying established the victim pattern, as if my reputation couldn't be changed.

A loud slam jolted the outer edge at the cat-walk, but there wasn't a hint of any aggression detected toward me. On the outside, I appeared to be cool and collected. I concentrated to focus out of everything at hand, but inside I was an emotional wreck.

The first step hesitated at the top of the stairs, where he curled onto his socks once the spiked iron stairs set downward, which was meant to be awkwardly encumbering. The prison was built for the stairs, who'd painstakingly calculated his oversized feet in his snail's pace, but it was my turn to show him some patience in return. I watched. I listened, when the latest advice in the academy remained fresh in my mind: "Kindness means nothing more than that." I had to set my boundaries, which was all the thanks I'd allow.

The control officer watched over me to go next. His expectations on the job had the routine over several others' acknowledgement, verbally requested its clearance all across the radios, but then it was up to me. I held up the next announcement by the next CO at the wing, who monitored the paraded set of eyes, as if I belonged and should've been there for me. Each officer had a specific post, when I'd been staged with each escort of the corridors.

I arrived at the security door, like rush hour freeway that was monitored at each exit merge for the foot traffic down the corridor, and for a moment, I felt accomplished. Except they flowed by, perfectly timed of each escort, while I waited in line to remain closed. I had been waiting, but any number of excuses must've required its procedures to be patient. Anything hasty could've been dangerous. I knew that I paid close attention at the academy, but I missed out a lot in prison. It was my radio to use its clearance, when Inmate Johnson was in another dead-stop for a timely nudge.

"That's right," Inmate Johnson offered a nod to understood that nothing was automatically opened. Each departure perfectly fed between each escort, but the pace grew wary with the pair of locksmiths who also waited for me.

"Any time!" I got that undeniably look by my locksmith who grew agitated, still hidden around the corner of his cover.

I could've ignored to blow off anyone else in the control with a known violent criminal over me. It could've been my own right to brush it off, but every glare was enough to disagree. I was clearly seen to show. I was the oddball, and nobody wanted the extra weight or weakling throughout the fiasco that initiated DOC. Each sarcastic expression further defined my incompetence with one down and three more to go.

"Access to visitation… from wing… one?" My voice croaked out each word in that high and girly voice throughout the entire lockdown unit. My traffic was heard by every two-way radio by everyone, but I might as well have said: "Here comes the fish, ready or not!" I could just feel the chuckles. Of course, they all looked up. I took the first steps for all see or pass it along, but I had an escort toward the phone-booth sized holding cells when I poked out my head to make sure it was actually clear before proceeding... trusting myself.

Inmate Johnson managed the farthest distance of the hallway, as I watched against the risks, like a lost a flip-flop's which he could've been drawn away from anything else. I focused, maintaining a steady pace, but even my fellow officers cut in ahead, who wagered an extra escort in between my sole efforts.

Every pod had been vacated through all four other veins in the same directions. It seemed to be so efficient, who were planned of my fellow officers, slipping between the equal spaced inmates, but I couldn't possibly had been able to make its lost time. I'd floundered with no apologies, or woefully burdened upon my partner, but she didn't ask to be issued for that post at the start.

Everyone seemed to cooperate into the extra routines, except for my first escorting inmate. Inmate Johnson was impossible to control anything, who could've acted out as if he'd been cut free. He was too restless, as if he'd ever been let out of a cell, during a well-deserved field trip or a petting zoo outing. He twisted all around, looking for anything more than a shuffle along. He had to check out every door left ajar of a peek, examining the supplies closet, electrical circuit buttons' cover, or the unisex restrooms unattended, while I dragged him along as my mind raced wildly, as I entertained some self-defense into practice, but I didn't want that either. No one ever wanted to resort into the clam-shell position on the floor to fight my own distance between safety, and my survival.

"Put 'em in V9." CO Sanders pointed in a direction behind herself as she approached, yelling it out at me. The wing corridor cracked opened through the squealing gears and the rising sunshine blasted through its echoing mix when I winced into the center courtyard of doors all around. I must've staggered or a bit dazed off guard where I lost my bearing.

"It's right here, ma'am." Inmate Johnson cued me toward the visitation door.

"Did you remember his ID?" CO Sanders snapped as she came closer.

"No. I left it at the cell." I spun around, taking my eyes off of my inmate at her, instead.

"How the hell are we going to know who's in each pen without an ID?" She hollered back at me, as she shook her head to loosen her hair in the cooling air gust blowing back from inside. She refreshed her doo, twisting her tightened bun again, who quickly disappeared. I realized how glorious it must've felt, while I was doomed, bald with its very little hope anymore.

When I got back for the next inmate's cell upstairs, I made it a point to return to the visitation department with two IDs stuck onto the Velcro patch sewn onto the front of my stab vest. Little by little I knew I would eventually use all of the still empty loops and clasps throughout my body armor. But then, I also knew how inexperience I looked, and how everything else looked besides myself.

The first pods were working throughout the wing to be relocated temporarily, while I began to empathize with the inmates. They seldom walked any further than the limited showers in the same pod, when they merely longed to be curious, until they'd be facing the same four walls to stay, while the locksmiths couldn't leave faster. I started to empty out the top pod cells, who were protected from the locksmiths' view, as I expected them to be sheltered from the inmates. That profession had a specific expertise by a private company, but they acted as if they didn't deserve the job for anything else, who treated me like I was a waste of time, who breathed down my neck with every chance.

The entire view throughout DOC had been turned into a mental condensing course, which was more than the training in the classroom. My aspired career was my highlighting joy that was only two days earlier. Surely, I'd surpassed the academy, but I wasn't nearly scratching the surface.

"Come here and help me sort the mail." CO Sanders unloaded the mail dumped in a pile in the CO office, right after the lock-smith's work in the emptied pod, who butted one task after another.

"Where did all of this come from?" No schedules or routines had to be read off of an agenda or calendar pinned on board in her need-to-know attitude in charge, when a piece or two landed on the floor. I picked it up, coincidently analyzing the different in-house and outgoing mail pieces.

"Mail and Property was dropped off at the wings." Her answer was curt. "It's usually picked up a lot sooner." She exaggerated with a breathy sigh.

"What are you looking at?" I had it in my hand, as she flicked through the mound at any direction.

"This is the inmate's ID number, and this is his cell number." She said, grabbed out of my hand to pointed it all out before she tossed it on the side for me. "Just make sure when you're delivering the mail that you're checking the inmate's IDs before you give it to him. The inmates get moved around a lot and it's not pretty when the wrong inmate gets a letter that doesn't belong to him." I picked it back up to figure the cluttered chaos in order.

I tried to remember everything she said with every question I asked, but I must've slowed her down. "Focus!" I snapped at myself. "Pay attention!" I scolded inside, again and again, trying to concentrate, as if once was enough to slap myself back into the moment. I had to stop my mind from wandering, but it didn't work. It only made things worse. I started to shut down, worried that I might've asked a question that was already asked, when I might've already been answered. I stopped asking her help, when I decided to hide the fact that I also knew that I was never going to be that smart, anyways.

I should never had been turned out to be much of anything, or too stupid to catch on. Ma was surprised to pass every year, after she'd advise me to "be nice to people and they would be good to me," as it became my mantra… for the family patsy. I was the casted role to satisfy my siblings, or whether she just resigned to the fact that I wasn't worth the effort to bother. Either way, I started to fear that familiar lump in my throat. What if ma was right, and what if CO Sanders knew? What if my assigned partner was too kind to keep me on by treating me that way, because I was just that obvious? Maybe she just couldn't say it in so many words, as if her cruelness were used to force me to leave. But, if that was true, where would I belong?

"They'd have to fire me!" I fought back. I wasn't done yet! "I'm not quitting!" I reconsidered about my fellow-officer, as I wondered about CO Sanders.

I felt badly for CO Sanders. It wasn't fair to be her partner. Her anguish was well deserved, but she didn't want my compassion. It would've been a lot easier on her if she would've been posted with another seasoned officer to share the load, but I didn't even come close. But then again, the other officers didn't get a partner at all.

"Let me have your keys." A locksmith reached out for his keys to add the recalibrated locks of the first pod. "You can go ahead and empty out the next pod," he said, as he returned around the corner again.

"Let's go." CO Sanders dropped everything and I scurried right behind her.

It was time to return with the same inmates, when she explained how I'd take the last inmate from the holding cells in reverse, finally finishing with Inmate Johnson to his cell for the rest of his television show. I had one inmate back in, while I'd swapped the next pod of all four cells of the upper tier by every inmate, who passed both directions.

"We need to feed." CO Sanders' voice made me jump up in her call to action.

A line of the aluminum food carts had been delivered by the kitchen crew workers' hot and cold trays plugged in against the wall corridors. My partner typically whisked by, as I took a quick example. The eight plastic food trays balanced four milk containers on the top, and I saw which meals were taken accordingly. As impressive as she made that look, I felt safer by carrying just two inmates' meals, and I chased right behind her.

"Look, I'm not going to bust my butt while you stroll along with just two meals at a time. Are you here to work or not? What the fuck, why me?" CO Sanders was asked for more. So, I made an about-face. I doubled up that trip for the same escorted inmates for the second tier. If that's what she said, who was I to say? A weakling? A wuss?

I had nothing available to hold onto the rails, towering the meals above my head. I squarely planted one step and then another, as I extended my free-flowing arms in front of my pristinely clean uniform, or at least the rest of the day. For a moment I tempted to further use my chin to stabilize the trays half way upward. I counted down every step that felt more rewarding, as if small things always mattered.

I cautiously settled down each step upward, except when I forgot about the top solid platform from the stairs. For just a moment, there was a thrill of success. It was the top. I was right there, until I bumped into a smooth solid block of concrete by my toes. In an instant, I tripped. In slow motion, I failed. I lost my balance, unable to catch my fall to my knees, with nothing left to grab onto anything (literally or figuratively).

Everything I carried, flew from my hands, up in the air, and all the way down where the meals immediately disbursed to the floor with their roaring laughter. I didn't think about the housed inmates through the silent audience, aside. I was in the highest sense of accomplishment that fell just as low. The embarrassment was excruciating, robbed from anything I'd hoped for.

I'd expected to bring each meal to the top tier. I was expected to be served at their trap doors to eat, and they were hungry, too. It must've smelled wonderful that invited each one to be fed, but they fed off of something else. Their hollering jeers and vulgar insults were held out for me. My total focus for that moment had their own bets against my acrobatic feat. Oh but wait, that was only the beginning.

I lunged at every direction, trying to spare against my total loss that escalated my entertaining performance. Every tray popped opened, while it was thrown into the air before, during, and after impacts. I couldn't stop anything left to salvage. I had to save myself, desperately grabbing at the guard rail to keep from falling backwards, while their meals littered a food blizzard all around.

Salad pieces that were smothered in French dressing had been stabbed into the iron spikes on the stairs. Greasy fried chicken patties bounced all the way down, followed by mashed potatoes and gravy that disbursed like marbleized plaster. Every milk carton was pre-opened and approved by their welfare check inspections that splashed across the room to mix the added slimy mix. Of what I had... was trash.

I expended every ounce of effort in a jaw-dropping silent scream. I was incensed, maddened and hot, when I inevitably broke down in tears that flowed uncontrollably. There was nowhere to hide, but my entire day was a non-stop failure. I collapsed in disgrace, when my partner had already finished her next pod of her floor level meals.

I got angry at myself. I caused the mess and the joke on me, but the inmates were right to laugh. Although, they had to know that they'd never go without a meal or be denied from their food. The inmates hooted and hollered with a new favorite story to share for quite some time.

"Did you make her carry all four meals on her first day of feeding?" CO Rauley shouted at my partner, who'd just arrived to see why the pod went off. I was then ashamed even further, publicly humiliated of my fellow officers, too, but CO Sanders couldn't avoid my partner's pleasure... who got caught.

31

I wasn't sure how I felt. I didn't expect anyone to defend me, ever! CO Rauley walked in some concern, when I had to think whether I'd apologize to my partner... like before? Wasn't I responsible of my own decision? That shouldn't have been her fault, which was my mistake. I didn't understand why he retaliated against my actions onto my partner, instead! I was the one who made the mess, yet another officer took the heat and didn't chasten me.

I didn't see anything wrong, except of my own inept. Blame never played that part that didn't occur. I had to allow the 'better man' to edify my partner, which was just like my loved ones. Who was going to apologize to me for my results?

I excused and I even dismissed my partner's behaviors that proved my inadequacy. I was challenged by every test of how vulnerable I'd been reinforced and didn't belong, amped up of the efforts toward destruction to tears. I'd been allowed, manipulated for her amusement... and then, but how familiar? I was begrudged by CO Sanders, and I tolerated it, until CO Rauley was my advocate. Finally, I understood the love and respect I deserved. CO Rauley demonstrated the right thing to do, and the consequences about abuse.

I began to internalize policy. I'd arrived when I didn't want her to cause trouble, when she was already mad at me for her own outlet, except I was expected to suck it up because I didn't rely or trust on anyone else. "Don't tell" had become my habit to protect the other. Why didn't I know better than to simply obey, regardless of my own limits? How many other ways did I want to say 'no' that had no effect? I shrugged by a perfect partner for the punching bag.

"Take these." CO Rauley handed me with a few plastic trash bags and a handful of sanitary gloves to stuff my pockets to use anything I'd needed. Then, CO Sanders disappeared again, only to return with a push broom and mop from the porter closet, without a word to say.

"Thank you, thank you," I repeated, almost stuttering, but I don't think he heard me.

"Do they have enough food?" CO Rauley rode her hard. She'd just come back with a few old bath towels, torn in half to be recycled towels with a pail of steaming hot water and cleaning solutions, who demanded her to jump, instead.

"Yeah, but it will take a while." She already knew and didn't need to be told, since the kitchen had been called out for the eight additional trays that didn't make it a habit. Anything was specifically limited by the daily food supply and eliminating waste, but she knew the meals would've been allowed of that much. In fact, she counted on my fiasco.

"Go finish feeding the other pods before everything gets cold." He ordered her out of the pod, but I was relieved to see her go. I was embarrassed and didn't want her to see the mess I made, when my stress level needed some relief from her unrelenting brass toward me.

"I can get this. You came to help. Why don't you work with CO Sanders?" I knew how much strength was needed to project it through my diaphragm, where that pod was so loud to be heard of each other. "Really, I'm fine." I further gestured to encourage him to go, but nobody had to deal the additional digs. I'd been able to handle through any denigrating barrage from the cells, too.

"You got this?" He yelled, and I nodded as reassuringly as I could. I plead to graciously allow him to go, without feeling like he was abandoning, where I was happier alone.

Piece by piece, I collected the hardiest meal to the garbage bags, while the all four hungry inmates had no trouble of my interruption or expense. CO Sanders, on the other hand, ran in to supply anything available to me, coming in with another box of sanitary gloves and her "no thanks", anymore. I'd lost count of how many pairs of gloves I went through, or I could've found more if I needed to get it myself.

The food shook off of each gloved hand that inadvertently claimed my trash, while I tried to understand the mindset of each inmate. I censored out their noises through their glares, but I imagined what must've been fed. It was every day and at the same time through their routines on time. What did they trust? Did they think I couldn't be relied on? I began to realize how disheartening it must have been to see their food to be discarded before them, who only watched nothing else available to them. I'd denied them. I failed to provide of what they'd hoped for. Were they robbed? Did I cheat them from being satisfied, even for a little while? They were totally dependent on anyone outside of their cells, as I started to understand their limitations which wasn't too differently from the short leash at home, remind of whom in control.

I had to stop and clean my mess, while CO Sanders continued the rest of the pod without me. I wanted to pitch in the load of my partner, when I didn't care about her personality, or an excuse for the bad day. The added escorts had been filled in between the locksmith's demands with a new fish that didn't want me, until CO Rauley's anger was directed right at her. Was she burned out, because DOC's denied overtime and pay, which wasn't pushing her above her choice, too? My choice was a clean slate, conveniently used to prevent her from any retaliation against the department, who could've been the perfect buffer.

Finally, CO Sanders came up the stairs with their meal trays, as if I was invisible. I leaned against the wall to let her safely pass by, and for a moment the inmates were quieted down to eat. Either way, I enjoyed the peace, knowing that it wasn't going to last.

I didn't like the inmates' entertainment who couldn't miss a single move, regardless of how it looked. I heard the derogatory responses, as if I'd been on display for their delights, throwing my rag mop around, left and right. They might've been the most dirty-minded men which was meant for me, but they were behaving exactly the way I expected. I could've been a private show in the prison, albeit a deprived grown man watching through a cage... in reverse. It depends how you looked at it, but it fit. They behaved like all eight irreverent pigs who moaned when I even wiped my brow. So... I accepted a self-satisfied moment of pleasure to concocted another twisted encore. They screamed for more when I'd had enough. It was time to draw the line in the sand.

I heard every imaginable name or cat call, but I didn't want to chasten anyone else to be shamed. That was not my style, but how? It had to be stopped, and it was my call. Hollering or anything else would've just fueled the fire, but I'd never learned anything else that couldn't be another argument, dragged into the abusive conducts to be amped up that would never end.

The basics were unpredictable in lockdown, but the inmates shouldn't have been planned or manipulate through my mess that hurt nonetheless. I wanted to run off and cry in defeat, but I stayed. I could've stewed in self-pity, but I'd need to restore the day. I was stuck in the middle, but it was up to my decision made it shake them up... for another surprise.

When the show was over, I wanted an impact on them for something else. I remembered how I graceful or ungraceful I walked all the way up the acrobatic balance was in awe, who anticipated every step. They must've held their breaths, hoping either goal to be accomplished.

CO Rauley stepped up, when an advocate should've come along that was too old for that, or finally "ripe". I could've picked up where I left off, but I wasn't needed and preferred to be alone from CO Sander or any other Sanders.

The over-used F-bombs or any other verbal adjectives in prison barely affected its language, when people lived on the outside who were even worse. I put up with the medical insurance phones, when I listened every caller that wasn't half of their foul language to fix the problem... for the next complaints. The anonymous faces would never be recognized with nothing more than the names, who slithered away in shame. A weak "thank you" was never heard from again, as if problems were my job to shine. Until I had that day: What else could save face, to see them again?

I thought about the training at the academy, knowing that my job wasn't meant to penalize the inmates. They were supposed to be in the wrong. Was that their right? Their incarceration was their sentence, which was their punishment.

"Dear Lord, help me out here," I pleaded the slightest whisper in my heart.

My uniform wasn't designed for the female body, as I wore a slightly oversized fit, to hide behind my hour-glass figure at work. I'd flattened down into a sports bra that covered a loosely bloused dress shirt, instead of the knit polo shirts that could've revealed everything. I even pulled the wider man's waistband slightly lowered to disguised away the curves, which was not that kind of attention in prison.

I put all of my cleaning supplies away, as the next security check had been required to carry on. I refused to shirk my responsibilities before I was all brushed off, when I wondered: "How could I handle that?"

The whole pod of all eight inmates either egged me on or finally cheered over the greatest comedy show's applause, when I did return with that final appearance, but the audience was my change to focus on them, instead.

One by one and I conducted the security check of the floor cells. No one told me how I'd conduct each walk that didn't cover the rules. It could've been a quick fly-by and a glance review of their welfare existence, but that time, it was all mine. I knew I'd make them nervous, and for a moment I enjoyed the bully empowerment over another, who were the violent criminals of the opposite side of the bars. I didn't just examine the condition of the inmates in the cells, when I studied each one! I memorized the finest details, until I finally included their faces etched in my mind. "If you know who

I am, now I know you!" was something more than a security check. I must've instilled fear in the inmates, when I realized that the next inmate took a slight step backwards with my arrival at the front of the cells, who couldn't read me... and my advantage.

My uniform was thoroughly soaked in the sweat. My make-up was melted off and still flushed, ragged, and worn out, while I stood tall and curiously composed... alone. Who was going to oversee that? I didn't even care if CO Sanders didn't need me anymore when CO Rauley put a stop of her contempt, or whether anyone else might've seen me from above the control room. It didn't matter to me that another set up of retaliation could've been saved, and I didn't need to get even or seek out any vengeance. I was the typical officer in control, and I didn't plan to take it out on the inmates... unless I'd play!

After all, they were playing with me, too. I passed one cell, until I'd recorded all I needed before I moved forward. The pod seemed oddly quiet as each inmate waited. There wasn't a word, but I was neither mad nor hurt. I was intense and determined, as if they needed to communicate another poignant reaction, since I had no real reputation... yet.

I finally headed for the stairs, knowing all the eyes were locked on me. I took one step, and then another up the stairs. "How nice and clean!" I was pleased with myself, who only focused to check me out. They were exactly where they belonged. In fact, it was the exact opposite side of imprisonment, when I was supposed to be on the outside!

I stretched over the railing. I was drained, hesitated for a second to lean in, who still focused on me, as I inadvertently arched into the low curve of my back and against the wall. So, I went with it, as if it was intended for the audience to show a bit sully attitude in a slight tease, for more.

I was still in center stage during a deep sigh, when I came up for air. Something had to end... or an encore. I swept the sweat dripping down my face, shaking my hand to the floor, as if even that was enticing to the inmates. It wasn't quite planned when I tossed my head back with a quick jerk in a little sassy reply. I rolled out my hip outward with a full slap on the ball of my ass saying: "You can't touch this!" as if I'd brushed off of the dust and didn't need to raise my voice, when I was just loud enough, and only once.

"That ain't right, CO!" The inmates comically moaned down lowly. They carried it on for a while, as I picked up, prancing through the rest of the way to my exit that never mistreated me again.

CHAPTER 3

Two cups and a string

I got used to the number of family during our reunions, who talked all at the same time and any room, while I cut some space to respect hearsay. It was unavoidable, but inmates communicated throughout the number of languages and dialects that rose well above of the typical roar in the lockdowns, who couldn't barely hear their conversations apart. Noise was deafening that continued all throughout the day. Its concrete and iron walls bounced inside that distorted anything to understand, since the time I worked at the old can factory with my Dad, when we lip read all throughout the factory. We could've been within a few feet up close or from either ends of the production lines, where we'd communicate one way or another.

The inmates seemed to come to life every morning during the day shift was the daily norm, unless something seems off, when I wondered something changed to perk up, straining to hear something important, or when I easily dismissed to leave it alone. The daily routines of the lockdowns mixed within the shouts throughout more than a series of numbers that resorted to communicate back and forth, but especially when specific messages filtered through the gang heads in code that reigned above all else, who bowed for their calls: reached and received.

The first week of orientation was scheduled on the days, when I began my first year of probation through the night time. The lights were turned down on the grave yard shift as sharply switched down that included its hush in the air. Good Friday Penance's mumbled a whisper below the fainting candlelight floating down the ceilings, when some officers swore that they saw ghosts. Holy or not, death-row and life-time inmates were made to respect the spiritual realm of life, regardless.

Inmates poured out their souls to one another, when it sounded like a mass rush through the rosaries in church confessions that penetrated across their silent hums begged for more. Imaginations might've satisfied another bedtime story, or impossible to believe anything between an issue or a lie to fill the time. Either way, I called it white noise, until a tidbit of truth seeped in, where I couldn't shut it off. The metal air ducts amplified it in the CO offices, as I worked along the functions inside the prison walls.

Details craved over something about somebody else, when my grandma was strictly forbidden its eavesdropping the phones (or prison), which wasn't anything private. Back then, any local households were alerted for its different ring tones to answer their specific phones, but the neighboring party lines were available to anybody. It robbed their privacy, but sacred thoughts were juicy, and addicting! Grandma crouched over so closely into the kitchen towel that muffled its receiver, which was anxiously saved for later. She was so popular, which drew Bridge Night together, regardless of what could believe or easily deny 'the unbelievable'.

The grapevines spread and the news also unified some of my night-shift co-workers, all over again. It galvanized its ductwork available, as if it was designed to be tunneled through its unending temptation, but eavesdropping was nothing new. I'd strained to hear about what I needed, since I was a kid.

I longed of what was denied, as if I had worth-telling secrets just above the second story of the farm house, who forgot about me. I wasn't expected to be connected all around, until I overheard a hint of suspicion that fed my doubt, and nothing was believable any more. Information had to get to the truth. Facts should've deepened understanding, but the worst thing just another 'pinch of yeast that spoiled the whole lump' in the wrong hands. I panicked. I was as intense as my grandma! A convenient point of view created confusion, mulling over the debates, intended to be fooled, or easily persuaded accordingly, when I grew nervous.

I crept across ceiling's floorboards without anyone detected, according to my needs. I remained there, disappeared where I could spend the whole day, who were just a few feet above them, who never looked up to the ceiling vents. My grandma listened to their business, except I overheard my loved-one's private space of my difference of the opposite gossip. I'd never tell, resisting to divulge all the harder... to make them nervous.

And then, law enforcement didn't persuade me against 'that career' choice, all the more. I held out, hoping of what I needed, where they hoping that I couldn't slip something I was denied. Either way, I signed up for the DOC team, while my family's joint decision got the cold shoulder. A time-out upstairs wasn't enough to be banished since I was still a child, during the silent treatment that eventually lost its affect.

"Plausible deniability" was a line I borrowed from the movie: *Independence Day.* There was a laboratory scientist who'd been isolated for a lifetime of confidence, until his underground research was ripped wide opened. And, that was like if the doors were welcomed at the academy, as if the germ-free zone didn't matter anymore.

There were two sides on the job who typically overheard the commonly known criminals, as if I'd already been born among them. My habits were kept in check, watched over, and closely groomed, since I couldn't be read of what they knew... closely to my chest. What could I lose? I obeyed because I couldn't be over-powered, until I had to climb out from my own sentence of impris-onment to be set free.

The "What if's" at the academy preferred to know, more than blind obedience, where I got its explanations that penetrated to my bones. Whatever was right or wrong was tore open, transparent, and impossibly faked out of the cowered smiles with its consequences that were out of hand. Of course! It made sense! I sat at the edge of my seat once nothing else was able to redefine or twist the laws, when I stood tall to complete Graduation Day for everyone in the auditorium, except for me. I'd been embraced of the elite behind the badge, but who could've been hurt, when I should've been proud?

I walked away toward something more important in DOC. I allowed talk that carried all throughout the night, while I focused on the tasks at hand, logging the timeline in the service logs, written where nothing could be denied. I heard and/or dismissed of what was important, but the prison wasn't only about the inmates' ears. Now what? It was just the facts... anonymously?

"You're giving the inmates the wrong message." My supervisor cut to the chase which he turned upside down of another barrage of forms on his desk, when I entered behind the door closed with its investigation... about me.

"Sir?" I was not about to jump to conclusions, but I didn't know what I did wrong.

"It's brought to my attention," he stopped for a moment, raising his eye brows, as if he needed to open his eyes a little wider. Taking a deep breath, he continued, "that you are a little too friendly with the inmates." Lt. Kershner pushed his chair away from his desk and sat there with his knees relaxed, uncharacteristically wide across of my supervisor, and then, he just stared up at me. It was my turn, apparently. I looked back and forth. I was cornered by two other ranking officers at either side of two witnesses.

Someone dropped paper on me. How did that happen? I'd hardly recovered from the last reprimand (there were a few). I trembled, worrying about my first year under probation. I faced everything to be addressed, but I didn't drop paper on them! My fears wore on my nerves. I was afraid that I could be stripped from my badge, stepping down of the fold, and I could lose my future, and all of the benefits above a mere paycheck, when a career meant so much.

My DOC family played interference, as if they tag-teamed against me, but by whom? Did the next group of my shift pick up where I left off... by CO Sander's cronies? Who would've gone out of their way to run me off the job something so petty? But, it was always about the little things. I grew indignant as I contained my emotions. They had something to caused trouble that wasted my time of something else more important. Was that funny? Was that serious? I didn't know which way I'd turned.

"I don't think some of those guys ever heard the words 'thank you' or 'please' before." I admitted every word I said that triggered me in defense. I barely read the report in front of my supervisor, where I noticed that it was cowardly missing: individual or clique? Whose credibility hurt who? "A lot of these guys will be going home when they're released from prison." I stood tall, brushed off through the training prodigals. "Maybe, with a little common courtesy, they could take back a few courteous examples and pass it along once they're out." I hoped that I might've rubbed off to believe in people like me, but I read it again. I slowed it down to process it more accurately. It had to be a joke? "I didn't single anyone out, sir." I searched out the written claim. Was I mistaking? I might've been wrong, as I raised my shoulders, clueless. "Wasn't it supposed to remain 'firm, fair and consistent' to everybody?" I mumbled to myself. I thought that I was treating all inmates the same, or drawing out the problem about me, when I finally ran out to be ready for his consequences.

It was his turn, and I swallowed hard. That lump was stuck in my throat, worrying about another attempt to be discredited that didn't fit. "The academy said that an inmate can sniff out a fake a mile away," and so much of my training was still fresh in a maximum post. DOC decided, who chose me. It was supposed to be the best fit, and I accepted the accused criminals in my care, unless that was the reason I could be weeded out to disprove the worse. I plead face to face some mercy…something, anything? Lt. Kershner had his orders, required of his procedures to follow with every allegation that were filed against me. I gave it my all as I studied his lead.

I handed in the final screens during my application through the academy, once when I'd been called into the office at the court house. There he analyzed every form when I stood behind doors to fess-up. My recorded history had the power to be pulled aside, or step down. His brows raised, hesitated about an issue or possible error, too. I'd accept the consequences. I answered everything honestly that couldn't be erased or changed, as if my answers were purposely filled in with the little bulleting dots. The results wore heavily on my heart. And then too, I waited.

He went blank, stoic, and stone cold, when I asked to be repeated (when I read it, again). Did he give me a chance to lie? I could've been expunged from prior drugs, since I had a tasted joint in the sixties. It might've been flippantly useless, but I was deadly serious. I did it! I was bad as I sweated the fear and loss, of the hope of that career.

He threw his hands up, ridiculously flagged right out of his office, but I wasn't playing with him then either. I was promptly dismissed, as if it never happened, but it did! A mistake had enough to know of every constant reminder like his frivolous time was a waste, or whether I was annoying him to be bothered?

I was forced to process an anonymous report through Lt. Kershner's procedures like a thorn in his side that didn't deserve their complaints. "Did I belong with the team or not?" I had nothing to argue either directions, when it was his call.

My supervisor balked, until he added a few extra pointers. "Perception is everything!" began to make me aware of how I looked to the inmates. "Good manners are easily misconstrued, when the inmates could've been an invitation to befriend any one of them. Don't give them any reason to get the wrong impression." And then I was turned away, concluding the talk that satisfied us both. "Be safe out there," which was formally concluded.

"Thank you, sir." I didn't exaggerate an about-face, when I just turned around and left.

I was relieved to leave unscathed, until I literally bumped into that little group of my colleagues. Their cute pranks muffled at the other side of the door, who were proud of their uncontrollable laughter, as my heart dropped. I ran away too embarrassed, which was just like another scar where I'd felt it pierce from an old wound, since I never quite healed from the prior schemes that started to get old.

I cut my losses, when I never thought it would've been that way with my fellow officers. I was played with, from something too familiar that was impossible to avoid. Did I merely resume, picking up with another 'working family' that depleted my emotional and mental stamina?

I willingly offered my needs that acted like a 'front-loan' to entrust another's gain, but my sacrifices didn't stop there. It felt like I'd been bleeding-out in so many ways, as if self-harm was an expectation. I absorbed a very coy hit or a bump that hurt, when it felt like the knife was held at the juggler. Wasn't I that easily fooled against another's come back, and ever rebuilt for me at all?

My decision moved toward the legal career, which severed my divorce of ill-gotten gains. I joined him when we moved away from my family roots that was traded off of another ruse. Wasn't I too friendly for a second marriage with a convenient scheme, which I misconstrued? Who supported one moment of kindness' perception didn't see the same things? I offered my ex with his promising chance, too. I saw his aspires toward his greatest dreams, unless I'd been cheated out who could never be satisfied, until I'd run out.

My earnings graciously turned over of my earnings as I covered the basics, and behind the scenes, he took more than triple of the amount he spent. Rick spent the money who made it look good, playing the part of a successful CPA, except there wasn't a single client. He enjoyed the perks of his immediate success on the outside, and then... bankruptcies were legal. It was seven years to be perfectly timed, for the third time, except I refused to play clever... or dirty. Expunged of all belongings involved us together, unless I'd detach my divorce that explained it in court.

How many ways had been padded on the back with the most slick people who wouldn't celebrate me behind the badge? Of course, I made them mad by a fearful requirement of the shrouded truths that twisted it around to blame me, as if my career put a wrench in their process without me.

I weathered every NTI (needs to improve) entry in my employment file through the completion of the first year of probation, when knowledge was power. Perception couldn't see another way to look at it, and when it's all right there in writing that had to be transparent with every example that became more clearly.

"Keep your head down and your nose clean." Lt. Kershner said. "The officers have a way of weeding themselves out." He continued with a good job nod, passing on the way out. That was his final day's review of every following complaint, which had been thrown out.

I focused forward while I ignored the rest, but my supervisor's words didn't fall on deaf ears. Some fell from the roster openings while I remained, too much determination to fight for more than a steady income. Maybe they thought that I was strong enough to take it, but eventually, I learned why they'd been weeded out, as my trust slowly regained from the damages:

My sister had no trouble exposing my darkest moments, as if I wasn't allowed to heal and recover. She had my rawest sins, as if it was her reminders' purpose was meant to keep it fresh: "I never smoked a cigarette. I never did drugs or hung around anyone that did." She began one day without notice, although a joint, depression-drugs or Ritalin worked which refused to be necessary. "I never got a divorce who had to raise my kids as a single mother on minimum wage. I never let myself get so low to consider suicide, and I couldn't image any of that!" She blurted it all out without a beat, unless she was the golden child and messenger. I was dumbfounded. I felt ashamed in front of everybody who heard, but nothing else was said.

I began to identify the inmates. If Allison said of all that to be true, at least I didn't have to imagine of what I experienced! Did the inmates succumb to be caused of another, which was exactly like my family? Which ones were pressured to act against their will, or too desperate to refuse not to? What happened on the streets, where I'd been kicked at the curb, too? Prisoners were filled of accused inmates, which had been worn down or pushed too far, provoked to the brink who broke the laws against their better judgement. How did that happen? And then, I wondered if any of them were in prison because they were caught, until it was too late.

There couldn't have been enough laws on the books that evolved over time, when I reconsidered the mindset about imprisonment. There was a part of the inmates who were banned, while society were spared or couldn't fathom of what I'd involved.

Criminal behaviors were hard to bear the pain and truth I studied at the academy, when I had to stop it or even back it up for a moment. I had to ask, striving to fully understand, when I had to know! I shook my head or didn't even care anymore. I raised my hand, regardless of the classmates' behind me, so urgently waited to be called for the instructor's permission. Whatever the lecture was being covered, I interrupted the class to be put on hold for my time to learn why.

"I understand what you mean about inappropriate behaviors." I began as I staged the question once I had the floor, "but, who decides when it's inappropriate?" I overheard a few snide remarks, when I didn't realize that I had the only hand to be called upon. I held it up in the air, or maybe I was impossibly stupid for real, but it was more world-shattering for my turn.

"You do." My instructor gave me the simple answer, as the classroom sheepishly settled down. "You have every right to say enough or say what's offensive." I paused for a moment to process something new, or maybe I just had to hear it, when I wasn't done, yet. The classroom was full of strangers who I'd never met before, but the class was all mine for a while. They gave me all the time necessary, and no one could've had anyone else heading the class.

"But, what if they don't stop?" I pursued. Did I just let them know how the word 'no' didn't apply in any other ways, or never allowed at all?

"That's called abuse." I heard, and heard it over and over throughout my mind, until I could finally say to it myself, "They shouldn't have done that to me!" And, I imagined how different things could've been! I was used of their ill-gotten gains, to fool me with every lie.

Instantly it felt like freedom, or did the cash cow sacrifices cut them off those holy secrets. Finally, I also understood why I was never going to return home, but I didn't figure out why I wasn't allowed to know it innately, until I put it to practice on the job among the criminals and the law. Even when I was a stranger, and even to myself, I couldn't recognize of what self-condemnation looked like. It tore at me. I was conditioned to be denied of any explanation or understanding. There was that edge! I was thrown into doubt under the ruse of 'inmate behavior', as if it was never meant to be applied by my loved-ones.

I wasn't even sure whether I liked something, because I was told. Their judgements were passed along with the double-talk that put me out of line by taking the blame, which was clearly inappropriate behaviors, but who could I tell? Hearsay of promises were nothing private or in confidence. I was sold out to accept the pat on the head, or when the dirty names made me cringe any other favors.

There was a time when I entered a bad part of town and inappropriate behaviors felt wonderful, where I had no business to be allowed or looked over my safety. I joined the Jesus Freak during high school, when I saw the reflections through the inmates of another sub-culture to pitch in the food kitchens. I sorted out bad fruit from the good, where I served the hard-luck and homeless, or where I stocked the food banks in exchange for free labor to feel satisfied.

Another time I sat next to a restless drug addict who prayed for death in the back rooms of a church sanctuary. There, adults took turns with anyone who'd swapped in, when I reached my curfews. I was a just a kid when nobody missed me. In fact, I counted on it. I was glad to be out of the way, where people needed me, or whether I was wrong for them, until I was an officer to be around the outcasts in prison to know the difference.

I trusted Inmate Johnson, who stepped up to help me, but I wasn't afraid of him. I was afraid of what I didn't trust that all came back. Inmate Johnson had a good example to compare CO Sanders' set up to fail, and my loved-ones intentionally put me in trouble... and didn't! The was a third-party culprit washed their hands from the dirt, when Ma was blameless who enjoyed the perks of the golden child, which was just like the telephone game. Passing through the connections made trouble to stir up a hint of truth... with a twisted turn.

"Hey, CO?" Inmate Johnson called me over to the front of his cell, several months later. I covered a double shift, carried over into the day shift to meet again. "Can you find me a packet of coffee?" He pleaded, knowing that I had access at the officers' dining hall. "It's not like passing," asking me to do something special for himself.

"Come on, what's it going to hurt?" Another inmate joined in, adding the pressure to give in. It really was no big deal about a simple request, which could've given him an extra cup of coffee, but that would have been something harder to turn down or establishing the habit in the future.

"You know better than to ask that," I said in a quick turn away from his cell front, when the word "no" made sense about inappropriate behaviors.

"Oh! She don't have no baaaaalls to make up her own mind," Inmate Gordon rang out from one of the lower cells, as I returned back down the stairs. "See, she's gotta do what she's told." I stopped abruptly. Of what he said, had nothing to do with a single packet of coffee anymore. I was hit below the belt, when I decided to establish my management style.

"Is that how it is?" I hesitated for an answer, knowing all sort of mind games in prison. "Balls?" I strolled over to his cell front. "See, my daddy told me something a long time ago." I built up their curiosity when the inmates quieted down, anxious to hear what I had to say. "He said, 'Smart people don't have to tell people that they're smart.'" The inmates seemed dumbfounded, and I paused to let them think for a moment. "So, you want to talk about balls?" They wanted the answer, and I had another twist for another perception. I waited for the pod's full attention. "Oh, you mean those little things?" I appeared somewhat proudly before my eyes, as I kept focused away from anything possibly accused of the slightest glance, avoiding their prurient viewing. "See, these are my balls." I covered a hand over each breast. "Looks like my balls are a whole lot bigger," and my answer... fit, with nothing left to discuss.

Time passed, as I managed over a thousand inmates throughout the lockdowns, which I should've done among my family as if I couldn't keep track of all that day forward! I'd sweat the situations between the slick and silk-tonguing criminals to think on my feet, when my pocket notebook became handy. It reduced my doubts to refer somethings that couldn't have been mixed up on paper. They'd tried for a while to trip me up, but I defended enough of the details that couldn't be argued against it, which included the notes about another fellow CO.

CO Chesterfield was assigned to another department to work among the inmates' kitchen crew. He applied that position for quite some time, but I didn't expect to lower his guard like that. The daily mind-games poured in an unendingly barrage through the prison units, who were particularly harsh for the taking behind the scenes.

The inmates got whatever they wanted, who helped themselves or swindled out of what didn't belong, regardless. They got what they could as boundaries blurred, which was barely familiar to recognize the difference over time. The inmates supported each other who sharpened up their gameplays, who collectively groomed my fellow officer. They found 'thee' scheme, but what a wonderful job he had been esteemed by all! In fact, he seemed to be the most enjoyable officer, so I witnessed the same scenarios I allowed.

I purposefully decided how I'd out-grow or heal from my residual crumb of skepticism and doubt, as I detached them with a wide opened range of blessings. After all, I had enough of my own issues, where I couldn't assume my fellow officer's concerns. He must've been the better man than me, where I didn't question his job. He was that good and there was no other purpose for him, as I bowed out and believed in him, since DOC didn't have to check up on him, either. The kitchen ran so smoothly as the inmates behaved so agreeable, but they carried out another set of demands, which started out so subtly. After all, nobody likes a critic when I didn't have to knit-pick.

I, on the other hand, didn't let a thing slide. I was tested by Inmate Johnson who involved the whole pod with the same plot. They ganged up against me to allow Inmate Johnson's gift and personal thanks who tag-teamed against me, before I realized how the entire pod pulled nothing so subtle in the kitchen. I was still a rookie in compared to the seasoned officer's choice, when I'd picked up the red flags, but it was his call.

There was one supporting the other inmates in the kitchen by any insignificant issue that accumulated, when I started to feel suspicious and distrustful. It slowly squeezed the pressure to say something, when the inmates were too smart. I was avoided of anything negative for anyone else to know, so that I'd been kept from any drop-papering need… to stay out of the way.

Being nice and polite was superficial. They appeared quite respectfully, while their illustrious officer began to relax. He cut it down, allowing the inmates some 'wiggle room'. Every ounce was enough to poured down their gratitude with a slow and false turn against him. His kindness was always thankful, who never asked it in the first place, until his gifts had been turned into sacrifices. I saw it, but our esteemed officer wouldn't listen, or refused to admit the mistakes. And then, I was pushed away by the inmates, who also protected their gaming conquest in motion.

CO Samson conducted the whole kitchen crew. Every inmate cooperated and gave it their best, but they had their rules, too. Something could've talked about any sport (or anything else like fishing). Regardless anything innocent abated his distractions, who purposely kept him focused away. Any personal hint of anything of worth was stacked against the officer, but patience whittled away anything incidental when nothing sunk in, as if the '(fishing) hook' barely noticed, who subconsciously cleared his throat, until he swallowed. My favored CO could've spit it out, but nobody seemed to care, when I tried to keep from overreacting away the slightest complaints against the claims thrown against me, too.

A little piece of information laid down the groundwork, while inmates visibly shrugged off its mere suspicion among DOC and the entire team. Each inmate had been inadvertently reissued new replacements, who'd been trading out the inmates in the kitchen that resumed their plan intact. Didn't anyone wonder why the inmates weren't upset to be pulled out of one job for the next? But, what a trophy they glowed? High-fives passed one for the next, trickling down throughout the inmate units.

The inmates made a cooperative stand, who focused for just one specific purpose, while CO Chesterfield's embarrassment couldn't backpedal out 'from the net'. Any verbal or written reports were impossible to stick, or spared of himself. But alone, no one was ever planned to be that strong. He couldn't admit anything to be detected, which was ever so slowly drawn toward their accomplishment.

Months had a pass for the champion's patsy, as if not one of them could be fingered by every conniving bet behind the (third party) hold, who coached every self-serving move forward. Every day CO Chesterfield greeted their crew who were transported from the lower security units in a joined effort, which overlapped and blended the same collusion that was unable to distinguish between the individuals of the kitchen crew.

The inmates supported the sole officer, when just one disagreed who ganged around their 'trouble maker' to be hovered and protected of their plan that was more important than anyone else. The inmates or officers were managed to be singled out in intimidation or beaten into obedience of submission, when fear and pain was just enough to survive the threats or a regular reminder, who couldn't escape from the 'hold'.

They were all involved, like it or not. Inside the kitchen was finely meshed on the surface, as DOC hired the inmates who were transported out to the other prison units, who reported (tattled) back to their head. The inmates were never too far away, which was intended to be kept from anything to unfold prematurely.

CO Chesterfield was perfect for his promotion by DOC's interview of choice, who got to fill a forty-hour work week with a bonus of an extra eight hours week's pay that awarded him in a time-and-a-half prize. It was sweet! It was a no-brainer, since his job was primarily meant to watch over the inmates who did all the work. How hard was that?

But the inmates were closely examined of their choices, too. The number of inmates went through them like water, who signed up for DOC's agreement at the kitchen's food preparations and cleaning, who diligently obeyed with anything they'd require. Everything ran beautifully. The inmates complied with everything, like when the trash was taken out to the compactor, which were strictly returned (wink) of the found kitchen tools at the end of the day.

CO Chesterfield had no trouble, which became incredibly capable to manage by another low-staffing mistake to be pared down for just one officer, instead. He boasted! He bragged and didn't need a partner, but it also enhanced the opportunities of the crew in the kitchen. A sole officer amped the inmates to flatter their leader all the more, as I wondered just how sweet who seemed to be phony, but I didn't have that amount of courage! Even if I'd seemed unkind, I'd come across like an insult, who denied to be checking anything out. I stepped aside, preventing from any move to 'rock the boat' and sit pretty, 'like a good girl' to behave.

I noticed how the inmates were so motivate, regardless of the most miserable chores that never complained. Imagine how they managed at the back compactor in the heat of the summer around the swarming bees, who protected their food source in competition. And, who scrubbed out the toxic sludge barely draining, or when they freed out their grease-clogged ceiling vents above the grill to maintain fire safety? I wouldn't have been paid enough to go near that sweltering stench at the rear sally port that the city's garbage collectors emptied every other day. Yet, the inmates did it regularly for about fifty cents an hour, and nothing was said (or wouldn't dare)?

On the surface, that may not have sounded like much, but that was money for an inmate who could spend it on himself. That came to about $12.00 for a three-day work week, or about $48.00 every month, which was tallied on their bank accounts with their direct deposits on their pay…, but that was discretionary income!

They could put it toward a flat screen television, or CD player and ear phones. There was any number of treats to be prized throughout the inmates' favors. It satisfied them all, regardless of what was really bought! They coordinated who held the power to the other inmates bribed or traded out the rest (after the 'taxes' were allowed) to pay their 'friends' with a Honey Bun to be sold for another's debt. Doritos and Coke next to a lidded and personal cooler refreshing their bags of ice available that came in regularly to buy for pennies. That was some big kudos of their paydays, which was spread among the other inmates, albeit another 'price'. One way or another, it spread the love, which enhanced their lifestyle in prison.

The inmates didn't have to worry about their next meal, clean hygiene, and well-suited clothes. They rested their heads in their own bed to sleep in. They didn't have any car payments and insurance, homeowner's maintenance expenses during their basic comforts, which was already been satisfied by the State. Above their hired earnings had been arranged to spend a wealth of amenities, who all played a part of the 'job'. DOC's catalogue continued to approved a plethora of items, which was provided by an invoice at the Property Department, but the inmates couldn't misplace every receipt of what they owned.

Once an inmate whined about his low wages that didn't impress me. I never complained to spend fifty cents to my name at the end of the month. I was a single mother of three children during a fulltime work week, but my paychecks didn't pad my pocket. My children's needs went first, when my income ran out before any discretionary funds for me.

The kitchen workers handled the foods during their metal cutting tools, spatulas, and spoons were strictly accounted by the inmates' uses. Everything was tied down to the cutting tables, stoves, griddles, and caldrons with every three meal days. In between the continuous routines to be prepared in the highest qualities of food, or when they were called aside to make it up later. Any inmate jumped up to assume any emergency or added chore that merely pointed out something else who took on the chemical solvents aside. Their officer barely snapped his fingers who dropped it in a moment, (which reminded me of how many chores waited on the next list that wasn't enough to do just about anything asked?)

Our food supply trucks docked at the tarmac delivers with enough food for about 1200 inmates to feed the inmates of that lockdown that replenished the unending job daily, which closely justified DOC's budget against the slacking waste. Its 'all's well that ends well', except for a frivolous catch here and there that was timely planted to satisfy their lustrous officer.

The inmates might've had a quick finger lick here and there, a nibble from a shortened snack sack, or a healthy and deep-throating spit, like they appeared embarrassed through a sheepishly smile, but that wasn't about being sloppy or careless. They were meant to be caught a few times with a slight 'slap on the wrists' that didn't have to go any further for just one CO in charge, but imagine how dangerous he'd lost perception.

The CO never lost sight of the inmates, but the kitchen crew held their officer within range, too. Nothing was allowed to start over, who had invested CO Chesterfield to ensure he'd relax, like when they almost tripped over each other in the walk-in coolers who went out of their way to show-off their 'boss'. How much naïve, fooled, and conditioned loved-ones dealt dual goals? Nothing meant hearsay that was easily twisted to stir doubt and confusion… to buy some more time.

The inmates were all too happy to include CO Chesterfield along with some small talk that up-lifted their crew bonds against anything needed to be reported to DOC anything further that also helped 'the lead's management skills' through all the merciful apologies second chances, as if he was too busy to see anything deeper. They loved him all the more (sprinted to the final goal), who desperately worried which was almost there!

The inmates were quite aware of their sentences, as if no one else could've helped them through their insatiable interests, when CO Chesterfield lowered his guard that extended his friendships into the families. He didn't hold anything back, while the inmates were satisfied of another hold, instead. Behind the scenes, or their undergrounding enterprise, was about to roll. The final details disclosed the conversations beyond the kitchen, which was far from private.

They'd been saved it (or held their breaths long enough) to cash out, when it was 'time's up'! Innocent small-talk suddenly playeddown the word "no" that wasn't allowed anymore. Inappropriate behaviors didn't sink in, when abuse was allowed and wasn't allowed to stop it. There was a lot more going on behind their own criminal agendas, when somethings were refused or withheld of an explanation.

They'd been knitted together (like a loving family-crew who took turns that lost track of the chore list, while I was cut out). They shared, whether it was accurate or not. They extended his details, (like the Bridge Night outing) when the prisons visited outside their families, as if anybody was ever that interesting to stand out who were involved something more than a grapevine of talk.

Every piece of information was kept closely calculatedly, like if their investments multiplied more valuable over time, as if they called in the selling portfolio that was more than a favor. The designed plan involved all different valuables during his guidance, advice, or service options... for a price. CO Chesterfield gave his private information in their hands. How serious and deeply profound apologies couldn't mercifully fit or protect that? Even DOC was unable to save or recover from anything left, as if turning himself in was preposterous. They ganged up, cornered, and owned him! He had no choice and took the fall! Was I wrong, and they were all right? Were they spared by the greater good?

There was a lot more than some money or a pleasant work place. It was always about business! The kitchen crew were sacrificed for CO Chesterfield's glory, which was an all-or-nothing in return. Didn't they make him look good? Didn't any of them do whatever it took? It was like a hotel's bedding had been swapped out of the freshly-folded laundry, except the gratuity wasn't negotiable... on the bill. It was life or death!

The inmate's cut was closely controlled all along, while the low staffing's were scarcely monitored by every inmate's phone privileges. For as much as the officers had been dismissed, too much went undetected. The outside of the prisons filled in the details across the internet, which reached beyond the walls, and into his home. Of what CO Chesterfield had, costed his wife and children, school, house, car, and on. What was it worth?

Everyone had to know how I plead, trying to cover my friends, families, or right next door of my apartment for their protection. I warned my ma's visit and didn't listen, where I understood how quickly their eyes could've been used against me with a fearful threat under an established and unfounded lie, since I regretted her daily walks who couldn't be stopped.

I grew all the more adamant. I urged. I begged to stay away from the local inmates, but ma strolled along the prison town where I lived, who pointed the out proximity of the well-known bald woman with a scalp tattoo about me on the job that was more than a pleasant chit chat. She volunteered my information, who blatantly flagged down the orange dressed inmates' attention, as if I couldn't be reached 2000 miles away... for the fall?

It was all put out there, who couldn't wager its worth. "They are so nice to everyone." She laughed it off too seriously, who knew better. Outside of the cleaned-up streets where the posted CO was harmlessly allowed and should've intervened, discouraged her to pass along. But who could turn away such a nicely old lady, when I knew that she was far from dementia?

I was a rookie when CO Chesterfield was a bit too comfortable in the courtyard during the smoke breaks for his kitchen crew that infuriated me, where I was a fellow officer who laughed me off, too. It was meant for me to 'lighten it up' and 'relax', just like when my ma flaunted about me in the public view among the inmate chores, regardless of the assigned officer who ignored the warnings, too.

Maybe I was just too sensitive. I sat on the edge-of-the-fence, but what would I know? Where was my mentor, guiding support, and reputation? Was I supposed to dismiss it, as if I didn't count or didn't apply on everyone? CO Chesterfield seemed a bit too friendly, when I got each NOI dropped on paper from every thorn-in-the-side that it didn't affect anyone else? And, who'd passed along every detail to the next inmate, all the way to the final delivery, a tit-for-tat arrangement, as if that was a fair 'price' in return?

Talk was mere hearsay, since there was nothing left to defend a paper trail. DOC never quite examined anything standing out, until that fateful day. The concluded plan was ready. An inmate asked CO Chesterfield something in return, except it wasn't a request. By the time CO Chesterfield finally realized what he understood was too late. Everything he owned was held dear at risk. In a flash, his first and only son had an unknown friend in high school who threatened whether he'd reach adulthood. He had to relent, and the inmate took control over. But he was a law-abiding officer with nothing done wrong? How much was entrusted by every left-handed desire to fool him so explicitly?

There was a head surrounding the cronies, who protect anyone from getting to close, or anyone else in charge, until he said so. The kitchen crew waited to respond with the calls. CO Chesterfield, any inmate, or all of DOC who didn't want anything to prove or disprove all around, as I was stripped powerless. I stayed aside and hid from anyone around to notice how I ached in my gut. I had to look away to experience it himself. The incarcerated criminals lived on the inside, while CO Chesterfield pranced home every day, until the walls expanded into his neighborhood for the 'package'.

Shrewd and cunning criminals created a dangerous trap all throughout the kitchen crew, who arranged the drug bust for his delivery into an inmate's homey. My fellow officer was charged and locked up in solitary protection throughout his sentence, who went from a badge to orange. I knew about a law-abiding officer, and just like that, he was gone! DOC found him at fault. CO Chesterfield was found guilty, where he was victimized as the scapegoat.

The news spread like wildfire, as I kicked myself. I couldn't help him, as I stepped aside to do nothing. I could've been the intruded rookie, but I was right between the bully and the underdog. Anger grew against the scum-of-the-earth… when I blew.

"Knock it off." I yelled, blurting out as if nothing was expected. My outrage couldn't contain among the officers gathered, status quo, for a quick smoke. "It could've happened to any of us." I aimed it to all of the hypocrites. "If you knew something was going on, why didn't you ask him about it?" I pointed each one out, who knew and refused to hear anything I said.

"How many of you opened their traps to hand something from one cell to the next?" I couldn't be silenced. "They made their special trips, passing back and forth." I continued who couldn't ignore me. "They all looked the other way, who refused to take the light covers down from the security lights after lights-out. You're here for a good reason, but not because of their crimes to go to jail. They're self-serving con-artists without a conscience!" I addressed everyone, who'd relaxed under the canopy. They didn't see that? I let my anger fly like a crazy lunatic without any regard to the feelings of my fellow officers. "We're supposed to have each other's back!" My voice raised, while they just seemed to stare, dumbfounded in disbelief. "All I see, is fingers pointing away to someone else." I threw my arms in the air, and stomped away without any concern how I looked, or what they thought of me anymore.

"That's fair play!" I screamed back, when I also remembered the final words that were meant to hurt me. I walked away and couldn't help but how I heard it scream at me, just before I left Wisconsin,

"That place is going to change you." I hung my head, even lower. What had I done? Did I blow which could've been anytime in the moment? Did I hold it in at the edge, and nobody thought I'd break? Was I hiding from home, where I could lick my wounds to keep it inside, until secrets were protecting to withhold the truth... in prison?

A law-abiding career fought against my family's support, whether I accepted the legal side... or leave? I faced too much of that amount of pressure that I couldn't handle, but I didn't mean to hurt them! That was wrong, and that was inappropriate and offensive... because of me! Did I require an apology? Did I harm my co-workers, and hurt them back? Whatever I got through the media news or the grapevine tablets, I'd reached enough payback... just the same.

"Hey there, Wilson." I looked up with a very weak greet of my co-worker and friend, where he found me at my office on my post, as I obviously cried it all out, hidden in shame.

"How are you doing?" He entered and sat beside me with his typical smile through a compassionate tone of his voice.

"You heard?" I smearing my tears away that couldn't stop.

"So, what's wrong?" He acted to be just fine. "Do you really want to take anything back?" He spoke through my sobs, regardless.

"No, I don't, but they didn't deserve to be at the receiving end like that." I was further ashamed and unable to face the closest COs of the shift.

"We all lose it from time to time." He didn't play it down, and I appreciated his honesty. "The trick is by restoring yourself back to your normal self as soon as possible."

"I'm not something that can be turned on and off like a switch."
I felt defeated, who cared about me, but I knew that my problems
were much deeper. I was afraid of what I'd turn into.

"How do you want to be thought as?" He continued. "Someone
who gets mad and hides in shame afterwards?" He had my attention. "Or, someone who had something to say, and said it with passion?" But he knew! I agreed as he pulled me up to my feet. "If
you offended anyone, you can apologize later. For now, let's show
everybody that it's all out of your system." He got up and headed
for the door that followed toward the corridor, as I was invited to
rejoin my team.

CHAPTER 4

Safety during the Risks.

The briefing rooms had everything mounted all around the walls, but safety was more than the first place to be reread daily. Phrases like "Stay safe out there" hung a few wooden plaques filled in a void after "Don't forget who you are dealing with" didn't really mean anything new, as if it went in one ear and out the other.

I stressed how I read the emotional climate among the inmates at the top of the first security checks with the grave's shift. I could feel it the air, as if I was born by an internal barometer, where a high or low weight needed its attention, which was especially when an emotional darkened sense was rolling in. I couldn't exactly say how, but the alerts resonated those times that demanded its most courage.

There were approximately 50 single bunks, or another 100 other area who housed the double bunks in the lockdowns in my care during my post, who could've easily been mixed up with the upcoming shift in the same bald officers in the uniforms of the inmates, when a nice heads-up was anybody's guess. The prior shift officers were already gone, too anxiously rushed out the doors without so much more as a quick high five, thumbs up, or any other hand gestures, but either way, I posted up as ordered.

I tucked away some kind of strategy in the corner of my mind every day, when I purposely planted a well obvious pause of the inmates about the other officer which was replaced, when I'd introduced the reset mode before I entered the pods.

Initially we (one CO overseeing from the controls and me on the floor) coordinated to work that day with a supportive thumbs up, until it felt that undeniable grab at my gutting core for a moment zapped my energy. A shallow pant robbed me from a toxic suffocating alert.

I gave it a quick scan to clear my partner's post, when I'd face any consequence to heal later, since the scars still played back. I double checked my safety equipment when we all were scared, so what could I lose? I had already decided to cut the risks free, since the years I entered the 'egg shell' pass, again.

All of the COs had been covered in the usual equipment of the lockdowns from the face shields to the black boots, when I entered and left each pod that slammed behind me. The inmates had been harboring their anger, until I arrived for another day to breathe easier the rest of the night, or whether the inmates looked in on me, too.

My safety worn its armor before I lowered the final face shield in the pods, which was also meant to be intimidating, but it was policy. DOC wore its appearance of power, but its respected came of either ends. I was able to settle down and unwind any inmate with a slow and patient 'mom type' officer as I'd replenished my night shift before it was laid out for the morning officers, where I left off to the higher hierarchical posts for the day. They noticed, but the day shift staff thumbed their nose, regardless.

In between the cycling continuum, Maslow's pyramid had a fly-by glance in the academy. The first and highest responsible decisions hit running hard of the earliest day. The second shift officers were made to overwork through the grunt-work chores… and down, as if I cleaned up after the 'shit rolled down hill' to be refreshed all over again.

I bided my time restoring the work areas, who'd trashed the prior shifts to be left for the grave yard shift's, when I'd push the reset with the rag mops to soak off the dried floors that was carelessly spilled on the floors or from another leaking trash bag, including the bathroom doors that didn't need a to flush within their general areas…and got away with it. My co-workers had every right to complain, who vented… and got away with that, too.

There was a limit that grew out of hand to be talked down, as if the day shifts were more important or just arrogantly disrespectful, unjustly dumped to respect my place, too. "Whether you think it's right or whether you think it's wrong, is what you think," coined another plaque from the wall, where I paid attention of what was in front of me.

My supervisors took precedence, where any upper ranking officer expected their broad shoulders to smoothing over any issue through the night, until I showed up for briefing, who looked particularly weathered that day I began to worry. The question was: How much more, how bad, or what else? I took my seat, as if I wasn't told, who saved together, and only once, wondering the whispers were bound to come directly from the report.

"There was a staff assault for the ambulance" had their full attention who he took a deep breathe in between "who had just left with Officer Jensen." We hung onto every word by the Shift Commander's bars on the collar, "and was taken to the local emergency room to treat the burns on his lower face and neck," every one of us had that audible gasp, "he was thrown on."

It could've been me! I imagined his way out in full sirens, or I just didn't want it know, burying my head from reality. How could've been anything differently? I could've been the inmate to hurt anyone. I could've been the one right after I'd slipped back on the roster, before my double shift raced through my mind.

An inmate laid in wait, who planned it in action. Every officer followed through the lunches to be fed, who routinely picked up the trash and meal trays. Most of the time, no one took a moment to think about anything beyond the job hurried along the rounds, but an inmate took advantage of the opportunity to hurt an officer.

CO Jensen generally joined the team of the four sectors down the entire wing that was efficiently swooping through the trap doors, who habitually operated the short cuts to be left opened a few at a time. The officers worked it nicely in unison, although the clock was allowed to fluctuate.

Any other CO was just as good as any other uniform, when an inmate was ready to stand at his door trap with an arm that was stretched out to make a point. He couldn't say or listen any wiggle room to finish his meal, when enough was enough. He wasn't done eating... again. He put his food tray aside, when the officers were going to be there to collect the trays, of something else.

An inmate was prepared. He heating up his hair conditioning gel in a plastic drinking cup by an electric stinger, just in case, but once more was the last straw. He was ready to explode, grumbling under his breath that brewed over time, and could stand any longer. At a perfect aim, he squatted down at the opened trap door, and upward.

Backtalk deteriorated, who had nothing to negotiate each rejection, when that last resort was his for another message to be 'heard', as if DOC staff didn't offer to communicate any other option, anymore. The word "no" was reinterpreted by the 'in your face' message... squarely noted.

The entire group of officers banded closely together, as if they were impossible to discriminate any one over the other, but it was CO Jensen, who instantly dropped to his knees in a split second. The excruciating pain landed underneath his face shield. "Bulls Eye" shouted out, when the officer was impossible to drown out his shriek, resounding its horror all around.

The first CO responders replied, but medical staff were the right ones in need, who their best efforts were too sticky from wiping anything off, where his flesh was fused as one. Cold compresses barely touched him, until the paramedics ran in with their first aid immediately treated for his possible graphs.

No one was bothered the inmate's insults against the CO demands' orders. But imagine if the COs had enough to be hired with an oversighting watchman. An extra set of eyes could've monitored the daily tasks, but the prison guards no longer applied anymore. I put myself out there to be proactive by looking out of each other, but at any time the missing signals "be safe out there" on the wall, was no more than a kiss of death on autopilot. We all just posted-up to take the orders, regardless.

I prayed silently, remembering how the scaring reformations were lifechanging in the Burns Center wing of the hospital. That level of compassion tugged at my heart. Nothing was denied whenever I dropped everything else to run in some more pharmaceuticals as needed, since I wore the titling Pharmacy Technician without hesitation, because I was there, witnessing their healing changes... inside and out. I felt his pain, knowing how the demands were merely swapped out, where DOC handed the next set of uniforms to a few other names next to me. The various shifts carried a different level of stealth, and impossibly forgotten of the consequences, knowing that it was no accident... in the Chicken game.

The inmate got a disciplinary violation, which was nothing more than a slap on the wrist with a known criminal history, who wasn't going anywhere. An early release could've been restored at the other end of their sentences, who believed good behavior would be earned right back. Any inmate misbehaved against their privilege's LOP (loss of privileges) status with a small sacrifice, while the rest of the inmates in the pod whooped it up with the same twisted sense of humor. Fair or not, it worked.

The Disciplinary Department reviewed the severity of the acts that processed his argument who defended the assault, and DOC gave in. What was the justice? What traded the orders with safety? Who was the one in harms way, and who'd wear the scars next time?

The inmates celebrated DOC's decision had the COs to be more considerate. The inmates were allowed a few more minutes to enjoy their meals, while the lockdown unit got a jot under the Officer Assault column with a newly designed bulletin. The monthly Status Report boldly advertised it to keep track, as if it was waved in my face any better. DOC could've been reconsidered, but there was nothing to be changed, but the follow briefings grew all the more vocal, pleading against with the liberal items remained available inside the cells.

Nothing could control against DOC, when the CO attitudes plummeted, too. Was I supposed to be that appeasing, regardless of the victim who was still healing or recover at all? My fellow officer was still off of duty, when I wondered how many other victims signed up for that, quit, or returned for more.

At any time was another situation, when a pod housed eight or sixteen double-housed cells of each corridor-length wings, as DOC further reduced the COs to only three or four officers on the day shift. They paired up to push through the lockdown's escorts and any other tasks like before, when the inmates got creative to push against the limits at the other end. The inmates were so clever whose homemade hooch offered a swig, until a bad batch rushed them to the hospital with Botulism.

They thought they'd be able to pull-it-over the officers, as if the inmates couldn't have been any safer. The water bottles appeared to take their belongings back from the exercise pen, except the same brewed alcohol remained behind for the inmates' rationing turns. The officers happened to avoid that particular pod, who repeatedly assumed their inspections. Somebody had to have checked that whole day... at least once, or maybe a dip glance for the cameras, as if no one gave it a second thought. They met the deadlines of their routines, until that was after the fact.

The next shift officer realized how the inmates were acutely ill, who didn't wait for the nurse's rounds. The emergency alerts wheeled them out on a gurney, one right after the next inmate for the entire pod to the medical unit. All of the inmates fessed up, who spilled it in a rushing ambulance to the nearest emergency rooms... and half of them died. The others survived their sentences for the rest of their lives on a respirator.

DOC took steps to prevent the production of inmate alcohol, as if that was more important than the dwindling officers who needed better coverage. The inmates started making some of the inmate foods from their trays, or they acquired any other items purchased from the inmate's state catalogue, that had been extracted from its yeast. The state already took their necessary measures to protect the inmates from themselves, but no change was deemed necessary.

"What the hell do inmates need all that shit?" Officer Rogers interrupted our shift commander in briefing, who hollered him right back... in close subordinance.

Didn't we all find that edge, when we knew better than the canned answers for something more? Officer assaults just seemed to shove the charted results forward for a creative excuse on paper. Our shift commander's job had to maintain the status quo of something more than a pat on the head, but DOC forced the ranking supervisors shouldered it all the more.

"Pull their stingers (an electric shaft at the end of a cord which was purchased to heat their water in a drinking cup), they're not responsible enough to handle them in the first place." CO Hallgrimson's baritone voice was easily carried across the room, but our supervisory staff just let us allow to vent. Were we just managing to cope, stuffing it, or exploded somewhere else with no change?

"What the hell do they need hair tonic for? Can you tell me that?" Another objection was well received with a rowdy applause at once.

"Leave it alone." My dad's advice spoke to me from the past. "You can kick a dead dog all you want, but at the end of the day, you still have a dead dog." I remained quiet, listening to my co-worker's voice with the same feelings.

It took a while, but eventually the angst subsided. We got tired of hearing the same answers. The administration justified their liberal direction toward the improved health and welfare conditions adjudicated behind the criminal consequences.

The locked down inmates lived in a cell, who were allowed and entitled by the State's dole. The inmates were expected to cover all of their basic needs, but I didn't take pity for them. They were in confinement by their own doings. They deserved it, restrained of their own disregard of the law. So, how could I ignore a lot of others on the streets, who did nothing wrong and got a lot worse off... in another form of confinement? The illegal swelled in prison, while the lawman lived on the outside to fend for himself. Abiding citizens expanded the laws to feel each fine, but LOP in prison, on the other hand, had a tool of gratitude or a temporary ding. The inmates and criminals met their satisfaction, when safety and security couldn't hardly compare the general public's welfare.

Medical and dental staff were always within reach to be monitored during any number of chronic conditions, or where emergencies were called out to see a specialist. DOC had a transport van with two CO escorts for the appointments outside of the prison walls, but he'd never worry about a missed meal. There was a sack lunch to be prepared ahead of time to keep it handy in the kitchen cooler.

Any financial benefits, such as earned military pay or retirement benefits, nicely padded their bank accounts throughout their sentences. The inmates' discretion, like a single room apartment, was quickly filled without the need for a job. Electrical appliances like a television, electric shavers, goose neck lamps, or a room fan arrived shortly, although the temperature-controlled cells were already set through the vents.

Toiletry soap selections include a variety of hair and body products to be purchased pennies on a dollar in comparison, but if an inmate didn't have the money to purchase the basics, the state provided to cover their indigent status, while the tax payers picked up the tab. The monthly supplies were required for his hygiene products that included stamped envelopes, writing tablets and a pencil. And with all of that, the state restored it with an additional $12.00 balance each month, as if welfare checks meant the same thing. It was automatically deposited into their bank account for their use in prison, by an extra or enhanced cable service television that cost $1.00 monthly, for example. Their personal choices were not negotiable to stay within the inmate's catalogue orders… for the 'door to door' CO's deliveries.

Their awarded income,(whether it was SSI, retirements accrued, or interest growth from the top, could've been ordered against anything, like over-the-counter (OTC) vitamins or other mild pharmaceutical treatments without medical need. Candy and cookies, jars of peanut butter and whole loaves of sliced bread, packets of tuna, beef, or cheese spreads, according to the inmates' needs with a receipt. Doritos and any variety of chips enjoyed their soft drinks aside a personal cooler right next to his bed, who kept their fresh bags of ice on demand at the kitchen locker, too. Their late-night munchies or afternoon snack time was right there for a movie of their choosing's, which was all to himself. Greeting cards, dictionaries in Spanish and English or a combination of languages in the same book for translating, and even ink pens could've also been found in that catalogue, although that was more than a pencil which was docked out of their money (on paper) for the asking. And at the end of the month, their bank accounts were replenished to keep the supply coming… for his records. No one could cheat anything out of a thing.

The inmate library provided a plethora of reading materials, who merely asked for a variety of college courses or a gained GED for free. Additional reading material could've borrowed out, or owned their own newspapers and magazine subscriptions to be purchased through the good ol' US mail, while the inmate banking department took care of the bills to monitor or intercede the undue debt concerns.

The inmates who lived alone in lockdown listened to music of their personally purchased CDs, who didn't have to borrow out any other inmates or damage their things, but DOC policy monitored his accumulated space. Over time, their limited amounted items had a simple form to be pared down of his choices, with the option to donate it out to their family and friends.

Visitation was encouraged, but only heathy relationships were pre-approved. Adults and children, family or friends could've been seen weekly, and/or talked by a monitored phone that was delivered in the privacy of the prison's cell-phones.

Programs aided each inmate according to their personal counselors for everyone to work through any number of other issues that was deemed necessary by the Psych Department. And, sometimes religions had just the answer by faiths and/or personal Bibles' readily available, supported by volunteers, or the prison Chaplin.

"Not bad!" I realized the irony. I began where I'd left to be relocated in a small apartment alone, where I started out on an air mattress to sleep on the floor before I bought my first coffee pot. I eventually accumulated to be satisfied over time, when I budgeted every receipt what I protected and safely owned from anyone else. I turned the dead bolt where I lowered my guard inside of my apartment, wondering whether the Parallel Universe should've satisfied the balance during the academy, as I faced my standard of living in my uniform.

"The incident is still under investigation." The briefings continued, but the sergeants and/or lieutenants had nothing more to add with my shift. Day shift, on the other hand, had three times the number of officers, and second shift had twice the number of the officers in relationship to the skeleton crew... who suffered in silence.

The workloads adjusted the numbers down of each shift, but especially when the grave officers were borrowed out temporarily, reassigned out from the other units to equalize its coverage. Another

CO came in to help, where the lockdowns were never sent out. We'd only received their backups in one direction, since I wasn't about to be swapped out to another unit, instead. The lockdown was my base, and the rosters merely filled in the blanks for a name on paper, and then it was my turn for some other unknown officer who was my partner. The COs were assigned out from the opened yards, who obeyed the orders... with no experience, or when they'd volunteered to fill in an extra shift, too.

Officer Alvarado wasn't any more anxious to pad his income to be jotted in. The roster called out everyone's post who took their equipment, but CO Alvarado was just glad to have the job or the reason the lockdowns held an additional hazard stipend. Nonetheless, he was welcome! Every now and then, the borrowed officers took the lighter job at the controls. We swap out the floor posts with the second half of the shift's share, where he was posted for the first security check, instead of me.

I had the service logs to be prepared as I listened by each squawk box from all of the pods that were quiet. The flooring post officer expected to arrive within the first 10 minutes, as I watched from the glass-bubble room that was built, (physically) suspended between the two-tier stories.

CO Alvarado assumed his post for the floor, and I'd operate the controls to managed the touch screen panels which was replaced from the clumsy knobs, when DOC evolved technology that covered two posts more efficiently. I chased across the cat tunnel of either sides, as if anyone should've been able to handle just a single review, figured it alone, or ever at all... but it was the orders.

"This place is really creepy." His voice spoke from somewhere as I spun around the chair, desperately looking around, and unable to locate his echo. I expected him who just came back from the first pod, and then he was gone!

I hit the day on the job as if nothing was anything differently, and I did watch! I saw the pod open. I saw his initial walk, and I knew that he returned. What happened? That first pod was success-fully finished and then I closed it to open the next pod walk. He was right there, and then the officer was just missing. Did he just leave? I stretching onto my toes. I scrambled around, while I kicked my chair out of the way. I jumped and for a moment I lost sight of him, as my heart was wildly afraid for him, when he whispered once again.

I had my partner, hung at the edge of his fingertips that framed a set of eyes right back at me. I dropped onto my knees, as his face strained to raise his chin from a short stepping stool who found that flapping hole at the floor, which was used to pass anything to my control room.

I had my fellow officer who arrived, but he didn't have a clue about the maximum cells risks, who was terrified. How vulner-able he'd agreed to obey the sacrificial gape of the roster for his first time!

"Do you want to continue, or would you like to switch places?" CO Alvarado's eyes were fixed on mine, who craved the courage that didn't just happen overnight.

I'd been able to detect its positive and negative energy, since I'd once hung on the edge of my fingertips, too. I understood his eminent fears, since I'd been conditioned to know about something wrong, but CO Alvarado couldn't have known. Suspicion could make my hair stand on end. I'd pay attention of its evil presence, when I'd walk away to survive unscathed, but then I saw how CO Alvarado was scared, too. There was an undefined sense of the crim-inal restraints, when there was a safer iron distance, apart in prison. I'd looked inside to check on every one of them, and sometimes they'd ignore my existence. The inmates were tuned out, staring in a gazing emptiness, when I constantly checked through the clear difference between the two, for safety sake.

I had the feelings that manifested any gaslight for the shock, when I'd flinch or duck instinctually. I didn't have to remember how my husband palmed my face with a quick shoved aside, stumbled against the countertop in the kitchen, who'd just returned home from a work day. I was pushed off balance, because I was in his way, but I didn't have to fall. Another second chance had another option, when I'd avoid it all together, again. Or, when I intuitively read the cue, which was planted by my teenage step-son that didn't need an explanation why he intended to hurt me. He held me up that had been set up to be rushed out to work, who planned to make me trip. He pulled a tightly stretched twine across the lower edge of my front door. And again, I didn't fall, because I could foresee the problem of my own safety. It was the same things. I'd gained an innate barometer to hone inside to "do the right thing" to do.

"No, I'll stay down here," He said, barely audible, as he looked away into the soft shadows of the security lighting. "Just let me catch my breath for a minute." He fidgeted for a few moments, who shrunk from my view. With a final glance, he said, "You'll keep an eye on me? Right?" And, he reappeared to enter the next pod for him, as I was proud of him.

It took practice to find the inmates inside of each cell to make out a shrouded image in a corner, lying on the bed, or unnervingly stood just inches inside the front of his cells that tested the wits of every officer. I watched him exiting with each pod, who looked up at me for another glance and a smile, visibly shaken through his courage.

CO Alvarado followed through every task, like when he key-turned the trap doors to take out library books to be returned. He'd fumble with the flashlight beam in the dark when he aimed on the inmate's forms to be signed out in exchange, away from their few seconds, but I watched. He had to take his eyes off of the inmate, while I focused on my partner through that first day for the pay, but the bonus was more than the money he actually gained.

All of the policies still remained written on the walls, where "Safety is not convenient", when nothing was discussed or explained any more. "It was just a matter of time," and after a while, the inevitable braced to wonder "What's next?".

DOC's Heath Center hired our Psychiatric Nurse, when he was escorted off the job. He made his rounds, dispensing the meds to the mentally unstable inmates at wing one. He spilled each envelope of the right number of pills in each inmate's opened palm. He moved along and visibly watched to make sure that Inmate Larimor swallowed after he wagged his tongue in front of him for the next cell, as usual.

With all the knowledge, we all expected him the finest details at zero percent error, when CRN O'Niel shuffled around in his medical supplies at the trap door that was still opened a bit too long. Inmate Larimor's poor communication saw the need to explain his message... by a healthy spit at the back his neck. He shouldn't have been teased in front of the drugs within range, who had to know how available it was, when CRN O'Niel wiped it off: understood!

He had the review who accepted the job. He could've been able to deal it with a paper toweling, thinking "Shame on me and move along", and the lesson's learned. He could've maintained his composure with a seriously disturbed inmate in his care, but he was incensed.

CRN O'Niel took the power in the wrong hands, but nobody expected to stop him. Every secure officer could've been armored that included their pepper spray. Usually shaken hand held can could've been enough to deter its two second burst, since we all experienced how it felt it in training. That lesson was meant to hesitate before its perfect aim and burst in the eyes, except our trained CRN couldn't have known how much pain he inflicted on everyone around.

He couldn't walk away, who couldn't control a 'tit-for-tat' response... that didn't belong, but who was the 'bigger man'... toe-to-toe with an inmate's response that didn't belong, either. He helped himself of the mass control tank of pepper spray, when he didn't confuse it with a fire hydrant of pressured water hung on the wall for a better choice.

CRN O'Niel lifted up the fogger from the emergency hook, as if he'd owned it and had no right or permission with the hose aimed into Inmate Larimor's cell, squeezed, and waved uncontrollably in the air, as if it was a room deodorizer that set off a cloud of the red/orange particles on everyone.

Inmate Larimor gasped with just one loud call for help, as he suffered through his nasal tissues, throat, lungs and eyes. He was unable to walk away. Our CRN cornered to inflict him pain. All of the officers looked up, when the results jumped into action... of the mistake. The immediate vicinity dropped everyone to the aid of the whole area, who scrambled as quickly as possible from spreading it any further. The issue jeopardized the entire health and welfare wing for its explanation later.

The first CO was able to resound the entire lockdown prison through the radios that initiated its procedures with one officer left behind all four other wings. The COs escorted out the inmates and their CRN first, in that order. The rest of the COs faced the compounding disaster against the clock. It was fought to control the clean-up, where the COs endured the most reliable 'victims', who were the silent 'heroes.'

I should've counted on our CRN. I thought his was certified to mean something better, but it was the COs life experiences that were beyond his book studies and grades. The wing was specifically hired to manage the mentally-impaired inmates' care, but no one expected the CRN to retaliate! He fully wore the blame. He was the cause, but the consequences landed on the CO's responsibilities, as if I (or any other fellow officer) was designed to make it fix, regardless.

CO Osterloh was the first officer who initiated the alarm, and not the CRN who worried about his own welfare. Officer Osterloh didn't ask why or how. He croaked out one syllable at a time to Main Control who carried that on from there, who only got out no more than a yay or nay response. The entire pod grabbed anyone in orange to be decontaminated in a safer location, while the others pitched in to limit and recover the least amount of the damages. Only then was our turn to collapse in exhaustion, later.

The COs swarmed in every direction, who were more than a job to police the prison of the Peace Officers. The control room officer engaged each paired-up escort to coordinate each lock safely opened, as the other officers poured in from the other wings, who lugged in the hurricane fans aimed at the recreation pen.

Everyone knew about the swamp coolers, anticipating its cycles before the pepper particles would be blowing through the vents. Their eyes seemed to bulge, almost panicking at the time to urge it along. I caught the attention for more, as I worked on an empty stomach, while others spit it up through their gagging reflexes, aside. Our tears shed and noses ran down every officer, who suffered to communicate with a wave and point, where the Main Control cameras had it all.

But, how much pain did I shed through the tears, when emotional pain seemed shallow to me, as if the CRN couldn't have been spared? He was safely removed by the first culprit, as if he was the "golden child". I had nothing to say, like I'd been shaken in too many other situations of my own. Our CRN was initially entrusted, but how much had he inflicted harm on others, too.

What was worse than a government job of the general public who held a higher standard? I could've been excused to step down or fired by the job of the State's income. That status wagered its integrity that also carried it against the highest penalties. I kept it under control, which was a greater demanded of any other officer swallowed hard, but real physical pain seemed frivolous in comparison to the emotional pain I wore down my sleeve.

I didn't have to sit with an inmate watch, but it was bound to be my turn. I was posted to stay right at his side, which was more accurately posted by a nurse's bed watch, through the shift. He needed to heal from a bullet in the gut after surgery, until each surgical repair was replaced too many times, and DOC finally decided to leave it alone. He wouldn't stop chewing through another hole at the bottom of his colostomy bag to play with it. His sentence could've been saved for another lifesaving to keep him there temporarily in suicide pod, as if I couldn't have enough distance from his frothy ooze on demand.

Inmate Collons was a fearless man in his early twenties. The medical ER was taken back several times to reattach its daily protrusion from his lower belly, when they decided to let him abuse his transitory colostomy sack. As long as he wasn't doing anything to compromise his safety, which was naturally collected or maybe saved up for the next one, until I realized how raw that fecal matter really was.

I learned how to focus into a bio-feedback technique to disassociate, mind over matter, borrowing an exercise, when I'd learned how to reduce my heart rate during surgery. It was a safer alternative to avoid general anesthesia during the procedure, when the surgeon hesitated and continue through my inguinal hernia repaired without incident.

Remembering how to ride a bike, was as easily able to keep my throat from closing up, was another skill I called back in practice. The stench of Inmate Collin's juices seeped into the clear sack for all to see... with another moment of truth.

Fortunately for me, he was housed at the farthest end of the cell's pod to be left opened for the rec door for any possible breeze next to me. The stench was still overwhelming through my crooked nose that was never set by a mouth-breathing habit's small blessing. His inmate cell stunk worse than a field of rotting cabbage in the Spring. I laughed right along with my coworkers, who congratulated me with a slap on the back to deal with it.

"CO, look at me!" Inmate Collons started out to get his seek attention, when I barely sat down. My clipboard began to jot down with his assessments every three to five minutes on paper, although everyone knew that there really weren't any codes to fit.

Either way, I kept an eye on him, squirting it from the sack with a little squeeze in my peripheral vision. I refused to connect or respond at all for a while. Surely, he'd eventually give up, as if I must've aged or lost my senses. But the truth? It was easier to control my gag reflex from looking up directly at him, while I didn't get his reaction to give in either.

He concocted another shock one thing or another, when one smeared his excrement onto his fully exposed body. It shrunk his skin like a facial mask from the neck on down that dried to flake it off, floating in the dust that began to collect on the floor.

"What do you want me to do?" I conducted as unimpressed as I could, while my throat closed up with every word. "There's the sink, wash it off." I pointed with a nod of my head for his stainless-steel sink at the front of his cell, which was about four feet from of me. It took him a while, when he ran out of anything else to get a rise out, who began to scratch and finally washed.

He had a 'bird bathe', when I looked up with a satisfying smile of a man, instead. For a moment, I think he wanted to apologize, as if I was seen in me the mother figure who was embarrassment, or whether he was just that miserable and hit bottom. Inmate Collins relaxed on a restful spot on his cot, who rolled his back to bed, but his body language was more important about his boundaries. I accepted my rightful place (post), and he had his rightful place in his cell, but there I drew the line. I refused from being sucked by a criminal's harassment, when he resumed in the most disgusted manner for the next officer.

Our shift commander made the right call to be rotated. One in the back line came right around, as if the complete circle finally ended after Inmate Collins was well enough to be relocated. All of my fellow officers were posted to closely watch his safety... to recover in prison during his gun wound, but there were others who didn't expect to live long out on the streets, as if that was the plan,

There was another inmate who didn't care whether anyone watched him or not... where he lived inside his mind. Inmate Luka had no concern for anything beyond his personal murals throughout his cell walls and ceiling. He was so busy, entertaining his finger-painting in the nude, as I glanced into every fifteen minutes, who didn't require an officer to sit at his cell front for a constant watch, which was in contrary to the self-destructive criteria.

Inmate Luka spent away the days that seemed nothing to bother him, while he strained to focus all of his energy to balance his weight, who stretched one leg to firmly plant his foot onto the iron writing table, as the other leg forced his big toe tip into the perforated wall of his cell front. That was his pose, who urgently reached down for some more finger paint that didn't need to be flushed, but his psychiatric drugs slowly adjusted him back into reality.

A can of pepper spray was enough to deter an inmate to stop head-banging against the wall, or when another inmate refused to keep his surgical stitches to put a stop picking off the sterile dressings. Pepper spray was needed to use it as a distraction that bought some time, which was never meant to be in the COs hands until its last resort.

And I had another young man, when Inmate Jerome was aware enough to conceal his behaviors between the random checks, but he could've been any other inmate who also preferred to be alone. The staff were entrusted to spend time with a few other things to be done somewhere else in the prison, since suicidal inmates didn't want to be bothered. Cutting some space of a twisted assurance couldn't have been any less. The coy inmate convinced his CO's focus away on something else, who might've tricked the CO's watch while Inmate Jerome resumed downward into his darkest moments through the nights.

Inmate Jerome was determined to keep his cell front away. He succeeded for a while, cheering out and loudly laughed hysterically, like a hyena, as if he was so excited to believe that he could accomplish that 'final line' of the (human) race. He couldn't contain himself, as if it was almost over to allow his success, when he seemed to invite the CO's applause for all to see.

The COs fought against his pulsated spurt, as if he was impossible to come near, since all bodily fluids were considered contaminated toxins treated it all more difficult, but he couldn't go down quietly, hollering out the greatest show over all other attempts. He had the sending out, which it got all the more dangerous every passing second. I saw it and at that time, I operated the control room by a birds-eye view.

"Wait." Sgt. Jeffreys took over Command from the first responder who initiated the alert system, when he swung out his arm like a driver who held back the passenger's seat during a sudden stop. "Is the gurney ready?" He made it sound commonplace without a doubt as my fellow-officers stood-ready, eagerly obeyed of his directions, while I turned up the squawk box in the pod to understood everything called out or motioned by any gesture from the control room. But how many COs could've fainted by the sight of blood, as if they'd never seen it before?

When I was a kid, I remembered the time I watched the farm animals to be harvested. The blood was drained to allow a controlled flow into the ground, as the full-grown animals collapsed peacefully before me. It was life's cycle and I participated it, but Inmate Jerome used his blood like a weapon, instead. Everyone feared his distance, knowing he could've infected anyone near, when I wondered whether he'd go down peacefully… or the fight.

"Where's the board?" Sgt. Jefferys' commands where calm and reassuring every step, but that in itself worked against me.

Inmates were not farmed animals, and I knew when excessive bleeding couldn't be stopped like a slaughter that wasn't right. I began to panic, while my sergeant looked like he was unnaturally patient. Where's the urgency? I saw the inmate sink, drooping to his knees, and collapsed into the pool of its thickening clots at his feet. I got outraged and he was under control! I was able to manage the control panels. I covered it all recorded, while stayed on top of the commands, but I couldn't turn off my gut that didn't feel right.

"Okay, NOW." Finally the sergeant's arm went up, as if I couldn't respond fast enough to engage the cell door to open. Sgt. Jefferys was the first one to enter the cell, who'd been slumping over. "Step aside." He yelled back at the other officers from their help, as I felt like I had to step back, too. He twisted the back of the inmate's tee shirt to form it in a few handles to gain a good grasp with a 150ish-pound body of dead weight. Then just like that, Sgt. Jefferys slid the floppy inmate out his cell and through the door. The upper level balcony slopped its blackened blood clots over the edge of the walkway and onto the splashed floor below.

But the mess wasn't about that bothering me. I didn't like the nonchalant attitude to submit my commander, who was allowed of an inmate near death. The audacity against my lead had an exploding fit inside.

I was aware of that weakening feeling of blood loss, experienced first-hand. I hemorrhaged during birth to my second daughter, when the contractions stopped with every precious blood drop was wasted. I needed my doctor's help, when the afterbirth refused to let it go, ripped out piece by piece that saved me. I was in a hospital setting, where I relaxed knowing that I was in good care, but it was a far cry in a congested prison cell with a sole man in charge.

I watched the time-window during blood loss, when grandpa relaxed calmly for grandma's forearm to pierce its blood-letting routine with a pan on the kitchen table. He said it made him feel better, and blood was assurance without any concern. Did my sergeant know how long he'd let it go, when grandpa never grew weak from **that** much?

Inmate Jerome's blood had been soaked on everything in his cell, where Sgt. Jeffrerys lost his footings that slid back and forth for the inmate. Both of them were in distress, yelling back and out of the away where he had enough space of the plastic board. They quickly scooped up the barely conscious inmate, when he had no fight left, to be carried out by the four officers down the stairs, and the nurse stood with its tourniquet once the gurney was transferred to the heath unit. There he was hooked up to a saline drip for the awaiting the paramedics with a ride to the ER.

When our job was done, and the order was 'cleared', standing down over the radio traffic. Inmate Jerome had been passed off to the health professionals, when the debriefings were held in the court yard. I was relieved from my post in the control room, who excused me by another team player, as the disgruntled whispers overflowed to the others: "Who's going to clean that mess?" which seemed to be the greatest concerns, who argued among themselves. The cell had to be decontaminated and sterilized, as if he could've been shortly rehoused, or had another inmate's cell.

"Job well done." Sgt. Jeffreys first words seemed to take off the pressure from a very stressful suicide intervention. "Did you see how quickly he bled out?" he continued. This was his way of offering an opportunity to address and settle the nerves of all involved.

"Why didn't we go in with the body shields? He wouldn't have lost so much blood that way." CO Hansen was trained in the tactical use-of-force who practiced it more aggressive of control, but our lead waited before he'd be able to intervene, until the fight was in submission. That would've been the safest way of them all.

"Did you see how much room we had to work with?" Sgt. Jeffreys went into the description of the space available, as he listed the problems that limited the amount of effort instead of tripping over each other, when he handed the first responders over to carry the heavy work of the lower level.

"Tell me," he paused for a second before continuing. "How quick could've been able to show up with the shields?" Officer Hansen repeated it as their sergeant resumed to nod his head, listening to hear and further analyzed the orders. It could've been their worse moment, urging the alternatives.

I also wanted to know. Sgt. Jefferys took Command, who seemed so confident, when they were held back who hung onto every moment. They feared Inmate's Jerome's demise. Officer Hansen pinned down their Command, who refused to be blown off, as if I agreed with the better options for that situation that unfolded, as we all grew. It defended a plethora of in the details to be recorded, until the fear and stress finally eased it to understand… into thanks. Anything less was cheated out.

"Where's Stevenson and Lopez?" Sgt. Jeffreys stretched out his neck, who couldn't see the entire responders beyond his view of the court yard, but no one wanted to say anything. We all eyed at each other, when the sergeant obviously missed two of officers at the entire debriefing.

"I think they're in the bathroom." I said sheepishly under my breath, as if I was a snitch. I knew Officers Stevenson and Lopez were physically ill after the fact, and unable to recover during an overly-emotional event aside. I couldn't laugh along or play down my co-workers, when I left with his head pointing out to get them.

I knew where they were hiding, who'd been afraid to deal the trauma in privacy, as I seemed to rush all the sooner. "They should be here to know this stuff!" I urged along as if I could talk them down. But I had too many things to remember about safety and the self-damages, like when I crawled underneath a bathroom stall to help get her cleaned up, once I knew about another woman who I stopped cutting.

And, I remembered how my fellow-cadets couldn't handle the violent reactions where I also watched the videos at the academy, when I held back their hair, as I began to worry, chasing down my fellow-officers to searching out CO Stevenson and CO Lopez, who might've been hung over the toilet to get it all out.

Did I forget about how fragile life needed to be there, who signed up, got involved, and anxiously intervened during the lowest moments? Who was responsible, which time was protected, or spared of their safety? We all (emotionally) bled one way or the other, whether my fellow COs and inmates experienced their lives to fight back, when I knew how important the options made me stronger for it.

Chapter 5

One Card Short

*T*here were plenty other openings throughout the State, but the officers were doubled up on the rosters in the lockdown unit, where I never expected to be assigned there any better. I took the assignment upon graduation day to think twice about it, as if the game of life dealt out the full deck around the table.

My mother was the matriarch once daddy died who rallied behind her, when there was no one left on my side, nonetheless. I showed up regularly, fulfilling the obligated visits spent time with my ma, no matter how I was rejected of the blessings for that career anything imagined against one excuse after another, when Allison arrived at perfect time during the dinner's dessert.

Ma welcomed her in, as she opened the news who decided to pass the application with something even better than me. She pranced in who was so delighted to be in the same field, as I supported Allison's choice for Probationary Officer (PO), instead. At first, I felt a relief to bond the career. I was enthusiastic to hear all about it. That was until ma directly turned toward me, as if I was pinned in completion to argue against my sister, but I didn't want to take anything away from her choice. Didn't she apply for that job, when I didn't want to take on that much for me?

"Oh no!" I relented, knowing how I'd be somewhat less than her field. I complimented her revered her choice! "I would rather work among criminals behind the bars. They would be exactly where I'd have them in each cell than someone else, chasing them down in their neighborhoods."

What? Did I say something wrong? But it was just like if played cards around the table, when I didn't drop the trump card for that trick. Suddenly the game was over, the hands were thrown in and Allison stormed out the door just as quickly as she arrived, when I realized that she never expected the oath of the law, and nobody needed to hear it again.

Eventually, it felt like I was being watched from the highest spectating sport, sitting in the bleachers behind the binoculars to see how well my loved ones followed up the scores... for the other team. Except 'the other team' was my choice. Of course, I made them mad toward law enforcement, instead.

Anyone of them could've played the all-powerful trump card over my decisions, who were coached through a well-played scheme. It was my savvy manner to decline and cordially beg to sit out, but the games weren't allowed to stop or ever end. A gamble of chance remained, tabled, and too important to be kept from my dream or my desire to try, but the ante could never settle high enough to fight against of what they didn't want me to have.

I couldn't have been more graciously respectful, while I had their hope to wish them well. My family rejected every effort to work in the prison, except where DOC believe in me. "Maybe later they'll see!" I shrugged, while I held out to let it pass, as if 'the door' still remained opened.

A second chance at the academy offered to reenlist after I'd been dismissed by a broken leg in defense training, but even that was a gift that offered a moment to ingest and reconsider. I recovered during a cast and crutches over eleven weeks, when a sabbatical had a wider perception.

Suddenly I felt selfishly needy, as if I was weighted down grounded, incompetently rubbed in, or worthlessly quit on. I had nothing proven, but either way, an abrupt silent treatment backfired, when I used it for a better look. I had to carry the papers walked out, but there was a promise to reapply in its best interest to start over. But even that when I thought it over, the decision grew all the stronger that was all mine.

I returned and jumped through just as many hoops as the next guy. The community billboard published every test result the wall in our classroom. I checked out how I'd meet the goals, passed or needed help, where competition didn't matter. My strengths and/or weaknesses, good or bad, involved all to see. The study groups discussed the key points, when no one had to realize how I struggled either way. "My loved ones would be so happy, knowing how I'd come along!" I thought, as we met gym after hours to practice our self-defense moves and worked to reduce the mile runs to exceed together. And I still held out hope, who'd surely believe me! But nothing was said, as I shook it off even further.

The state paid my way through the training's expense that didn't take it lightly, as if DOC also demanded the sink-or-swim 'grade' for me, instead. My attendance had been embraced by the classmates, who invited me to celebrate along the graduates to join the backyard party, but I cordially bowed out. It was their day, not mine.

Eventually I didn't need to tell anyone about my work in the lockdowns, where the inmates were housed of all ages, cultures, and socio-backgrounds that were segregated between the criminal categorizes, which was also well-spelled out in my space. I could physically meet and touch a visible sense to communicate anything interpreted, where prison dissipated its confusion, which also enacted out what I had experienced inside.

Soon, I no longer needed its inhalers. That breathless wheezing was gone. Chest pangs raced my heart like a revving engine was over. I was still nervous, but that kind of stress was different. I respected the finest cues put into practice, like how I used to watch over my shoulders to avoid trouble from my loved ones. My home-roots had all females raised among the lone exception of my dad, called: family. Genetically we all seemed to look alike, except for the color orange where I wondered if I was adopted out… in the uniform where I'd never fit.

Sometimes I imaged as if I was a badly worn power cord that nobody cared or bothered with it, until someone gets burned. Using black tape was enough to push it a little too far, as I did what I could hold it together. "They can't help it," I'd forced the hope upon hope for that breakthrough.

Years had passed when I began to realize about prison, as if my world had been closing the walls all around. "It just geography," when *The Pretty Woman* movie wasn't that funny in that apart, too. But the scenarios repeated the same places… in my mind. I'd been turning myself into a sentence of imprisonment, when an epiphany saw a day-certain toward its release. I had the habits for too long, until I'd faced the courage toward new and strange territory.

I came in with the same situations through the academy, when the rules at home should've already knew DOC's right and wrongs. I felt like it was time to brush myself off, where I had to dig in to find out what I deserved, whether I'd move to live to either ends of the country or where the most vicious criminals lived right next to me.

I was captivated toward something else, as if there was a whole a new concert artist on stage, which drew me out to join in and dance! I felt like I was wooed, regardless who would've been the lead or the followers to move with the flow. The tempo or genres didn't even matter, but a private song played the music in my soul to notice the subtle signs… up on my feet.

I was that illusive wallflower to be invited onto the floor with an extended hand. I should've been old enough in the 'finding myself' stage, since I was mocked to grow up, which was underhandedly familiar, delayed and held back.

I wanted to believe the benefit of the doubt who were just as firmly stanch in place. I remained bounded to my loved ones, while I didn't want to play anymore. I grew too anxiously annoyed, when it was just as easily dismissed to blow it off... but I'd been mistaking.

Too many tempers flew, who slammed me down the impossible trick bag of lies. I vacillated to give it in long enough, 'fool me once, shame on me. fool me twice, shame on you' turnabout had forgiven too often.

Playing cards illustrated their skills shuffling out the deck of cards, but Classic Solitaire counted on the full deck easily proven alone. I could've been fine to allow cards during the open yards during rec, but not in the high-risk gambling debts in prison, either.

What could've been hurt, as if my loved ones didn't mean any harm? It was just a game, as I fought against the opened seat, constantly invited to play, or else that would spoil the 'fun'. I heard the rules and all questions, until I wanted to see the directions, which was jolted out of my hand.

CO Sanders' interruption had also been reenacted through my family's shame, who looked down my nose. Didn't I hold the cards, until another person got caught, lie, or fess up? Did I rob their joy? my turn? or just a sore loser?

The card gambling inmates scrambled away from any direction. They clubbed together with one aside of the 'look-out' in orange, but I began to realize how I'd decipher between the black or white hats which also broke up through their guilty 'fences' to protect.

I went through any number of situations that finally sunk in, when somethings were not my place to be suckered in, anymore. Maybe I was too slow, naïve, or simply stupid to embrace peace management which was wrapped around me. Was that possible? Could my loved ones be right and I was wrong? And were there sides at all?

I chose law enforcement before I ignored the subtle hold, as if I carried the 'scapegoating bank account' with my name on the bottom line signing out every sacrifice, forgiveness, or emotional bankruptcy. It was my signature, my decision, and my responsibility, but I was cheated out, who didn't want me to sign up for THAT (in law enforcement). A need had been generously provided by any request which was my gift, unless the needs of obligation hurt, when I stopped to chase after anyone or beg to break their silent treatment, which seemed calming, instead.

There I investigated the answers, when I compared my apartment by the prison events written down from my chest pocket. I noted to substantiate everything valuable at work, when I began to note my progress inside. The window ceil was bare, where I had a little flower pot taking root by my two hands... to nurture that, too.

I studied the chaos, as I reassessed everything from my mind onto every page. I analyzed the magazines, catalogues, or mail junk ads, where everything affected my opinions. I was alone, but that meant I had 100% there.

Furniture styles were appealing, but what did 'I' like? I enjoyed it all but then I evaluated between the Victorian Era or the Southwestern flavors, aside any others that satisfied me of my choice. I tore in (literally). I began to spread out the snips to research 'me'. It truly made a mess but it was my mess, and nobody else had to see it embarrassed by anyone else. I taped and/or purged my desires onto paper... for me! It must've looked like the magnitude of the big bang, as the whole place sent particles wider and more finely defined... on a mission.

I split down the topics that expanded another 3-ring binder even further. I'd took over to reconsider and change my mind as if I wanted to 'buy' the best stamp of approval inside, but there was real debt to rebuild back my credit score tightly budgeted to balance my own checkbook to manage... of what I owned in both inside and out.

Thrift clothing filled my wardrobe, where I found a few pieces of furniture to make it work. The things I had to do at work became all the more anxious of mine home, too. I picked up across the living room items, as I put the air mattress away with a real bed. Isolation learned to enjoy selfish protection, as I relaxed from anyone else's judgement or competition, who didn't have to see what I had.

There was a time I learned how to negotiate when I was happy to let my husband to be the head-of-household in charge, as if the man was supposed to be a pride thing that didn't matter to me. I stoked his ego, until it got out of hand. Slowly, I couldn't backpaddle to submit to his command, like when he practically pointed to the mat to 'stay' or when I was summoned out in service at any time.

I sunk into depression, too tired, and impossible to meet every challenge that was important to be appeased... to the winner! I had to allow it, unless the 'debate' was too easy when his menial conquest wasn't enough, and he'd retaliate. I had to play, the right way! It was like I would scream out 'uncle', like if it was the code when I threw in 'the towel' that wasn't high enough of his victory to be disqualified. A rematch never allowed it to quit, which was planned out that way, but there was no one to turn to or deal it differently.

I didn't see the need for failure, until I didn't care anymore and I stopped to supply the blame game, which amped up the 'scarlet letter' for everyone to boast the most ridiculous things against me. Why even bother to appease anyone, who robbed my own personal right? The cameras or property also whittled down me into damaged goods, except I had something better to recover through my career during the solitary life apart.

Once at work, I had another inmate in the lockdown who wanted to provoke me. I could choose any other reaction as I'd listen to think about how I'd react to try out some other diplomatic styles of my own. And sometimes I was wrong. It was hit or miss, when I hurt him to take the blame.

Inmate Cortez was atrociously obnoxious, as if he couldn't be stopped. His mouth was loud, vulgar, and raw every time I looked in to check on him, but the security door squeaked open for the pod into action. He merciless kicked up every night that would never let it go, but even negative attention got his attention.

He wanted to interact, using any other things to get under my skin for a rise. He begged any kind of response in return. It was just a game. I knew it and laughed it off, until he wouldn't leave me alone. He egging it on that started to spill over the rest of the pod. I could handle him, but then the other inmates shouted back and forth to stimulate the fight that involved more than Inmate Cortez alone. Nobody was taking sides or gang up against me, who just wanted some peace and quiet, but how many begged me to give in what he wanted, too.

Self-disciple and control could last all throughout the day, until I was forced to do more than a cordial 'no thank you' for the rest. I was fine, even proud of the due diligence, except when the other inmates' patience ran out. They wouldn't tolerate Inmate Cortez's disruption from their sleep long enough, but Inmate Cortez didn't care about anything but himself. I had to, but now what? Did I cause trouble by doing nothing, where I had to face the instigator! I bit my tongue. I stood face-to-face and accepted the challenge. I could give in just enough to satisfy the fight, but I did it wrong!

He quieted down low enough for only him. I thought I'd spare him from the other inmates in the pod, except he got it personal. He was a little too cocky and a bit too close... between his suited cell: "You're just a little man in a little cage."

It wasn't meant for an audience. It was meant to just him and I, alone! I thought it would hurt with a swift slap on the wrist. I had enough courage thinking, 'You want it? Here! Now it's my turn!'... but it was just words?

Inmate Cortez went ballistic. He turned the pod upside down, who didn't have to include them suffer. Maybe I should never have said anything, sucking it up as before, until I was under the pressure to force my hand. I had no choice to sit out and do nothing about

Inmate Cortez, until the other inmates in the pod added its pressure on me... to do something!

I through about switching places, as if another seat around the table had better luck. The cards were dealt out, since I was bound to lose... for something else. I watched how the bets filled the ante that went out to the other players, hoping it might've balanced out my pockets.

I didn't like to play it anymore, when no one rallied around any better than I expected. My hand was dealt out of the exact 52 cards of the full deck, as I wondered how long I had it pass, until I threw my hand that was never supposed to be my trump card. "Show me your hands!" I made the 'table laid' call for everyone's hand shown all turned up. I went ballistic. It was always intended to be stacked against me, which was why the players urged against taking that job. "Who learned how to deal from the bottom?" Their 'best interest' worried about the sharpest games, who also played in prison. But by then, I was already... in DOC.

CHAPTER 6

For the Taking

*I*t only took a moment to complete every security check
throughout the night, as I walked softly in the pods, counting
down the stairs to avoid the clanking screws through their sleep.
Although, some officers found it amusing to use a well-placed
stomp, as I conducted the exact opposite of the accused criminals.
The security devices from the control rooms operated my computer
sensors by tripping it out prematurely. Stopping a fully opened door
from a full speed slam was that little hint of respect that made the
biggest difference.

The inmates were conditioned to lie down at the same time of
the lights, as I anticipate anything to enjoy the peace. Whether sleep
ever came that easily, a diffused flashlight bounced against wall or
floors to process their surroundings propped against the far corner
at the foot of their bed or paced in circles, hardly taking three steps
in any direction in an effort to walk off enough energy to sleep, as
if they seemed counted on it.

The scheduled chores supplied another task of each walk, while
I anticipated ahead to thwart off any attempts to end their sentences
planned by an escape or suicide. At any time to end their torture to

find rest only needed about a ten-minute window, while I held out the hope for the best of the inmates, instead.

There were no ugly faces jumping out for a nervous rise or any ghostly images spooked by the night reaper through the shadows, when I turned to check out and dissipate the thought about suicides at all.

I began to practice another habit with an intentional pause that kept me from overreacting rashly, as I studied each situation before I'd act. It caused a moment to listen before anything I'd say, which was how their silent treatments became a well-expected default response of my loved ones, as I sorted out to process the opinions behind my back, like I tried out what to obey and what no longer applied. I was going to be involved to play the game of the rewards and winners, regardless. I'd never been allowed to accept the trophies to be cheated out, when I realized that that was the game!

I couldn't open up or divulge every secret, who tried to pick-my-brain. I was baited through every scheme to be fooled to remember how the shrewd insults empowerment them, when the inmates were also very clever to catchup with my skills, too.

Any gamble was what they wanted more desperately, who were just as staunch as before. The consequences only knew one thing, behaving to feel more confidence stronger, but some inmates loss ground, spinning downward in prison. Isolated lifestyles grew more anxious. They couldn't see it any other way out to contemplate suicide, while I fought against them to complete their sentences, as if I couldn't escape the rut, either. I was posted to face each suicide watch in real life and death danger, since I already experienced it through... to pass it on.

Every onset was always welcoming it to figure out the unspoken thoughts about a repeated dream that turned into nightmare in my childhood. I dreaded it. It terrorized the same panic when I awoke and no one there next to me. It could've recurred at any time, except when I wasn't asleep. I accepted to step up and take the post right there, when I was next to him, wishing it could've been me in those lowest moments, instead.

A dream kept coming back and I was enthusiastic to welcome the chance to be played out, which robbed me up in a jolting screaming jolt, when no one else heard me beyond my mind inside. I got too scared, willed to be awoken from my dream cut short, knowing I'd try again.

One part of me negotiated one for the other to beg, when nothing was going to cooperate. The one part of me was just as appeasing, which was just as strong on the other side to fight against it. I truly cared to pick either one of the more responsible one, but I didn't concoct my dream that didn't consciously plan the plot which I couldn't forget.

There was nothing more than a glimpse, when a split second flipped into a panic. Nothing could've been explained to anyone to know about it, when I was very young of the first time. The quietest morning was when I yelled out, who said "It was nothing. Go back to sleep," but I couldn't stop worrying, craving to understand, until it kept coming back that expanded and never let it finish, but it was also like I would never be left alone... inside. It further unfolded as I grew older. The more details I got, teased both sides of pure joy that made a turn shuddered in fear, but I just knew something was important.

"Remember how it turned out last time?" I pleaded with plenty of time to know... intensely obsessed a little longer, when "It saw me!" In all of the great vastness was nothing in the way throughout its unimaginable and breaking speed, when I lost reality. I was lost into the delight with just enough time to relax, while I got in trouble to heed the warning: "Please, please wake up NOW!"

A loosely wrung of its existence was more than a speck of light when I could see how a hollow and transparent ball became so enlarged that split opened by the energized strands to engulf me, as if I wouldn't dare look away for even a second. I was so afraid to be slipped inside, and taken forever, when I awoke, drenched in sweat, collapsed, and exhausted. Lying awake didn't offer any relief, as I wept in silence.

"Can't you go cry somewhere else?" My husband was irritated, turning around back to sleep. I knew that I was going to wait out the night, at the far side of the house where I could cry freely in a place to let it all out. I huddled inside my afghan on the couch as hours passed before I crawled back into bed carefully undetectable, like if nothing ever happened, but it was my problem to wonder why.

I relived every browbeating into submission, who sympathized my husband, instead. I was pathetic through every criticism to measure up, knowing how I believed his unfairness, as if that grand orb in my dream was the unconscious life would never win... who'd consumed me. Nothing mattered how hard I tried or whether anyone cared to help me, as if I was just a waste of money to bother the expense of therapy.

Bob was surely the better parent, even though I was a very nurturing mother of my family. I took on the adult roles, when I gave in that never meant to be the 'perfect' couple from the start. Our marriage was never planned, when I was shortly out of high school and play time was over. Eighteen years old was legal enough after the drafted army had to grow up, too. Nonetheless, I truly was too immature. I was a giggly mate to satisfy his insatiable need, when he came back our land.

Abstinence was spent during the Vietnam War once he returned, as I simply obeyed because I was glad to meet his desires... for the mistake. My babies followed every miracle to know when kissing or hugging was supposed to be meant for the children, and I was supposed to behave and be mature with every 'guided' detail.

I was stuck, wondering if he'd reach wit's end, tired of me, or whether I was burned out in prison, where I had a place to monitored and manage criminal life all around who still remained. On the outside I looked like everyone else, until I wore the undeniable stand behind the uniform. There I was defended behind the policies, but there wasn't enough to find the answers on either side.

"Pruitt, you'll sit on Inmate Enoch tonight." The roster was read out loud for my post to take the rest of the equipment on my way for the previous shift.

Inmate Enoch was admitted to be housed among the general population of the wing for his sentence in the double-bunked lockdown, but there was no one else in that cell. There really wasn't much available to have. In fact, it was actually quite sparse considering the first three or four months that didn't really matter either way.

Sometimes it was easier for me to watch over a hundred inmates than an entire shift with one inmate to keep a close eye on him, as if no one else had anything more important, except I took each suicide watch seriously.

Inmate Enoch had given up on himself, or maybe the whole system let him down, but it didn't have to be like that, or whether my social status, economic situation, or age meant anything else. If fact, my presence might've been irrelevant in his eyes, unless Inmate Enoch had nothing to fight over to want anything, empty and immeasurable... plus one. I understood the need of its worth to make it matter, for no other reason than me at his side. Connecting one with another couldn't cancel out zero to zero, because that in itself outbalanced the need to hang on.

He was physically extracted from his cell who stopped him slamming his head against the wall, but the suicide cells of that pod were almost always full, teetering the edge between life and death. They all needed their attention, but my secret stared right back at just one inmate in trouble, and nobody else had to know why I had empathy for an inmate of imprisonment. It would've been his decision to take his life, except when it was in my hands, and never allowed to be abandoned for a moment that affected me in the darkest nights... alone.

I rotated out the other officers who made themselves comfortable at the front of each cell, as if it was nothing more than a blessed reprieve, except for the laminated and indestructible card remaining handy with each daily review that was considered part of the uniform. I knew how much damage could've been done in a very short time, but Inmate Enoch couldn't have been oblivious of the change-of-the-guard... when I arrived.

His mind was on other things to babble, or things I didn't want to hear. He grumbled all the while he was stripped down for the suicide smock cover, after their last emergency was set up with another cell and his personal belongings were temporarily safe in storage.

Inmate Enoch sat quietly on his mattress against the far wall, rocking back and forth, with his legs crisscrossed in front of himself, when I came to realize how different each CO worked the same posts accordingly. Some were better skilled and some things were just not allowed, but then it was me there, and I couldn't be ignored with an inmate.

Inmate Enoch sat totally deflated like a limp rag. He was reduced to a self-dehumanized shell who couldn't even consider an escape, which I'd make sure he couldn't have made it any lower. I looked upon him in as much as I saw the lowest and most desperate moments, who once looked down my nose or looked the other way, since he'd climb out... for himself alone in a cell.

He was extremely protected from any eating utensils or napkins that was limited with the basic finger foods, which was unwrapped by the paper or cellophane that was passed through the trap of his bare hands from anything used to be choked from everything that was removed to the trash when he was done. Toilet paper was handed as necessary and visually flushed to make sure the wadding paper couldn't jam down his air pipe, and when he didn't find a cup was nothing more than a drink of water from the palm of his hands. I separated his pain to keep his distance from his crime, who needed a well needed break... together.

"Enoch, Enoch!" I called into his cell as discretely as possible. "Enoch, don't fall asleep like that." I urged it on more and more, as if I'd eventually quit. "You need to keep your head and arms visible for me to see at all times." He finally laid down and slid out of sight inside of his blanket. I saw how he'd been curled up, but even that wasn't safe about the suicide pod's policies from his prior location.

The shift commander and a few of the male staff entered the pods twice a night to inspect the blankets that had been changed by another DO (department order), since Inmate Turner scratched a hole in his suicide blanket who never thought it could've been torn. It took him all night and by morning he was found blue, where hanging didn't have be suspended from the ceiling. The officers went in non-stop when CPR lasted about a half hour. They wouldn't give up, when the paramedics arrived who restored the vitals before he was taken to the hospital. Inmate Turner had been transported back to his cell just 3 days later with no memory of the incident to resume his sentence, but DOC found that 'loop hole' that filled in the addendums to make sure the blankets remained intact.

"How's this?" He shuffled around inside of his cardboard and densely felted bedding, which was all he got.

"That'll do. Thanks." He made enough of an attempt to comply, as he uncovered his head to expose his face by his hands showing.

I had my own come-to-the-Jesus moment, when I wanted to surrender it, too. I was stripped down and too exhausted to continue life anymore. I didn't even care, since I had no fight left in me. He could find another and better woman instead of me, I thought! He could have it all, and then, the plan became convenient, who was more than happy to enjoy it during the upcoming visit to his folks. Memorial Day was set aside for a four-day weekend that should've allowed enough time to be spent the in-laws, which was really the other big event designed to be freed of me, knowing our marriage never wanted it in the first place.

I couldn't handle it anymore, while he put on the face for a good idea to be cleanly cut it out of the picture entirely, and Bob was pleased! I had everything prepared and ready to succumb to the fumes that coughed out of the old car. I had a few magazines to slowly relax silently, suffocated of the final breath. I planned to leave a full tank on idle in the garage, while I felt that sense of euphoria with the end in sight to all my sadness.

In hindsight, I didn't realize just how wrong that happened about me, until I'd understood how susceptible suicides needed, and its importance about me at the academy. Bob could've been charged, under the categories of many but specifically in the 'deprived indifference'. He hid it from anyone, and the whole time he decided to assist my death. (If you're not a criminal, what kind of people are you? If you know about pain, who looks away?) By doing nothing to stop it, he facilitated the ability to follow through with the plan. He had an explicit agreement for the death of his wife and/or mother of his children.

When they returned, Bob left the car at the end of the driveway by the road, who was told to wait and check the car. Did my children wonder, or whether the car was even road worthy? He told the kids not to come running out without an explanation, who obeyed. He walked all the way up the driveway alone were his car still remained, parked far enough and out of their view. He took a look into the side of the garage window, who cupping his face to strain to see the slumped body into of his 'hobby' car. I saw it, while stood trembled away from the kitchen windows who never took a glance back at me. I was supposed to have been dead, after all the time he wasted the whole weekend to watched over my children's holiday, instead. I changed my mind who felt cheated! He though he could've trusted me, or rush back in my arms to be there. He came into the kitchen's back door. I survived... and he was pissed! And, all I could do was just take it.

He kept my children greet me back home from the outing either. They all walked right by me to go unpack, but no one had to know what they held inside too.

If I called 911, if I told someone, or whether I'd talked with the police about the trouble I feared, I would've had the police witnessed what Bob did from the other room. I had the power to see him haul away in cuffs, except that arrest would've left a mark on my children's record, and I walked away.

I just took it. He didn't feel bad, beg for another chance, or profusely apologize, when there was no remorse... since we shouldn't have gone through a shot-gun wedding. He didn't come to our wedding night, drunk after the reception, more interested in Johnny Carson's "The Late Show", instead of me.

Bob was a war hero from Vietnam who swept me off my feet. I was smitten by an older man (6yrs older than I was), who couldn't get enough, and how could I say no? I couldn't let our age difference show or tell him that I wasn't ready. For about three months we were inseparable, with one thing on his mind and nothing else mattered. Our whirlwind romance took all my time. Then one day, he was done. Finished. He had no explanation, and there was nothing to discuss. I thought we'd been making love, but love had nothing to do with it.

"If he's good enough to sleep with, he's good enough to marry." I was ordered to find him and tell him that I was pregnant a few months later. Although he wouldn't give me a reason why he no longer wanted to see me, but it didn't matter. Just like an inmate who was removed from society to be handed over to the state, when I was entrapped in marriage.

Every shift supervisor came around to conduct the random checks a couple times every night. Inmate Enoch obediently stood up to hold his blanket by the corners in front of himself, in a broken sprit and stripped naked to validate policies. There was no fight left in him, and when they finished the check, he went right back to sitting on the mattress, rocking even faster than before. Sgt. Willowby didn't need to say a word as he observed the yard staff who swept through each cell for any tampering signs, then they moved along to the next cell to repeat the same.

Another inmate above him tried to sing the songs of yesteryear. He subbed in some of the words, partially-forgotten lyrics, but no one reacted either way, and so was Inmate Enoch seemed unaffected, too. At times I worried that he would topple forward, exhausted yet still there while I watched, hoping he would lay back down again. But I didn't say a word. I knew his mind was racing and I did not want to interrupt him face his own demons locked inside there, too.

At times I saw him broken down, and cried. And, I saw how hard he tried to conceal it from me. He lost himself for a moment, swiped across his runny nose when he realized that there was no sleeve, and he lost it again. He flagged an arm, slapping himself in the face, taking out his anger with his fists while he muttered vulgarities to himself. I tried to offer some space to look the other way, but I saw it. He was reenacting a scolding, like the browbeating I used to do in that private place on the other side of the house, where I didn't have to hold back, when no one else was around.

Whatever he did or whatever I heard him say of what little dignity he had. I checked my watch and lowered my eyes, focusing on him with my peripheral vison, but never losing sight of him closely. He didn't need to feel my eyes connect or appeared to be stared down. They say that your life passes in front of you when you die, as if I let it pass by on the edge, searching for a reason not to that could've been me.

I pushed myself out of the sunken seat into my chair, which was worn beyond something a second-hand store made it work. Not that it was ever in good condition. It was passed along from the Administration Department to the floor officers in the prison to get a few more years out of it. I had to stand up and walk in place to restore the circulation in my legs throughout the night. An edge protruded frame bar across the chair frame, cutting into the back of my thighs, but he didn't need to know that. I didn't want him to see how he struggled inside either, while I wouldn't dare leave the front of his cell.

Every time the control button pressed the security door opened with a full-powered stop slammed hard that amplified the cement and iron pod in the night that was purposely disrupting of what little peace robbed out, with a reminder that there was nothing but a barren cell to stare behind the spiral remaining to restore or salvage what was left. He jumped, startled in a high pitched "fuck," between the grumbling underneath his breath to identity of whatever he owned to be damaged to him, or whether he was victimized in an unholy manner, who couldn't wrap around his thoughts, where prison had no apologies and no mercies for him.

He was only a twenty-six-year-old kid, barely grown, as I wondered of what could've made the difference in his life, instead the housed the state prison that was paid back to the lockdown. He wasn't forced to steal drugs, commit petty theft, or vandalism for something more firmly embedded with a permanent scar that stared right back at him.

The parallel universe lesson at the academy was that correlation, until the questionable claims didn't fit. There had to be some big mistakes to sort out, and someone had to be the big enough person to own up. Someone had to be called upon for another decision, or choose to point something out to explain of what no one could understand. There had to be answers, blames, or pushing the buck on someone else. Either way, whoever owned or claimed the responsibility to deny or expunged of what they could, until imprisonment paid.

Had he hooked up with the wrong gang for acceptance? Did he flounder without any direction, approaching doors that were not meant for him? Whatever he missed or should've gotten, didn't matter anymore. Even the soothing love songs from the second floor had grown distantly isolated, staying there with him in silence.

My shift ended at the crack of dawn, and I was happy to see when the relief shift arrived on time that I could walk away where a tree was planted just outside of the entrance and/or exit door. The doors were held wide open. Nothing stopped the foot traffic, but then, and a noisy flock of birds flew into the sky when I passed by. I joined the caravan of old beaters migrating out of the parking lot of another form to leave.

Luckily for me, I resided nearby in town, without the temptation to stop and pick something up on the way home in uniform, where I had no need to broadcast my occupation... just around the corner on the outside. We knew each other, identified and greeted, like a secret vote from anything standing out to move along, or where the perpetrators raised concerns behind their best behaviors to see right through it. In public, they were everywhere, when I believed that I wasn't off the clock until I removed my uniform to drape over a kitchen chair to dry, with a line of uniforms ready in the closet for the fresh one to finish out the week.

"Are you ready for another watch?" Sgt. Willowby had another fill to run the show, who greeted me from across the room just as I entered the briefing room the next day. "We've got Inmate Pina back again." I was specifically selected for the order.

"Sure. What's his problem this time?" It wasn't as important to know whether there was another post back to back, as much as something asking how I'd handle through another night.

"I don't know. Whoever knows with that one?" Sgt. Willowby leaned into his computer screen to update the roster to put me on another watch. "Just let me know if he gets to be too much for you tonight." But he didn't have to say it.

The shift commander had the daunting task of positioning our staff on the daily roster for full coverage every shift, who switched out the different stressors of each post by minimizing burnout on any given officer. It was obvious that he tried to change it up as often as possible, but some of us were better at some jobs than others.

"Hey, CO!" Inmate Pina called me, wanting attention before I had a chance to sit down and arrange my service log and observation forms to start my shift.

"Come on, man. Wrap yourself up!" I scolded him like a child, who knew better than a man running through the house without clothes on. I was well aware of his shenanigans and there was nothing he could do to make this ole girl blush. Besides, his commando dance was nothing short of ridiculous. In fact, it saddened me to see the depths a grown man would reduce himself to.

The inmates were generally cut some slack in the suicide watch pods. Basic infractions could've been otherwise penalized on another continuous watch. They were considered mentally off-balance, subsequently voided disciplinary tickets, who wouldn't have known better at the time. Inmate Pina, however, was a frequent flyer who'd learned how to play the system. He knew that every threat or cry for help couldn't be ignored regardless. Inmate Pina displayed a few distressful moments and that was enough to set himself up for another constant watch, as our CO's were paired up to sit with him throughout the evaluation period allotted for review, again. It was a game to him to get of what he wanted, but my fellow officers had to operate one man short.

I readjusted my stab vest for a little roomy fit to settle down, according to the amount of the minimal risk post that didn't need all that in a chair, as I fussed the knobs at the temples of my face shield to a slighter notch upward in place for the shift. That made quite a difference to breathe easier, since it had to stay on at all time of the continuous watch. The shield compromised the air flow when I raised it up between every pods' walks that felt suffocating, like it recycled its depleted oxygen from a broken nose. But it worked for the camera.

Inmate Pina clearly was not a suicide risk. He knew it. I knew it. But this way, he had a convenient 'front row' audience for some undivided attention. Regardless, the effect was made to put up with it. Maybe I would've done the same thing but I abide my temper by the senseless check boxes, dutifully filled, per policy.

I tried to gain a better perspective, but then again, I remembered how my second husband loved the seclusion at his desk in the basement. Rick was perfectly content in front of the television, and any other creature comforts. Inmate Pina's name could've used Rick's Freudian slip, who knew how he'd get his undivided attention whenever he was ready to call me out as needed throughout the day, and something's never changed. He was completely satisfied in his element. Prison cells counted on their food to be delivered and was picked up behind him, except for his toilet which was just a few feet away from the television, but who really needed, a remote?

I reviewed the inmate's psych evaluations and each housing restrictions on the wall next to their cells, and then, my bases were covered. An active taped camera recorded my every move, but that also used to protect the inmate from any part to review their accused abuse to replay its proof later.

"Yooo hooo, CO! Are you deaf or sompthin'?" Inmate Pina hollered out some new material for the show in line to get it going. He was a well-practiced egoistic inmate, which wasn't much more than my step-son wannabe stepped in with next the chip-off-the-block.

The briefing room had laughed in a roar with Inmate Pina. "Enjoy the show tonight, Pruitt!" Heads turned to watch the reaction for an old-mother type with old-fashioned principals to absorb their applause for his debut.

"She's gonna whoop his ass tonight." High fives mocked about the personality clash that made each double take... for my turn.

"I'll kick his sorry ass if he tries anything, Pruitt." The offers were in jest as I took it on the chin, thanking everyone for their tongue-in-cheek sendoffs.

Inmate Pina was a scrawny old man with a filthy mind, and no boundaries. I heard the stories of him masturbate and climaxing in front of the young female officers, who were too appalled to complete the night, but the sight of a man's genitals didn't produce the same reaction in me. The days of a hole for any man's 'toy' didn't stir the heat of passion. That wasn't any other kind of raise anything for me.

Quite the contrary, sexual gratification ran it in full throttle for a while when Bob came home from his tour of duty for some services of his own needs. It took about three months to get it back under control to manage another overactive libido of my second husband too, except Viagra came in all used up after Rick's computer's service too late in line for me. I was just done, pleasantly relieved and entirely celibate.

The space between the real thing was always a handy second option to know about being satisfied, who forgot a head's up or even ask. His surrogate computer with a steady supply, who called in for me to take him in for another 'real' emergency to spare his embarrassment. Desperation grew out of hand a little too greedy to help him, except the male imprisoned criminals could've eliminated that entire part of the challenge, as if that was tempting at all.

"Hey stupid, can you do this?" he bellowed for all to hear as I paused to glance into a controlled stare, rather than a rewarding double-take for him. He tried to start out with a bang to get my attention. The posed: turned around and bent at the waist with his palms flat on the floor who had to get up soon enough. Looking through his face turned bright red between his saggy sack swung to and fro below that framed his grin between a pair of hairy legs.

"You'd better stand up before you pass out." I laughed inside with a visual. I shook it off or cursing the thought I'd forget it entirely, but he wasn't done. He had to open his mouth and wag his tongue to point back at it for me.

"Goddamn, you're ugly!" No sooner had I glanced down to record the observation form, he slapped at the cell front where he pressed both hands, stopped in a rush toward its barriers. He needed a bit closer, squinting through one eye back at me. "No ring, huh?" He strained to get a clearer view. "Nobody wanted you?" His voice was melodramatic to drive the insult home.

I sat coolly unaffected. "He's exactly where he belongs," I thought to myself, even though I couldn't imagine anything worse for what he'd done to me than else. I was content and let go, sparing the shame of my children that I personally was responsible to expunge his rightful criminal history, forgiven.

"Whatcha got on 'er head?" He stared at me a little longer when he realized that there was a tattoo on a bare head. "Huh! Nothing!" He stepped back into the cell, laughing like a hyena, so proud of that last dig once he put it together. I lost my crowning glory after childbirth, but he didn't have to know that. I was only in my early 20s when I lost my hair that wasn't just shaved off of the choice. It slowly fell out and finally gone, when I coward behind a covering wig, towel, or turban to hide a perfectly smooth scalp.

"Grapefruit Gale, won't cha come out tonight," He began to sing about one of my most painful burdens to wear it openly from wearing camouflage in prisons. The inmates from the other cells throughout the pod enjoyed his performance, heightening the decibels of the echoing laughter for all to hear well down the entire wing at my expense. Coming out was hard, like a freak on display with one spotlight aimed solely on me, as if I was his new material's jokes to share throughout the echoing walls beyond the pod, but it was cruel, not funny.

"What's the matter with you, CO?" He stepped up toward me with his suicide smock finally wrapped properly around himself for some decency after hours of the incriminating abuse, already filled in with anything else. "Why don't you say somethin'?" He spoke somewhat calmed in a sincere concern. "Defend yourself." He urged as if he really cared, but I did not speak, controlling my facial expressions and body language to guard my thoughts. "Somebody's gotta toughen you up!" He began to pace, confused in the lack or pleas of another reaction from me.

"Oh, oh! Sargent's coming. Better behave myself." He tiptoed back like a prancing girl with a classy upbringing and cultured pose, who sat with his legs crossed and hands folded on his lap, when the trio arrived for the blanket checks.

"How's it going, Pruitt? Is he bothering you?" Sgt. Willowby came to my post in his dry demeanor and canned questions along each officer through the pod watch floor.

"Not at all, sir. He's behaving exactly as I expected." I matched my supervisor's response with the same lack of energy, as he signed off my observation forms that I used to fill in each inmate response of his behavior.

"Looks like he's been doing just fine tonight." Sgt. Willowby summarized my coded overviews, knowing that there was no way to feed his propensity to act up.

"Yes, sir." Inmate Pina, after all, didn't do anything toward self-harm during my watch.

"Good, good." He handed my clipboard back to me and continued with the other officers following to complete each task, approved, and he passed by.

I knew my shift commander checked off with every officer's emotional wellbeing, which he included how he checked on the incarcerated inmates on both sides of the enhanced security beyond the cells. Sgt. Willowby watched suspiciously over Inmate Pina's mortified and verbal language with the offer to switch posts, just in case the pressure was too much to continue.

But I heard so much of that before. I learned how I purged from my life by any other inmate, as if Inmate Pina had been removed from that part of my life to enforced my solid core, except for the pain that remained behind, unable to shake the remorse or believe of their denials.

There was no shame behind Inmate Pina's snide remarks directed at me. He was just as mean-spirited, like so many others. I hung onto the hopes against hope, who'd tried to run me down. He wanted me to get down and nasty like himself, but that kind of behavior didn't take that kind of strength to cause me to fold. Bullies were not the ones holding the power and control, when a stronger person stood against the evil and nasty minds... like him. "Anybody could lose control?" I thought, while Inmate Pina gloated in his abolishment's, challenging with one insult after another. Except, I sat through his watch, looking upon those who were locked away, separate, and detached. Knowing of what "You can't touch this", really meant.

"What's the fuck's wrong with you, bitch!" Inmate Pina was furious with me after Sgt. Willowby had completed his inspections. My report was going to be reviewed by the psychiatric physicians who authorized his continuous watch, and I had the ability to influence his chance to be held over for a few days of care, which was not meant for his pleasure.

"You're a real winner! Sitting there like a damn mutt," he continued, pacing in a circle, who wasn't able to shake me on the outside, but inside he was hitting me where it hurt. I knew how unnatural it was for a woman to be bald. Even though it was quite acceptable for the men to shave themselves. I learned how to view it as a gift, a blessing that kept shallow people at a distance, by those who can't or wouldn't handle their unjustified damages.

"I bet your mother can't even look at you." He was outraged and began shouting at the ceiling like a wolf at a full moon, determined to hit a nerve.

My mother didn't feel any pain for the cross I had to bear. Her response was simply, "There are worse things," but it affected every part of my life, including my sex life. It hurt when Bob held onto my turban in place during sex, as if he couldn't have understood the desperate climax who lost the amount of the pressure applied, squeezing my cover from sliding off. I had to lay still and stay in place with both hands tightly on my head, as I waited out the intermittent reward (and a true miracle) into his favorite missionary position with the plea "don't move, don't move" until he was done. He couldn't stand looking at me without my head exposed for the truth, as if he didn't want to know... where all of the inmates had a good look.

"Here, look." Inmate Pina acted like if he was the professor behind the podium, staged in the center of his cell for a lecture. "I'll give you some," he said, then, pulled at his pubic hairs with one hand waving it at me. "Oh shit, you're bare there too!" The light went on, and I buried my smirk into my paperwork. "You got some sorta disease?" He almost wondered or tried to recant, hobbled to the front who slapped the perforated wall with those skanky hands like I wished he could've taken my 'hand wash' squirt into his palms first. "You got cancer?" he whispered.

"I'm fine." I answered, finally hearing a respectful tone. What was I supposed to say? "No, it fell out due to a medical dysfunction by a survival mechanism, when my body was depleted beyond its limits?" He was too small-minded to grasp it.

"Good." He stepped away, thinking or walking it off, until he gave in and lied down on the mattress, when I savored the silence.

Inmate Pina threw off his game, who seemed to run out of energy, trying to get me fight back. He wanted to make me angry enough to lose control or lash out just like him, but cruelty was something I'd never understand why anyone purposely wanted to make a person feel badly. It just made no sense to me. He was as revolting as I had ever seen, but of what he had to say was a reflection of him, who couldn't repent either. The years threw at me to become conditioned to accept what couldn't be any different since I absorbed every blow, every verbal bout, I'd already heard from the same people who'd stepped over that line to love and forgive, as if I'd expunge every dig who might still respond in return.

"Shit! You're a frickin' nightmare to wake up to!" The peaceful pod was rudely awoken by the man with a mouth. It was all about him with no regard to the other inmates, who were so troubled and in need of intervention. "Don't you ever get tired of scaring the shit out of people?" He'd only taken a nap to recover and came back with a vengeance. "Why did you take a job to work here? This place will hire just about anybody, I guess." The degrading resumed.

I'd been called 'monster' or 'a leper' for as far back as I could remember, albeit in Parochial School. My classmates exaggerated a wide berth to make a safe pass, or when they'd scream out an alert all around especially at recess time who jumped up and laughed, when I was the entertainment who made fun of me. I knew of what it felt to be ugly, but being bald was nothing of what ugly meant.

Back in the elementary school years, eczema caused its problems in class. The thickened crusts made almost impossible to manage a pen or pencil to write, when I took a moment to lick and moisten my knuckles. I spit through the lesson or tests as I traded each finger to suck them to avoid it from bleeding a quick 'catch' to during class. Hand written lessons were the only options, but especially when I got it handed in, soiled. There I had it taken over, and aside.

That was at least until I'd saved up my babysitting money. By the time I was in my tweens, I walked for a doctor's visit close to the high school. Now that I think about it, a new appointment didn't meet the age authorization for treatment, but I was seen. I saw a doctor when I learned about the largest skin organ, which was expected to be my targeted weak organ. Even though I was able to have it manage the eczema of my own, the damage was already done. I wasn't meant to be well. The immune system was compromised, worn down from its chronic and untreated infections that carried throughout my early years of development. So then, the hair loss was no surprise from the specialists, and the consequences.

"Hey Sarg!" Inmate Pina hollered for the shift commander as soon as the second cell-search team entered the pod.

"Hang in there, Pina. I'll be there in a minute." Sgt. Willowby looked over toward me to see if there was any urgency before answering.

"What's up?" Sgt. Willowby asked when he arrived with the hand cuffs opened for the trap door, but inmate Pina didn't turn around to be cuffed up right away.

"Come here, come here, come here!" Inmate Pina whispered to draw over the Sargent for the furthest corner of his cell front, sheltered from my chairing in place when he thought it was clear to bend his ear for a moment. "I worked on Pruitt all night, and she never stood up for herself. Someone's got to help her stand up for herself. The other inmates are going to destroy her if she doesn't toughen up." After a few moments, the Sargent left him to talk to me.

"Pruitt, what's going on?" He asked while signing off on my paperwork.

"Nothing, sir. Why?" I was content with myself, just as before.

"Pina tells me that he was riding you hard all night and you never stood up to defend yourself." He spoke loud enough to allow Inmate Pina to hear of what was being said to me, so I did the same.

"Yes, sir. He was pretty nasty all night but I didn't see any reason why I should have to defend myself to an inmate." I didn't mince words and drew that line-in-the-sand for Inmate Pina to take a closer look at who was at the inside of that cell. I didn't see any reason to argue with someone who already knew how wrong he was, and if he didn't think his actions were wrong, defending myself wasn't necessary to waste any energy on him.

"Pina," The Sargent took it back to the inmate. "Don't take Officer Pruitt's courtesy as a sign of weakness. She is plenty tough enough." His response was the sweetest thing I ever heard! Finally, someone understood why I didn't argue against the cruelty of another. When I walked away in tears that was never meant of the insults to hurt me, but because how I hurt how badly abusive it was about them.

"The shift's almost over, Pruitt. Good job." Sgt. Willowby returned my clipboard for the last time.

"Thank you, sir." I resumed my watch in silence until morning when relief came for me to leave and I walked away.

CHAPTER 7

Free-range life

*T*he day arrived and the transfer request finally approved, which was the medium or risk-level-three unit of the lowest security level available for the violent offenders, but that was both good news and bad news.

"You're not going to like it there." I overheard some two-cents worth. "Watch, she'll be back," he continued just loud enough to be annoying. "Didn't you hear what happened last week?" Another night-shift worker joined to discuss my decision to leave, and I took the bait.

"Okay, I'll bite." I gave them a "this-better-be-good" look. I wasn't in the habit of sharing my personal business at work, but it was too late. The news was out. "What happened?"

"A new recruit never made it to his post last week." CO Kirchner puffed up his chest as he broke the news between a quick pull on his cigarette. "It shocked the shit out of everyone," he said, looking around for support, jokesters invited to go along with him. "You heard this, didn't you?"

"You're not talking about that guy that made it halfway down the center fence and then just turned around and left?" Officer Salinas smacked CO Amodor's shoulder when he finally realized what they were talking about. I smirked that sounded just plain silly to fall for it.

"You guys are so bad," I said, shaking my head as if they'd have to try harder than that, conning me with something so ridiculous. "There's no way! Who could to put themselves all the way through nine weeks of training, who just to walk off the job on the first day?" Half of me wanted to blow them off like another scheme to see if I was still naïve.

"True story!" CO Kirchner coughed a bit as he tried to talk before exhaling his last drag. "Ask the Sarg!"

Oh no! Now that must've been playing with me. I wasn't about to interrupt my supervisor to suck that in too. I almost smiled, grateful to prove them all just how 'quick' I had to catch. But there was no let up, challenging me to make it any more believable. Besides, I had too much respect for my supervisor's time. 'Wouldn't they love to see me follow through it?' I grew indignant. Did I have to slap the floor, as if I had enough shouting: 'uncle'?

But still, I felt like seeds-of-doubt still carried the wind in the air. I was thrown. Imagine the benefits of the caging lockdowns away from the high risking inmates, who were mixed along in an open yard. I had to trust the rehabilitated inmates all together. Except, a new rookie officer was just too much for the job. The fear gnawed at me. Was it a cute trick among fellow-officers? Or, was there a true warn to think it through? I imagined whether that edge was behaving through the sentences. I couldn't tell. I was confused to be all that gullible again. Did they test out that embarrassing spectacle to show just how much I'd grown? Were my team players trying to plant fear to protect me by staying?

Fact-finding studied criminal behaviors at the academy, and I paid close attention to the warnings: "Inmates are smooth talkers who twist their words just enough to plant doubt," but, that same swathe covered everything I'd encountered for a quick moment to remember from before DOC passed probation. "Pay attention

119

to your inner voice. If it doesn't feel right, it isn't." My instructor stopped to discuss the videos quite often, pointing out the details on the screen, but he wasn't showing me anything I didn't already know, or miss? I recognized the patterns. Forgetting the past was like bringing everything to the table. It wasn't the first time. I remembered to know about the conniving schemes to deceive me, trap, or was meant to harm their gain over myself, or just for the kicks. Either way, I listened; surely it couldn't have been true!

There was no shock or surprise at the work-place a little wiser. I had to look, really look at every detail. I'd dissected and broken down to match or compare. I analyzed each separate (puzzle) piece to contemplated and reason out the bigger picture. I needed to put it all together, which was also its depth by a wider view with another perspective like a different brush stroke, color shades, and effects determined every intense or subtle impression. It all mattered, even negative space like ignorant compliance in a blind objective was concerned. That was when I meant to be 'a good girl'… for another reason, too. Certain compliance was restrictive. It robbed me from it, straggling away the needed oxygen, which limited obedience deflected its responsibility and blame.

I was told to know one thing or another. I was conditioned to believe their narrow minded, or near sightedness, until everything took focus. I was sharpening up to recognize the difference, appreciating 'the better picture' to see it clearly. Each characteristic or personality was a conglomeration, visible to see of what was exposed.

I didn't design the spinning mess to live in confusion, which I didn't create of what was within its own cultural diplomacies and judgements. Traditions or selfish assumptions had been acquired to be made understood. Right or wrongs were established. Familiar behaviors came from the originals passed down, and basic morals were like gold. Yet, crossing social backgrounds were expanded to feed the evolutionary growth… or fed the mutated monsters for misuse.

People were a lot like an artist or painter who were specifically in charge of their own skills on paper. There was a certain, unique, and recognizable its distinction between the innumerous groups or cultures according to each forte', and common belief was acceptable to manage their home and/or family rules. Certain talents were complimented... outside to 'play', which was smoothly designed to run it among themselves. Except, I couldn't dispute, when I badly recoiled.

It was as if their ongoing artwork could've been imagined to appreciate the collective pictures to be stacked, down-loaded of the ongoing snap shots of still-life pictures. A slight advancement unfolded a continuous story, which was quite visible to be evolved before anyone to see, but families' photo albums changed their own accumulated pictures, too. Their history could've been a family video show, which I picked up something off... and one look was enough to keep it to myself.

Anxiety grew. Something was either wrong or just didn't make sense, but if I didn't figure anything out, since no one would tell me. Something gnawed inside against my will and core. Life's stories flipped through each page in as much as another soap opera and I missed a third dimensional view. It reminded their connections each act or event, captured by the proof I saved, which was selected of each posed by 'photographer' that wasn't the same things.

Initially, every natural response took years of practice since birth which were conditioned all together. Siblings grew to be out-grown for more space. Anyone either bumped, pushed, or was moved out of line of the consequences. Cultures branched into a new beginning for another homebased claim to be grounded. My family conformed in time to mark each unique member, labeled for keeps, unless I broke away from the bond of the results within a basic form of understanding.

Spoken words were harmless against anything elusive, and nothing had anything to prove or resume inside, exactly where it had to stay. Anything else was either imagined or easily denied, which pulled the most empowering vortex in any direction to become nothing more than hearsay, as if the family core made the call for the stand. It ran itself aside the legal magistrate for the home when I realized I had no power over the rules. No one would mess with it, while 'Reverse Psychology' was not proudly commendable for me to defend my ma's technique.

Suicide watches were hired to know and interfere the quitter. It was a real scream of attention in prison, while I sat down each one, regardless of their reasons behind it. That was not my business. Acting out to demand death, the desire to be erased, preferring to be left with a voided existence was shallow in comparison to the alternative. Why was death beyond anyone else's demand without any other answers? Unless, that demand was a hold over the fight to stay closely.

The real answer about suicides should never had been an issue to fight against the worse possible way. There were no other decisions allowed. How could a suicide candidate had been crushed out against the ultimate stance... broken into compliance? He gave up who couldn't be meant to win. He couldn't be allowed any permission. Of what or whom was under his demand was more important? And then, I understood about the purpose to live their sentences, who graduated into the open yard of the lowest inmates, facing through the process of freedom.

Escapes were not allowed in prison, nor imprisonment! I had a commendable job of responsibility to be involved where I was needed. The masochistic attitude of reckless life on the job wasn't suicidal worthlessness! In fact, I experienced it. I'd never hit the bottom until I'd bounced back up on my feet to show them how. It fit because I literally acted out of what I could say or explain of what I wanted! Then I couldn't have been empty! And, the first step was: "I want...", and I looked at that same enactment to the picture and whole photo album in my lap. I no longer could quit when I couldn't 'get enough'. "What else did they say (in body language, too)?"

I went face to face to know that important 'part' who didn't want me to have it. It took all the time I replayed back of what I couldn't have seen before I got the 'whole piece of the jigsaw puzzle' together, and I had nobody to argue against me to recover. I saw the answers, since that missing emptiness of hunger was satisfied, how I finally realized of what was so important during a time certain release! Unending stress and tension couldn't have had an end, unless I knew where I was protected from anyone. The opposing threats had that line in the sand, boundaries of the law, or even concrete walls wrapped all around, which were heavily monitored to trust which was clearly spelled out. My own imprisonment sentence offered enough time of criminally accused inmates for the process.

Secrets who were hidden had to know what was withheld to feed another. I didn't turn my back to disagree. I was anxiously driven to law enforcement that shouldn't hurt anyone, but it did. Nothing shouldn't have affected them to achieve my own choice as a CO, unless rehabilitation and corrections was not the plan.

Any missing piece of being totally unaware, naïve, or ignorance of the results weakened the fight which was driven away from the hope. I didn't care to compete or overshadow my loved ones, as if I couldn't have turned out to be much.

I'd been shown the taped videos to see the threatening which was used to be kept closed during their silent treatments which weren't a punishment against me at all. I was the threat, afraid cut me off who wouldn't hear it. I made them nervous from being exposed. I fought against their degrading and contempt in law enforcement... who'd backed off. Their twisted picture was in the reverse. I was being accused to blame me, as if I was the one walking away from them, except it could've looked bad who'd fooled me all along. "You're dead to me" was the sweetest blessing I got, when I was cut off of the hold.

Courage, bravery, and the hope to endeavor had nothing about being called a coward, as if it was an insult. It was about the highest amount I endured throughout the risks of imprisonment. I already fought to live above the pain threshold with enough strength one step at a time forward... without the goal, yet I was that determined. I was hooked for the drive, when our new CO turned right around half way in, and just left.

Why wasn't important to face suicide with more than the status quo who'd stir up trouble to be kept in place. I didn't expect any help or encouragement, and I didn't want any of them to be hurt by me who got mad. I was farmed out, sent to 'my room' upstairs, or at least not allowed to agree the fun away from me, knowing that I wasn't better than any of them. I took the blame. I was the black sheep of the family, a 'bad seed' that couldn't let them to be allowed any more than that.

I imagined about a row of a lot of bushes for a hedge. That might've had plenty of uses, unless I was supposed to be a tree. It was frustrating to demand a lot of maintenance, since I was cut down more often than anyone else, who resented me. That couldn't have been able to stay it shortened to grow offer its shade, or the fruits for the takings. I had the ability that was not their intentions. I didn't know. Did they? Jealous? Who were mad, retaliated, and hurt?

I was never expected to be smart. Isolation kept me sent upstairs, farmed off, or where the most constraining life existed in lockdown. But the life in prison was insignificant in comparison. Inmates could've been kept safely housed apart, when I worried to be thrown along with the inmates among the open yard, as if I had all I could stand. I was too ingrained to be humiliated, mortified in disgrace, but really... an official CO?

I saw things differently in an old phrase: 'The truth will set you free' was truly my ticket. My ticket was a one-way pass, and never returned back. The courage wore an all-or-nothing kind of job, where I had it applied, reassigned, and moving forward.

"Does anyone know why he left?" The talk was publicly opened in the courtyard, but I already knew. Another year had been passed by the usual crunch time, and I pitched in for each other, just like anyone else. I wasn't anything special or anyone else who noticed me anymore. The time was up, and social time was over.

"Hey, let's go. It's about time to get the next walk." I had to be nudged, to be posted-up. I had so much to say, trying to be involved, and still I felt like I lost another opportunity, and not a word, but there was always an officer nearby.

I had the fifth week of training with my OJT (on-the job-trainer) when I was the cadet's first experience for the right decision to go any further, but I was anxious to strut "I can do this" attitude. The thought of the post ended shortly of his first day on the job, when I didn't hesitate the prison's example of the low-level yard by the petty or short termed slap on the wrist prison, regardless of any level I accepted. That was all I had at the time I spent the open yard, which I was about to face the hard-time inmates, in comparison. I just did it, convinced that I'd believe or even trust the dutiful assignment, where the inmates graduating out of the cells had a huge difference between the different prisons yard criteria. "Surely the Department of Corrections had to know what they were doing."

I took a dry run to the desert the day before I found it the day ahead. I was responsible, and on time. I'd assumed the speed and distance to be prepared, and calculated perfectly. There was no doubt that I was going in the right direction toward the prison complex, until I passed a sign at the side of the road: **Do Not pick up Hitchhikers. State Prison Ahead,** as if that much was shocking already. I could've turned right around, heeded the warning, but I didn't. I knew that I was onto something I needed, and I continued.

I didn't have the privilege to draw any courage or the needed support, like the five cadets' introduction in the lockdown. They stood at the security door in the lobby for CO James from the Administration Department with the lead, when I was alone.

The low-level security perimeter was framed in, whether the maximum lockdowns didn't really matter. My gut wrenched to search out the exact opposites, while I sought out a well-preserved secret in the outskirts of town. There was a solid fortress who were quarantined far enough away and in the other direction, which was designed to shelter the healthy segment of society.

I just needed to be generally pointed, and the detail were all mine. I'd remembered the road names and landmarks besides the etched notes next to the map, but ultimately, it was up to me. I was driven to pursue only one specific career choice and a purpose. An elusive prison had to find the answers of my own.

I arrived as expected, perfectly on time. It was a paramilitary setting that I blocked it out on the calendar to demonstrate the guts to complete of what I'd set aside for more. I was directed, waited for CO Mendoza standing exactly where I was told. I obeyed, but I had no clue to know which a man or woman was in uniform. There were a few other women at the academy issued to the opened yard that day, as I wondered how well I would've been accepted the all-male prisons.

I cheered myself on, but I really wasn't looking forward to another repeating induction of the female in a workplace commonly known as a male-only occupation. I was one of those government enforced hires in factory work back in the sixties when sexual harassment had no repercussions by the ignored cross lines. That was then, when there were laws against that kind of behavior to protect and put a stop to it.

I had nothing to compare the lobby or sally port's first impression, as I relaxed, confidently knowing I had the right to be there. I'd been cleared inside, when the security door bolted with me in from the outside, as if the tour began with a real wake-up to see what vulnerable really meant.

I was inside of the prison, when my knees weakened. I worried who I could count on the line of communication that had to have been passed on to the next person. What if CO Mendoza didn't know that I was waiting? Was I being tested to see my reaction, or holding out my patience? There had to be a camera somewhere, just in case. I couldn't tell if it was my turn to figure anything out, as anxiety drained by with every minute.

I had been left behind several times, but especially when I was just a kid even years ago. A trip included my whole family to an amusement park in Chicago. I knew how much I anticipated and full of excitement. I remembered the awe, enamored by a ride high above the ground during the event. It was fabulous, and then, my family was gone! I was among strangers in a strange surrounding. I was so scared to be left alone. I panicked, running around relentlessly, until I had to wait for them to find me. I wandered the parking lot that wasn't marked throughout the trampled field, where I waited next to the car to find me. I watched families driving by with me sitting, as if I was busy. I knew I'd be rejoined, knowing I'd sacrifice their outing to enjoy, and my choice was forfeited of the greatest carnival. At least, no one could've left without me, where I waited.

And, it didn't surprise me when the police picked me up, playing in the middle of the street. I wasn't missed, until it was important. Ma thought it was funny to be handed over at the police station to wait for Daddy to go get me after work. Was she inside, on the phone blocked of anyone ringing with the news before work was home that day?

And each time I had recovered another time, when I woke up in a darkened bedroom or why I'd slept before bedtime. That should've been a typical pass time upstairs to doze off, but the noise and sounds of a large family was replaced by an emptiness that I could not explain. They went to a drive-in movie and forgot about me. Nobody noticed, as if it should hurt anyone. I did something wrong. I panicked and I ran next door. Initially, they'd all laugh when I was discovered alone. I should've been patient, to wait.

My neighbors had me watch the car driving home from their windows, where the headlights turned in. No sooner had Daddy's old station wagon poured out after the show, the phone rang for my ma, who'd been left behind. She was pissed, which was my fault, who scooted everyone else rush to bed, which affected everyone. I listened, who I couldn't tell if they were whispering to laugh about me, or giggled among themselves as they shared their favorite parts of the movie.

Maybe I couldn't have known right or wrongs, but it was the way it was, except I'd never do that to my children... when I'd grow up. I changed to be overly protective, hovered over my children until they graduated to leave, by a helicopter mom. Did I just repeat the extreme opposites?

I had to suppress all of those old feelings back where they belonged. No one had to know about any of that, while I'd nagged myself to watch my posture straightening up over the years. I'd rolled my shoulders, shrinking 'over the weight' to carry.

I waited just around the corner or their briefing room... without me, pouring out in every direction, who were dismissed to carry on. All of the same looking officers wore the same uniforms who swarmed around me. Their day's assignment rushed by, and in a moment, I was alone, again. I was in the path of every single officer, and nobody thought I was out of place. That's a good sign? I worked to stay positive. None of that was typical? Invisible? But as the final few, filed in to replace someone else, when all of the officers had disappeared, too.

Inmates came out of the Quonset huts who were unmistakable. Orange glowed into the morning light, which stood out like bright warning signs in the distance by my heart that felt like it was punching my chest pound, and I wouldn't move where I waited. I froze and didn't call in, wondering who would've known I was there? Was I supposed to be waiting? Did I come to the right Prison? Is it Monday? Questions bombarded me faster and faster. "Hey!

Where is everybody?" I wanted to scream. "They're not restrained!" I panicked to hold it together, just a little longer. I needed help, as the inmates got closer and closer, sprawling all throughout the yard from their sleeping quarters. No one but inmates were around, and all that I could think about the inmates who got out. I imagined that there had to have been some unruly criminals who were just like the flickering videos during classes. Did I really see that I had to watch them out for it? Did I imagine the worse to assume, or do nothing for the right responses?

It might've been nothing more than a minute or so when the inmates started to come too close for comfort. And then, CO Mendoza slowly made his way over, greeting me with a wide grin. His timing had a perfect cleansing breath when we met. Or, did I want to run to his relief, who was a perfect stranger? But I adjusted, as he began to explain the role of inmate management.

Throughout the same punctual weekday mornings at the other side of their entrance gate, except I didn't need the entrance door at the scanners who just walked in, whether I had already been proven. In hindsight, it must've been easier alone than when the five newly arrived cadets were made to spill it out for all to see, where I was almost excused from my personal invasion at the low-level yard. In comparison, OJT cadets felt insulted, distrust, and contempt by another budding officer that was handled differently in the lockdowns.

I followed CO Mendoza's lead, adjusting my stress level, using him as an emotional barometer. He was my only source of protection, and I trusted him. I had to. He was the only officer around, and an ever-growing number of criminals surrounding us. I admired how well he carried himself so nonchalant, but tension weighted on me. I was forced to cling onto a stranger with my life. I couldn't trust anyone imprisoned without respect for the law, marked in my uniform, and obviously noted to be there without the badge.

As we walked along the yard, I must have looked like that skittish little Chihuahua pup, anxiously jump back and forth in the "Kibbles and Bits" dog food commercial, and Officer Mendoza was my 'bulldog'. We could've bumped in together when an inmate passed us on the sidewalk, afraid of getting too close for my guard dog at my right-hand man. And yet, another time CO Mendoza even stopped to ask how he'd demonstrate an inmate to submit a pat-down. It took all I had to keep from shaking him by the shoulders and asking "What the hell are you doing? That's an inmate!" Everyone knew that the very color of orange represented poison to innately 'beware'. I held back, or jump into action to watch his back. He might not have noticed, but I trembled the conflicts inside. On high alert, I anticipated a set-up to attack us, but he didn't appear that kind of danger he'd instigate on us. And then, it was over. I could breathe normally again, recovering like an old dream that reenacted a turn into a nightmare, when I finally relaxed.

"Let me show you something." CO Mendoza encouraged me to cut across the yard one afternoon and I followed closely. The inmates, who were spread all throughout the yard, started to regroup around their Quonset huts in designated groups of twenty or so. "Don't worry about them," CO Mendoza assured me. "They're getting ready to turn out for chow." He motioned back to pick up the pace toward for the opposite direction with a door ajar. Even I knew that any kind of warehouse or any other kind of storage structures should've been locked, shut. I didn't say half of those unspoken alarms for a panic look, but didn't say a thing. His reaction was enough to know if something had been wrong. "The inmates don't have keys." CO Mendoza kindly put my concerns at ease. The side door had a latch that could slide up and down, similar to that old barn door. A ladylike welcome gestured and held the door open for me to enter.

"No way!" I stopped dead in my tracks. I was amazed of the room that I'd entered, which brightly shone from above of the ceiling skylights. It was an arena fully unveiled, and my jaw dropped of everything spread from head to toe. Musical instruments were perfectly positioned or hung, when I first saw of what might've been an underground treasure trove of keepsakes. "They play instruments?" I cried out in a jealous surprise... of prison life!

"Some of the guys are actually pretty good." CO Mendoza didn't seem to share my surprise. "Here, let me show you something else. Wait here." He went out of sight for just a moment. "Check it out." He called me out to watch while the curtain opened like a practiced rehearsal, or at least, a garage door that rolled away to the ceiling. Any other inmate's audition 'on stage' was readily set up under a small canopy for enough seat benches outside. "They have concerts almost every month, too." I barely believed of what I saw.

"But?" Again, I hesitated. How could I question what I couldn't possibly assume the inmates to have or lack of it? Shouldn't I had been concerned to be left out with all the musical instruments accessible to the inmates? Was that automatically understood, when nothing was automatically meant for me? I would've worried them trusted to respect what didn't belong or just borrow.

That was a managing prison, where I applied what I knew. I wasn't able to trust what I was told or when DOC policies had the same to everyone, until I understood everything explained while he further demonstrated his examples. The academy training was important beyond a classroom when I'd realized why I wanted all the more to experience. Teaching lectures weren't enough. I was both exhilarating and relaxed fulfilled in confidence, which I missed before! Was I mad, penned up in resentment, where prison was motivated for more?

"By the time the inmates make it in here, they know they've messed up. This is a place for them to turn their lives around. Once they're removed from the streets and all other influences that caused them to make some bad choices, were taught another way to express themselves to earn respect. Their fists had another form to beat down or the use of intimidation. That was never going to get head of any of them after a while. But here, they have no one to blame for lost privileges. And, no one to cover them anymore. They learned to accept the consequences of their own actions, or count on their just rewards for good behavior." I wasn't worried and CO Mendoza was believable. I actually felt hopeful in prison. He thought the inmates were expected to go back into society, as a better person than when they came in.

I felt the passion. I was touched. Prison had second chances and I thought about their ruined criminal history who were made to face reality, but that didn't match. They could've been saved from that indelible mark against them for doing time in prison. That should've been the honorable and decent loved ones. Is that protection for them? I'd dismissed and forgave the chances to let it pass. I saw who were expunge of their consequence, while I'd worn the results against me, instead.

That was about the needed secrets. Conspired belief was how they'd been given a pass, while I recoiled in denial. Reality set in for just a moment. The unthinkable plagued the unfair blame, which was my lifestyle, my role of the family. Unless the state prisons had second chances, I had been held back, separated, or isolation, too.

I reflected my own imprisonment. I could distinguish between any mind-games, but especially the 'gotcha' excuses slipped through. Rick used to explain it away from the need to bail his son out of every bad situation he'd gotten himself into. His son relied on his dad to be brushed off. Redundancy got exhausting to get stronger in one way, and the destructions continued to be denied with no way out, who wouldn't listen. He pushed me too far when I'd given in, or when I was never aware of the trouble stirred behind my back. One was spared by another mistake, who just laughing it off, when I knew and had nothing I could do. He was convinced that it was his parental duty, and not mine. I was the wife and not a disciplinarian. I was stripped of all power over a step-son. Rick relieved me from all his son's repercussions. But it was a flimsy excuse to dismiss his bad decisions, who further used me to be the fool. The clever skills were schemed toward perfection, which was granted toward the wrong goals.

I believed to do the right thing who used his own system against the academy, because he wanted me to stay out of it. Rick refused my part of the remarried family. I was saved aside as his wife. There was nothing to discuss about my step- son, who was thrilled to use our double-income household, but the debts included his financial restitutions, bail money, court costs, and legal defense expenses. Troubled behavior placed an insurmountable burden on the both of us while his son enjoyed a world with no boundaries. For all of that, Ben was protected from a criminal record. I'd just married into another and familiar situation... again.

That burden affected my husband's mental and physical health. Our marriage was dangerously pushed against the wall, until there was nothing left. He pawned my valuables, stolen for cash, or was traded for drugs, but by then I didn't even care why. Deceive was used to look the other way, which denial protected me from it turning the threats. The police photographed my marks. Ben was 'smart enough' who felt above schooling in truancy. Court appointments were unscathed, while shady foot traffic began well before I tiptoed throughout the house. I was powerless to stop the sabotage, in fear.

Imprisonment constrained my own perimeters, while I recognized a real hope for those in orange. There were so many men dressed in orange, where my guiding OJT spoke proudly of every one of them. My closed-mind attitude turned it around. I couldn't help but to see the potential for change. Inmates were given the controlling grounds, who quickly established softball teams to suit up for practice. And, I wondered how different things could have been. I struggled to make a buck to stay afloat, after I walked into the job fair. I was totally tapped out, when I signed up DOC, as if I had to sign up for good the second time.

I was immobile, centrally located during my broken leg from walking away, as if the decision was easy. His earnings had to stretch it a little more... but that broke, too. My husband and the father of his step son tapped into his 'creative license' into his own private practice. He got nervously private, when secrets came out all the while I knew. I couldn't agree to live like that... clenching the proof.

He wanted to be bought out! It was something meant to spare out another trust intact on paper. At what cost of too many 'clients' lead to another file against bankruptcy. But he got better with every swindled scheme to repeat another seven years to work within the law. Nothing was meant for me to gain anything that was impossible to ignore, or fool around with the law to be caught to live in my house. I understood how dangerous who couldn't be blessed for the badge.

But then, didn't I do the same thing? We co-signed to own my home when I was remarried and sold. I got half of our down payment, while he kept the balance well-above its value, as if my children's father would've been better used, or swindled out of me, too. I excused Bob's gain to hope for the best, but my heart was heavy, and the both sides of the problem.

"Don't kid yourself, there will be some of these inmates who will return to the streets no better than when they arrived back in." CO Mendoza seemed to have a few specific inmates in mind. "But someone always pays restitution." He said as if he knew, and I smiled in return.

On the other side of the supply rooms had all the sports supplies in the same condition. The musical instruments and everything else in anther far corner of landscaping and cleaning tools was ready at the back exit as I watched, about accountability.

"First things first." CO Mendoza counted down the preprinted inventory sheets by the missing mops and pails, trimmers, and rakes from the bare shadow images painted on the wall that corresponded the sign-out sheets. Then, we left through that opened door left behind as it was from the beginning, as I continued his tour for the other side of the yard.

The prison grounds were gorgeously pristine without a weed in sight throughout the desert landscape. We checked out the kitchen trash times, documented a few times a week. Tell-tail signs of the garden rake combed the dirt into Zen-like designs swirled around the budding succulents, which were consciously planted near the smooth river rock borders framing each one. The trees stretched beautifully-shaped canopies over the walkways, which had already been swept free that lead the wooden picnic tables, albeit mounted into the cement floor down the center thoroughfares. A team of inmates were busy taking out the lined trash bags from the cans that stood outside each of the inmate sleeping quarters aligned like a small village and hauled it out with an adult-sized wagon without a care in the world.

"I never got this kind of cooperation at home." I said under my breath, remembering how full the kitchen basket had been over-flowed. Eventually my husband took it out instead, realizing that his son's promise was expunged out of a few simple chores. It was another look which was enough of the message to avoid a crooked smile to end an argument with no intention no follow-up, instead.

"Rules don't mean a thing without consequences." CO Mendoza said under his breath. "It's all about balance." He grinned, guiding me away from a newly planted yearling. "You need to show respect, too."

One week was not enough time to get comfortable to work on the yard, where there were only about 300 inmates during OJT's yard, serving out their sentences doing a job. Before long, I had to return to the academy to finish four more weeks of training, but I was the lucky one to have been introduced to an opened yard. I didn't care where my assignment could've been, regardless a lockdown.

Maybe that young officer who walked inside the open yard of the medium-level security never belong inside by himself. If that was the case, I wouldn't have known how far I would've walked inside by myself, turning right around and heading out without a second thought. But that unit was about to transfer and manage over 800 inmates in a far longer yard than the one I'd accepted without hesitation.

"What are you going to do if you don't like it there?" CO Schmitz didn't want me to leave the lockdowns, as if I'd be gone. We'd worked so well together, but our friendship didn't extend beyond the workplace.

"I'm going to keep graves." I appreciated her concern. The turnover for both officers and inmates was typically expected. "Who else can you call at two o'clock in the morning?" We laughed. "Hey, let me show you something." I took her radio and flipped the channel to another unit. "CO Young, what is your 20 for a 21?" I used the proper codes required on our two-way radios, closely monitored by the FDCS. She covered her mouth, shocked to see me do something under-handing. "4331" the radio traffic response was clean and crisp. "See? Now you know how to find out where I'm working without going through Main Control."

CHAPTER 8

Teetering on the Edge

"*R*osy!" There was no doubt. I heard to know exactly who greeted my attention across the opened field in play. "Hey, Rosy!" I raised another arm, nonchalantly walked through the yard of the very first day of my debut. Head turns, and a few longer looks stared who checked me out, while another CO was paired up for another induction.

A new transfer was set aside the whole week to the day shift's orientation crunch, according to policy, which flipped over my usual sleep's routine. Still, returning to work was nothing more than a nap through the duration to go back for the night shifts later, as I relied on the coffee and sleep aides to make it work.

The walk stretched all across the administration building, which was assigned halfway around to the other side of the recreation yard, which wasn't the original unit sealed for the opportunity forever, but the open yard remembered it quite differently. There were no trees or any lovely succulents, wide-emptied fields of softball or soccer teams that used to sprawl right up to the fine-lined perimeters within respect. It might have been the lowest low risk yard to be reconsidered, but the medium level yard was the lowest risk level of security allowed among the violently claimed criminals, who hoped for their eminent and/or pending release. There they learned to enjoy a full-sized basketball court for the busy spot, and the volleyball net was set up for a group of inmates to choose side rotations after each point. While they walked two by two around the outer track with no concern, some joggers passed their inmates, or pumped their exerted repeats around their personal space for each other.

Anyone who knew me waved, although others took a moment to gawk at that bald woman with a rose tattoo on her head, but I didn't mind. Of all the nicknames from the lockdown work place called "Rosy" that stuck, and I did nothing to discourage it. It made me smile, an inside joke for all those nuisance complainers who filed against me with a grain of salt, knowing some would not.

"No, I was not on a first name basis with the inmates." I defended myself, pointing to my name tag pinned to my chest with the capital M clearly marking my first initial. Since I had no control over the inmates' acceptable name, the accusation for being 'too familiar' with the inmates was thrown out against DOC.

I held my head high and mustered all the confidence and poise, passed the half way in, as if it was that center fence decision, and I took it all the deeper. I had no one able to dodge with every head stopped for a look up upon command, like the trumpets were immediately known about my arrival, or when the highball bounced laid the bets. It took while to make it to my post, and the hot roulette table's final spin crowded a little too closely settled in for the decisions. And then, the stares dropped off. "Oh her?"

The lockdowns began with training grounds where I completed the first year of probation that started it all over again, except I had a reputation preceding me. The inmates had their ways of staying connected, while they'd complied within the system's step-down programs, wondering I'd been clinched for them, too.

My work history also established their long memories that followed. With every ticket I wrote against the inmates who refused to comply with the most basic rules, jeopardizing them to be awarded or denied from their privileges along the way. I'd caused some of them to lose ground, and some extended the same allotted time for anyone, when isolation was or wasn't ready.

I made a lot of mistakes, and sometimes I'd overreacted a little too close to heart. There were the times when I pushed to stick my neck out, to take a chance, or try something new, and always a little too nervous and even timid, while I faced a prison system full of some very deep wounds on either side.

I hauled that same mind-set baggage all around, unable to drop or resolve to be hurt, which I'd merely picked up or where it left off that I did on myself. It was of what I knew because it was all about survival, as if my life had nothing to risk of anything left... at first. Maybe I'd been merely lanced and redressed on the right track at the academy, but the rest was ultimately all in my lap, with that firm slap on the ass to 'go get it, girl' attitude nonetheless. I surly needed its assurance and comfort to heal, but there were times when I took it on the chin. I sucked it up, as if it was no body's fault. But how would they know? I weathered for each hit, stripped, and exposed to be chastised, as I prayed every frightened moment on the right or wrong side, to get away.

Whatever happened was the easy and established scapegoat at home. "Sit or you'll rock the boat," was the phrases daddy used with every lesson, when the times flew over my head too often. It was my own fault when I should've known better, but it was 'a dammed if you do and dammed if you don't' entrapment against to fight, or cried empty. It was never an option in between. Issues weren't able to be satisfied, like the boat made the waves, frightened to hang on for dear life. Survival was well trained as if that was all I knew. Total submission was nothing more than a game to play along at my expense. I wanted my turn to win, and occasionally I was sparsely handed under the table with slight wink for a crumb to graciously take of what I could, which was more accurately their catalyst. How was I supposed to know how to manage limits of that job in prison?

There was no such thing as 'right answers' into real trouble. I swallowed hard to remember that "Inmates have long memories", but it wasn't just the inmates. I got the gut warnings, when all else didn't matter and didn't care anymore, until I matched up my principles, matching up with policy to be put to the test.

I'd tried to redirect bad behaviors on the inside of a cell. There was a barrier of safety, until no one was stopping anyone walking into an overabundant amount of danger surrounded on the open yard, worried about the consequences because of me. But that was when I realized the blessing, wondered who was in charge of whom that wasn't a one-size-fits-all job. Even inmates got the second chances, or whether anything was slightly amped up or was barely noticed. I'd lost that edge in an area I was really very weak, both physically and mentally clumsy, when I should've been mastered years ago.

One night, Sgt. Caruso took me to the side and called me a kick-starter, but a label like that should never had been so quick for the next time he'd dare to pin on me... for the efforts to try. Imprisonment was a mind's eye view to reenact my memories that were played back for a few of the casted 'soap opera'. Imagine imprisonment when I was held up, like a concrete and steel echo inside my mind, where I remained hidden and detached there too. I was a CO facing an inmate, equal sides of the steel-iron barrier which wouldn't budge. Despite all of that, the inmates needed to be seen and heard, which gained a barrier of my permission to establish credibility, when I discovered how it went on either sides of respect.

The deeper I walked into the open yard, I was visually exposed who had seen enough of me in an uncomfortable distance, who'd gawked in a mutual shrug.

I physically carried its protection with my lone radio at my side in my belt, instead of the original vest. There was no need to lower its risk level on the open yard. I'd changed to reflect my appearances to entrust the inmates and CO's safety, hoping to respect likewise. But I inadvertently created enough attention who'd monitored the cameras into the farthest depth toward my post. I didn't know how cheeky I'd gone right through the opened field, when I brazenly walked right through their field player's who held up the game to stop and let me pass through, as I sweated the slightest mistakes, fearing everything accumulated to continued.

I had a wide-opened berth through my safe space, because they personally accommodated my short-cut. It had to have been annoying, except for their forgiveness... for me. I was too preoccupied on the first day of the new transfer day, when I ignorantly barged through their field in-play that was hardly courageous. I should've been embarrassed, until after the fact and a long way to go.

I was more scared of the old recordings, knowing I'd catch up. Not that I didn't try, but arguing just seemed to be more of an 'I'm right. You're not.' shake-down that originated by my loved one's conditioning. I didn't see the point and walked away. Grampa said, "It takes two to argue." while I grew more and more reclusive to embrace solace. It was relieving, or at least, I stopped their insidious badgering the choices for the less and permanent affects still remaining. And yet, I wondered how much worse could've possibly been able to manage hardened criminals?

Confrontations got stuck in my throat, choked up inside by withdrawing to heal. Of what I was really made of, wasn't as important as the right or wrong decisions to appease above all else, but the thought wrenched a knot in my stomach. I forced myself forward, even when there was no way to hide the fear about imprisonment. Any inmate could've been cornered with any other inmate's opportunity. The open yard had access from the barriers and no walls of protections, regardless. I had to be visually shaken, but any chance I had to return to my old unit was gone, for another year of only one direction.

"It's unlocked," I heard him call in as soon as I entered the day room for the first inmate's housing structure.

"Hi, I'm Pruitt." I entered the day room when I'd introduced myself at his control room, centrally located to be monitoring the surrounding movement. "Am I your relief?" I threw my backpack toward the corner. My two-way radio down was placed on the counter from my duty belt instead of the suited stab vest left behind, and retained its enthusiasm with enough coffee to fight against my sleeping routine.

"No, you'll be shadowing me today. Didn't they tell you in briefing?" CO Montoya continued as he closed out his service log for the previous shift. "I'm staying over for a double," he mumbled under his breath. "What do you know so far?" He asked quickly, turning the page, filling in the heading on the service log for the next shift.

"This is my first day in this unit." I beamed, pleased enough to have completed the walk on my own.

"Great, so you don't know anything." He whispered the words with such distain that I swore I heard the f-bomb a few times. "Do you know how to operate the control panel?"

My ambition fizzled. I was looking forward to see the results of the step-down programs who had been rehabilitated into a communal living environment. And, my first day was all set up by an overtired officer.

"It doesn't look that difficult," I said passively, careful to keep any additional burdens onto his day. "What's this about?" I tapped a fingernail on the Plexiglas cover over the control panel.

"Wow, you are green." He had to push one more dig in my direction, but I raised my brows, knowing that it was a valid question to ask. I was well over the grabbling stage, although I was also at the mercy of another to succeed. I waited.

"This used to be a GP (general population) unit," He said, as if that was enough of an answer. "Those guys were good!" He snickered a bit. "They had to cover the controls because the inmates were able to fish into the control room and press the controls to unlock the security doors when the officer was out." I smiled back in a coy reply. "Do you see where I keep my bag?" I looked around, confused. "It's hanging on the wall in the bathroom." He nodded with his head toward the door behind us.

"Okay... what are you talking about?" He knew my wheels were turning, but I was lost.

"I'm not kidding you. They could open your bag and help themselves to your sunglasses, pack of gum, smokes, you name it." He finally looked up at me. "You don't believe me? Go ahead, leave your bag there, but don't say I didn't warn you."

I picked up my bag and hung it in the bathroom on another free nail. There was no need to tempt fate with my Tums, lunch, energy drinks, or a travel-sized bottle spritz of air freshener that didn't need those questions asked to be passed along by a CO's better judgement through their scans.

"Alright, let's do this." He kicked out his small wooden stool, which was lying down at its side and underneath his writing table. Slid out toward me to sit, "Your post orders." CO Montoya stretched his arm across my writing surface, as if I bellied up for more, but he dropped another generic and three-ring binder in front of me. "I'm not going to go over this with you. You can read it on your own time." I pulled it over, as if I should eat when its ready to take what I could. Wondering what he had in mind might've been tempted to steal out a chance on 'his' time, but then, there was a row of faces peered inside both sides of the runs.

"Now I know what the animals must've felt like in the zoo," I whispered with my face concealed lowly enough from the inmates able to read my lips. I didn't want them to misunderstand, and afraid that I might have been referring to them for zoo animals.

"Oh, you'll get used to that." CO Montoya stood up and most of them scrambled away.

"CO, CO, do you know what time it is?" A single inmate remained and asked in an almost whinny voice. "Are we going to have modified rec tonight?" One final inmate timidly pursued.

"You'll know when I know," CO Montoya barked at the inmate barely visible from the other side. "Now, get the hell out of here." His frustration wearied me. How would he handle any questions I'd have? "They'll drive you nuts if you let them." He shook it off as he sat down again, justifying his style of discipline. "Here." He pushed the service log in my direction. "You might as well get right on it."

I entered my name as I continued to fill in the assumed work space like always, but every time I glanced upward, eyes glared back at me. It was unnerving to have someone watch every move I made, not by CO Montoya, but by inmates.

Orientation Week was more like Transfer-tweak Week, while I stayed on top of everything opened to change each assigned post. The control room was also its office that adjoining each elongated runs of either side. I did one thing at a time but I couldn't barely keep up between a few moments to take down every word in the service log with every step, when solitude never appreciated like before. There was no getting away or space to be alone anymore, except in the bathroom, which seemed to be more like an equipment room with a toilet and sink added to it, other than an excuse of distance with a real physical place... to squat in the corner to relax.

The other trade-offs excused the COs to relax more casual in the lower risk level yard, unlike the heightened safety equipment to be changed. I was stripped down to a bare minimum with all I had, which allowed the pepper spray, two-way radio, and a set of keys still clenched at my side within reach.

There was the time since I had the same old habits back in my high school days by Ms. Vohler's lifelong career at the Home Economics Department for the lead. She'd discussed the ways we were predominately raised, coaching her the up-and-coming, grown and independent women, who might've been unconsciously left open and vulnerable. But forty years ago were before her time, since her self-defense moves were embedded, well before my induction at the academy. She demonstrated just how dangerous it could've been, standing next to a locked car parking lot, digging inside our purses to be focused elsewhere in the sixties, when her teenaged girls had been persuaded to change.

She wanted to embrace lady-like femininity and/or helpless woman persona, while she guided their fine lines to be protected of themselves, like after a long tiring day at work, or groceries carried outside alone without a head's up from being blindsided, "like a sitting duck", just waiting for trouble. The academy lectures were also reviewed to know anything beyond a prized predator. It might've been simple, but I still fisted my keys in between the fingers to be prepared of any sense of caution that was carried over inside prison.

"Check the time," CO Montoya said once I barely finished to push along. "Get used to stay on top of the time." He handed it to be set aside of its turnout sheet, which was a coded printout for the inmate's daily agenda. "Right now, we'd better take care of the initial security check down each run." He stood up with his keys in hand, ready to lock the door to the control room behind us as we stood in the dayroom swarming with inmates. "It will be faster if we each take a run." I gasped and stared back at him like a deer caught in the head lights. "Just kidding." He laughed at my reaction. "Come on, I'll show you what to look for." He took the handle of the security door and opened it for me like a gentleman. Letting me enter first, I instinctually responded just like I used to step aside, when I cleared the door for his lead.

I followed him into the bathroom area for the inmates, who also took a quick glance to turn for my reaction, except it might've been different if I was still 18 years old. I'd worked in the factory to clean the men's bathrooms' that was so disgusted that I might've been chased out of the females from a man's place, who forced the women to quit. The young hired women accepted so many jobs, regardless how bad their atrocious tricks 'passed every test' through the 'man's passage' who finally gave up and let them stay... one at a time.

And DOC counted on the natural design to be weeded out, just like the good- ol'-men attitudes also opened the door as I watched my back. A swift whack on the ass was fun with the factory workers who were handed over to the next one of the winners to gladly fold. It was a joined effort, just like all of those nuisance reports that were thrown out, or when sexist harassment could've been insulted or misused too often before, but it was the job.

I closed them out. I had their rest rooms clean, until I was done. The talk whispered through the door, worried or hoped against a long and very distraught female, except then, the door was opened like they had never seen before. And, the urinal mounts on the inmates' bathroom walls before, and my reaction? Well, there was none.

Although it was a bright and sunny day, when CO Montoya pulled out his flashlight from his personally purchased to the duty belt. He used a purposely chose the lightest beam, where he exposed and pointed out of the most likely places to find contraband. "Sometimes there won't be anything but a small piece of string stuck in the drain." He bent over for a closer look at the floor drain in shower stall. "It's a good place to hide a shank dangling inside the sewer pipes." He stood up to continue, focusing the light beam as he moved it along the tongue and groove metal frame of each shower stall. Then he moved the clear shower curtains behind him on his way out to wave open the folds. He repeated the same routine for each of the shower stalls, and each time was just as thorough.

"Remember, it's just as important for the inmates to see what you check, as much as what you don't check," he added, swiping the top of each well-buffed aluminum 'mirror' when he slid his gloved hand underneath at the bottom edge of each sink where he pulled out a rag draping over the plumbing underneath for a quick shake before it was returned.

"If an electric outlet is loosened, check it. If a ceiling vent has finger prints on it, check it." He talked as we made our way across the room to the porter closet and started checking off the inventory by another clip board that was left behind on the well-advertised hook for all to see it.

"Is that really mild acid, or disinfectant bleach in those gallons on the floor?" Each bottle had a tinted hint of blue, yellow, and pink which corresponded to the colors of the spray bottles on a shelf. CO Montoya didn't answer right away while he turned to look at every direction to find the rag mops, bucket, scrub brushes, push and angled brooms allowed, according to the inventory sheet in that tiny closet.

"Why? What's the problem?" He didn't seem to share my concerns. "Can they really be trusted with this stuff?" On one hand he was searching for any inclining or possible foul play, but he dismissed the fact that three gallons of chemical solutions were in full view.

"Yeah, those labels are deceiving," He turned the gallons around to read each label. "But, this stuff is so diluted. All of this will be used up in one week," he said, backing outward, still giving the closet a final look for anything out of place. "The inmates know it's pretty watered down," he was finished as he pulled his disposable gloves off and shoved them into the back pocket of his bloused work pants. "Oh, watch what you throw away, too."

"I know. I've seen how resourceful they can be." But he wasn't telling me anything new there. "Where did you get your gloves?" There were boxes of gloves readily available all throughout the lockdown units.

"I'll get you some before we take in the next run." He said, heading for the center aisle of the run with bunk beds on either side of their elongated dorms. Most of the inmates weren't there, enjoying the beautiful weather, but a few inmates always remained behind to enjoy some personal space away from their bunkies. The bunks only allowed about thirty inches between them.

"Hey," CO Montoya stopped at the head of a bunk and tapped his foot attention sent into the iron bed leg a few times. "Take that down." He pointed out a line of towels draped from the upper bunk's mattress who'd turned around, which was mounted to the lower bunk's swing arm seat. "If they are that wet, throw them in the dryer for a while." His words were clearly understood with no room for debate, as I made a mental note to ask later: "There's a dryer?"

"That's a little full, don't you think?" CO Montoya kicked the waste basket a few inches toward another inmate, who was lost away in a television program. "How about emptying that out before the trash crew comes through?" The inmates typically didn't hear us, wearing ear phones to listen to the television or music played from tapes or CDs, but once CO Montoya message was clear he continued on.

We walked slowly, mimicked down the center of the run, and I learned who swept his head back and forth in the few minutes to complete the security check, but when we turned around to finish that walk in the opposite direction, when I realized how stealthy the towels disappeared that had been already taken down.

I'd already carried my own flashlight, since I crossed by the cell fronts that mimicked their shadows rolling with my night shift, but then I realized his additional importance on hand from then on. Blind-spots created some privacy between the bunks, but they couldn't quite hide from anything more than a slight moment that aroused suspicion, who made my heart jump that put that to a stop to that, just the same. I got the message and just as relieved, when I saw of what was missing by their 'clothesline's blockage' as we passed by it in the opposite directions, for my own safety as well. Disappearances should never had been a mystery, including to know what was missing, too. I got to see everything seen and unseen behind my back, when denial and forgiveness was never meant to be ignored.

"Are you ready?" CO Montoya asked while fingering his key set behind me.   .

"Uh huh." I'd hardly settled down and it was time to check out the runs again.

"Here are our gloves." CO Montoya brought a box down from the top of the EEBA (Employee Emergency Breathing Apparatus) box, mounted on the bathroom wall next to the escape ladder for the roof. "Take a handful and fill your pockets on the right." He urged me along. It felt like the days-of-old, taking only two pieces from the candy dish. "You'll never know when you'll be needing some." I dug in, taking his advice to heart.

"Let's go, I'll be right behind you." He said, deliberately seemed to define throughout his set of keys, while each key was specifically meant for that housing unit. "Take a look at each key. See how each one is numbered. This one is for your control room and the control room on the other side. It didn't open any other locks because it's made for this building only." I noticed how the last digit reflected the building number which I felt blessed to be able to understand my trainer so easily.

"What's the Folger key for?" Folger keys were used to unlock the trap doors in the lockdown units, but that didn't apply in the open yards.

"Check this out." He pointed to a key hole on the side of the security door. "You'll want to check that lock from time to time too. The last thing you'll want is to be inside of the run when the door locks behind you. You'll have to use the radio to be announced. You'll know exactly where you'll just wait to be helped out (and everyone else would hear their particular unit's channel, in your voice)." He laughed as if it had happened before, possibly to himself. "Here, let me show you. There's a bit of a trick to it." He pushed it in to hold before turning the key. "There's a spring inside that will give you some resistance. It's not really hard, but it would really freak you out if you didn't know this." I smiled with a nod, glad to see how thorough he was, but it wasn't any differently. I remembered where I purposely locked the kitchen cupboards from my toddler's determination, protected in my absence.

"After you." He motioned to take over. "Oops." He stopped me before I opened the door. "Always lock your control room when you leave." I searched out the correct control room key and he waited for me to be locked out again, the first time.

Knowing which key became familiar, reduced the amount of time and redundancy, since I also exposed the inmates of any other unconscious act. The open yards' eyes and ears were beyond the dayrooms, as I grew accustomed to the wider ranging things as I stayed attentive on the job, but that could've lost the habitual or sloppy complacent edge.

I locked the control room door and opened the security door to enter the inmate's run a second later. Although that might not have seemed like too much of a big deal, knowing which key unlocked of which door in hand made a big difference. I was told to open the electric fuse breaker room during a thunderstorm at the lockdown once, but it must have taken almost five minutes in the darken corridor, testing out every key of my sergeant's set, before finding the right one. That was not something I'd never cared to do it twice again.

Upon entering the inmates' run, I tried to mimic CO Montoya as we worked along to see any kind of contraband. I examined everything that might've been tampered, didn't belong, or out-of-place, until I stepped out of the shower stall from the far end of the men's bathroom that jumped to my throat and I found myself alone.

"I thought you were with me." I talked through the screened control room on the other side of the inmates, when I saw that he went ahead of me.

"You have to keep an ear open for your radio. Remember this inmate turnout sheet I showed you?" He was not pleasant. "They're calling for the kitchen workers and I'm checking to see if there are any from our runs." CO Montoya looked tired, and I knew that training was like doing the thinking of two people, so I simply continued where I'd left off.

Looking over the bathroom area and taking inventory of the items that were written on the prepared worksheet was easy. And, maybe it was because I was a mom. The woman of the house was always expected to find something right behind an inmate's attention to explain or plead leniency. I held the officer discretion as CO Montoya didn't hang around with their excuses, but I wondered if I could be as effective.

"You weren't locked inside?" I whispered as I turned my key in the security door of the control room that didn't trip the lock.

"I'd like to know that I can get out right away," he said. He knew to watch after me. "I lock it when I am doing something that keeps me from watching my back, or when I'm in the bathroom so no one comes inside or was caught off-guard." He didn't seem too concerned and I wondered whether the inmates were simple opportunists, intuitively. "You'll figure out how much security you want, eventually."

I took the post orders onto my lap, flipping through to read the inmate sanitation and grooming requirements, in-house and transport dress codes, property limitations, clothing replacements, as well as the daily routines including the turnouts for inmate jobs both inside of the unit and for those who were bused to another unit.

"You don't have to memorize it." He chuckled, not knowing that I was a slow reader.

"There's really a lot in here. Is it true that the inmates know all of this stuff backwards and forwards?" I was a fish all over again.

"What's more important is to know what's in there so you can look it up." He started to slouch into his chair with a toilet roll supporting his head against the wall. "Pay attention to the radio." He said as if I was the one to take over.

"Watch-swallow meds turnout," didn't come over the radio like that. I was familiar with the radio verbiage in code, as I asked the last radio traffic to be repeated, but there was no response. I was holding a radio that was held together with a rubber band, which kept the battery in place, the antenna's plastic housing was cracked, and the wire coil exposed from inside, when I realized how unsafe I was personally heavy-hearted. It was no secret that the lockdowns needed priority above all the other units who'd been selected out the officer's equipment which was saved for others.

"What did it say?" I asked nervously left sorely in charge.

"Yeah, some of these radios don't remit very well." He grumbled before sitting up and bellowing: "meds turnout" down each run and quickly returned into his sunken seat and paper-roll pillow.

In a moment the loud speakers were heard from the outside for the same things. There was no doubt. The inmates who needed to go to the Health Unit for their prescribed medications knew it was time to go get them. Games all across the yard were interrupted with the loss of an inmate here and there who headed for the gate in the center fence. There was another CO to be reassigned, who'd been unlocked to be passed through the locked gate. The inmates were resided for the more seriously sick inmates to the Health Unit of the other side, which were monitored right back.

The first few hours were full of commotion, and then just like that, the radio traffic was silent. Once again, I took advantage of the moment to read, knowing how quickly things could change. I was impressed with some pictures to recognize their contraband which was found by their fellow officers, just like me. The inmates seemed to use just about anything to carve out a weapon or tool. I delved into the department orders, regulations and revisions, and every single line, separated into codes that were further broken down into several other additional sections to cover even more additional details in the back.

"Oh man." CO Montoya struggled against his fatigue. "Let's knock out another walk." He was awake but not too alert and I knew that if I could see it, the inmates could too. But, what could I say? I didn't look any better. By mid-day my eyes tearing from the strain to keep rolling over the lines as I read. Reading the post orders were filled with legalese, and not exactly light reading.

"Good." I skillfully kicked my light shifted stool under my reading surface to display some agile practice for anything.

"Hey, don't let me keep you," he said with a touch of sarcasm, and a crooked smirk.

"Is that okay?" I did a double take, surprised that he would let me go it alone, and he sunk back into his comfy spot.

"You'll be on your own soon enough," he said. Then he closed his eyes as I slipped my radio into its side-holder and I locked my trainer inside the control room, waiting a moment in case he told me otherwise.

We were shown several tricks to fight fatigue during the training at the academy, but ignoring the need for sleep had its downside. That lack of sleep affected our cognitive reasoning. I'd seen it. There were times officers were more like jittery drunks, hooked on caffeine and energy drinks, who filled in the short-staffed rosters. We overlooked each other to keep from going on a heightened security mode, where the controlled movement was slowed down to allow a minimum amount to continue on less. For as much as the inconvenience was obvious, that also meant the inmates had to be locked down into their housing units. It reduced the number of officers who came in to work regularly, or the ones who were there to stay over twice as hard again. The tradeoff begged to stay over another shift, but it was an unending problem to exasperate the officer level risks as well.

Sometimes we stayed over to work sixteen hours straight through without getting a scheduled break to eat in between. CO posts didn't schedule the ten to fifteen-minute breaks on the general

OSHA law interjections. However, we knew of what it meant for the officers who came in refreshed, as needed. It was a more selfish need when I enjoyed the boost in our paychecks for overtime, and also the fear against the threat to face it mandatory instead of the alternative. Either way, the demands gave more than anyone else, which became a regular occurrence of overtime pitching in on a daily basis.

I pulled open the security doors of the dormitory runs that were left unlocked to go in and out all throughout two hours of rec time. Knowing that however, was a lot fewer inmates who were outside, and a lower load to go it by myself who were still remaining inside.

'All I had to do was walking down the middle of each run, turn around and come out. How hard is that?' I thought, giving myself a little pep-talk before heading into the dorm of about twenty-six double bunks, but my trepidation was well-founded. I argued against the reality of my job. Never mind how many of the inmates spent their two-hour rec time would bulk up. Never mind about their heinous crimes they'd committed, which I refused to read, imagine, or visualize. Never mind how many of the inmates had been forbidden conjugal visits over several years' sentences. I could've thrown in the towel at any time. Nobody would've held it against me, and I couldn't fault that officer who saw the dangers of the open yard full freely walking around without restraints or bars. I questioned the kind of people who faced the dangers daily and, yet I'd become untouchably complacent. What kind of person would purposely put me in harm's way? Was there really something wrong with me, and what did that say about me?

No one sat in the audience applauding my graduation. Heck, I was the only one of my class that didn't have the untouchable family for the fall, when someone had to be selected... for my instructor's honor, instead. He stepped down from the platform, who interrupted the commencement in salute to accommodate me. It wasn't shameful, since I had the rightfully applause.

I wasn't looking to make trouble for anyone, when I walked into the local employment agency. I just wanted a job to get myself back into the workforce as soon as possible. I thought I could ease myself back into medical billing with over twenty-five years of experience, but I was wrong. I was over qualified, but I had no idea how much that line of work prepared me join the Peace Officers toward law enforcement to check out any other careers that I kept coming back.

It took a lot of effort to promote its dedicated programs, as if I could fix anything on the job, while my callers misused me for a sounding board of their rage. I had to be able to maintain a level head regardless of the kind of language, which was used in the prisons, too. The only difference was my callers who were faceless cowards, and I could face anyone.

The Career Center probed into every aspect of my life, dissecting, and analyzing every answer I openly provided as much as I could, when the final analysis was summarized with the results. I was anxious to be best suited for the career change with its recommendations for the offers considered.

I'd studied to discover the necessary skills already needed, benefits, and pay. Clearly the computer had to have seen something in me that didn't point me in another direction altogether. The programs were designed to take everything about me the most likely able to succeed to disclose all of my inner core strengths against the recommendations, when I'd been strongly advised. It should've felt backwards. I'd always looked at the job market, instead of the skills required to fit the job, when I finally made the decision to pursue the career as a correctional officer. I went after it with all I had. The Career Center did not recommend a career for me toward work, it found a career based on what I had for me!

My life all played a part to see it myself, instead by the defaulted decisions who'd been entrusted by someone else. I sweated it. I was afraid of the fore coming retaliations against my better judgement… that took a lot of work behind the scenes.

CHAPTER 9

Misconstrued facts

"**Y**ou're new, huh?" Inmate Aldridge said once he got my attention. I didn't invite him over, or wish him away either. Inmate Aldridge was just doing his job, wheeling fresh water jugs to every picnic table throughout the recreation field, dutifully trudging that flatbed wagon all around the yard, when he slowly strolled his way toward me and the hairs behind my neck stood on end.

"Not really." I spoke just loud enough for him to hear me. My response was curt and uninviting as I maintained a steady gaze across the yard, hoping to discourage any form of friendly chitchat. What was his game? What did he want to talk to me for? Was he that duck I related to a story heard at the academy? Was he a decoy? What did my body language say, or gave it away?

"Where did you work before you came here?" He gently persisted. Inmate Aldridge looked harmless enough, but I couldn't trust appearances. He was an elderly man with a few grey hairs that sparkled in the sunshine, well maintained, and about the same age. His soft and passive nature was a direct contrast to the lessons I'd learned about their inmates to be typically conniving, when my self-defense walls went way up. Sex offenders were generally expected from the white-collar workers with a higher than average intellect, while I wouldn't take the chance of being found out.

"I took a transfer out of the lockdowns." I continued with a stoic attitude and he finally walked away, visibly shaking his head back and forth, lowered down away at the ground. I didn't like myself for doing that, but it was much too early for me to lower my guard.

Every day changed during orientation week, when I was designated to shadow the yard officer, which was one of the most demanding post of the unit. Tired and drained, I came in all pumped up on coffee to take on anything, which was like a new job all over again.

CO Rayburn knew where I obediently waited, exactly where I was told until she greeted me halfway down the stairs from the yard office. "The kitchen's just about ready," She said, arms wide opened to help with the supplies, as I fumbled to exchange the adding machine through the load. "Prepare to meet the residents of Hamilton Unit," we laughed.

"You like it here, don't you?" I got mixed opinions from the officers in the lockdown court yard, in the first place.

"I do." She seemed cheerful, despite the usual harried routines among the all-male prison.

"What can I do to help?" I could see how she rushed to get the day underway, but an instant pang knotted up inside, "Don't try so hard." I was afraid that I'd appear too eager to please, since I knew what that means! Bob redefined every intention, saying "People only like you because of what they can get out of you," since I edified my spouse's influence away from one family's patterns into another.

"There really isn't anything." She began to tell me how unnecessary I was before the day even started. In another day, I might have taken her rejection personally, but the way she said it was nothing like those comments of old that cut to the quick. I didn't need to worry about the phrases in my mind like "Leave it alone" or "Just stay out of the way" which still tried to seep back inside. "Except maybe," I perked up. "Try to pay attention as the inmates call out their bed numbers before passing through the scanner. Sometimes they rush through too fast, and I end up missing a few."

CO Raynard's duties were pressed to meet the demands. She assigned the inmates movement of the meals and there was a 'second' yard dog to be coordinated on the other side. I paired along, although I was mostly meant to observe. The unit's functions communicated all of the posts throughout Hamilton unit. She orchestrated everyone to be involved, who had the right to overshadow me with a pompous attitude in charge, but that was not the way she conducted herself at all.

"What are they like? I mean, do they give you trouble for being a woman?" I needed a head's up with some idea of how unruly the inmates were with a woman in charge, as if she required a different mindset than the men under control.

"If there is, I don't see it." Her self-confidence was admirable, but I also knew that there'd been another era for men having women-in-management issues, when I was that age for the change. "South yard, put your early chow on stand-by." The inmates needed to be fed resounded all across the yard by every hand-held radio.

"We're good to go." Officer Lopez gave the thumbs-up. The air waves were over the inmate dining hall with an announcement systematically understood all down the housing unit officers' directions, audio and visual, to conduct the inmate population. My trainer was already arranged with my temporary coverage, who'd been handed on down at briefing, but there were other officers pulled out temporarily, too. The officers were willingly issued for the job, until all the inmates were fed on the north and south sides of the fence took all four housing dorms, who returned to his original assigned posts at briefing when chow was over.

"North side buildings, put your early chow on stand-by." CO Taylor ran the north side of the yard, who echoed his orders almost immediately, while I watched my trainer's south side of the yard.

The announcements caused everyone to listened on standby for the details with the inmates, who were excused ahead in line.

"Turn-out insulins." Officer Smythe worked in the Health Unit at the medical staff of its routine, injecting one diabetic inmate skipped in line to eat, while a few other inmates didn't want to go out to the dining hall at all. They had their own piping hot cup of (instant) coffee from his own microwave on each run, for another meal at lunch.

"Southside buildings, turn out early chow." The security doors of every housing unit swung opened for the inmates that thinned down the last group of inmates. Groundskeepers were sent out before the hot desert sun who were chased out before the heat, which also specified the morning classes or any other schedule appointments, who turned out by the early inmate calls, who'd left with the rest.

"North side buildings, turn out early chow." The inmates overheard the officers' radios and stood ready, crowding at the security doors for the okay from their control room officers.

"Buildings seven, eight and nine, turn out your insulins." The Health Unit was located on the north side of the yard and was usually called out before the south yard, while another officer was needed to monitor the center gate who'd been pulled out of another control room post temporarily.

About 100 inmates came out of every housing building, rushing down toward the kitchen, and medical facilities accordingly.

"Permission to turn out the wheelchair pushers?" Most of the housing officers knew that they needed to be turned out as soon as the first inmates were let out to eat, when a courteous reminder took precedence, which monitored all of the inmate movement by the COs.

"Yes, send 'em. Turn out the wheel-chair pushers." Just one of the yard officers needed to make that announcement to avoid confusion.

"Kronberg, Heath Unit." CO Kronberg, the security officer in the inmate kitchen, wanted the Heath Unit to respond before sending his message.

"Medical, go." CO Smythe told CO Kronberg that he was talking to him directly.

"I'm sending an inmate to the back door for insulin." Inmate Begay had been worked through the night to prepare the morning meal in the kitchen who needed to eat by cutting through the back tarmac behind Health Unit's access.

"I copy." The CO simply communicated his promise to open the back door to let him inside.

"Feeding order on the north is six, seven, eight, five." Every week had the lists for the houses to be fed which were moved up to allow another building for the chance to rotate weekly.

"Feeding order on the south is two, three, four, one." I looked over CO Raynard's shoulder and saw how perfectly she'd arranged her papers underneath the paper clip in the wind gusts. Her podium's surface was jotted down by each inmate showed up for chow, which eliminated each ID checking off their options, as she flipped through the pages with admirable speed. If she saw one name missed or when another inmate was already marked off, she stood to believe it with enough proof to send them away, who could've tried a second tray through the line again.

CO Raynard glanced back and forth in the dining hall by the inmates evenly spaced across the room, which could seat about 200 inmates at a time, but it was never filled to capacity. The inmates segregated themselves, refusing to fill an empty chair that was affixed to a table meant for another race. Nothing was done to prevent it and the borrowed security staff allowed inmates to stand against the wall with their tray until a chair waited until it was opened of his choice, who couldn't go against any other officer.

"Building six, runs A and B, put your inmates on standby" was hardly put down between announcements, between the forms calibrated for our supervisor, before I was offered to eat at the end.

"The inmates eat better on the open yards than in lockdowns." She treated me like if it was my turn. "I never worked in the lockdowns, but you should order a tray sometime." She glanced back. "Today they're getting pancakes with butter and maple syrup, scrambled eggs, hash-browns, canned peaches, coffee, and milk." I had a surprise, a double take wondering just how to process, or believe. Everything I saw was new to me, and I must've looked like a kid at Disneyland.

The overhead run lights of every dorm were turned on at 0600 hours and a lot of the inmates stayed in bed until the last minute. I didn't blame them with the only thing on their minds. There were only three sinks, three toilets and three shower stalls in each run.

I was just a kid when I waited to keep the peace of the family. Eleven people lived in a one bathroom on the second floor that was upgraded since it was first built. I learned very early just how important it was to respect the time needed in the bathroom. But the 'understood rules' were never written on policies, since chaos also learned compliance. No one took skips, who took turns "on standby", like when we were ready to meet school's schedule.

The inmates had to be clean shaven, hair combed, and appropriately dressed to be out on time as well. Inmate educators (or turors), grounds keepers, landscapers, and maintenance crews called for their inmates clearly taking precedence by enough reminders through the strongest channel used from the Main Control over the open yard and dining halls, with no mistakes. It was impossible to ignore, although the outdoor sound system was not as effective, who also shouted out the runs without the need for the radio in a one mind attitude on their toes.

"Kitchen, yard." CO Kronberg's abbreviated radio traffic who didn't have to specify which yard dog he needed, but understood.

"Raynard, go." CO Raynard worked the south yard once it was already known for the day.

"Chow is completed, cleaning crew and porters remain. All security doors are locked and dining hall officers are no longer needed." CO Kronberg's update kept all the officers throughout the unit on the same page.

"Copy, Kronberg." My trainer paused for a second. "Good job, Lopez and Gibbons." She thanked the officers who were pulled out of their control rooms and cleared them to return to their original posts.

"No problem, ma'am." They almost stepped on each other's radio traffic in return, and we waited for the same response from the north yard security staff before chow was considered complete as well.

"Are you good for a walk?" CO Raynard wrapped up everything from the podium and headed for the stairs to go back into to the yard control office to be handed in to the shift commander.

"Sure, where?" I was glad to be partnered with her, although I needed to take a break to get rid of my morning coffee. "Hey, is there a ..." The doors slammed too quickly behind her, cutting me off mid-sentence.

"Did you say something?" she said as soon as the doors buzzed one at a time that let her out a moment later.

I wanted to cower. Wasn't there enough to pay attention to her load? Do you have to ask for a bathroom too? But she didn't let go of the doors slamming behind me on purpose.

"Come on. I'll show you my office." I followed with a spring in my step, until I realized how awkward and clumsy I was on display. I felt worthlessly needed by an extra, when I also recoiled and gave all the space she needed, like the children who encircled the 'cheese in the center' that played during recess until the song was over. The inmates encircled me. The food line passed by one at a time to be checked off at the podium, where I must've been checked out by the convicted criminals in line, who were once housed inside the cells.

"Sit down for a while." CO Raynard sunk into an over-sized office chair, also handed down from administration, while she invited me to relax and savor the moment to join in when she over-reached her cup of yogurt that mysteriously appeared. "There's going to be a bus coming through the back-sally port any minute, so we might as well wait for it." She said as she spooned her mid-morning snack with gusto. "Did you bring anything for the fridge?"

"Not really." I helped myself to an extra folding chair, smiling more content by taking the load off. "I cook once a week and freeze my meals. That way it's thawed by the time I'm ready to eat to work daily, and I don't have to worry if there's a refrigerator around or not," pulling out my drinking cup from my back pack of my own potion. I sprinkled in the right portion to rely on my fortified drink, until I filled my cup at the water fountain (or bubbler for those in Milwaukee).

"Here!" CO Raynard called out to stop me. "I have a whole gallon over here. I'll never use it up." She immediately urged her carried water from the refrigerator.

"Oh no, I'm okay." My heart wanted to giggle inside in comparisons, when she jumped to help me. "I used to bring my water in too, but I really don't have a problem with this water. It's actually better tasting than I get from the faucets back home." I sat back down with my sweetened drink, and the water fountain water was cooled enough to chug it down easily without getting a brain freeze. "Thanks, anyway," I said when I resurfaced for a breath as we both enjoyed a few moments off of our feet.

"You started to ask about the inmate population out there?" CO Raynard remembered where I'd wondered about the SO (sex-offender) yard after I wanted her opinions. So many officers were widely known who refused to work with them.

"I did!" I sat up forward on my chair. "I didn't see a single inmate give you any trouble, even when you called out and stopped a few of them to take their hats off or to tuck in their shirts. They almost seemed eager to comply. I just didn't expect that." I was both full of praise and amazement in her ability to manage, who'd been turning out of almost 425 counted inmates through her side for the chow line.

"Well, don't forget. I've been doing this for a while," CO Raynard said humbly. "Were you nervous?"

"I was at first," I answered, rehydrating myself.

"Well, see!" She said looking for one more taste from the bottom of her yogurt cup.

"But the academy...," I started and she began to laugh.

"Forget what the academy taught you," she said, rolling her eyes. "Most of that was just to get your attention."

"I dunno," I mumbled. "I really got a lot out of it," I confessed.

"Oh, don't get me wrong!" She seemed to recant. "Most of sex-offenders in here are not the monsters everyone thinks they are." She tossed her plastic cup toward the trashcan but it bounced back out, rejected from an overflowing situation for the next guy.

"The officers in lockdown told me to make sure you read some of their escape files once I get here," I said. Turning, I gazed back for just a moment toward the locked room, when I slowly picked up her cup rolling away.

"Why would you do that? You're already freaking out!"

"I guess," I shrugged, "finding out about these guys capable of..."

"But that was out there." CO Raynard seemed to make it sound like there was nothing to be afraid of. "Their temptations are kept at a minimum in here."

"What about the rapists?" I looked at her who was just as young and beautiful.

"They're not interested in a good-looking woman wearing a badge." She laughed and put an arm around the back of my shoulders.

"Let's go. Traffic control just announced a vehicle around the perimeter in the back."

CO Raynard had several sets of keys hinged around her waist that jingled when she walked. I had to believe that she could open any lock throughout the yard, but that thought alone gave me pause to believe that any inmate could've had the opportunity over-powering her.

"Hey there, Villa!" She waved to the officer posted in the watch tower. "Who is it?"

"It's the milk truck." He hollered down to her. "Looks like we got a new recruit today!" He added while CO Raynard turned another Folger key to release the crash gate.

"No!" she said with enthusiasm. "This is Pruitt. She asked to transfer here from lockdown."

"No shit!" CO Villa slid opened one of the windows who pushed the buttons to let us into the sally port's office where another service log left our last line that was picked up by the supervisors to be swapped out later for the day.

"What's this?" I couldn't help to notice a framed newspaper article on the wall inside.

"Oh yeah, you should read that. It's about an inmate who tried to escape when he hid himself in a box of the back trailer by a vendor's supplies truck." But I scanned it too quickly for the details later, when another vendor entered the sally port, puddle jumping to each unit deliveries.

"How far did he get?" I asked, hoping that I'd misread the news about the inmate who made his way out 'at the front door'.

"He was found at Traffic Control," she said both relieved and angry, knowing how many COs let him slide through. "It could've been me," she practically whispered, who were spared by the officers involved. "I check absolutely everything now, knowing how easily a box was overlooked in the truck." She pointed to the picture of an emptied trailer with one box that had been left behind, placed upside-down like some insignificant trash to ignore. "After a while you get to know what belongs and what doesn't belong." She added as we stepped in and jumped out who took all the time necessary. The inspection held up the truck to be parked, frozen in place before any move forward, as if nothing was more important inside the sally port or any other part of the walls surrounding prison.

When she was satisfied with her inspection, legitimate and safe to enter, she was the only one to do the work and the shift commander was permitted for clearance, as if it took two people to agree or any other officer was announced its head's up through every radio in the unit that also kept an eye on the cameras in Main Control. The inner gate rolled all the way to the side until the driver cleared the crash gate, and the gate quickly closed behind him. I had its first-hand routine beside CO Raynard who made sure to impress its importance, but all of that effort 'turning over every rock' was comforting in my routine. Only then the driver was compliant for more, walking in front of the truck to escort him to the dock behind the kitchen.

It wasn't more than a moment later when the kitchen crew were anxiously unloaded and relocked inside the kitchen's presence to be physically seen and/or counted out of their clearances, too. The milk truck was emptied at the delivery dock of the kitchen. Everything was done methodically, finishing one job to be starting with the next.

"Thanks, Villa." She acknowledged the officer in the tower. CO Raynard noticed that she had the incoming sally port from the Traffic Control booth by another truck approached around its perimeter, while another one waited in line and in full view before anything else, one at a time.

Orange was all I knew about a group of inmates who waited inside of the bus, until I knew that nothing could've been hidden by its contraband who were returning from the lockdown from their night shift job. Two driving officers were strip-searched down of the inmates, where one watched inside the strip shack to be built for its privacy, except for all bias that caused policy to step the women aside. Only the male officers were allowed to screen them.

"What's so funny?" CO Raynard asked one of the male officers, who'd stumbled out of the strip shack, clearly unable to control what happened inside.

"CO Belshaw... that guy doing over-time?" The transported team returned with a newly arrived officer. "He's a true Brit, alright!" His accent was undeniable, who didn't mention his acquired jargon. "He kept saying, 'Lovely...lovely...lovely,' with every inmate he cleared to get redressed," as tears flowed down with every hysterical repeated clearance. "Damn, you just don't say that stuff like that! I mean, it was after every inmate who passed along after they lifted each sack!" I spontaneously cracked-up right with them, when I the shock settled in and immediately my jaw dropped in the fear. I wanted to backpaddle and warn them all, but I didn't know whether some things could go very badly.

"Did any of the inmates take offense?" I was glad CO Raynard asked, but as funny as it was, perception could've faced a lawsuit.

"Naw, it wasn't like that. It's all good." Her reaction was the initial and short termed thing. The same reactions of the inmates trickled out that got even louder once they all seemed to stumbled out the other end who couldn't contain themselves. The inmates and officers mixed along who let them laugh, as if there were no sides for a while. But I froze. There was always that fine line. Some things should never be crossed, until there was the heaviest laughter about an inappropriate 'joke'.

I didn't know how to laugh and I stood out. I didn't want to be fingered as the scapegoat, or did my fears make them worry because of me? I was so sorry. Why couldn't I just let them laugh, unsure if I could've been just as guilty, regardless? Someone was going to pay, but it would've only been just one culprit directly or indirectly... involved.

A sobering concern weighed on me for days afterward. I'd hoped that no one would drop paper over the situation, to trust perfect strangers with my job, my career, my reputation. There was a zero tolerance for sexual offenses, and that went right along with the racial bias implications, too.

I remembered about another officer who dropped papers, who had the duty's follow-up. Who else could be the target, who was freed from a reprimand, as if it was the example for the rest? I'd already lost the trust of my coworkers during the lockdown unit who didn't think twice about dropping paper on me, when I worried to be like everyone else, changed to be spared at the same level. What's wrong about me?

I took the hits, and I got angry at myself inside, regardless of some pay-back of their own medicine. It felt trivial and petty, like an annoying thorn in my side who wouldn't leave me alone. I got all the more stubborn, refused their cruelty, no matter how many times it had been done to me, but nothing was ever excused scot-free in silence.

I couldn't shake a nagging issue cropping up a persistent and residual element of guilt that wouldn't go away. I mulled over between discretion and judgmental fear, but CO Raynard could see right through me. There was a connection who supported me through it, but so many loved ones intended to make it an issue that would never end. How did she do that, and my loved ones made me grabble an apology. CO Raynard was confident to assure her coworkers who'd understood that, without a word in defense, who blessed me with an explanation. That was not like the catty officers during probation at the lockdown, or any other sibling's secret which cheated away the answers left festering. I couldn't let go everything dangled over my head. Doubt embedded an incomplete or undecided fear that grew more sensitive, riding on the edge... until I understood how important 'all on the same page' had nothing cut out.

Fact-finding disputes didn't mean very much for the written claims against me; officially placed on notice to prove or disprove my defense, when it wasn't allowed to be erased, changed, or mis-interpreted. And hearsay wasn't allowed to be disproven through the twisted faces and daggered eyes, shouting that washed out anything to be said, which also included silent body language couldn't communicate any debate that could never be changed. Dropping paper on the report was the same things thrown out that was altered by a devious misunderstanding, that was clearly spelled out: worthless. Once everything was exposed, I was cut free. But I wasn't meant to be easily recovered behind a lifelong history.

Chapter 10

Take a number

I had a few days off of work to recuperate after the day shift week when I swapped back to the graveyard shift... on the open yard.

"CO?" An inmate peered into my control room, just after the lights went out in a now-darkened room. "Do you remember me?" He waited to give me a moment, as I needed a moment to respond. What happened? I'd almost forgotten, and possibly mistaken.

"I'm not sure." I hesitated to buy some time, knowing he wasn't the same inmate I looked into the cell from time to time. "Where were you housed before you came here?" I saw too many to see anything but orange, but then again, maybe I just didn't want to remember him in his lowest moments.

"You sat up with me all night when they put me on a suicide watch." He seemed so sure that I'd remember him, or maybe I began a new and strange surrounding that were impossibly unrecognized by anyone else anymore. He was hopeful, as if he carried a memory of me, but I couldn't tell, and I let him down. Apologetically, his posture dwindled with nothing to say as he turned to walk away. And that's when I saw him! He might've decided to give up through a dejected look, when I should never had to see it in another. It was that empty look of nothing left and nothing to fight for, who remembered with me glued in my chair.

"I really don't. I'm sorry." I piped up as if I called him back. I actually didn't recognize him, at first. "But it's good to see you here." He knew by the sound of my voice that I didn't recognized the man he was before. He stopped with enough of a smile back at me before he returned to his bunk. He was nothing much more than a shell of a man locked inside of a cage some time ago, but was no need to recall or looking back anymore.

For some, the transformations took months and even others took much longer, but that did not deter me, when my hope swelled more deeply affirmed as the CO. Some of the inmate sentences ran out like an early release or the incarceration didn't fit, who'd been thrown right back whether they were done with the programs, or not. The inmates sporadically trickled back in, as if sentences were perpetually tied up for life. About 90% of the inmates were eventually integrated back into society, and any one of them could've lived right next door, which boiled down to the same thing. At first blush, that in itself could've been a scary thought, until I saw how incarceration offered another chance of life, that was deserving to aspire again.

Every inmate had been plucked out of what they grew familiar on the streets, which was enough of a reason who'd been reclassified to another form of containment. A pubic and gated community was designed for the adult-dependents of the state's living quarters, as if they belonged to stay there. Their colors were no longer defining their neighborhood, where prison took them all: big and old, tall or short, political beliefs or gang. They were as one. Their new color was orange with big black letters down their pant legs, which also received their indelible letters abbreviated across their backs. Because that's where they were boldly labeled, all under one roof. They were all marked men, mixed throughout a new and strange enclosure within their impenetrable walls of every direction… which was no mistake. Where ever they went, their clothing announced their unique residence with no way out.

They were made to attend classes like "Back to Basics" and "Breaking the Cycle" who were plugged in right away for the next open seat to be reprograming. Cuffed in belly-chains and leg-irons were well aware with the inmate tell-tale sounds shuffled along the corridors in the lockdown unit of the typical background noises throughout the day. For only an hour or so, their destiny was locked down in place which felt no more than a phone booth who were all set around to sit, bolted onto the floor alongside a few others, while the COs lined in any possible moment who leaned across the back wall safely against the courtyard to regroup. They had their purposed to be moved over for another area for the inmates' expanding use of the breaking room instead. The inmates were reclaimed somewhere else when the COs waited just on the other side of the next escort, or wall.

Sometimes the transfer of an inmate came from one cell to another that seemed unkind, especially when an inmate tried to fight off an escorting officer, equal to or larger than himself. There was after all, no honor in striking or overpowering a small-statured officer. An inmate would've been mercilessly jeered by the other inmates for doing that. Still, inmates tested the officers' control, or of what little control they thought they could claim or take back.

I'd seen my share of bloody noses that sprayed onto the floor or walls, a little bit unexpectedly. As big and bad as they might have tried, every other day had another inmate who gave in to their angry thoughts or opportunity who tried to regain some sense of power and control that made me cringe, since I saw their final attempt into submission.

Officer Wytte looked like an oversized Norwegian from a long line of Viking warriors. He towered over just about any inmate in height and strength, as I felt every bit of compassion to stop or avoid it. A lot of the inmates' façade' needed that final stand to at least look like he was against the system to be used or absorbed to demonstrate it through a fight.

I overheard how CO Wytte warned each inmate who'd step out of line, but I expected him who repeated his canned monologue every time he cuffed the next inmate, regardless. 'The Brick' was built contrary to his unintended intimidation, as if he was the magnet for the next invitation to 'give-it-your-best', or when I screamed 'uncle' that wasn't going to be enough. The game seemed to offer any other chance to be cleared away from its guilt, but nobody would buy it. They were sized up to meet the match of the challenge, even though CO Wytte really didn't want the job, without a mean bone in his body. It fit, but I was also conditioned. I had to accept of own skills to award the badge, since I met every challenge that I accepted in the academy's training, moving forward through probation in lockdowns, as I graduated forward. Obedience and compliance needed the balancing, for a price. And I repeat: 'it was never meant for everyone', since I returned for the second time to start over in the academy, too.

The graveyard shift was nothing like any other graveyard shifts in comparison. It offered a peaceful sense of solitude in contrast. Safety and security were actually refreshing against the day's chaos. Boredom and fatigue tempted a lot of them who relaxed in a state of repose, but that carried a severe penalty to be caught. I'd looked the other way, and seen too much. I was always on high alert, watching, listening, and remained intent of any slight movement throughout the security checks, and the inmates were still inmates, left in that same care.

In the silence of the night, I used my time imaging another scenario, trying to work out any other various ways to be prepared. I knew the propensity of rage, or the fallback responses to concoct another outcome of the worst. I wondered how I'd picture or erase reality with any amount of effort it took, and anything could've come across to sweetly deal my way through, regardless if anything that might've happened, or not. I created another cache in my mind when I finally accumulated enough of the options, after I purged to save only the best garbage bag of my own.

I paid close attention to my speech, knowing the strength of the tongue, but I watched to conduct my body language, too. I enacted how I'd drawn back with a deep breath, a pause in thought, and its poise without abusing my position of authority. If I talked too fast, he could feel railroaded. If I talked too slowly, he could feel demeaned. If there was too much eye contact or had too much intensity in my voice, I might've appeared to be inviting a show-down. There was no doubt that my responses had the ability to escalate or deescalate of any situation, but even that was nothing new. A thousand other inmates met face to face, which defend law abiding policies that also supported me.

The academy explained that fine line that I'd endured most of my life, but I didn't want to be gently tip-toed or overly cautious anymore. I had to decide of what kind of reputation I'd establish and portray my own stand while I wondered if I could rely on a "firm, fair and consistent" moment of growth... toward excellence.

There was bound to fail, going two steps forward/one step backwards... for more. I lived a repetitious dance, although the fol-lower caused another dizzy spiral in 'a new song' with a different tempo to establish in any direction forward, nonetheless. I wanted to redevelop trust, and mutual respect of myself first, regardless of the either lead. I already knew how I was treated. I knew how it felt before, and decided how to treat them to impress my own options which I'd enact outside of my head, since I was enclosed in an imprisoned community, where I belonged, on purpose.

I thought about the possibility, tripping 'to the floor' during a security check. I wondered if I could recover quickly enough to help and remain whole until help arrived, who might've cut in for the dance. It was as if another inmate was that perfect contest to overpower me. Everyone gets stepped on my toes too, but anything was thinkable below the atmosphere that glowed no brighter than candlelight from the ceilings anywhere else. The dorms were so dimly lit that the security lighting didn't even cast shadows on the floors, much less a silhouette strong enough to draw attention from anyone on the outside, or a cell. I found out very early on the job's daunting work in lockdowns, when I also knew that I couldn't rely on my partner on the other side of the building for help either. His eyes were on the inmates.

Some of my fellow officers set their wrist watches to go off every half hour to take their walks. To be honest, a lot of the officers, especially the ones working a double shift, planned to sleep on the job. Their rebuttal was that they'd be woken up if there was any trouble, but that was not how I understood the job description. I couldn't submit to even a hinted sign of shut-eye. As irritated as it got sometimes, I was a team player who'd given them a ring on the phone for a heads-up, when I knew the supervisors were coming through for the frequented inspections to be spared, in fine condition.

But the inmates knew what was happening, too. They studied my routine and learned my habits, just like I studied theirs. It wasn't too hard to figure out, but my fellow officers didn't hold back, as if the inmates didn't have ears, hoping to get me on board with them, but I couldn't shirk my responsibilities. I hid it under my skin, as if it wasn't enough to watch my back behind the cunning tactics of the inmates... to change sides since I expected to cover and forge comradery of 'the brotherhood'. I felt threatened or tested in the weakest moments, but I was used to that too. Regardless how I stood 'in the center of the cheese', unable to count on their support for help, finally lightened up to be bought into the work ethics of the inmates. That couldn't be that much with that powerful word: "no", but it put me in a very precarious position where I stood apart, alone, and vulnerable between both management and criminal sides.

There was nothing quiet about the locking mechanism that unlocked the security doors, announcing my return to enter every half hour all night long. It had to be annoying. It had to disrupt the inmates' sleep every time the hinges squealed, but it was what I was hired to do. Clenching my keyset like a weapon, I did my job.

Between walks, I thought about what I would do if my radio slid out of my duty belt during an attack. What if it slid too far away from me to reach and call for help? None of that was too farfetched. There were always a few inmates sitting up in their bunks, and I wondered just how many more were either already up or I'd been awakened when I entered. Still, I was one of 30 or 50 inmates entering the darkened dorms well aware of the chance of being ambushed or raped by any number of them, ready to take an opportunistic moment of bliss at my expense. But I already knew how I'd been taken of advantage too many ways and times before, enduring to survive, and healed later.

How much worse could it be? I laughed it off, lifting myself out of the chair, wondering if my knees would ever be the same again. With my flashlight in one hand and my set of keys fisted in the other, as prepared as I could be. Another touch of the control panel flicked the indicating lights on red on my panel that further indicated the security door lock release for the runs again, and again.

The inmates really didn't know me, although they might have heard some stories, but what did they really know? Every night felt like another inmate was signed up for the one who'd finally entice me into sex that disgusted me, which wasn't their fault. There were a lot of woman officers who did, but I didn't see how it could imagine a fellow officer laid in their dorms, but that was as far as I could go. Aspiring any kind of pleasure had been burned out of me years ago.

I gave in to every quickie Bob was few and far between once we were married. I complied as if I ruin it, or any other protection to accept the consequences. I obediently lied still and never refused him, as if was something better than nothing. I knew the rules, when I also spared him between a blessing break to warn about my periods. He hated to wash off the blood afterwards, but he had to know when it wasn't menstrual blood that irregular. But he knew. And, when I remarried nine years later, I cursed my husband's damn that little blue pills on computer sex.

There was nothing the inmates could seduce me for their fully erect penises... in hand. I'd had enough of that sweaty desperation and the snorty grunts with every thrust. So, if I was attacked... I'd heal.

I also wondered how I would handle a choke-hold from behind, demanding my keys and access to the control panel? What if I was stabbed or got my throat slit and couldn't call for help? What if no one came? But that was ridiculous and unlikely happening on graves. There just weren't the opportunities to carry out an escape on the night shift when everything was still, unlike the chaos of the daytime. I played out different defensive moves in my mind with every scenario I could think of, and I escaped unscathed every time. Facing my fears was a 100% success rate, as if I could handle anything, but reality was always something else.

I was surrounded by sex offenders, but of what about the predators aside sex, who bullied and beat down on people like me. They might've appeared kindly, patiently schmoozing who whittled in to gain my trust, as I kept my guard up. Sex offenders were described to be the most cunning and luring type, where I was mixed in, as if I was fresh 'blood' turned against me, cohered and eventually trapped with no regard to the damages they'd left behind. Could I handle emotional abuse? And, how much more of that could I take?

I knew that I could take just one pill, and all my nerves went away. I could heal any bruise, tearing, or infection, but there was nothing that could eliminate the scaring pain left on my soul. My spirit was something enjoyed in my rocker, since I still cradled to soothe my soul, which was also a constant movement that protected anyone too close. I needed some quiet space, where the deadliest wound couldn't be fixed with a tube of ointment or gauze to heal from the damages inside. Nobody either had to know, didn't care, or too ashamed to admit and live on, since denial was too late.

The three-ring binders didn't have any snips added to my research, to look deeper. Why was my spirit reaching out to be an active part of the prison system? Why did I pursue a career surrounded by violent criminals? Something was not right. Was my self-worth so deteriorated that I subconsciously put myself in harm's way, as if it was my calling?

Working the prisons should've been enough to disprove any situation to live down any alarms to be afraid any more. Weary remarks got old and irritating. That wasn't the problem, except there was nothing I could do to change anyone else to believe me as the victim. Why did that start, and why did it continue? I was shunned, impossible to redeem myself with a fire that still burned deep down, as if I could never put out a forest fire with a tea-spoonful of water that got too exhausting.

No one stepped in at home, but who could've been there? Sometimes I couldn't be too sure, wondering who was more angry, me or the ones who just disagreed to believe, looking the other way when I took the blame. And... I kept returning. I dutifully came to visit my loved ones to appease their affection to connect, but it was futile. Time after time, I crawled to dread the next time, when nothing changed, just a little older. They were more interested in their self-preservation. They were the lucky ones aside of myself who maintained some common consensus before I'd arrived, already pegged to play nice, like if I was the guest. Anything I had to say fell on deaf ears, while their preconceived notions would never end.

I'd learned about the better-you-than-me rule for survival at the academy. It may have been shown all the way through of one of those videos, which wrenched at my gut tore that didn't sink in, unable to understand... why? That couldn't have been about me! But I was already in denial, to excuse anyone else. THEY LOVED ME!! I had to force myself to believe anything else, but there was a force at work even I couldn't break.

The gangs on the streets were initiated to their neighborhood who met the tests of the bond, or like the skirted cliques in high school dressed and acted alike who were easily excused by all others. It was like they had secret codes or handshakes that only understood among each group, who were aware to recognize their unique and common behaviors to be distinguished apart. They knew. I knew, too, but the basic assumptions were quickly enough to innately understand, except for my loved ones. I simply missed it. I didn't pass judgements or blame them for anything, as if I didn't count or possibly affect me of anything wrong. I empathically forgave them and I assumed their behaviors, but I also knew how I wouldn't dare jeopardize the fold.

My absence disrupted the family dynamics of my father's death, when ma took the reins. There was no mediator, and there was nothing I could do, secretively wishing it would've been me instead. I even prayed for them, but I no longer had either side left, as I tried all the harder to maintain the peace of the family.

No one had anyone to talk with me who pursed their tight lips that further whittled away my self-confidence, as if I was thrown to behave the exact opposite with my children. I stood in front of anyone, in between and go through me, as if I was able to absorb anything painful of anyone else. I protected my little ones behind me, who would have to come through me. Invincible like a super mom! I invented a new purpose, as if I was catalyst to spare them for me. But I was expected for it, which was never meant for me to succeed that passed down the generation.

I started to question myself. I questioned the uniform behind badge. Was that just a cover? Was I an imposter, a fake, an undeserving, or another achieved title as a CO who couldn't stop me?

Was that the actual joke? Was I that stupid to have been sucked up to be completely rewritten? Did they know something I didn't know? Yet, I still asked: What did I miss?

I needed to find something to validate, something based it on. I needed to know why I couldn't just shut off my brain that felt like a broken record kept playing back in my head. When did it begin, and why? I earned the right to be a correctional officer just like every other officer who was tested and tried, pushed to their limits and came through successfully. What happened?

Since I was alone, I had all the quiet time I needed to think on the graveyard shift. I got busy, purging the right from the wrong to make more space to cleaned house. If there was a broking record replaying in my mind, it was time to get rid of anything worthwhile, but telling myself to "stop it" wasn't working.

An open yard of criminals all around couldn't compare of what I had inside... of the job greater than anything amped up all the more vulnerable. I tapped into the lessons I'd learned at academy to probe for answers. What planted those deep-seated conflicts inside? Why was I hanging onto anyone else's opinions which was deemed to be more important than my own? Yet, I chronically struggled with that situation.

I searched my gut feelings to read my body's reaction to put those feelings into words. Was I a masochist? Was I self-destructive? I started throwing out questions until something hit a nerve. Did I take a high-risk job to hurt myself, didn't it mattered to be all thrown in for the final fight, or did I do it for attention? My feelings vacillated, teetered on the edge without a care either way. Was I setting myself up as the martyr? The victim? Nothing, nothing, nothing!

I thought about talking to someone, anyone help me put my arms around it. I needed someone honest, face to face, hoping something could tell me what I must've overlooked, someone from outside what I couldn't see for myself, but there was no there to think about anyone else. It pierced through my heart, when I learned how important solitude and detachment was just mine.

I remembered about my dad's funeral, silent and still, as if I was mourning the loss. I stared down at me in an empty control room, since I was just another outcast still alive in the deserted end of town. Even they got better treatment, when I had no visitors for me.

I held on every word the academy, knowing how that career wasn't meant for everybody. Was I a weeded out, just like the noxious tree from the hedge that was never planted there? What choked me out to spare the best, but the roots kept sprouting back? Did I leave that purifying my family? Did they feel relieved or mad? Or was I their embarrassment, unless I'd be redeemed back to fit in somewhere else?

It wasn't that long ago. I was gently tolerant near ma's side, when I stayed over that visit by myself, who usually called one of my sister's to be there alongside of her. She trusted to be just the two of us that day, as if it lowered the guard to protect me from feeling so defensive.

Initially she shared some pleasantries together, but the conversation returned to the same story. I was oblivious who innocently compared me to my cousin Patrick. She thought out each clue or hint, one after another, which remained so subtlety determined, until she drove it home that finally hit:

"He was lucky to be alive." I patiently coddled her noble love. How sweet she was! I listened, as if she just needed someone there to appreciate its situation. I allowed her ramble, as if it was just easy babble that meant nothing. Ma stressed how her son who carried out the caregiving roll, as she unloaded her sister-in-law through the aging years. "It was a miracle, God's will!" She poured out the praise regarding my cousin's abilities, managing any task or chore, who'd survived an awful car accident. Patrick moved in with Auntie Lorraine for the best possible life under her roof from the severe brain damages.

My ma had nothing new, but I casually listened about the years she reminisced who wouldn't let it go. She was so glad, regardless of how awkward, as she raving about how well her sister-in-law was there who helped out by a full-grown man in a child's mind body. The talking passed as I'd spilled into my own heartbreak over the loss of my second husband, but the conversation eased back of her own agenda. The thought never crossed my mind of anything more than some company spent together. It seemed so trivial, as I let her talk continue.

Ma seemed genuinely happy for my aunt, and how well things worked out for her. It was a devastating life change, who'd been reduced of her vibrant and handsome man, as I sat to appreciate their life in general. Regardless of how many ways had been said, the same subject was more than a gentle pastime through the visit.

Ma never seemed to open up like that, or allow her feelings to flow like never before. Over lunch, the topic returned. Drying dishes and a few more comments came out. Watching the evening news, during the commercials, and nothing else was on her mind. I was glad to give her all the time in the world, and I gave her all the patience needed to let continue. She had a sharp mind, so it couldn't have been her memory slipping, but I didn't see the need to interrupt her, even though there was plenty weighing on my own mind. It wasn't about me, and gave her all of the space she had.

I was facing an uncertain future. After almost sixteen years of marriage with my second husband wasn't going to salvage anything headed downward. There was no peace, or hope to repair a damaged marriage anymore. I'd struggled to achieve harmony so late in my life, too, but there was clearly a void to share the pie of the extra wife to be crowded out of the family's go-to man. Rick also began gentle and accommodating, who was easy to fall in love with him. He was that rock who made everything better, except I was his supportive partner for his lead. At least that's what I expected, until the fine lines were spelled out between the lines.

I should've kept my mouth shut. I'd known he had a bad heart from the start, so it was easy to explain away his lack of ambition and energy. He didn't shovel snow, mow the lawn, or do any kind of household maintenance, and I didn't mind. I was used to doing all of that. I was independent while I was a single parent of three, albeit grown and moved along. He didn't complain to manage the household chores at the end of the day, regardless my classless style of tee shirts and stretch pants that was just fine. I maintained to dress professional at the clerical scene of work, but the exorbitant expense spent Rick's private practice, instead. Why couldn't I have just left well enough alone? But I just had to know where I stood.

One day I complained and compared myself with Donkey from the movie "Shrek". I reminded him in the moment when Donkey bounced up and down behind a crowd of others, shouting, "Pick me! Pick me!" and then I told him how I finally felt. When was it going to be my turn, who was just too busy? I wasn't interested in 'stuff'. How much longer would it take before I could have him all to myself? But of what came next, was nothing like I'd expected... either.

"My sister and brother come before you. My children and their mother come before you, and you came after all of them. It's in that order." Rick was overwhelmed by the first born of the family with no parents left. They were welcome to pick up where the folks died with no one else to fall back on anymore else, but him.

"But, I'm your wife! I'm your partner. I stand beside of you." I tried to define my rightful place, until I realized why I enhanced the marriage, like an extra paycheck adding to the pot.

"You and I will have our day after all of them are satisfied. You knew that I put their needs ahead of my own, so when it's my turn, it will be your turn." He made it very clear. I came last. No wonder he was upset who pointed its example for me to understand. I made it an issue to refuse my husband's co-sign for a student loan, which he couldn't refuse his ex-wife's third husband's purpose, to be satisfied ahead of me. He would give the shirt off his back to anyone who asked. Although, it was up to me to buy him a new one (so to speak). Of course, he didn't want to get a divorce! When I married, everything was bound with him to everyone else before him, where I arrived after the vows. Right in that order. But didn't he look good? My life was the gift which gladly amped up his reward that enhanced the greed, and his glory. My turn was never going to come.

Ma was offering that same role for me all over again, but she didn't want to be interrupted to stay on point, until she boastfully hit a nerve, explain how lucky Auntie Lorraine would always have a strong body with a weak mind at her very whim. With every nod, every time I agreed with her, she was one step closer to convincing me to become her own personal 'Patrick'.

My jaw quivered. I was still suffered over the pain from one bad situation, for the offer, facing the loss to another's gain. My heart grew heavy, despairing a well-focused fist to my chest. How long had she planned to suck me in when I was already emotionally shaken? I wept bitterly at the thought that I was being groomed to be incompetent, forced to believe that I was never meant to live outside of menial servitude.

I sat in the faintly-lit control room throughout the dark of the night. The inmates were perfectly still when I started to fold within, too fragile into a total collapse. I felt as if I was spilling in a mental slow-motion slide downward. My hands couldn't hold onto anything. I felt like my life was shattered by a glass-built jigsaw puzzle that had been dropped in a million pieces, crumbling apart against any vast area, splashing into the finest splinters that flew in every direction beyond anything to be restored. Maybe I was only in deep thought, but then I scrambled as fast as I could to pick up every piece in a panic against the worse. I was in serious trouble! It was as bad as if even one piece could've been condemned, doomed too big for the job as I feared self-destruction.

I fought inside, to accept the challenge! I demanded the undeniable truth for once, but it felt like the first time when the baggage was spilled out in front of the back pack to expose everything spread across the counter at the front scanner, where nothing could be hidden. I either stepped up to join in or demanded anyone else to step aside, as if no one could steal anything from me, when I realized how the inmates protected what they owned... in prison.

If I was in prison and limited to the finest things I needed, I grew indignant who took something missing who touched my things it all over again, when I'd noticed something withheld, cost me something very valuable that was intentionally kept from me, and I deserved to find what was always supposed to be mine.

Materialistic property was insignificant in comparison. Of what I turned out to be as an enabled behavior, deserved to be entitled back. I behaved. I cordially endured every ounce of patience or sacrifice needed. It was fine, so long as I sat fully able to feed their needs, unless I was treated to be the house guest: shallow with no depth of gratitude.

Easily manipulated to give into every whim, eventually reduced to win out the hearts who should've loved me. Subtle cruelty broke my heart, too many times and too long ago, although I would've done just about anything that spoiled the fun, who laughed it off behind me.

I'd gotten used to being treated too dumb, who counted me to remain ignorant. I wallowed in the timid attempts to prove otherwise, who kept it that way, and I kept hostage? Inmates were transported during the night, but I had no idea how far I'd been removed from the family's good graces, without answers in the dark.

I finally flipped through the set of keys to open the same doors to the control rooms according to each housing unit for the inmate bunks, when there was more than one key on that set.

Philosophically speaking, I needed to start unlocking doors without permission, since I already held its equipment every day!

It had the ability to explore beyond its safety range, stepping out of my comfort zone. In some ways I felt more like the only thing that drove me by those damn pinball flappers, impulsively controlled to keep it in play, bouncing all over the place to tally up and applause the greatest score. And it must've been exhausted, shot back in again and again, for someone else's pleasure, too. Was I ever worth more than the quarter I held, by the need to appease the demands?

I sorted out the easy stuff. "Why didn't anyone care to know what was happening? It felt like secrets whispered behind my back. When did that start?" The quiet of the night had plenty of time, without the need to hurry through the chaos in my mind. I could go at my pace, honestly and confidentially, just like I did at the Career Center. There was no need for intervention with me as my own best advocate. There was no one to argue against, twist my words, or downplay the memories that were all mine.

I was in charge where no one else could see, spy, snitch or tattle. And then, all of that aloneness tossed me back and forth: "What if something would have happened to me on the job?" I debated as if it was so bad with no emergency contacts so far from home. "Stop calling and see how long it takes for anyone to call you," Bob told me. "You're just handy." He couldn't understand why I was put out for any of them. "It's embarrassing how you jump to do anything for people, who don't give a damn about you," things like that had never been forgotten.

It was more troubling every day. I waited for that call, and months had gone by, which was enough to prove his point. "Sure, go ahead. See what happens when you ask them for something," and still I waited for the courage to dare "go ahead and try" to prove him wrong. I didn't want. I had to wait, until I checked to see if he was right. I made the call. I took another call to me... who blew me off. Of all the things that sunk in, HE was right! I caved in to plead his forgiveness to conduct him accordingly. I relived out my memories for a while, but behaving wasn't the answer.

The only direction to strive and rise above, when all it weighted down. I'd never quite let go of all those examples that met his expectations, which was his standard to meet his call, instead. Was he smart to take advantage of a good thing, consciously or unconsciously? Although, criminal conduct took one step over the line, I couldn't bear to make him out of the narcissist.

The inmates in prison had no history with anything more than they had to offer or share. Although many of them didn't even speak fluent English, one way or another communicated body language to get their messages across quite clearly. The look, glare, gesture and the like spoke volumes for me to pay attention and watch of what I could understand. Side by side rehabilitation sat in for group counseling or behavior modification training through the penal system. Except for me, I was all alone to manage self-discipline and hold my tongue.

I was limited to eight hours on the job inside of a dim room full of men. And when I left, I took that mindset home in my small apartment. Days went by, then weeks, and every night I sat in a different control room, in a different building with different inmates, but it was always the same, as if it was merely a scratch on the surface when I had to dig deeper.

Some COs relaxed into the more mundane posts on the job, who lost forty hours without pay for the first suspension. It was all about its significance handed out. I could've spared my partners to assume their responsibilities, in the remote chance I'd be the hero which should never been honorable at all. I was handy, and Bob was right about that much. I couldn't be the responsible one to stroke their favors. It was a 'damned if you do/ damned if you don't' fall-guy either way, while I grew numb to it, when that example of my CO team was meant me. It was not me when everyone was blamed, for the real 'wake-up'.

The COs on graves were just gutsy enough to be caught, who got mad at me for it. My work family turned on me, but who was supposed to watch over me? Nonetheless, they argued against the least amount of blame that was passed on the next guy to be hurt... anybody but the supervisors.

Any CO forgot about the officer working in the prisons who relaxed back in his chair, when random checks made his supervisor's rounds. Even though he'd said that he wasn't asleep, even a moment who nodded off for a just second. I kept my mind busy throughout the nights, but I wondered if I should've been watched, too.

Some of the COs relied on any number of things to keep awake on the grave yard shifts, but especially Hamilton's open yard of inmates all around, like when the co-working staff talked for hours that tied up the phones. It was supposed to be a vital secure device with each breach, but one penalty after another dismissed the rough times that bent a few policies, like a slap on the wrists' warnings. The boundaries had been allowed that had also been pushed into compliant, or when someone expected to be too clever. There would always expect the one just around the corner, who let me do the worrying. I sweated every little thing to spare the rest and didn't have a clue until it was too late.

Each side of the yard had a game room of supplies which kept a plethora of things were catalogued away that shouldn't have been used by the inmates during open recreation. COs felt entitled who helped themselves, as if the inmates where glad to see them distracted. Even law enforcement protocols carried a different standard, when the prison's populations got mixed together.

Didn't I want to be included? I wanted to be welcomed, when the look-out made it possible to join. I felt like I participated, but it was my part and purpose to protect them. Some officers played cards or dice throughout the night, breaking a few rules now and then which was painless, but not entirely helpless. Reprimands curbed the changes... about the risks, as if those old school tendencies were too extreme to bend, until I was in... and everybody liked me?

Sometimes it was the smallest things that needed to turn it around. It was that fine line which affect the unresolved issues in my head of some new groundwork to branch out that didn't necessarily mean improvement.

Impulsive behaviors couldn't catch it, by sparing the fall-guy. I had been collared with every jerk backward or a swift kick forward to take it seriously, when I missed two of the finest official COs of the same graduating class at the academy. I was one of the same 48 classmates, and both of them committed suicide... on the job. Was that the end? There wasn't anything to do anymore, and I wondered about the threshold on the other side. But..., what if?

Who would've missed me? Who had my back? Who would've caught or saved me... from what? I asked myself who would've known and looked the other way. Or who didn't want to break the pattern when redundancy might've mattered. I understood the repetitive lessons who lost the contacts by old neighbors, classmates, childhood friends, co-workers, husbands, and family and it meant it all. Oh sure, I had a few girlfriends who I could call tomorrow and pick up a conversation like it was just yesterday between months or years apart, but that wasn't it. I was bound to no one, about prison.

Aww hell, even my ma was at wit's end with me under foot. I knew just how I could hear every scowl encrypted, and no one else had to know. The last thing I needed was to show weakness, but how close was I in line right next to my lost classmates?

That door was always there. I had the power to walk through the right button at my fingertips, as my keys grasped for its return. It was about to finish, and my decision was no one else's responsibility, as I followed a small beam and straight path of my flashlight. My job didn't stand in my way of success or failure, but whatever I delved into or uncovered anything else was my business. I couldn't be second to anyone or any more chances in line anymore.

CHAPTER 11

The SO yard

I added a spiral notebook to my grocery list that approved the Warden to bring it to work. Taking notes was nothing new. I kept the notes in my uniform chest pocket note book, which allowed another spiral notebook of my own.

I picked up the ongoing list to take care of the week's chores and sometimes I'd inadvertently leave behind to the list for next trip. I kept a close record of each receipt, when I wrote down to keep track of my budget, which validated my belongings, until I realized about the other things I owned. But I also noticed how chaos needed to manage the things I had even more valuable than monetary and materialistic worth.

Anything weighted on my mind deserved to upgrade or replace the old recordings took form on paper, one letter at a time. My notebook wrote down its memories that extracted thought to look at it, really look at something out of my mind to reevaluated it like data.

It felt like there was a constant background left on that couldn't ignore every sound, attitude, and message that I could never turn it off, until I could control it on paper. I carried my notebook back and forth to work, when I'd close my notebook, since remembering wasn't needed to pick it up later. Rehashing the thoughts had been exhausting, as if I'd lose the thought of the most important issues remained up front on my mind, as if that needed anything else could wear me down. Constant anxiety was stressful until it was cut in half, which separated my personal work in prison.

I borrowed the 'cluster fuck' description left behind of the other shifts for me to clean the mess, which was exactly how I lived inside my mind, to do my housecleaning. My mind was trashed all around, where I tripped over a lifetime of collections which was nothing mishandled, safe and confidential. Everything had its purpose in an orderly manner to spread everything out of its proper importance's for its place since nobody was pushy. I monitored the pace to manage the constant taunting, still spinning around its own life against my will to protect every event, situation, and its unfinished projects... but it was all mine, when I was uplifted in a surprise for more.

A slow cleansing breath didn't use my inhalers any longer, as if it was going in the right direction. I wasn't medicated, counseled, or shunned in the opposite direction, which was cleared to walk into prison every day. Everything made each dead stop to answer each inspection but there was nothing to fear the right to substantiate my notebook at the scanner. At first, I panicked. I was afraid that someone could take my personal notes spread it around, except I waved the pass with a signed form to prove and defend my needs, and then none of that was further necessary.

I carried in another tool, where I didn't have to worry to keep it handy... for me. Anything new or troubling moments went into the details on paper, like the inmates where I listened to let them unwind before he was unloaded and finally put to bed. The spiral notebook was a real place, too. It unloaded anything resurfaced, like when my hand was raised for the chance to either understand or argue against its principles. There I interrupted the train of thought as if the lectures didn't end until I 'got it', or where I also accepted the challenge to use it for 'fact-finding' answers. What I knew validated the moments that never let go that was put to the test under investigation. I had the right to dismiss anything to pass forward, while I still searched for something missing.

Days and weeks went by in the quiet of the graveyard shift. I never let up and no one else had to know the secrets that cropped up of my younger self... with another rule, like an OD (Ordering Document) to try it out before it evolved into the law that made it harder to change my mind... etched in stone. But how many things had to accommodate everyone one of them before me?

Something pushed the buttons, like when I opened the next door who didn't enter until he came to face through the flapping pass in my control room who needed to explain before he went ahead, and I looked to see what happened with another example... in my memorial.

Every jolt of the truth alerted each experience, like where only certain officers were given clearance to 'make way' of cadets from my classmates, which was my turn, and my accreditation, to proceed. But that wasn't just an expected practice at the academy. I was the one on a mission to be stepped out of my way with no resistance. I was in charge more important than anything else, demanded to respond immediately, which I respected and nothing forced.

I was the only to feel suspicious that fought against its unrelenting tension, when blind obedience robbed what I wanted. I became restless that further scolded myself in line, since I was conditioned to behave.

I kept jotting down anything, as if I had nothing else on the job, when I opened up the next notebook to be filled. I entered anything still bothering me, as if I couldn't have been any lower that I hid every embarrassing scar that couldn't hurt anymore.

There had plenty room to write off what I remembered to examine everything exposed, as more resurfaced to refine each situation: Who (interacted with me)? What (happened)? Where (the present place)? When (how old was I that long ago)? How (the cause and consequences of the results)? It was more than any simple pleasures of the pasts, but my notebook closed when time was up, and I could stop my fact-finding on command.

Days and weeks of my secrets who didn't need to discuss what I knew before, which was how I saw things spread out and looking into the moments of my younger self. It was more than permission, which I advised a new rule. I swallowed enough, and everything had to come out. I was safe to be okay, for another look and a slow walk around my mind. I faced every interruption to better understand from anyone else's opinions, judgements, or anything other than its private objectives, when nobody could rewrite the past for me. I collected to list all the facts to accumulate every face and names that unfold that also popped up something else.

Nothing was that troubling to manage piece by piece, when I also looked up to enough attention paid the here and now assigned at my post. My career took precedence aside myself, which ought to stay on top of the inmate's sounds just as easily reopened later. The only sound for a glance interrupted in the night time to understand its urinal flush, or where a snort or two interjected a brief inmate rolling over in their sleep, which I went down to check on anything until I eventually realized what was needed to know typical or not.

It had to learn to become familiar inside the dorms filled on either runs, in compared to realize how little privacy was offered to themselves, as if I scratched off the lists in my mind to be concerned or not. My personal research didn't detract from the dual watch against the potential dangers, where I picked up where I left off.

I meshed along the inmates with a clean slate, since I didn't have to play down the labels that were imposed on me to believe that I was an introvert, a loner, or spineless coward, but none of that was true. Although there was no doubt that I withdrew to close up inside a hardened shell, when I felt more susceptible where I lost the prior armor of protection into the open yard. Either way, that was not the way I heard it on the inside.

It took a lifetime to keep my opinions to myself, but my inner screams remained silent. No one had to know about each hypocrite who looked so pleased back at me, where I was surrounded by the inmates in a safer place, and also called 'the drudge of the earth', inside the prisons to find peace, too.

I thought how some people say that 'your life passes by in a flash when you die', except my life meticulously examined it backwards. Sure, there were times didn't need it, as if I flipped through my life of the same patterns still remained in a life of servitude. I obeyed, which was not wimping out submissive as a suck-up through the same insults that worked against my will.

The memories were not kind. Was I sorry for something that couldn't be forgiven? I was accommodating behind my own self-loathing mask to overshadow all other qualities, questioning myself, as if I was a fake to blend in and remain anonymous. I was expected to do the same things with my fellow officers, but I had no place to go home on guard in high alert there, too.

That proverbial stone wall felt safe. Was it protection for me, or from something else? I was on a mission with the success through probation and into the next transfer for more. Did time wait out and let it pass? But it did pass and surpass the test against all odds.

I looked around to keep a low profile in the SO yard. I was surrounded by people who did some pretty heinous things. Did inmates succumb to the will of others, or were they the perpetrators who repeated the cycle? Why did I want to be accepted of the request to be involved in a SO yard? What kind of people could drive people, like me, into submission all over again?

I tip-toed between the double bunks and I could feel the threats through my bones every time I cleared the security door to reenter each run, hypervigilance by every little change was important to wager every step... while they slept?

The irony wasn't fair. Both inmate and family member loved who visited regularly with so much encouragement and hope for the future to carry on after their release, except me. They quickly greeted without any apprehension in orange, but who would've known that I wore the officer's uniform and I didn't belong? I didn't have to watch the love, as I concealed a glance to see every extended touch, back pat, endearing stroke, or the initial hug, where I wasn't allowed. What did the inmates have, and I didn't deserve to be kept from that, too?

From what might've started out who fished out any number of questions during a criminal investigation show on primetime TV that intrigued me through a storyline. Each character considered the forensic proof lead to the undeniable truth, as I studied its continuum formula. One question led to another, while my notes kept on track with any piece of information that was used to drive toward it the same way. At work I sat up and watched over the inmates, while I also brainstormed all the details to validate everything sorted out to narrow down what I looked for, good or bad, right or wrong... I didn't care. I just wanted to know what happened.

I showed up for work and took a seat in the briefing room just like everybody else. I checked the roster and collected my equipment, while my partner filled the room on the other side. I overheard their conversations, but I didn't have the time to reestablish friends or relationships, when small talk didn't need to lose any time. I had to catch up of my own needs, which was easily returned by anything set aside to assist the team.

Random checks and interruptions had each useful moment to stop and check how my mental stress level reread it on a regular basis. I had to review how I was feeling, moving deeper into my youth. Did something trigger the onset other than more of the same situations? Eventful moments were easily weeded down its senseless repeats, as if the elite few remained all the more valuable. I could feel it. But I also felt more cautious, warned by the heavily watch on guard that I treaded forward to slow it down. Something happened, as if I had done so badly. It wasn't always that way. What humbled me? What kind of shame made me cower to submitted so obediently, or shut down to make way for others? Sure, I had plenty to say, but I choked on my words since I became the perfect listener when I shared very little in return.

Every night I came to work with that kind of enthusiasm since all of my supervisors loved to see me, but I suppose some of them thought I was even a little weird to stay up all night alert and attentive in the dark. After all, how many night shift workers can handle eight hours in a room under a twenty-watt gooseneck lamp with a rickety old chair? But I completed every shift, certain that I was on the verge of something big day after day.

I trusted my gut and I would know, which was in parallel in training at the academy. I remembered: "If you want to know the future, examine the past. But, if you want to change the future, learn from the past." I forced myself to remember every incident, recalling everything younger and younger which I'd discover something more profound, but I started to get nervous, worried that something went horribly wrong.

It felt with a death-defying blade dangled over my head, like a sharp guillotine threatened that could've been for me. Who could've ever been that angry, or even that hateful with me? Every memory was slowly and methodically tip-toed to uncover anything detrimental. I recalled as if it was yesterday, when I worked of my own advocate to detach myself.

I had their same look or expression, a tone or voice in the way it was said, or recovered something too ingrained, or not quite ready to surface. How many times had I stepped out from the classrooms at the academy when I was so disturbed, dreaded to my bones, that also removed the wool from my eyes, again?

That immature innocence wasn't going to be easily forthcoming. At any moment I was expected to have an epiphany. Maybe I was going to be re-welcomed, like I was allowed back downstairs to become part of the family again. I wanted to make that happen for her. For her? I questioned the slip. I wanted to tell the younger me to take my hand. It was safe, I knew it! It was alright.

I remembered school age, which was just refused to talk things out, slammed with comments like "Why don't you just bury it" or "Stop bringing up all that garbage," that still bothered me. They had to know that I was in pain, stuffed down too many times kept to myself.

The slamming doors at the lockdowns made anybody jump, terrified, as if I could see it in so many others' eyes held behind every security door. Was I supposed to bottle-up my feelings held inside, forced of rejection, or safety? Maybe I should've left well enough alone, and that didn't need to be brought up out in the open to see at all?

I began to emphasize the inmates. Although I didn't break the laws of the land, I definitely deserved in isolation. I had become an inmate of my own right. I was in disgrace, there I remained to be the problem child. I felt accused with its unanimous agreement that backed my siblings which was justified, except the jury debate a proper defense, and no place to go…lost in the State of Limbo.

I could even admit an embarrassment, but I apologized any-ways. I wanted to be treated like the rest of them, but I couldn't sell myself to anyone. I was beneath them, expecting nothing more, unless I'd jumped in full gear to be bought out of a favor, but then, it was over and done, until something else might be needed.

But I did that. I scribbled down notes to see that it happened. I looked up to every loved one, putting them all above me who automatically forced them to look down on me, a notch below. My loved ones didn't want to be around, as if they couldn't possibly look up to me behind badge. I wasn't allowed to stand as tall as anyone, when I realized how daddy came to press my shoulders against the kitchen wall to straighten up. I slouched and rolled my shoulders forward to appear smaller.

I stepped back in time to think beyond my immediate family. Who else saw me like that? I could name every aunt and uncle who took me in as an uninvited guest through the summers, when my sister got married to be dropped off with her when I was around ten years old. But that wasn't it. Donna kept me in her bedroom, until I was grown old enough in my own bed, but that was not vacation time.

I could've been raised by my Auntie Marge who married Uncle Howie Pruitt. I spent the first summer who had no other children, where my uncle worked the lifelong Chicago Police career. And I also remembered how their family of seven children spent the summer on welfare, knowing I didn't belong, regardless.

I returned to my post day after day, as I scratched out to eliminate chunks of time reminiscing on the good times, while my gut had nothing to say. I was at peace to stop and enjoy, while my notebook stayed at my side on track, beyond kindergarten age.

I spent a lot of time with my dad when I was small, knowing every tool in his garage, hung and retrieving every one of them on command. And when he laid on its cardboard underneath the cars. I knew he'd work on anything, and he also counted on me scooting down any hand tools needed. He'd disassemble the engines with anything in the right order, which I proudly entrusted the utmost respect in his garage, knowing its manners put back together, restored or replaced.

And how I loved the of baby chicks that would hatch from the incubator, and he needed his help there too. I handled a hundred chicken eggs who showed my daddy's shadow by its faint look to believe beyond life taking form. He held up their shells patiently measured according to the calendar, who had my help. It took exactly a quarter turn of each egg, and he had another painstakingly time-consuming examined through the embryos that was pulled down on a cord with a quick jerk and it rolled back up, which was amazed by everything. My daddy was awesome, but how much he also enjoyed to watch the fragile eggs... for him! In hindsight, that had to have been an incredible task for a four-year-old kid.

Again, my gut feelings were at peace. I was his boy, since they were all girls and ma picked me out, instead. He even took me to the barber shop for a buzz hair cut to cinch my heightened status. And the, the slip came out! ...Naw, I must've been wrong.

I remembered about the feed mill, where I was rewarded a sucker to finish before we got home. That might not sound like a big deal, but back then, having a piece of candy was rare, especially a piece of candy that was all mine. Or, holding onto my own fishing pole sat still in the row boat far from shore, loving the shimmering lights that rippled from the bobber at the end of my cane pole for my dad to take over in the excitement of another fish to add to the pail. And when I hung onto the back of his John Deer tractor seat, until he stopped for me to jump down from the spade hoe at the end of each row. I was needed for that extra weight on the plow to turn over the soil. Or where, I remembered how eager I ran from room to room throughout the house where he was exactly expected with each window unlocked before he climbed up the ladder to switch out the screen or storm windows, as we inadvertently got soaked once the hoses were more than our spirt guns playing.

That was about the same age I met my first best friend, who was a bittersweet warm spot in my heart. George lived in the salvage yard about a mile down the road from that old farmhouse. I discovered a fence that framed out the junk yard that filled a plethora of the old cars left to rust outside the elements, even though nothing really kept anything inside or out, when I just walked in to visit any time I wanted.

And then, my heart pounded as I stared down, frozen into a new page of my notebook. There were no words. I had trouble deciphering the feelings of excitement or chaotic panic left behind our friendship.

I paused to take a deep breath to calm myself. I could take it. I had to! But the shift was over and I was off work for the next two days with chores to do.

CHAPTER 12

School

*T*wo days off of work didn't necessarily define Saturday and Sunday weekends. Two days were scheduled for my Tuesday and Wednesdays, when the mid-week mail and online flyers worked in the best deals. My errands shamelessly made it an art form around the specials beyond groceries during back-to-school season. There were kids running back and forth who couldn't be missed. I had to watch over the children, but it also pointed out their favorite selections aspired to gain their parents' approvals. School supplies weren't on my list, which I couldn't ignore.

Competition became demanding that escalated down the aisles in a frenzy to allow the children all the space they needed, as if I'd relive through someone else's shoes. It seemed all so urgent among the children, who stressed out the credit limit. The final decisions took what they could, when nothing was left to discuss. Their packages had been tabulated through the cashier's receipt, and then, the family car disappeared.

I relying on the sales to fill the needs, but it could've been the time I was the single mom, remembering how firm the boundaries had to cut it off, except when I had another chance to make another choice for myself. Temptations drew me in like it was contagious. I enjoyed the craziness about the children that safe enough to set aside, until I could've been just crazy enough to be swept in school, too.

For as much pride they had, I realized about the supply bins who dug in that satisfied it enough left behind for someone else. I understood how hard the parents checked the tags before shaking their heads, leaning on the phrase, "Because I said so." insisted on less and look for something else.

The children scrammed from one item to be dropped for another, until everyone was satisfied, but going back to school meant more than a new year's supplies. It was a chance to reunite their friends beyond the neighborhood.

All throughout the day, I could not stop thinking about the school's opening again. I caught the bug that spread, swept up in the excitement to go back to school myself. No one would have known, and no one was around to tell me that I couldn't.

I tried to fight and shake off the thought. Sitting in a classroom so late in the game was ridiculous. It put my children and spouses with each new year applied its higher education, degrees, or additional letters behind their last name. I was truly happy for them all, wondering if I would get the chance to enroll for me.

The academy completed eighteen college credits. That had to mean something. "Why waste it?" my emotions ran wildly tempted, as I swallowed hard. I was embarrassment and jealous, "look but don't touch" where I saw rejection that pulled at me through every aisle.

My heart was stuck in my throat. I knew I would've just set myself up for failure. Rubbing elbows with the elite students of the class of 2017 would've been a far cry from 1970. The newly attended high school graduates had computer technology from the beginning in comparison. I could hardly turn my digital clocks back, since the daily crank only needed a swift rock on the evening's alarm clock. I couldn't possibly keep up, and another chance would've been laughed right out of being made the fool. I'd lost all hope, knowing that being smart couldn't excel any better than another dinosaur.

Even when I got my grades high, I earned the honor roll a few times before I graduated from high school. I surpassed but only because of the menial courses beyond their real sciences. I could only admire the college-eligible students from afar, and way out of my league. I courteously smiled throughout the packed corridors who pushed the baby boomers through the system. Sure, I could get the grades, but not without a lot of help from after-school tutoring programs. The LD (learning disabled) classes did not offer much more than the basics before ADHD was ever understood.

Maybe I should've been satisfied with a high school diploma, but I wanted more. I brought it up with my dad on our drive into work one day, but he talked me out it. Even a community college with courses scheduled in the evenings wasn't something he could support. It was his belief that a female did not need an education. He wanted me to build a life behind a good man who would provide for me.

The world was in a state of flux, back then, when females were finally offered jobs that were typically given to men. My dad didn't mean to be condescending. It was what he knew. It was how it was, but he also wanted me to be employed with him in the factory where I could get a head start on life with money on the side, in comparison to the college kids burdened with student loans after four years. He told me that a paycheck was a real thing, where by a degree was a hit or miss opportunity for a career. He was right, but somehow, he might've arranged to take me alongside of him. I believed that anything else was selfish, once the paychecks were hard to give up.

But it was no use. My curiosity got the best of me. I had to check it out, and turned the car around for a slight detour on my way home. A naughty kind of thrill stirred deep down, when I had no one around to discourage me. My grocery items were safe in the back cooler that followed everything through town to wait a few hours. I stretched to see the lid of the cooler, hoping to find a shaded parking spot, and I took the plunge.

The parking lots were filled like Christmas time at the malls, except there was no way of knowing whether I was in a good spot or not, but that was about to be the least of my worries. I got out and followed one of the footpaths with a **'you-are-here'** campus sign inviting inside.

My stress level wasn't nearly as high as when I drove my daughter tour for a few college options in her final year of high school, but my suggestions didn't meet her expectations. I didn't have to be that pillar of strength fighting to contain my reaction with her attitude, which I dismissed away any form of separation anxiety. I wasn't going to be that picky, anyways. Close to home suited me just fine. If it really mattered to have my certificate awarded by a specific university instead of a community college, since I practiced what I preached. I'd have my credits transferred later like I still believed, or whether I had any of that important down the line. Either way, I could leave it open.

Volunteers swarmed throughout the campus with that youthful energy, quick to welcome everyone entering the Admissions Department. The double doors received their greeters, who were probably the upperclassmen, readily run to reach out their new arrivals. I vaguely remembered who asked a few questions throughout the commotion, when I robotically followed their advice to go down a corridor toward a door slightly ajar.

"Hello, Ms. Burdy?" I peered into her office, reading her name from the door.

"Come in." She gathered a few papers to the side of her desk. "Have a seat." She continued as if there was nothing more important, stretching out her arm toward the empty chair next to the front of her desk. "How can I help you?" My eyes must have locked onto hers, stunned, like a deer in the headlights, and swallowed hard. She was right. I was in need of help!

"Ma'am, I earned eighteen credits last year when I graduated out of the academy to be a correctional officer." I swallowed hard, poised with my arms down to the side while I started to sweat, agonizing, whether I was fit for the visit. I forced her to be honest. I braced to be informed, who would kindly decide for someone else. I sat, raw and vulnerable. How was I going to persuade a well-dressed professional to explain, as my office door was privately and cordially needed to spare the shame of the truth, worried that I was too late for a degree? "I wonder if you could tell me how many credits I would have to add for an associate degree?" I spew it all out at once.

I was never a fast talker, but I prepared everything out in one breath. I didn't want to waste her time with the eye roll message, "here we go again!" It was "just the facts", which was all that was needed, quick to the point. I felt like I entered a job interview, ready to argue against "You're too old" but of course, she wouldn't have used those exact words. She could've been oh so finely dressed in her suave look of the times, and her politically polished lessons to meet the counselor working in admissions, but I also knew that that was mere policy. Still, I had to sell myself.

I waited, trying hard to detect her subtle expressions for her reaction. It wasn't possible that someone had been tipped her off of her first impression, too! What could've reached behind my back for a mouthed message? First impressions of the moment must've realized how many applications had to juggle their curriculums deadlines, except she had no reason to waste her time that ended too sweetly in comparison.

Maybe I was too determined, too stubborn to force her move, but my inner noise couldn't to shut it off for just a minute. Thoughts bounced through any different responses, while her pause must've filled a lot of other options to prepare, too. She must've formed her words carefully, and I refused to make the run before any chance at college.

"So, you work in the prisons?"

I threw a double-take. Was she going to play nice first? Was she going to act like she was my friend before lowering the bomb?

"I do." My defenses were high, already defiant when I had nothing to back it up. I disobeyed, with no one on my side.

Ms. Burdy projected the perfect example with a successful career woman. It was the kind of daughter my ma would've been expected to succeed. But I was never expected to climb to that level. I could still hear her voice saying, "As long you pass, you won't have to repeat a grade."

"You must have some interesting stories." Ms. Burdy appeared delightful, asking about my work, but I knew that I was not the first correctional officer who had ever come and sat in her office, but there had to be a catch. Still, I played along. She was another example to remember about the same aged group among the smart kids who went off to college after high school, where I was off to work in the factory, in the first place.

"Naw, not really." I smiled with a drop of my head as if to say, "Let's not go there," but, she didn't leave a hint of arrogance toward the parody of our posts in life.

"What did you do before you became an officer?" She speeded up her typing between the computer screens, for her eyes only, and down to business between some small talk.

"I worked in Customer Service at Conquest Labs." My answer remained dry. It wasn't the career path that would've made me rich, but it was a job I grew from the bottom up for more than twenty-five years of training and advancements. My heart felt heavy, stuck in my throat to struggle through it. "A lot of those callers weren't the easiest people to work with." I believed just how challenging office work shared who also offered a moment of empathy in an equally amount of stress together.

"So, you have computer skills, communication skills..." She paused and looked squarely at me for a second, when a look felt more like the compliment I didn't expect. "I bet they use a lot of language in the prisons, too." she fussed a bit in her chair to get started again, realizing how their vocabulary was well-founded in abuse.

"Not as bad as my step-son." I was slow to answer, keeping my voice down. How easily I admitted the shame, when I recoiled. I listened between their most distasteful attitudes which accentuated their colorful language that couldn't be found in the dictionary, wondering whether the anonymous callers demanded to resolve their billing mistakes or my husband looking the other way who didn't care either way. It wasn't more than the first few minutes, who would let me down gently. "Look what you did! Oh, you poor thing! You're pathetic!" My head hung, showing the real me.

"Oh, I know what you mean." She spoke over the conversation, breaking in the comments bombarding inside. There was no hint of degradation, since I expected to lapped up every ounce of guilt to own the blame, personally.

"How long did you work in the medical billing field?" A slight grin was pleasantly satisfying, asking to boast my own success to come through, who understood or let me crow for the first time.

"Once you separate the government-funded plans from the commercial contracts, and recognize the various products underneath the umbrellas, behind any number of insurance companies, they aren't really that difficult to understand." I blurted out office jargon as if I was used to hearing it from our work team meetings. People who spoke their own language automatically connected perfectly. But, no sooner had I finished, I put my hand over my mouth (metaphorically speaking) to apologize. I didn't mean to outshine her, gloating about another career that took years to master. She stopped typing and started to sweat.

"You'd have to be pretty good to do that kind of work down here." She was interested who appreciated the difference between Customer Services and Patient Services, when she spoke just the opposite manner under her breath, by the way I was restored back into balance.

"I'll tell you what." Ms. Burdy pushed her aerodynamic chair away from her desk and crossed her legs, mimicking my posture. I could hear my pulse pound as my face flushed. I must've offended the very person I came for help, but I was wrong. "I'll bet you can qualify for a few more credits than the eighteen you earned at the academy." She had my attention but I had no clue of what she meant. I was confused. "I'd like to send you across the hall to see Mr. Crawford. He pre-screens our new students to get a basic background of knowledge to see if we can override some of those prerequisites."

Okay, she won. She wasn't about to join me in a pissing contest. She decided to send me away instead. Then, she started to stand up to see me to the door when she noticed how heavy my heart was. "Was there something else you wanted to ask?" She stopped as I tried to control that lump in my throat.

"I have not gone to school since the sixties and even then, I had a hard time keeping up." I extended my hand to say good-bye. "Ma'am, I want to thank you for your time."

"Oh no. You misunderstood!" She refused to take my hand. "I believe you may be surprised by how much you already know." I saw her enthusiasm but I already had her figured out. She was hired to fill as many classes as possible. It was just business. She just found me to fill some of the extra-help courses. I gave her all the information she needed, and I made it easy for her to validate the very proof I thought I could break.

"Prerequisites?" I said with attitude. "Doesn't that mean that you have to get me up to speed to prepare me for college?" I felt defeated.

"That is exactly what prerequisites are for." She gently lowered herself back into her chair. "Those courses carry college credits too, but I don't believe that you will need to take some of them." She dropped that jubilant smokescreen. "I believe you could be scheduled directly into our college curriculum just by-passing those courses." Her words were slow and calculated. "If you test out, like

I believe you will, you will be directly scheduled into our Freshman or Sophomore classes. If I'm right." She stopped for a moment to make sure I was listening to her and not the noise in my head. "You can pick up extra credits by overlooking some of the prerequisites."

"What makes you think I can do that?" I wasn't proud of myself for the way I reacted, but I needed to keep it real.

"You didn't stop learning just because you didn't continue to go to school after high school." She got me to smile as my head lifted a bit. She knew that if I could keep up with the ever-changing medical insurance industry, since I could satisfy dry call-ins' problems who counted to be expected to fix, so I also had the stuff to earn a degree.

"Where did you say his office was?" I asked again, as we raised my chair together, leaning across her desk for that hand-shake.

"You're going to do just fine. I'm glad we met." She closed, freeing me from the need to apologize anything misunderstood, as if the special needs department was right behind

By the time I was ready to leave for Mr. Crawford's department, I was, once again flying high with the thought of being a college student. "Sir?" I walked quietly a few steps in his direction with respect to the people who were busy filling in their bubble sheet answers, who were just as intent as I would've been. "My name is Pruitt, Marion Pruitt," I said nervously. "Ms. Burdy sent me here."

"Wonderful!" He greeted me with a handshake, since I unconsciously had mine extended. "Let's see what you're made of!" He quickly left his desk at the head of the classroom to lead me toward the back where the computers were already set up. "I have a few computers still open." He talked while I followed closely behind. "How much time do you have?" Then, he stopped abruptly for a closer look at me.

"Is it possible to come back on another day? I have groceries in the car." I wasn't prepared to spend the day on campus "How much time would that take?"

"Oh good, good." He sputtered, deep in thought for a moment. "I will be here all week. Can you set aside a few hours for me before five?" he asked with his eye brows raised, giving way for me to reply.

"How early do you start? I work the night shift and return after six. Is seven good for you?" He seemed to wince. "How about eight? Then I can shower and change first." I smiled that accommodated it a little later.

"Tomorrow then." He shook my hand again, and I saw myself out.

Outside, the campus was still bustling with people, stopping in front of billboards, or wandered aimlessly around campus layout maps from their brochures who studied out every other building. It was wonderful!

I returned invisibly mixed in all around the crowds, who darted through the foot paths without a care. And for just a moment I believed I'd fit in, until I could see how I needed some work. I still wore the second hand stores, looking like I was somebody's mom, when I knew that I needed some new clothes shopping, too.

Mr. Crawford had several programs prepared for me as promised. Each test covered abstract thinking, reading comprehension, and grammar. It didn't take him too long to review my scores, and we sat down to discuss my curriculum, starting with ENG 101. I had surpassed my expectations, but there was a lot more to overcome. The thought of entering a classroom filled with teenagers, scared me half to death, or when I pictured where I'd sit in the back of the classroom, pushed forward, and afraid back to cut the grade... for the second time around.

The tuition expense was nominal in comparison to the emotional cost of failure. The pressure was on. I needed to get an "A" to qualify for 100% reimbursement from DOC, which counted by another boost with a 1% increase upon completion, as if that would've satisfied the first associate's degree. I could almost taste it. I saw a climb, minimized within my earnings, still paying off my divorce attorney, used car, and the household furnishings, when I kept a close eye to manage my charges against my bank card.

There was another plaque prominently displayed the briefing room. I read them enough, as if it was ever there before, *"If you think you can or if you think you can't, you're right."* The answer was always mine!

There was no reason to hand over my paycheck to anyone else in charge. I could eat peanut butter and jelly sandwiches for dinner, when no one was around to complain to me about it anymore. My job required the same uniform that everyone else wore, when a nice pair of jeans easily replace my clothes to stay current with the times in school.

Nobody had to know what I was doing, where I was going, or answer to anyone else. By living alone, I could do anything to take all the credit or downfalls, as if I was going to become a bitter old woman. In fact, it made me angry. Who needed to plant that believe it would happen? Either way, I was enjoying life with no one else's opinions, proven all by myself.

All my three children made their own personal college fields of study. They left home, as if the back door was always opened to remain handy of the love and support. They grew self-reliant, adjusting their standard of living which was their decisions, since I co-signed the loans with all the faith I had in them. And pushed sixty required self-reliance with the same challenges. I strived to achieve the grade; except when I pushed all the hardest with that final sprint.

The application processed through which I registered of just one course, but it was limited to only fifteen students. It was a first-time basis, or when SAT scores had the flexibility to change out any one of my classes. The colleges limited forty to fifty baby boomers with one teacher, as if any class I wanted would've accommodated me.

DOC also opened up its benefits after the first year of probation to offer the state's expense of tuition once I carried my curriculum in line for the campus student ID for all to see, before purchasing my school supplies. I thumbed through the more frugal-cost with the less writing in my book at their college bookstore, but I help someone of the same book who thought I was the clerk. Any one of them might've been assigned to that class, when I worried whether I could withstand the younger minds learning at thier pace... next to me.

I entered the right class room for the morning classes, freshened up to change right after work. My classmates jumped with every enthusiastic high-five flowing in, where I found a seat that must've been mistaken for a visiting parent or guest speaker. I was a fellow student, inviting myself right next to another young woman, who finally figured out the real professor, who became friends.

Differences attracted inmates to compliment the prison system, too. Those goal lines defined their sentences in any number of ways, as if the final line didn't have anyone rush through the race. And illiteracy didn't require a crash course that was both humbling and sobering, which I saw their strength and courage at the open yard. Grown men in prison felt humiliated, where I couldn't hide from being dubbed the slow learner, either. My heart bled out to that inmate on track to get his GED, where: *You are right here.* Truancy was no longer an option for the inmates, or me. They'd avoided an education back on the streets, but I was not about to accept that either.

The state government funded the prison system, since the public schools missed out and their education still carried... a second chance, as if imprisonment carried its benefits which required the basic skills to read and write. Both older and younger inmates who drew out each letter of the alphabet in the nighttime. At first, they shrouded to conceal it in shame until they couldn't be ignored, and I smile back, instead. I checked out their workspace passed by with my flashlight, when I wouldn't dare tease or make fun of them.

As word traveled, inmates stepped up with its encouragement on a regular basis, wondering how they'd catch on so quickly, when others sat out who deserved to admit the need for help, as the doors of hope stayed open.

Fortunately, or unfortunately, however you looked at it, the state prison housed a lot of their inmates who sponsored them tutoring, on call. Help was all around. Inmates were available with all the patience the world, as I saw about rehabilitation besides the structured programs from DOC. It was awesome, who looked out to me. I had a pair of inmates asking permission to sit in the day room, to study away from the sleeping inmates in the runs.

I was supposed to keep the inmates behind a locked security door through the nights. They knew it, and I let them out. I briefed them to stay inside the building, away from the windows, but they already knew I'd take the chance. I had an inmate asked me to take the risk, putting myself out, again.

I listened with regard of the sleeping inmates, who asked to move away from their lamp burning in the dark and irritating whispers. They were better outside of the runs to the day room table, instead and I gave in. I wagered against the potential threats against their drive, on me.

One inmate might have explained everything perfectly, but another inmate came across altogether differently or maybe it just needed enough sleep the day before. It was no body's true answers from a book that took no offense to help each. I saw how one thing had the most difficultly, and then it turned around by the next inmate further down the line.

I could relate how the inmates fumbling through the sounds of each letter to pronounce each word, who seemed to be hoping for the tutor to pitch in, which wasn't impose on anyone to work it through his own. And sometimes I'd look upon them and think, "what a waste". What could have made the difference, or what were they handed in life toward that spiral? Didn't they have a choice born into anything better than that?

I cried bitterly at the thought that I could've turned out better, and still envious fighting against it. Even my grades proved to otherwise, except where the prison system put a lot of stock in their education. But who was I to judge?

I used my erasers to a nub, when transferred my lessons to the computer lab at school, since I needed my tutors who worked readily available at the college. Every computer designed its programs, which I also learned how I handed in my homework through "blackboard." Nobody turned in their lessons on paper anymore, and the days of actual chalk in the classroom was a thing of the past. I was greeted by name too often by a team of tutors, who cheered me on with every lesson I completed, which I included the writer's club to critique each other's work as confidence grew.

By the time the semester was over, I achieved an "A" that surpassed my expectations, with a lot of help, as if that wasn't good enough. I wasn't convinced that I truly earned that grade. So, I expounded the next semester, loading down all of the more demanding courses covering the other professors. And again, by the end of the year, I finished out an amazing 4.0 GPA. And that did it!! I finally believed that I was "A" material, rubbing elbows with the most competitive students of class 2017.

For the first time in my life, I studied one book after another authors, subject, and/or genre to the next. I drank them down like fresh water on a hot day. I was done questioning my scholastic ability, now flying high with the thought of being normal. ADHD poured all of the advice to see how different it meant, which also redefined my gut instinct to believe what I was supposed to believe. I felt normal. Better than normal! I even believed that I could've earned a degree greater than that, when I had to crow and call ma.

"Hello, ma?" My call was not surprising when I made the call.

"Well Marion! I'm glad you called. I never know when to call. I don't want to wake you," as if she was glad to hear my voice.

My ma loved the telephone, something I'd just never learned to enjoy it like her. Once I even checked the clock who picked up to see how long she could go. I gave her all the time she had and just wouldn't let it go. My arms cramped, holding the phone for so long, switched one ear to the other. I tried to put it on speaker phone, but she complained that it was difficult to hear me. I had to hold onto the phone, no matter how long it was going to take, as long as I could promise to call back, again.

She'd never run out of things to say. She'd tell me how my sisters were doing, their vegetable gardens, the weather, her health, the health of others, home improvements, the news…it didn't matter whether I had anything to add or not. I hung onto the phone, listening to the things about the economy and how it affected the cost of things, how it affected my sister's families, or the need for a part-time job about the ones and who empathizes what wanted instead. She knew how my nieces and nephews were doing, who was dating or their choices. I heard how her neighbor came over who cleaned fish to share their way home from the inland lakes of the areas. She knew who'd bought a new car, and she did not hesitate to share her pride in her children, one after another. All it took was an intermittent, "uh huh," to let her know that I was still there, but all the while, she never asked how I was doing. She already knew how I was doing. She said that she watches TV and knew all she needed to know about prisons. However, that day, I had something to boast some sense of pride added to her list.

"Ma, I went to school last year." I got a few words in before she got started on a new topic.

"What do you mean, you went to school?" I couldn't tell whether she was happy for me or not. It wasn't like me, initiating the conversation, since it was mostly listening.

"I picked up a few credits to put towards a degree." Her hesitation was genuine. School was never something I'd considered something like that before. "Work benefits kicked in after probation,"

I continued, taking advantage of the silence. "And, I got 100% reimbursement for the cost for all my college courses." Breathing came through the wire like she was inadvertently exhaling into the receiver. "I didn't want to waste the eighteen credits earned from my training at the academy." Silence. "Ma? Are you there?"

I was thrilled with excitement. I didn't lean on my loved ones, who couldn't have known how I did without their help. I lived alone, except for the time away from the job where I achieved top grades at college. My sisters and extended family members were gone on to college, as if I pulled my weight at the end. Surely that news had to make her ecstatic! I made the call to give her all the more surprising things to be spread around for her. She collected to hear about anything that might've perked up by the next callers to hear about me, but nothing could have been farther than the truth.

"What good is that?" The tone of her voice changed. Her energy was flat. I must've misspoken. She was thrown, about something, anything? Maybe she wasn't sure about what I just said, so I slowed it down more clearly.

"I sat in their classes, with kids right out of high school, and I pulled off a 4.0 GPA." I couldn't contain myself with such wonderful news. Surely, it should've been my turn to give her something else to feed.

Unlike myself, she could stay on the phone to say, and didn't want to hear anything I said? I thought I'd just offered a bulletin of fresh material, as if it was a gift. In fact, I finally counted on the grapevine to enhance it for her., although I didn't follow up anything further, like one ear passed through the other ear. But it was important! I was giving her an exclusive to go viral with a first exclusive.

But there was no doubt that she understood exactly what I said, when I worried that hit a nerve, as if a repeat was everything passed by the second time... undeniably underlined in bold print, and possibly rubbed in. She reported all the stats from her grandchildren's achievements over past telephone visits with me. The only thing that was different, was that I knew what I was doing and she didn't.

"What good is that?" Her response zinged me aback. Certainly, she didn't mean that!

"Ma!" I called out, almost laughing in my announcement. "I went to college for a year and got an 'A' in every subject I took!"

"What would you do that for?" She sounded confused. How was I so misunderstood?

"Well, since I had eighteen credits already, I visited the local college to see how many credits were needed to get an associate degree. Work offers a 1% raise in pay when you get a degree, so I thought I'd try for it." I spoke as if I was trying to convince her that I did a good thing, but that was not what she wanted to hear.

"So, what do you want from me?" She was annoyed.

"Well, I guess I was hoping a pat on the back, Ma." The tone in my voice lowered to a whisper. I felt like I'd just gotten slapped. I thought she would've been happy for me. If I had to tell her that I wanted a compliment, turned around as if the compliment wasn't worth much. "I was thinking that I could even become a writer." I grasped at straws for her to get on board with me. I really didn't think about how I was going to use a meager associate degree from a community college. I could've even played down the basic courses, or any kind of field of study. What went wrong?

"What would you write about? Me? And, say what? Lies?" Her voice was harsh and filled with disdain.

"Ma, I don't understand? I thought that was good news." My joy turned into sorrow with that lump tightening my throat to a higher pitch.

"That degree don't mean nothing! Why would you waste your money like that? How old are you? Why would you take up a seat that some youngster could've filled?" She ranted with all her reasons at once, like pulling the rug out from under me. I started to whimper. It didn't matter what else was said. It was nothing kind.

No matter what I did. Good or bad. The tears fell. She heard me crying, expecting me to profoundly apologize like I'd done something wrong again, but she did not let up, to be scolded back in line.

"I have to go, Ma," I said without knowing if she heard me or not. I flipped my cell phone closed. I knew she had enough to pass it along for her next caller, and tear apart my joy with someone else.

CHAPTER 13

Account-ability

Safety was about my survival, as if I was stripped from DOC's armor during the open yard of criminals, when I was selfishly self-defensive to protect the rest of the inmates. The runs stayed together with all different personalities. It was like my family crowded eleven people under one roof, as if I couldn't manage at home, but the land of the law governed DOC's written policies, handed down by my discretion toward peace.

'Eyes and Ears' required more than the post I took, watching over the inmates, which was short for the Peace Officer into practice. Some people kept their heads down with respect for the rest of the inmates in the runs turned down to sleep, while I'd detect the warnings to pin down the problems. Phrases like 'Don't touch me, Move over, Shut up, or I'm telling' stayed just as secure on the walls screwed into the walls in the briefing room, just like back home.

Change was the trigger when my presence was enough to step in between. I couldn't change them in prison, until I purposely stood out, sticking out my neck, to look for trouble. The job was dangerous to notice the boundaries who shoved and pushed a little too far. Some were expected to be stronger than others, but I studied their different skills who didn't choose their bunkies mixed among their backgrounds, which was my job to make it work.

It was like I had a prepared meal to be set up in a pressure cooker to cook on a stove burner. The weight floated from the raising heat that should've rocked and know how it adjusted smooth and regular tempo, looking forward to a perfectly fixed dish. A little too hot could've been turned down, unless it was left unattended, horribly exploded. Nothing was ever taken for granted, like if the ordinary behaviors also steamed inside, until I saw all kind of raised flags jumped into action, as if the risk took the immediate chance by sliding the pot off the burner entirely.

Recognizing the triggers, affected others as well. I couldn't hide or deny the problems among inmates, except when I intervened. I'd become hypervigilant to the finest nuances no one else could pick up on the job, when a survival mode wasn't enough anymore. I honed into my gut like a barometer to read my protection, besides the criminals who leaned on each other.

"What's up?" I sensed a pair of eyes glaring down at me, as if he patiently waited to fill in the service log set up at the beginning of my shift.

"Could you wake me up for work?" Inmate Jimenez fidgeted. "I'm a sound sleeper and..." He paused long enough to read me. Some officers would have slammed that sucks-to-be-you attitude, instead.

"Yeah, no problem. What time?" I didn't hesitate, knowing he was concerned about something else.

"About 01:30?" he answered, when I knew more than a simple wake-up call.

"What's going on?" I probed.

"My bunkie's mad at me." His eyes locked intently onto mine. "He's tired of being woke up every night. I always set my alarm because I don't wake up to go to work, but then he kicks the bottom of my bunk to turn it off." He explained a problem above his bunk, as I waited for the rest which was a good start. The lower bunkie rushed to get the alarm turned off before the others could've been disturbed throughout the run to keep just one lost temper, asking my help. But that was not the job of the officer, who was afraid to step in, instead.

"Don't worry. I'll be taking my walk about that time anyways. Now get some sleep." I assured Inmate Jimenez.

Inmates cooperated to live by a set of rules, as if there was one leading inmate 'under the thumb'. Each run of the four housing structures accepted the inmate heads to do job, unless I could manage another option through a wink to take over. A wakeup call had been slept too sound through the alarm clock, as Inmate Jimenez cautiously trusted me to come through for him.

One by one the inmates gradually turned off each television, turning in for the night. Of course, there were those few moments still lingered. And then I saw him nodded off, who didn't need to know that I was going to be involved, regardless.

No matter which run was posted to check over the inmates throughout the nights, there was always one inmate left on-guard, too. Their makeshift lampshades were concocted nearby, while I also set my watch perfectly timed down the run with each security check, when I avoided the inmates' detecting my help with his black eye the next day.

I adapted the typical officer's concern to manage the inmate's mental and physical welfare, except an inmate's situation desperately saw the difference between unfairly leaned upon or bullied by its consequences. They were grown men, when I had the power to stop any one of them to grabble, by empowered fairness.

The run was calm throughout the night, but I never forgot. My flashlight made the inmates squirm through every security check from disturbing their sleep. They might've shrugged to put up with my relentless checks, except they seemed glad that it was me.

And then I was there, which was in perfectly timing with Inmate Jimenez's alarm going off.

"Jimenez, turn that thing off." I hushed it under my breath at the head board to get ready for work with the breakfast crew, and the inmate below didn't have to be disturbed, when I indicated a tap on his iron frame bed just enough to appease them both.

"I got it ma'am." he said, and I continued to move along as usual. I had a few hours to think about how I was going to wake him without making it look like I was doing him a favor, and I cinched it. The social skills, as I had been under control of my best interests at heart, completed full circle.

The academy, however, didn't cover how I'd awaken a deadly asleep inmate, but I learned what not to do! I tugged on the corner of a sleeping inmate's blanket when I almost got myself killed once before. I got a phone call posted in my control room, who needed an extra inmate 'on stand-by' to get up around 2:00AM in my run.

It wasn't his fault when he lunged up at me when his eyes were impulsively opened, and apologized profusely once the brain caught up. He was kind enough to explain the trick, tapping on the iron frame to resonate its vibration that aroused from his sound sleep. I was in a safe distance to protect myself when he didn't understand how to react.

The academy didn't mention how PTSD, ticks, or brain damaged inmates. Medical conditions were meant to be kept confidential, even though the inmates were considered dependents. Custodial care of the inmates stopped its suggestions box to administration, as if it was no use, impossible to believe, or remembering them all at any given time. It was unnerving who filled the sexual predators and social deviates, yet knowing a trap was a given.

I slowly evolved to remain guarded... among inmates. Imprisonment was purposely lived in harm's way against another, as if I didn't expect anything less than a warped sense of right and wrong. They were distorted by the lack of conscience and no regard, with a second look to remember their names easily changed back. It reenacted every generous gift or whether it was aggressively taken through its experiences with a deeper perception.

I'd been forgiving, allowing its generosity continued beyond my ability until it hurt, as if hurt back was done name calling, which included: The Victim. But their title should've been pinned with: The Abuser.

Perpetrators were victimized so subtly conditioned of *their* crimes, which was criminal! But how many weren't incarcerated, imprisoned, and kept handy to be fed on the outside? Of course, who wouldn't want me to change my career? Denying 'who was who' retaliated against me to stay away, when I faced prison. I made them mad, only a mealy victimized survivor, until I brushed off of the dirt from my pants, and I got back up.

There was another time when an inmate came to me for some help. Inmate Swartz had a speech impediment, and I had to listen intently with his question. I was fine, until Inmate Borche urgently tried to cut in.

"CO, CO." He was as annoying as a two-year-old calling his mommy's attention, demanding more important than anything.

"Hang on. I'll get to you in a second. Right now, I'm talking to Swartz." I frowned at him, scorning to wait ahead of him.

"He wants you to..." he wouldn't let it up.

"Wait a minute. Can you understand what he's saying?" I interrupted Inmate Borche mid-sentence, with an even more stern look than before.

"I know what he wants," he emphatically continued.

"So, you can understand him! I get that. What makes you think I can't?" I slammed him. "Let him explain. I think he's doing just fine." I played down his need to help, refusing his uninvited aid, when he walked away.

Inmate Borche needed to ask me for something, who didn't invite to come up with anyone else. I understood the amount of courage he'd manage alone. His words were slow in coming, who might've taken a little more time to get out. Inmate Swartz tried to interpret our conversation, and I was not about to refuse his trust in me, when I noticed how Inmate Borche began to shrink. I had to put a stop to that, too.

Interjecting his help was condescending, and actually enjoyable to stop taking over for me, for a change. Was I better than the wasted time? Did he come through for me, to spare the bother, since I was a CO? But I wanted to show the right decision to talk to me, well enough to resolve it himself. He felt whole, and deserving at the end.

"Borche, can I talk to you for a minute?" I met up with him afterwards, and I asked to follow me outside. I didn't want the other inmates to overhear our conversation, so I decided to separate him from anyone else. "I would like to explain why I needed you to leave Swartz alone with me."

"I was just trying to help." He admitted, knowing that I inadvertently hurt him. I had robbed my inmate from being the hero, and I'd denied him from his kindness.

"But you were trying to tell it better!" I started to explain that nothing was wrong. "I know you didn't mean it, but you were using his disability to put him down..." I used a measured 'pause' to leave him think, where he had no one else all around, solely in front of him to process... "by doing it for him." through my body language tilted in the illusive hat.

His anxiety diminished with another message I had for him, as well. "When you showed up for him, you were actually telling him to step aside." I described Inmate Borche to see what I showed him to see, when I gave all the patience needed... to listen.

He was defensive and on guard, who expected that I would've called him out to be reprimanded, believing that I was mad to scold him back in shape. He obeyed, brewing and biting his tongue, but I couldn't just let go as if nothing happened.

"It wasn't needed for anyone else who was better to come to me. I wanted to show him that he was right to trust me with a lot of effort, alone." Inmate Borche's eyes looked up, when it sunk in. His good intentions were being analyzed. "When I told you to let him explain on his own, I gave him the chance to do exactly what he thought he could do." Inmate Borche listened while his head visibly sunk lowly. I'd deflated his rage, but I didn't have that intention either. He not only restored himself after he felt rejected, cut off, and sent aside during his best efforts of another's help, when he held a greater form of respect with me than just another CO of authority.

"What you wanted to do was a noble thing. You wanted to help your friend, but sometimes helping is also hindering." I said to restore his dignity.

"Sorry, ma'am." slipped out when he realized that I wasn't mad at all.

"Let's go back inside." I smiled, and we both returned whole, too.

I was always a little scare to address another inmate face to face. Maybe it was something I would've had explained; except it could've been me, spitting and sputtering to be laughed off, which could've been two vulnerable inmates undo all the worse.

I kept coming back to work, like my pension tenure was a set goal with a time-certain release during my own sentence to deserve what I missed. I didn't need a common consensus decision, a jury of my peers, or among the family of loved-ones, since I was driven to accomplish rehabilitation about crime.

I didn't need it, but there it was, pulled out of the kitchen table chair to the center of the room. I waited for the licking, stood there until everybody was called for the last one inside. They all knew the routine. Every one of my sisters lined all around the cupboards, to avoid the leather switch by every word. I obediently pulled down my pants to bare my bottom bent over, as if the cuffs had a dual affect around my ankles, who made them all watch.

The message was slow in coming, except when Inmate Swartz calculated each word, didn't matter how long he needed, or anyone else's business. I focused on him that didn't need it beaten in or aimed with just one final hit...in reverse, when I left them happy to know of what just happened, instead!

In the past, I'd easily bow out, until I got the option in prison. I stuck my neck out in ways that should've wrenched my gut, except I couldn't back out from any number of inmates watching, witnessing, and studying the chance to overpower me with the slightest opportunity. Telling one inmate to comply or correct something else, seemed to spread within earshot, as if they'd lick their lips on high alert. But a hand gesture was enough to set off the domino effect throughout the yard, like a target had been slapped on my back, feared at all times. My posture, my approach, and attitude were constantly scrutinized.

The pressure was ever-present. The phrase "pick your battles" didn't apply in prison. There was never an expected response to anything. And then, there was the all-powerful race card which the black inmates used as necessary. That accusation worked to back off, which made me bring the conversation to an abrupt halt. All efforts to move forward were immediately done. There was absolutely nothing more to say after that. It was dirty, meant to piss me off, as if they were just expected to be like that, but the state understood that specific 'panic button' fear which was more than money. Evolved attitudes wield the threats that pulled down DOC's reputation all the way down, too.

Racial accusations grew all the more sensitive that applied enough damage for any given excuse. Its reckless use became its greatest fear, when the greatest blows inflicted the twisted words that you couldn't take back anything more serious. The mark stuck, even if it was just once, could never be erased in ruin.

The lawful government stacked against the standard comments expunged to be restored to its cleanest level to shine, except for my sisters who were more important than any other loved ones to be sparing them... for a good example. They were taught how they'd line all around to see the pain, but never affected to feel it.

Racial bias placed a mark labeled it to be prepared for redemption, which it never really was, until I'd seen it happen. I lived it. The state's response jumped to hurry the quick fix, as if I had been pinned on my lapel, to be thrown under the bus. "Three times and you're out" was spread out among my fellow officers. Who would know? but it worked. That fear was so unruly spun, and it was all better, plunked with just one to step down. DOC's black eye could heal, but somethings remembered all the more incensed, when I sweated forward in wishful thinking.

"You know what I think?" One of several black inmates said, glaring at me from the outside of my control room. "She's got something against the brothers!" Another piped up to fuel the outrage. "She don't like blacks!" Their coy conversation further escalated under my skin.

"Okay, now we're done." My hand went up to the talk-to-the-hand gesture. I dialed the phone, while high-fives celebrated my defeat right next to me. But I was not done, or alone. "Hey Bilal." I called on my biggest, black, fellow officer, and friend.

"What's up, darling?" His wonderful baritone voice was like music my soul.

"I have a problem. There's a whole bunch of inmates, ganging up against me. They're singling them out because they're black. Can you talk to them for me?" My voice was shaking and he knew I was in trouble.

"I'll be right over," when he practically hung up. "Listen here. When I get there, give me a big hug before I do." I chuckled his afterthought, knowing how that would look, too.

"You're serious?" I had to ask, stealing a piece of love shared in my heart, but at work there was always that fine line, while I remained professional.

"Trust me," he said. He was just as annoyed as I was over that misused race card.

I hung up the phone and I kept my back against the cocky little group still going at it, as if I was supposed to be more and more afraid with every minute who continued. Their street talk accents and slurs got worse, drawing attention throughout both runs. But I just waited.

"Hey darling." CO Bilal greeted me as soon as he entered and I met him halfway into the dayroom for all to see, as he opened his arms for my embrace. "Where are they?" He looked around as I pointed to Baker Run when the jaws dropped. I had them caught in the act.

"So, what's the problem?" he asked, entering through the security door. But the inmates, who were trying to stir up the wrong issue against me, had nothing to say.

"She don't like rap." I overheard a mousy voice cower in response.

"How did she know you were listening to rap?" My fellow officer and friend was quick to realize that the music was too loud. "Weren't you wearing your ear phones?" Their heads went down, knowing exactly that I'd asked it adjusted appropriately. "Bring it here." He had the right to seize their property.

"That won't be necessary." I piped up in the good cop/bad cop fashion. "I just need that music turned down." I offered the same option as before.

"Is that what this is all about?" CO Bilal's voice screeched like the fingernails on a chalkboard, shaming the young blacks for their bullying, tough-guy stance. "Get over yourselves! Officer Pruitt is trying to show some respect to all of the other inmates in the run who don't want to listen to your music playing in the background." He reiterated my words practically verbatim.

"Sorry, sir." The apologies came out one by one.

"So, what's this about? Pruitt's racially biased?" He wasn't going to leave well enough alone... silence. "I thought so." The young overly-confident group slithered away one by one, and CO Bilal didn't leave the run until the last one went back to his bunk.

I loved it, and CO Bilal almost seemed to savor the chance to put an end to it. His attitude meshed with mine, fired up against how harmful racial discrimination got with the easy pass. They didn't want to argue about equality to get their way that cornered against the ability to get out of their trap trick. That was, until I had the right person to my rescue. Race or ethnicity had no place in a multicultural country, but that was not exactly the same message DOC taught, and how others were refused their promotions. As for me, I just liked to work hand's on corrections' management besides any other rank. That gotcha hook involved all DOC, except it weighed more severely differently, since somethings weren't about to be treated the same for everyone.

I wished they were all the same, as if we all carried DNA to blend in all countries from the human race, but that wasn't enough. DOC coordinated to manage the different races apart, who particularly paid attention to the young black inmates, segregated safer that way. The inmate housing couldn't accommodate anything else, matching race or gang affiliation with each bunk to keep the peace, as if it slowed down its evolution to avoid the liability of the state's civil suits in prison.

Inmate culpability, however, was the single most important thing to check inmate accountability. Everyone stopped each face to its pictured ID, who was undeniably validated to the population counts. Sometimes it felt more like it could've been more than a dozen times a day, although only four mandatory counts actually mattered when I had the reports went back to the State.

That actually played the biggest part of the general public, which the inmates located on either side of the fence, but my concern was about the inmates inside. The formal counts were conducted state-wide that never changed the same times every day. COs counted out the inmates, and then it was ready to repeat it again.

At that time, I expected the inmates next to each bunk to begin the moment, checking off the inmates in the run that I forwarded back all the way to the shift commander's completed reports. There shouldn't have been a surprise. It had been repeated enough times, like the back of my hand. I saw a nod and moved forward, but I also expected an inmate pushing it. Redundancy should've been easily trusted through every routine, especially taking inmate count. One hour was enough time to have all of the housing officers checked off the first few minutes, but assuming anything invited trouble.

The hourly count delays ate up the rush at the end, like when a van or bus arrived in the sally port, which affected the present inmates from another unit in between the register sheets. The CO's held up to wait for the inmates chased back to their bunks, before everyone received the announced count, and at that time they all conducted face to ID on paper. Easy-peasy. Everyone heard the radio traffic, who physically watched each inmate to their runs, and the inmates knew that, too.

Pencils or erasers, black pens or black-out dabs weren't allowed. It was correctly completed with the only right answers the first time, when no one had to start out the CO's formal counts until the inmate's movement had been held up, and only then. It was a collective decision in a joined effort, except sometimes the inmates plead a little wiggle room, since the ID to face inmates were expected to be recognized automatically that seemed ridiculous. Enough was enough who decided to squeezed in another delay for the COs to catch that, too.

I couldn't deny an inmate taking a quick rinse in the shower from the hot temps outside. I could bend a little to coordinate it all in on time, but I couldn't play around a missing inmate at the bunk bed that affected a domino effect on down, as if we were all connected to the hip.

The shower was running when I could hear it from the control room. I could see the steaming hot showers left on that didn't have to shut off. I saw the towels swapping in and out, anxiously pressed in line, as I hollered out the seconds ticking along on standby to pay attention to be cut short and dropped everything… on my call. Start time was ready, and they all scattered in place, as if it was always about the little things.

I entered the runs, scanning to take in the nuances of all the inmates waiting for me and present to be accounted for, but that wasn't the case. Nonetheless, I focused onto my paperwork matching each person at their bunks.

I only took about four or five minutes for them to be patient in place until I completed the report, and then they were good to go right back to their showers. They didn't have to realize how unnerving it was at zero errors since I was too serious who stopped trying to catch some quick movements from the corner of my eye. I had to look onto the paper clip with each jot correctly.

Throughout the units all across the entire state stopped all movement for the formal counts with each announced clearance, until the inmates knew the consequences who were issued by a disciplinary violation, when my warnings were ignored to explain in the Disciplinary Department.

My reputation spread my tickets among the inmates to think twice, when I used "that voice" to mean business. Most of the inmates knew how far they'd try and push it, while other inmates stepped aside to stay out of the way.

"Stand by for count." bellowed loud enough to be heard into both runs through the caged control room, as I projected the beginning announcement down either sides. Any derogative growling's were ignored, which might've appeared to be too busy, when I waited a pause for a minute or so at the door for all to see. "Hurry up in there!" I put that extra effort to hear me in the showers, wrapping it up to scoot in place, which was nothing to see or show off, either.

All COs had their own style carrying their own quirks, and some inmates did whatever they were doing, as I tried not to be too disruptive on the job. It was their home personal space, as humbling as it may have been, but everything was that important regardless how valuable.

On the top of every shift felt like I was goggled through the model runway down that first walk, when I also examined the audience as I greeting my debut, in return. It really didn't mean anything more than some anonymous sounds of the jungle which was the nation of the beasts, who were more cowardly than anything else. I couldn't exactly finger "the wild" when I'd consider the source, mimicking grown men acting like children making squawking sounds of some bird, clucking sounds of an old hen, or long drawn out moose calls in mating season, where I worked the high ground.

"What the hell, you act like we're in some kind of boot camp or something," an inmate called out as I was about to leave. For a second, I wanted to laugh out loud where I stopped with a slight tilt of my head from behind that went dead silent, but no words could fit, when negative attention was attention, nonetheless.

I worked inside the walls, but the same people on the outside were unseen or ever recognized again by the cold call medical billings, which was just another place for that job. I managed to take care of the two-faced adults, where I also took care of them, too. I held my tongue for the same and familiar cowards, unable to face me that expunged all their guilt and denials, cut free. I was verbally browbeaten, subjected to their taunting and insults, when I raised above the stronger one, instead.

The most spiteful and cruel were encouraged to be toughening up. Or at least I was supposed to believe that... by my loved ones. They were the chosen, and most successfully crowned bullies freed of all guilt, while I buckled under the pressure that was never meant to win.

Undeniably, some of the policies were actually quite petty, when the most rudimentary rules needed the basics displayed on any run. They had to live all under the same roof of all ages, races and beliefs, challenged my own self-control by an unspoken hope left behind. That could've been easier said than done, but I made my share of mistakes along the way.

A large percentage of the inmates had some very deep-seated behavioral issues, but so did I. I imagined how the typical child was another set of grown adults, when I savored isolation for a reprieve away from the pain, as if I repeated imprisonment with no place to go, and the paradox was my life for the career.

The inmate items rightfully claimed his own precious few commodities in the open yard, unlike the contained or locked cell, where their boxes were left unattended underneath the bottom bunk. I had to appreciate just how vulnerable all their things rechecked from time to time, and the inmates did the same things.

The double bunks were bolted immobile to the floor, which was no further than three feet apart. There were no draping screens under the top mattress for privacy, who slept fully exposed, until I saw who tried to enclose a partition curled up to hide in a fetal position. There was no escape who also used their woolen blankets created too many shadows blacking out the lower bunk on either side, but I couldn't allow that for my safety needing everything wide opened by a glance.

It could've been harmless, who secretly hoard over his personal belongings. His inventory spread everything out to review his inventory, like an inmate concoct something incredibly vicious in the lockdowns, since I remained in high alert by the inmates relocated to the open yards.

"Sarge? It's Pruitt. I'm having an issue with an inmate. I'd gone down the runs with my security checks, and Inmate Larew hangs back his blanket, blocking off the lower bunk every time. It's a stupid game, I know." The issue blurted out and my supervisor listened with a very condensed version. "Can you tell me what else I can do to get him to comply?" It just wasn't something going to carry out, like a set-back, who ignored my clear re-directives. Frivolous disciplinary reports could've escalated too severe, but he wouldn't budge.

"Fill out a seize property form and replace it with his blanket." I could do that and that was okay? My supervisor did not talk down to me for an easy answer, as if I be afraid that I'd cause an inmate fight back or retaliate, which I couldn't think 'outside-of-the-box' for me. "Then write him a ticket for improper use of state property," which he further encouraged its empowerment, by breaking my old school style by the rules, like if "I said so" would actually work.

"Oh look, the blanket police!" An inmate piped up on my way back to the control room, dragging Inmate Larew's blanket behind me. I ignored it, and as I stayed as professional as possible, when Inmate Larew got the message. I acted out my call, when words didn't work. 'I took the ball away' and the game ended to accomplish the impossible.

It was years before the extreme use of authority played the risky 'war' games of the inmates, who complained to my supervisor against me. Wasn't it enough to have my own co-workers drop paper on me frivolously, too?

"You know... I think you should attend sensitivity classes." Sergeant Blakeman listened to gather any officer complaints from one building to the next throughout the night, as if he was also collecting the officers' condition of each building.

"Really?" My supervisor might've resumed the day, until he spilled. "Why didn't you ever tell me?" It felt like my reputation could've been smeared.

"Cuz I told Inmate Wallace to stop making you mad," Sergeant Blakeman frankly talked directly at me. It felt like anger was the only language to communicate the problem. I didn't use profanity, leaning fully on policy that couldn't change an all or nothing walk on that fine line and no soft shoulders on the side. Wondering how I struggled for dear life at the edge.

Sergeant Blakeman was known to be thought of as a real hard-ass, and arguably, a love/hate relationship, but that problem was never a problem for me. He was available and I reached out an occasional no-nonsense reply, or cut-to-the-chase kind of approachable. I was a quick in and out, just-the-facts kind of "ma'am, yes ma'am" response and it was over.

"Thank you," I whispered to Inmate Conally on my next security walk.

"For what?" He seemed oblivious to the redirective, since I'd just been through just a half hour earlier.

"For putting your shoes underneath your bed." I reminded him further seasoned with a short and sweet double-take, too.

"No problem, ma'am." He realized how a simple "atta-a-boy" gesture worked both ways.

I stopping at each bed to review the ID's prominently displayed on the end of each shelf at the center walking aisle, and each inmate stood between their bunks until I was finished. "Thank you" became a new announcement on my way out, who didn't need to peek around to see how far I'd take when it freed them, too.

But no sooner had I sat down to calculate my count sheets to justify the empty beds of the runs, I heard a slapping sound from behind. Baker run had an inmate-on-inmate fight rolling on the floor.

I remained safe inside of my control room for a few moments to realize a few inmates' horse-playing, but I was wrong. They were in full blows, like a back-door brawl behind the redneck bar.

"Knock it off!" I shouted down the run, which also initiated the emergency call sequence carried over the radios for help. "That's enough now!" was the next call, as if they actually heard 'the timing clock' crunching in as many blows to get in before the first response closed in.

All the other inmates cleared away from getting involved, which was so familiar and no different in prison, but I wasn't about to enter the run to break it up and get hurt myself. All I had on me was a can of pepper spray, a set of keys, cuffs, and a radio.

I'd watch and fill the report later. I'd learned about the ability to know which one was the aggressor or the victim, which wasn't that difficult to figure out. The older man was no match for the younger and more fit inmate, who targeted in a few more kicks to the ribs, preventing the older inmate from getting to his feet. The younger one grew wildly driven to the older inmate's face, as he'd tried to crawl away. My fighting skills were meant for self-defense, which wasn't trained to engage between two grown men with a beef. The best thing I could do at that point was to observe and document their assaults.

Out of respect for the men living in that run, I chose not to use pepper spray, since the effects of just one short burst knew better in the lockdowns. Accumulated experiences had my own first-hand experience at the academy with a direct shot across my face. But what's more, I'd also suffer enough about the residual particles that couldn't be blown away during the decontamination process at the lockdowns, or anywhere else down the run. Pepper spray inside of an elongated sleeping quarters would've landed on everything, burning their nasal passages, sinuses, throat, and lungs to make them all miserable.

Help arrived swiftly, when the aggressor surrendered to Officer Brown immediately escorted behind his cuffs, who could barely catch his breath when the fight was over. One interviewed outside, while the second inmate remained in the dayroom. Two officers assisted Inmate Georgio to his feet, already expected a wheel chair from the Health Unit, while CO Brown took charge of the emergency Command, who appointed my partner from the other side for the C/D runs. The fight needed to protect the bloodied crime scene to be saved for the camera.

The initial emergency system used the exact call codes over the radio, like a brief review that passed its headlines through me. I was relieved of my Command over the entire unit, but the first responder took precedence that happened to interrupt formal count, when our Shift Commander stepped aside, and sweating on hold.

Both of the control rooms picked up, which was no more than ten minutes of the inmates on hold, reissued into separate holding cells. Any signs of blood required the toxic clean-up, undecided, pending their investigation… and then show was over.

I didn't see the first blows started, but it was settled peacefully with the details forwarded from the forms. I asked around, curious by any other inmate along their run, but their eyes dropped, silent, and pinned up tightly. They didn't confide anything to add, since I wasn't considered to be one of them to prod any further.

Formal count made it, cleared on time. And then, the two inmates were separately interviewed after the medical staff cleared their injuries. Inmate Georgio, the older inmate, returned wearing one arm in a sling to protect the stitches on the elbow. He got the bumps and bruises, which were deeper hurting with his feelings, at wit's end. He couldn't tolerate the lack of respect from a younger inmate. DOC's altercations mad arrangements to be relocated to the other side of the center fence of the yard, who seemed to arrive a bit prematurely from the level four unit, to try it somewhere else.

Too many inmates struggled among the inmates who were selected by the state, but one released one with another coming in, but Inmate Richards wasn't ready to know the hierarchy's macho powers with Inmate Georgio too intrusive in his space. He was improperly trespassing, and refused to back off. There were enough signs, who ignored them. He didn't care or its significance called 'home', loitered… in his face, as if there was an unwritten rule inside of the runs, which wasn't any differently than a family, traditional, or cultural conduct in prison.

Some common courteous was either too simple or too blind to see beyond their own self-righteousness. Impulsive attitudes were 'thin-skinned' for the limited judgements gone wild, but no one had to stand between the bunk beds. Inmate Richards came over to talk to the inmate, resting his folded arms onto the upper bunk. Inmate Georgio whispered, growled, and then, it was just the right tone… and that's all it took. Inmate Georgio didn't like the low waistline view, while the eyes were still opened and lying down to sleep, but that's all it took.

No one complained before I rushed in with all of Inmate Richards' belongings to move out that run. I knew it often enough to take it all out without notice. I spread the first sheet or blanket onto the floor to drag it all out at once, but moved to another bunk on the other side didn't need to notate his inventory within the unit. I gathered it immediately, before anyone could've swapped out like a better item, or whether anything inadvertently disappeared to admit it at all. And Inmate Georgio returned just the way it was.

If I looked the other way for even a moment, his belongings were cleared out. I'd seen how he could've lost every piece of paper, envelope or letter. Every bar of soap, toothbrush, or old magazine that didn't matter, regardless anything of his things or not. His possessions were meant to be taken from him. But every item was precious to him, which I carted out in a mess for himself.

I remember the old farm house between the summer the day my family moved, literally reloctated, since I accumulated my things underneath my bed between the schools closer to their new home. I was going to high school!

I'd counted back the number the summers to each family who took me in, like my things were relocated across the fence, or over the tracks somewhere else. I had only a paper bag carrying home every year, except it wasn't any better than another assigned bunk, which was anybody's guess there, too.

The final three summers were when ma made my married sister take us in, regardless of the burdens of their new baby on the way. Back then, telephone service calls were only free for local calls, when long-distance calls were too expensive to talk to any one back home. I was completely detached to leave the white community to move into the Hispanic part of town, suffering through the deseg-regation of the 60s (albeit their culture opened the doors regardless of our appearances were just as important, or any other color). It never occurred or grew to accept the love, until I was returned back home. It was the final summer that ended when I was driven to a custom-built house.

"Ma, what happened to all of my things?" I finally asked with a stiff upper lip.

"How would I know? You must think I had a head the size of a horse to remember everything." She took no interest, but she had to know that my possessions were gone.

My things were either destroyed, left behind, or was buried in the rubble where the old house once stood. I kept my lifelong valu-ables that compared the same things with an inmate. I protected my items from anyone looking under my bed, when I wasn't there and nobody had anything to say, "ask ma" who passed it down, face to face. Nobody looked after my things, which was just like the job I protected the inmate's things relocated, as if my loved ones turned away that should've meant more.

All of my memorabilia fell along with the farm house that was condemned. I turned thirteen that year, but the thoughts remained all the more important. I went back at sixteen to pass the driver's license on my own, where I believed what I understood. It was impossible to recover everything I had. I had to see for myself how the fire shrunk into the pile, knocked down into the basement with nothing left to salvage. So much time had passed, when I under-stood prison sentences, since I bided through enough to move on for another chance, too.

It's funny how quickly I had to know the things disappeared with nothing to discuss, as if they looked so innocent among the inmates which I protected their things, like vultures demolished it into dry bones, scattered of no recognizable value. There was no proof or no signs to admit anything. They kept their heads down the run, since I had no one to tell me. It was true about the inmates, which wasn't up to befriend me on the job in prison.

Maybe I should've deserved no more than a brown paper bag to spend the summers away. And, maybe I was taught how to respect the value of the things that never expected an answered for it. Either way, the inmates hoarded their things closely to his chest... just like me.

CHAPTER 14

Does pain hurt?

*G*ames were played all too often, and when they were done, it was only entertainment as they laughed and good sportsmanship. Pleasant stimulation introduced play time to socially interact harmlessly, until the 'I win, you loss' pattern repeated beyond words. Games were expected to face the challenge and shaking hands congratulated with every meet. I did. It was fun and I loved to watch their moments of glory, unless I liked it so much that spun my life style off course.

The inmates signed up DOC's programs, as if it was a time well spent to rein in their 'Break the Cycle' meeting on the inside, or where monthly 'Lady's Night' continued to spin harmlessly in between, who had to come back for more. No one could let it go, who craved for another meet that seemed to lap it up like a sponge, which wasn't about the clean floors.

Sometimes I wished I could apply to be transferred to guide the rehab programs, but I wasn't incarcerated among the inmates, where I didn't belong. I would've taken the training to support the inmates in another direction, but I knew I wouldn't head my loved ones, either.

"Kids will be kids" was the mantra of the times, although we all knew better today. That kind of behavior should never have been allowed to continue. Seldom stepped aside to let it spiral out of control. What was the uninvolved innocent, when the COs purpose needed to interrupt the spiral back into a peaceful place? So many things felt backwards.

I remembered how I ask my loved ones with nothing to say. I wasn't allowed to head the course or involve it either. Their strength grew in every puffed-up reward in character to toughen up their dominance. When I realized how I saw wrongfully gain in practice around inmates.

Everyone headed something, where I carried authority without the closed-fist attitude of power. I already knew how harsh the inmates reacted in prison. They learned to control against anyone to be beaten into obedience. I smiled quietly a bit lower when I submitted down to obey, like if all children craved guidance and approval. They learned their own needs through trial and error, who relied on their support and encourage guidance. Subconsciously, moral beliefs established their base one way or another.

I experienced to learn fear about aggression, where I was planted through the yard like a referee. There, the training grounds practiced self-control, as if the arms swept over the 'safe' calls. I read its results, except when one thing couldn't develop a conscience for the easy victors, intended or not.

I stood back, just like the job, and I watched, but I wasn't hardly a spectator's sport. I was out there for another round, as if a lot of the inmates had their games for the fun of it. They laughed, but I studied to include their body language of what I saw or lacked. One point was up and one mark went down, but it was always about the final score.

I wore enough of the scars to leave the marks that couldn't change the results that never healed back the same way. It was like its final blow justified to throw the game, given in to the warrior, when I learned when to bow out.

I could've been standing among the open yards to monitor its safety all around, when I also saw another sister who wasn't allowed to win, and laughed it off, but the damages remained that imposed its fear on both sides. I'd hid to lick my wounds, while the next blow was about to swing again. It was every-man-for-himself attitude, when kids were told to fight their own battles that never really ended.

The videos, which were played out at the academy, reflected the same situations through the pages of my notebook. Of what had festered, stuck, and trapped inside was it so unthinkable to face, or hidden. It had to be the training's scenarios. That had to be blamed on criminal behavior, fit for the incarcerated punishments in orange, but that was not what tore at my gut to see the same destructive behavior played in my memories.

It had to be more through the floor vents of the room upstairs through my aged eyes among inmates. I questioned the kind of people who took pleasure from another, or was that a cover-up? Did they strut away, perfectly content within themselves having no sense of guilt? Or was it about the shame which was hid behind something else that was the furthest from the truth?

In a lot of ways, living in denial was easier to accept any excuse. I couldn't possibly blame what they were doing that I couldn't change. There was no one allowed to consider the very people who should've loved them. I was the problem to retaliate against me. Or did I have to retaliate in return, by walking way? I couldn't imagine domestic, verbal, or sexual abuse.

That 'scarlet letter' had been riddled with my fault. I was labeled who counted on me, covering throughout my family, as if it was the norm. I had the people who relied on my slow side, somewhat deficient, simple-minded, and spared on someone else. I was a waste, the proven loser with no backbone to make a stand. I couldn't stop the badgering... I deserved.

Just like an inmate who patiently groomed their victim, I was first hand exploited. Like the scales that fell from my eyes, wondering who'd made it wrong. The good graces looked the other way from being tormented to appease them. Early development was embedded all I knew that defined me. I was a yes-man. I was raised to expect a pattern of servitude, because it didn't have to be right or wrong anymore. I didn't care, numb and easily taken advantage from a moment of hope, who laughed back with a crumb, which I graciously thanked a distorted offer of gratitude.

The inmates bartered goods and services all the time. It was a tit-for-tat or quid pro quo kind of atmosphere down the runs, too. I knew it was going on, but couldn't do anything without catching them red-handed, in the act. They were shrewd people who conducted their business and settled their debts, which it felt so familiar with the in criminal inmates. So, I watched.

The inmates held their bank account which was managed through the prison system. It was right and legal, but it was customary who were able to purchase goods from the inmate canteen and the catalogue of commodities. And then, another inmate might've offered to do his laundry for a week in exchange something else to purchase. What was generous to one, and cheated another? But nobody was giving over their edge for just enough to survive. Of course, how stupid I'd been. I didn't ignore to notice the sly one who took advantage through its deceit, alone.

I was the one carried for my sister's clarinet in its case all the way home from school. There was nothing else I had any books. I was also the go-to person for their hand washables, and any other favors I covered for them. I was the nice guy, which also kept them out of trouble, too. But wasn't what people do for each other? That much was no differently. Imprisoned methods had traded away the debts… undenounced for my own dignity.

I was shyly, defined to be an introvert, although I had plenty to say. In denial, tolerance couldn't oppose their outbursts, and into tears. Unleashed risks were groomed to be told, when I saw fear across the room... all the way back at the convicted criminals. I wouldn't dare make them mad! I had to appease that temper, that rage that made my knees weak, as if I really was spineless, afraid of anything forced back in my place. But there was nothing meta-phorically speaking about a rabbit cage. I was stuffed inside for a punishment. Although, I couldn't be sure if they just wanted to see if I fit, until they laughed secretly let out who forgot. Prison was supposed to be the punishment; except I wouldn't forget about the short fuse to restrain their rage as I watched to snip it in the bud, or when I called back up needed more than just one me.

I knew when another came through with the local police, but Bob had no right to look over my shoulder, anticipating the time I'd leave the house during our divorce. I believed it when it was no game. The police pulled in the drive way right behind him, who snipped it in the bud for me. *The Eddy Haskel and Beaver Syndrome* described the situation by the police that regained my confidence, when negative reinforcement didn't need anymore.

I skipped out of all the English courses to perfect my reading ability, before the next science field. My degree was reachable, and I could've showed how much better I'd do that became more important with a new hobby, so I began to read... everything.

My English Professor showed how I'd think on one thing at a time. I thought I was slow, who taught the opposite noises inside. I closed out everything else, tracking through each word and sentence to help cognition and retention. None of that was explained the way my brain worked before I learned it a half century later, when I aced the first year to believe in myself.

ADHD managed how it explain, knowing something wrong with me when I gave up the degrading insults. I tried to win them over. I pleaded to be like everyone else, until I was at the community college. They coached me, when I'd discover the bond and friend-ships of the tutors, who were happy about me, instead.

Did I need a controversial drug, as if I'd outgrow it, who lied of what I'd believe at all? I was the dummy, the family embarrassment, the idiot, and family joke. Help would've made all of the difference, further defining the LD (learning disability) classes. I finally assimilated to be just like them, when I knew where I didn't belong in the wrong group, until I took a second look... again. I faced all of the possibilities against the fears, and disabilities. Although, I still didn't get why I was so strongly fought against my career.

I didn't mean to hurt her, but I suddenly realized how blind I'd been. I didn't burden or lean on anyone to carry the load, unless I really was naïve! I showed all the proof for an astound applause. I held off until I specifically made the call. It surly was good news! Go ahead BRAG! But her life-work had been invested, like the stock market fell. She created her own purpose, her design, chosen of her use... accordingly. I cried. Oh, how I cried in perfect sequence backwards, to proving the rest for my awakening.

I saw when she sent out with my sister to see it for herself. We weren't friends. "Just because we were born by the same woman doesn't mean we're family" Janet was well-rehearsed how she was told. Just the right things were meant to break me down, but I refused to hurt them back. I wasn't wrong, just different. I just didn't realize how I was supposed to crawl back to fill in her needs, until I proved her otherwise. Detachment cut her off to a stop.

I bought one book after another, which had actual proof as I reinforced how I had an easier active mind change. I even got the blessings of my supervisors, who allowed me to carry my book of choice, to work.

One good thing about being a poor reader became a new hobby getting expensive. I lined my library across the kitchen counter top, like trophies were all set up in pride. It was a real solidly believable thing to admire, became unstoppable. I bought to challenge it more difficult to read! I reached out to study and open new horizons, but eventually that wasn't enough.

"Read the bible." The thought of picking up the Bible with my next book was easily dismissed inside.

"Read the bible." Those three words would not leave me.

The thought seemed silly. Who says, "Oh, I think I'm going to go to Barnes and Noble to find another book to read", and walk out with a Bible? I smirked to myself. It was preposterous! Besides, I knew better. I remembered how sacred that book was when I was growing up. It was *that Book* kept on the top shelf saved for a visiting priest just in case one of us needed Last Rites. I remembered how the Catholic Priests only used those specific fingers to handle the Bible. How could I possibly let anyone read, much less hold both hands with every page like if it was a secular book? My early Parochial training was sketchy at best, but I was not about to tempt insubordination with God! How could I dare to compare myself to that level of priesthood? But I also couldn't shake off that thought, of permission?

I had to argue within myself. I knew that I was not the brightest bulb in the chandelier. But that if I misunderstood the passages? The Catholic Church was very aware of its issues censoring out the monthly missives to follow His Word from the church pews, which were prepared to allow only the right verses, which were only and specifically allowed of what to read in church. No one carried their whole Bible into church! "You just don't go buy a book like the Bible", I shuddered in fear. Surely, they had a reason to keep the Bible out of the laymen's hands. I wasn't sure about the courage to step out of line.

I was a Jesus Freak where I joined a club with the high school teenyboppers bonded together in fellowship. I was a just a kid studying the Bible which was mostly a social time, when we had another book called the *Good News for Modern Man*, instead. That made it okay, but it was definitely rebellious to push it. It was that time in my life when I craved love and kindness, but I kept my secret from anyone else to ruin it. I couldn't imagine of what the consequences would have been, and especially if the church ever found that out, too.

Not that the Catholic Church ever did me any favors. I went to the convent after I graduated out of Parochial School. But I wasn't good enough. In just three days, I was rejected. It only took one look at me sent home. My eczema was "an undue expense for their non-profit organization to afford". They had every right to be selective for the more godly people.

My teachers were nuns throughout the eight school grades, but who was I? It shouldn't have been any surprise, although I felt hurt. I took it personally. They should've been drawn to that holy occupation, but not that! Every part of my body could've been hidden underneath those black and white habits.

Every day I change out of my clothes after school. I had to undress into play clothes, just like the rest of my sisters. The same outfit was saved by everyone who folded or hung their same outfits for the next day, who wore it throughout the week and I was no different. Washday was Saturday, which had to be inundated of eleven in that house.

Although my sisters were long gone before I hardly got stared, but I couldn't hurry outside with the rest, until later. The chunky eczema scabs glued into place with every move throughout day, when I had to pull my tights down ever so slowly. I opened up the raw nerves for each leg, leaving in my leggings of the following days. I was teased for being the last one to come downstairs, who didn't have to withstand how pain shivered it to myself.

My skin wept from that yellow ooze, tinged with blood that ran down each leg to freeze in a new crust, which got easier as the week got closer to the end. The older scabs coated the inside of my tights from the day that created it between the sagging tights. Within a few times I changed my clothes, and into play clothes. I eventually didn't care, when I stunk like a dead animal, making a face back at me in class. Who was ever going to be friends? as I grew to ignore what I'd accept to manage. My weekly clothes were turned in to the laundry, and then it started all over again.

I was ugly, as if the eczema had to know how heavily laden my clothes carried a foully stench, except Sunday Church services. There my family was all proudly lined in one pew. There, I was fresh and clean, sitting poised and well behaved for all to see.

I don't remember how old I was when I got my own bed, but the rest of my sisters paired up with the full-size beds. I didn't even mind the teasing for being 'The Queenie' who got special treatment. I was relieved to sleep alone. Finally, I could sleep through the night without a bed partner, who pulled at the sheets in the night. I was re-glued, and then ripped away again, which was soiled, or complained about the crumbs crawling to bed... with it.

Grandma thought she was doing a good thing one day. I loved her, until the day I stayed away to hide. She held onto my arm and wouldn't let me go. There, she lived at the old dairy farm house with the surfacing cream for herself, until she wiped me down with its raw milk like a fresh (natural) skin cream. But I screamed in agony! She'd never find me, like if I was set on fire. My head hurt squinting too afraid to move my eyes. I vomited on all fours, when I was finally found later. I was carried to soak a cool bath, who hollered at me from going all the way in, like I couldn't even sit up. Why didn't she know that I was allergic to milk? Wouldn't that have been something people should have known?

I was no stranger to pain. Pain was intended to be held down, treated at the doctor's office to lance my boils for an appointment. There was no escape from the torture beneath the weight of my ma, who had to keep me still during the procedure. I remembered the doctor's knife as he protruded each rock-hard mound that punctured its head, spouting at the doctor who wiped himself down, too. He squeezed out each boil until it bled. But didn't he see something wrong about a child with boils?

Yet, I still wondered why I had to endure instead of prevention? My OB/GYN punched his fist inside because he had to rush from bleeding out. He manually tore the placenta out of my womb in pieces after birth. There was no time for an anesthetic. All he said over and over again was, "Take a deep breath," while I felt him claw at his fingernails and a jerk with every grip, trying to tear out the no longer needed living tissue still attached and unrecognizable to weigh.

Years of chronic illnesses could've caused the death of my second and third child with each born earlier. It was the result of accumulative trauma that damaged the autoimmune system had been worn down. My adrenals allowed each pregnancy that shortened the deliveries in neonatal care, as if going bald was only emotional pain that followed.

It only took about three months after my third child was born to lose my beautiful head of hair that once flowed like golden silk in the wind, as if medical treatment wasn't necessary. By the time I showed up for my monthly steroid injections to my scalp, I couldn't tell the difference between physical or mental pain any longer. I flinched with every stick as I frantically tried to adjust and gain some sense of normalcy, but by then it was too late.

I tried to be the best mother and wife to compensate my appearance. My house was kept immaculately clean. I cooked every meal from scratch, and I worked out at the fitness center before day break, giving my husband the firm curves any man would wish! There was nothing I wouldn't have done to make up for the embarrassment I caused. But, no amount of effort was enough. Some things I just couldn't fix.

I thought I was careful to cover my head outside of the house. Even when I walked to the mail box at the end of the driveway, I wore a scarf or wig out of respect for anyone who might see me. There was no need to traumatize anyone exposed by something as odd as a perfectly smooth scalp on a woman to prevent the double-takes and stares over the years. I was very conscientious to avoid any negative attention in public. But one day, my precious daughter was tormented because of me. Oh, how I hurt for her, and I had no power of the injustice.

Bethie ran through the kitchen one day after she came home from school crying hysterically, angry and mad! "Honey, wait! What's wrong?" I chased after my little girl, who was always my little charmer.

She turned for a second with her little hands fisted in front of her. "It's all your fault!" She tuned me out, slammed into her room.

The news spread all through school. She was mercilessly teased, called for being the child of a skin head. But they were just children. They didn't know! Suddenly of what she'd known to be common and usual, was the root the pain against her. Some school kids were ridiculed her to take the heat, and some things didn't matter, as if pain played the part of life. How could I had been able to protect or forgive anyone from that? I was helpless against the pain, aiming at my child instead of me.

I mourned the loss over the years, since I'd turned my pillow over to hide the nest of hairs matted onto my pillow case, and at the end of the day as I swept the floors to chase the rolling hair balls. I knew every strand in the trash, but I also worked to reduce every static-electric tell-tail sign. There was no secret, or any reminder. The washing machine backed up with every cycle through the washer and rinse loads from a clogged filter before the additional drains coughed up another mass from the bathtub, as if it my job to throw every strand to protect their embarrassment.

I couldn't even mind my own business behind the line at the grocery store. There was a lady who thought that she was kindly concerned, slowly pulling off one strand after another from my shoulders, but even that was a pubic admission to all of the other shoppers. I had to turn politely to thank her, swallowing that lump in my throat as I fought back the tears.

I couldn't keep it to myself no matter how hard I tried. Bob couldn't look at me without a something to cover it up, but it was obvious. He didn't want me from the start, disgusted as I went bald with the last straw. My dad said, "You can't have a team of horses if only one pulls," but I didn't care. I couldn't cut him loose. I latched onto him all the more, hanging onto what I'd overcompensate, and too scared to go it alone.

I behaved for the neighbors, relatives, or friends but they were all outsiders. I was a guest to take what I'd get that I couldn't fill my precious children. I would've comforted their love in every way possible, since I remembered the early summers' I looked upon my cousins, too. It was time who'd know where I belonged to sit it out... sat aside for someone else's comfy chairs, who silently rocked to sleep in their arms in my auntie or uncle's family rooms, who had enough arms without me.

I taught myself how to cry silently asleep, when I eavesdropping through the other side of the wall. I hated that damn telephone over time. The telephone was unendingly attached for my ma's privilege and right, where she sat in the corner dining room. That last straw grew into a panic, as I listened at the end of every school year. I expected of what was about to happen, hoping against the inevitable. I overheard my mother's desperation pleading, wearing down my relatives who finally took me in to agree their turn.

I'd stuffed out the kitchen towel, immediately shoved into my mouth when it was time to hide every sound of the next sob, ready to come up for air. Every frantic call jumped to the next personal phone book down the line, as I heard toward that final rejection... for her relief.

I didn't blame anyone to take me in. I was miserable, but especially since I was made to eat all my food allergies. I knew of what I was supposed to stay away, as if I would never remember the doctor's advice. I would've gladly been able to fill my own plate from the pots left on the stove, but making a plate for myself was not allowed. My dining seat was set at cutting board, where I stood at the perfect height. Eventually, there wasn't enough room at the dinner table to seat the whole family. I didn't complain, realizing that my crusted and sporadically remaining eyelashes, and bloodies "dry lips' wasn't very appetizing, to see me like that either.

I knew exactly of what was caused... in obedience, who counted on my flare ups, as I whimpered with every bite to clean my plate. I knew that I'd suffer for it later, but then, I'd inhale my food with that uncontrollable sob to choke on my food, that only scolded for acting up. No one showed me any mercy. Nobody dared to speak up, and oddly enough I understood that. I forgave them for that "better her than me" mentality, and the repeating old patterns. They all had to notice what was wrong, and then, ma accepted her order of another loved-one to watch every bite eaten, before my plate was reported back, all cleaned, for the pass... intentionally made sick.

Saturday night bathing had everyone quickly jumped in and out that wasn't freshly warmed for me, saved at the end of the line. The bathtub had been cooled and the clouded soap water stung my skin as 'everything' dissolved to the bottom. But I wondered how my clothing or sheets who added it through the wash water, as if it was ever seen at all? Anyways, my job was the last ring in the tub to be scrubbed down, squeaky clean for Sunday's mass.

Was I hidden from them, or was I protected for them? And I still wonder why my badge desperately frantic against the work in DOC. No reason could've been explained, but the rage and anger remained, who were tag-teamed from my choice in the law-enforcement... unless there was something too threatening, or too guilty to hide from my career.

In the mornings I waited my turn, since I was able to take all the time I needed at the end. I soaked each finger apart, as I moved onto my warmed washcloth to peek open my eyes glued-together in the winter months. The dry air was the worse, but even that was all backwards. I should've been miserable in the summer months during the raised air pollens and mold with my relatives without a word, or step in between, just not her again! Ma had to share the burden, who allowed my prolonged illnesses in early development that shouldn't have been the livelong results in my lap. My silence was meant to protect her! Dubbed: "The quiet one of the family"

My success to achieve straight As in college was more than her fear who was afraid I would tell. She went numb at first. The silence was disturbing for a few seconds, and I didn't know how to interpret that reaction. Did she come through, unbelievable of straight As to prove her wrong? Wasn't I supposed to do something good, unless she kept it from finding out that I could? Her knee-jerk response set her off. It terrified her! She'd cried to anyone to complain about her lot-in-life with one like that, unless they would "make her look bad"?

"Read the Bible." That thought gently crossed my mind. I had to realize how much I spent out every week, like I'd never read before. The New Year's Day was just around the corner, and there was a challenge. I'd realized how to meet a resolution. I decided to read the Bible, announcing to complete it cover to cover.

Some of my fellow officers took up the dare to read the Bible with me. Since they weren't all Catholics under the same God., they didn't have the same hang-ups. Never closing my faith from the stacking Sundays black by the collected mortal sins I'd missed. I should've been condemned, excommunicated by my soul, but what could I lose? I'd just wing it! When I knew: *I will never leave you, I will never forsake you.* and, I smiled right back inside. I couldn't recite the specific verses which had already been etched on my heart.

The first NIV Bible read more like poetry. It was not fluent English to me, but I still read every word, including every ancient name agonizing through every syllable. Sometimes I'd stop and even apologized to God for the mispronunciations, and just kept plugging along, but four months ended my resolution as if I just got started.

I was ready for my next book to pick up the St. James Version, and learned even more. There was no sense to over-step the boundary in the Bible, or the additional six commandments of The Church. Reading the Bible should've been anointed to the priests and up. They were supposed to preach "the Word" for my congregation to join their membership. But nothing stopped me, and I absorbed the transcribed "Word" from the American Standard Version Bible when I was addicted. Even though I had been drilled from youth in respect of the highest order, I didn't feel guilty. I jotted notes in the margins of my Bible like a workbook to reference anything else to relate, while I highlighted and continued to personalize it all the more.

At first, that confused me. Sometimes the actual Bible didn't make sense. I worried that I was feeling too much freedom to continue, yet so many inmates seemed to justify their own criminal deeds. "Paul?" I read and talked to Him at the same time. I asked for His guidance and understanding of His will… which was unchangeable and all written down. I began with a continuous service log repeated at the beginnings every day, which also logged the details of my life in my notebooks that I compared by the olden stories in the Bible.

Opening in the Bibles, weren't contradicting to study with the wisdom of the spirit. A deeper understanding offered both carnal and soul. The flesh was bound to die, rot and be nothing other than a cycle on earth. But I craved more than my thoughts which was for and living by my unique soul. The period of the Parochial, Freak Jesus Moment, Catholicism, couldn't touch like I held Thee Father reached out of the Word. Remembering that the written word was unchangeable.

My decisions and choices were all mine to come together, which was as wide as the East to the West, communicating spiritually with God. I was physically alive in the carnal moment, but the essence of my spirit existed with God's presence without flesh. My consciousness was unleashed without the risk on the job, as if the physical fear didn't matter anymore.

His presence recognized me, as if I always knew that He was just invisible. I lifted my prayers, whispering a miracle between us, who'd never believe me:

> I flew across the country to my ma's side to be operated from a growing spot in the lung. I could've stayed in touch with the news, but I had to be there. She went under surgery. The surgeon adamantly searched, destroying the lower lobe of the lung, but the spot was gone and no need for cancer.

> And, I couldn't have been talked out of a late time visit to the hospital where I went to see my father-in-law. He was unresponsive and the family discussed to be unplugged the next day. The nurses were amazed when I ran down to ask for water, because dad asked to wet his lips, who'd visited at the nursing home for one more year.

> Or, how sick my son was born in critical condition, and no one could tell how he'd turn out, where I prayed, too. Michael grew, surpassed all the way to the Master's Degree, as if it was all a lie, who made it on the Dean's list.

> And then, I also touched my Father's anointed oil to my forehead, when I recovered from a ruptured vessel in my brain. I would never remember six days in ICU, but He did.

I didn't tell anyone that I talked to the Father, as if I was supposed to humbly pray only to the saints that never made sense. Weren't they all dead people, except only the Church summoned the right ones after death? Either way, I couldn't convince anyone that I was always heard. Bob told me that I was 'praying' to myself. He told me that I'd think it out, hashed over inside. Was I too immature, who mocked Him and finally outgrow Santa? But nothing could've been alone, because I also heard His inspirations. The Bible and of all of His guidance was an extended hand, which wasn't an overbearing arrogance under someone else's control to be used into submissive, unless our love was mutual.

Flesh inflicted pain, unless abuse was tormenting, wield by a hold, unable to be afraid in the same place to pick it back up, where my Higher Power was always there. I'd grew to assimilate tolerance, just like the inmates getting along in the open yard, where I managed forgiveness in a gated community. The inmates were kept under control, but I was never been able to appease the fights against their will, who were stronger than my relatives, family, or loved ones. Some things were easily shrugged out of my hands. I relaxed, walked away by anyone else, except I relied more importantly in His Word, as I drank down His Book in the quietness of the graveyard shift.

Nobody needed to be assumed at the posted COs... at the pulpit. I understood the blood sacrificing offerings, like I didn't need to bleed for anyone. I threw the thought right out the window, which was explained by the ultimate crucifixion. Flesh couldn't meet the numerous amounts of the unblemished animals that couldn't satisfy atonement. I swapped the translations back and forth to compare its meaning. I had a perfectly unblemished score of my 4.0 GPA, as if I didn't need anyone else's help to disprove or believe the second semester, too.

I read the Bible from any of His many books, which was like The Chronicles finale compiled by C.S. Lewis of about 40 other books. St. Paul (Saul) wrote several books of the scripts, building the final chapters all the more. I attended a mental feast; an opened unending smorgasbord that was never cut off, like I'd never been so hungry and so excited to dive in. I imagined to be fed, which wasn't an issue about glutton, for the fill. It was God happy for the taking, and holding nothing back.

When Jesus died, that curtain was torn from top to bottom, when God welcomed all peoples into His Holy of Holies! My eyes kept coming back that explained how Paul died daily, too. And then the few Levites, the esteemed few, who granted His access, but after the curtain was ripped wide opened. Was I invited in? since no one was kept privately aside for Him alone. I thought the most crucial training allowed the cadets, who'd been saved aside of the badges into the prisons. But it got it backwards, as I questioned the rules of the Bible.

God the Father invited me, like He wanted me to stand up and walk in. But it was at any time, where He was handy...for me!

Sometimes Hollywood reproduced the favored Bible 'stars' in the movies, as if Christianity was entertaining... for thought. A theory, an idea enticed an audience that impacted on people. Were these real advancements meant to improve a morality in society? An element of truth, recreated drama to influence their curiosity. I watched enjoyment, TV stories that touched the heart, or had been messed with even worse.

I envisioned the characters from the Biblical versions from the original scripts, but I never got bored. He got my attention to flip through His stories beyond Hollywood, of His unchanged productions.

The book of Job was captivating, astound how he'd lost everything when he should've been doing so well. Then it changed, like the rugs were pulled out from under! He had so much, and then he was stripped away... of God's gifts. How many things did I build up, and experience how I had been taken away in so many ways! Why was that important to be told... in the Bible?

Job's friends mocked him, demanded to repent when he knew that he'd done nothing wrong, stayed fast, hung onto the truth no less. He couldn't be persuaded otherwise. Did my loved ones persuade me into a family's shun, too? Job suffered horrible sores and boils, as if I pushed it aside, wondering if I could ever make a comeback.

Job had a full life, while I also lived into the years. It was just an interesting story, until I felt his compassion, like I had nothing left meant for me. Did I get too much? Did I defeated who deserved to help themselves and have it all, which backfired of my success for repentance? Did I deserve that, too? That was a famous Biblical story that I'd had trouble getting past it, replaying in my mind. Sometimes, going through the motions didn't need its painful, as if I was determined to relive it over through my notebook, until it was time to close it aside.

Prosperity was not in the future for me, accepting nothing more than the best I could hope for, thinking how I could never live long enough like Job. Maybe I hit the end, the last resort when I walked away from my second marriage. The only promise he kept, was asking him not find me and cut me free. The divorce was a clean break, and I'd 'lick my wounds' in emotional and financial ruins. I fell in depression, too old and exhausted to barely redeem myself, which was easier to give it up.

Ecclesiastes caught my attention that repeated: *there is nothing new under the sun.* I must've read that book over several times, regardless how another Bible couldn't spell it out any differently. I had nothing more to prove toward another New Year's resolution who stopped caring who'd watch me… publicly. I was the next joke that didn't even hurt anymore, as if my purpose was theirs to enjoy my expense?

I slept alone in my cheesy apartment, when I returned to prison with an ignored career. It was already written in my heart that emphasized my story in the Bible, until I got to the Book finally sunk in. It grabbed me, like an epiphany.

The graveyard shift had a low-lit atmosphere day after day, managing the same things, as if there was nothing more than a team of COs stirring conversations to pacify time, and I resorted to believe that I'd never amount to anything. I was institutionalized to assume another kick in the teeth, as if ma was right. Prison was a dismal place to work, depression spiraling downward, except I was not ready to be the next officer to quit. I filled several notebooks to face the truth that I knew... *under the sun* by the new day to dawn and rise! Remembering: *I was with you in weakness and in fear and in much trembling.* (1COR 2:3) as if He extended His hand to get up with that look in my eyes.

Once the Bibles had been read backwards and forwards, it didn't require the book to be read in sequence anymore. I picked up with David who fought with God, and God was pleased, Who wasn't looking for a Hothouse Lilly! He believed in me, when I should've been from a waffling reed: *lukewarm water to spit it out* (Rev 3:14-16) feeling harsh to know better.

The more I realized, the more I wondered *who* pacified *who*? What held my diligence and self-control, under what control? I didn't just float to the top of that special cream of the crop, through every ounce of stubborn courage to face some very deep grounded fears. Facts couldn't discount blindness, as if the wool was pulled over my eyes in the dim light through the night. Did I fight against God, as if David fought with God, too?

Pain conditioned both mental and physical in the academy, as if each lesson faced it to feel it themselves. It planted each hesitation once we all accepted pepper spray across the eyes one at a time, or when we first saw the gas cloud that affected the pain to walk in. How we had to make it through that made involved one reached out to another's leads seasoned through the way out. What good would've made out alone? Once my shirt was grabbed onto one clung to the next that created the chain along. There was no one's fault, or pointing the fingers wondering who was who. The only goal was to minimize the pain, like the first blinding cloud needed help from each other's exit out.

The academy positioned crowd control obstacles. My classmates screamed out to the knees, crawling around every barrier which I moved toward another. The size, age, or gender didn't need to inflict the embarrassment. *We are all one body with different abilities* (ROM 12:4). Unidentified: The victim or the hero? No one said anything who ignored the glory, as I walked away, content alone. Was pain just inconvenient, and not damaged?

Any amount of physical pain couldn't compare the emotional pain, graduated forward in prison with the most vicious inmates. Every day were obstacles facing the State Prison risks that didn't scare me through the worse and extreme level... of rejection. I was no longer useful or missed by anyone which was my normal. *Don't worry about what man can do to your body, be afraid of him who can kill your soul* (Luke 12:4-5). I lived too far away from my loved ones, emotionally hit too closely for the additional brink toward collapse, but in my Father's eyes, I was an Honor Student.

I went back to the three ring binders a few years back. I still had the pictures to review it all over again. Every picture I gazed every page, like seeds began to sprout. Whatever I was told to bury, forget, or drop was a lifetime... to dream! *Delight yourself in the Lord and He will give you the desires of your heart* (Psm 37:4). I was *possibilitizing*! I laughed to myself, tossing back the ridicule my first husband gave. Bob refused to answer me, unless I used proper grammar. "What would he think of my new word?" I puffed up inside, with no regard of the exhaustive effort he wasted on me.

I saw myself in the woman who just wanted to touch the hem of Jesus' robe. *"Who touched me?"* (Luke 8:45) Jesus asked, when He felt His healing pass through Him. *"What do you mean, 'Who touched you?'"* Jesus' disciples thought that was an absurd thing to ask, since they were being bumped from every direction in that crowd. *"I did."* the woman said. She was scared! She wanted a healing without being noticed, but even a touch of His hem didn't get by Him. (Matt 9: 20-22) *"To **God** be the glory!"* rang through my mind, just like I couldn't steal from Him. All of my needs would've been met, but His generosity needed to be received graciously. I had to say, "Thank You!" The woman's faith had the gift of healing, granted the healing she expected. But God wanted her acknowledgement for it.

I had to learn more about God's nature, wondering about His Entity. I wanted to know about how Jesus examples in life showed it just as important to understand my Father's feelings. *Don't cast your pearls among swine* (Matt 7:6), was by it's true value and it's rightfully credit of it's worth. Just as He withheld the Promised Land from Jacob's sons who whined and complained, with no thanks or appreciation of the taking, God's special peoples were never quite able to recognize His true value. They were offended by God who didn't know the differences between the pearls or the gravel. God was dissatisfied by His generosity or sacrifices as He was well said through His disappointed, angry, and hurt. And, I was insolent that I held back as well.

I stepped back. I wondered if the pendulum hadn't swung a little too far to the other side, until it broke. I couldn't bend over that far, comparing myself to God! I wasn't able to meet the level of my God, but His desires of His love was humbling. I shuddered in shame, bowed to apologize, but instead I felt Abba's smile upon me. His love was something to go both ways when He wanted my hand. *"And the Spirit and the bride say, Come. And let him that heareth say, Come. And let him that is athirst come. And whosoever will, let him take the water of life freely"* (Rev 22:17).

I knew I was never going to be able to give enough of my loved-ones, even if I couldn't value my own worth. They didn't want my 'pearls' to be offered, trampled down into the ground. I'd offered, and impossible to be appeased. Any amount of appreciation was flippantly given away, in the hope of my offers or were abused. I was horribly derided. But then again, it wasn't them. It was me! I readily forfeited ahead of anyone else on my own. Did I hurt God by my misused worth, when I gave of what I had to someone else, instead?

How much had I been cutting Him short? I must've hurt God's feelings all the while He watched as I failed, as my loved ones were more important. He called me *His child*, when I'd been blowing Him off, like a nobody. "I'm so sorry, Abba." I whispered a sincere apology, spirit to Spirit. My Father's love was there for me. I must have been insulting to dismiss His love. I craved a pat on the head that was never meant its worth. I looked for approval who kept it coming all along, but their habit was counted to be exploited of their gains, and I esteemed them, instead. That was not how God works, but just like Job, He knew I'd rise to the top.

My eyes started to well up in the fear of doing it wrong. "Please forgive me (so small-minded)." The convictions of my past crept up in shame, feeling too bold to hand everything over at His feet.

I couldn't let the inmates see me like that. I was supposed to be their sense of protection and safety, but nobody cared to pay any attention to me but I didn't think about anyone cutting me out, either. In fact, most of the inmates would've just as soon stayed away. I wept. Was that a pity party? I sassed inside, but they were typically separated, asleep in a crowd all alone. Even inmates got visitors! I sunk deeper than I could say any less for myself.

I stepped aside to let my own children venture out. I gave them all the space needed, where I watched from a distance, who moved forward. It was supposed to allow their bonds of marriage of their greatest wedding day. But my gracious submission, felt more like a slap in the face, ever so subtle. But especially where I was reserved for a table to celebrate their feast, which wasn't the head table for me.

There was nothing to discuss, and I didn't interfere, anticipating the moment to applause or celebrate my first-born daughter. Hand in hand they faced their chosen officiary, undenounced to me as planned. I obliged, as I swallowed hard. The arrangements were moved after their marriage vows, where I'd celebrate at the kitchen's serving door at the far end of the banquet room. My daughter's wedding took the head table, out of sight from me. It was a public display, a public humiliation for my daughter that day. I was cordial of the best of it, but I'd arrived, deserved it or not. Their best day had no regard of the disgrace, but I endured it, like I couldn't be noticed through that stiff upper lip.

At the end of the day, the wedding cake was served table by table after the meal. One table at a time was ushered in line to go next, until there was nothing left, not even a slice of cake. Crumbs were left like it was all over, and I returned to the seated place empty handed, which displayed my insignificance at the tail end. I bowed out gracefully with their first-hand experience to understand them. I didn't want distance, isolation or shun, but they didn't learn a thing against the blame they put on me.

In the First Book of Corinthians I got my answer. It was there where I learned about discernment, more than righteousness. I questioned to justify their actions. I kept myself available when I had nothing to give. I was rejected, let down with no conscience to cause the harm that continued to ripple down to heal in private.

Be wise in understanding righteousness, but as babes in malice (1Cor 14:20). I couldn't accept that level of malice for no other reason than any other reason to hurt me, who was an intended scheme to cause enough pain to create distance. I ran away to hide, which was self-satisfying by another that wasn't meant to be resolved.

Reading the Bible taught me to see more and more of the examples so callous, which validated my weakness by my loved ones. They'd acquired a sick kind of underhandedness, which didn't have the kind of mind-set to be forgiven. There was an embedded seed of contempt, refused to be dealt or anything else to be settled.

What kind of game was perfected and purposely allowed of the insults? It was natural whim ahead of me, like when I realized how nothing but a crumb was left, who further turned their backs for even a taste for me. I return to my seated reservation, walking across the banquet room, openly shown all around to be carried back with my emptied plate. What kind of people would do that?

I could've made a scene. I could've demanded something for myself, but I was impossible to absorb their insults, to heal in forgiveness. My children followed suit, who felt to be the greater one, like their tag-teamed cheers squelched me down, and wrongly judged, who only got more demanding and more abusive in the continued cycle.

Unendingly? Didn't God reach that limit, too? I wouldn't have done that to them, pointed in my face, anger with nothing resolve, which I offered a place to vent. I had broad shoulders, but that spiteful behavior turned it around. Hollering "Grow-up MOM!" put a stop in my tracks. That lack of respect was just more of the same, but my place didn't belong like that.

Even Jesus found no honor in the town He grew up in (Luke 4:23-29). He was run out of town by those who had been raised by the same people he knew His whole life, too. "Dear God. Was I in the same things? What did *He* do wrong?" I called out, with no words to follow. I thought I was doing my best, and yet, my best was not good enough.

"Did it hurt?" An inmate was suddenly stared into the cage of my control room, when I was disrupted from my downward spiral.

"Excuse me?" I was startled, unaware of Inmate Munsey who stood in the shadows, not more than a few feet in front of me.

"Did your tat hurt?" He was captivated while my presence offered him enough to study my bare head, reflecting the glow from my desk lamp. "How many tattoos did you get before you decided to have some work done on your head?" He implied the need to be conditioned for the pain of a tattoo… and finally close enough on my scalp, and its message.

"Oh, wouldn't you like to know?" I bounced back playfully.

"But, did it hurt?"

"Compared to what?" I visibly shook up Inmate Munsey to take a step back. He was suddenly aware that the hair was gone in a hint of curiosity. It was merely a fainted shallow for the glimpse who had to ask. There were enough other COs and inmates shaved clean, except mine was smoothly bare, who finally wondered how much of the indelible pain was etched into my flesh that was also visible on my face.

"What is it?" I could feel him study any kind of tattoo of any specific markings that could've been noted against me, attesting to my allegiance to a specific gang or belief. That took care of all the (secretive and well protected) details, to clinch the sides which was enough to be decided, where I'd been respectfully kept aside.

"Oh, you know." I had to think for a moment. I knew that whatever I was about to say would become known across the yard by the time I would be back for my next shift. "Aren't they all personal?" I knew that tattoos were as intimate and specifically chosen by every individual, trying to be self-expressive.

"Why did you get one on your head?" He winced though the additional body language. Hearsay or unspoken quotes communicated back with something more in return, and he probed. He had to know in the wee hours of the night to pass the time away, or an exclusive report could've been available to cash in another bartered bonus.

"Well, since I can't have hair, I figured I'd put something nice up there." Which was well involved to play the game, like that first dance on the floor. I hesitated for his turn when I wondered who had so little to realize, or how accurate really was.

"When did you get it?" He could see that my tattoo was nothing new. In fact, it was put on well before tattoos were popular.

"Quite a while ago," I said with a smirk.

"Were you a biker?" His questions were non-stop.

"Oh no, nothing like that." I paused, and he saw me give in with the possibility, as if I wasn't ashamed, but there was no reason to fear the truth. "I had the tattoo put on shortly after my baby girl came home in a fit one day after returning from school, upset for having a bald mom." I was smiling. It was a long time since anyone had asked me about myself. "When I got a tattoo on my head, it did exactly what I hoped it would, and I became the cool mom." I enjoyed the recollection and the successful way I redeemed my daughter.

"Yeah. Kids can be pretty cruel." I saw him pause, most likely reliving some of his own pains from yesteryear.

"So, why are you bald?" He gave me that look as if to say, "Don't stop now."

"I was a sickly child and finally my hair fell out." I stated a fact.

"But, doesn't it bother you… bald?"

"It did, and for a long time." I had to take a deep breath before I could continue, but in prison, there was no hurry. "See, one day I had this revelation." I was so self-consciousness, carried the burden since it started. "I am the same person with or without hair." Inmate Munsey waited patiently. "You see, I don't see me. You do. So, the problem isn't with me. It's with you." My spoken words seemed to cement the fact. "I almost see it as a gift," I continued. "I can sort out shallow people by the way they look at me. Some are distracted by a bald head, and others overlook the surface and easily talk to me, and some just can't get beyond that." Working without having a wig on was my choice.

"But, that had to be hard." He offered some sympathy.

"Sometimes I feel like a highbred." I thought about all of the different color and wig styles, but I left enough, perfectly groomed on my dresser. "I don't have to get haircuts, worry about a bad hair day, or waste time in front of the mirror… like everybody else."

"I can't imagine you with hair."

"It probably was the last straw that caused my divorce. I think it was harder on my husband." I showed some remorse for the consequences of my hair loss, something that was blatantly out of my control.

"Well, he's a moron." I had to step back when he said that.

"Maybe." I didn't need to feed the conversation in the direction it was going, so there was no need to do any male bashing in an all-male prison.

"Do you think you will ever have hair again?"

"It's up to God now." I quickly remembered reading that God can *count every hair on my head* (Luke 12:7). "I figure if I look good enough for God, it's good enough for me, too."

"Did you lose all of your hair?"

"Okay, that's enough." I took back the control as the security officer. "Get some sleep."

"Okay, ma'am." He seemed apologetic and satisfied at the same time.

That inmate would never know what he gave back to me that night. As if he was heaven-sent, and I didn't feel empty anymore. It was a clean slate. When I was ready for God to take over, He refreshed my soul with: *"You cannot earn my love."* (Rom 3:20).

CHAPTER 15

No other Perceptions

The job needed some time to recuperate, but the school buses turned over one after another that permeated through the walls, rattling the windows of my apartment at the end of the graveyard shift, breaking dawn with the same diesel engines right next door.

Our neighborhood picked up our young and aspired students rushed away. The retired savored the freshly brew left behind, waving back at the final few toddlers locked in their car seats, as if no one really noticed the heartfelt rhythm and balance for another day.

The public media diluted the daily morning bites, as I passively tuned it for bed. I easily dismissed the entertainment in comparison to the actual emergencies at work, where I shook it off for someone else. It was my time, and then it all started over... again.

Many years passed by the work at the prisons for another day switching the shifts, like I was an empty nester all to myself, but many parents, grandparents, or any other extended family members lived somewhere else watching over each other. Except when I'd become the spare, I magically evolved and barely tell the difference.

All of my equipment was perfectly accounted for, before it was passed out to the next shift. Main Control handed everything out, except for a few problems saved aside, however a pile could reconsider a nod and a promise. It gambled one over the other that outgrew its guarantees who took any life-still-reusable equipment as needed. No one complained, and we also knew what had been specifically handed out, and I collected my way through like anyone else.

I was aware of the indiscernible radio, which was all it had... for show. A hiss or click signaled that intuitive heed to another, who also paid attention to the slightest hint for the phone call. The yard officers were specifically provided for the most frequented traffic calls, but someone always responded, but the inmates tuned in to listen closely, too. Whether the men wore orange purposely overheard by an officer, but the uniforms didn't matter who worked true emergencies together for safety.

The state budget cut every angle, especially during the recession. It was the need to watch costs, but our work took in the basic community's concern. Enclosed civilians in law enforcement took priority, but politics compared us against their duties on either side of the walls with any option needed to think outside of the box, too: Their two-family earnings in the same workplace wasn't unfair to make a choice, when only one could keep on, asked to step down the other, but the idea to save just one DOC employee to the single households doubled its risks in half to remain on.

There was an impossible amount of pressure to force them apart. Fortunately, I was unaffected to be trimmed down any lower than alone, while the newly trained officers jumped at the chance to take over another fine officer that soured the seasoned unity, instead.

On the same hires on the bonded security staff created another family's opening otherwise unemployed. Their work had ended, forfeited who closed down the firms, as the mortgages were about to fold, like any other threats against their standard lifestyles. DOC's decision recalled either badge for just one to each family, but the arguments couldn't stand water.

The claims were filed in dispute, as if DOC could force the scapegoats that hit a nerve. The COs fought against the proposal leaning toward corruption, who stood behind the oath. The very suggestion was preposterous! DOC delegated the shadiest thoughts, who tried to be hemmed in officially.

One security officer chronically doubled up on the tightly shortened staff, regardless of the newly assigned officers had been scared off, when the seasoned officers pitched in with the sole medical staff working too highly at risk. Their CRN had to respond, while the inmates cried all the louder and still in line. Inmates' medical conditions just weren't going to be enough, but who'd make those calls, either? *Let every soul be subject to the government authority* (ROM 13:1).

DOC officers defended against risks who supported each other, but it was like a family who'd been pressed in trouble at home on both ends. Even one esteemed officer couldn't manage the budget at home in another risk situation in harm's way. Doubling up left another unattended, which spread it out even less... as the prisons ran. *The Lord is a refuge for the oppressed, a stronghold in times of trouble* (Psm 9:9).

I accrued sick time on the books, regardless how I'd been worn down to press on. Some of it was sick time used by DOC benefits away at home. But I adjusted to let it sit on the books, like I was nothing more than a warm body who was enough to show up on the job. Sometimes the nastiest viruses, migraines, or a serious surgery relied on its back up. It padded the paycheck on a nice cushion, but even its appropriate time away, encouraged against the guiltlessly benefit. It could've been an accumulated margin on paper, but the excuses didn't matter. I kept a close watch and used it wisely, but then I wondered why my dad just never took off all through the work in the factory, who refused to stay home... raised like me that way?

The COs were a highly respectable group, who developed sense of responsibility among a strong and loyal team... of whomever remained, but the self-sacrificing attitude took the job that was more than its pay. It was just business, like when my dad illustrated how "one hand washes the other" into the family. The heads-of-household expected to rely on the other half in marriage, in a joint effort who negotiated to cut back. The discretionary spending barely stayed afloat, and DOC's pressure dumped over into the domestic decisions, who couldn't meet the last straw.

I pitched to offer another option, by finagling around our RDOs (regular-days-off). I was assigned to keep my same 'weekend days' that just happened to land on the worse two other weekend days for the other officers' schedules. So, I got creative. It could work which uniquely cooperated with DOC's blessings.

The same Wednesday/Thursday's could swap a holiday off. New Years, Christmas Day and July fourth's Independence Days could've been better to give family-man's day off by switching our weekends. I had nothing to do a holiday by myself. For just the same 'hand washing the other hand' covered DOC. No harm, no foul!

I felt a sense of satisfaction, watching to see how nicely that turned out. It was a warm delight inside, of no obligation in return. That was, until I realized how my sacrifice expected more beyond my calculated donation up front. Was I being fed off of, when my personal joy dwindled?

Daddy never called off work by swapping out in return. Was he teaching me how self-sacrificial concern for another was just like him? He was an expert factory mechanic, like he married a career and his work was the break! He worked... regardless.

He checked off the calendar at work. He had his operation, who was released right out of the hospital and immediately returned to the job. He needed to recuperated, and he did! But not at home, as ma boasted and commendable by his dedication... or another victim for nothing?

For the most part, anyone had his own business who'd enjoy those rose-colored glasses just to get along. But it wasn't necessarily needing an eye adjustment, when blindness was more importantly needed to look the other way.

Rehabilitation in prison was meant to aspire more, compliantly broken in, or institutionalized... for success. The inmates were graduated to the double bunks to be crowded in to fit, as if there really was no place to turn away from the highest alert moments.

Stress tightened it in just a little more. The officers were thinned down while the inmates reached capacity, and still I was there. Fingers-crossed, swallowing hard to proceed, as I still looked at each other, when one more partner bowed out. *From that time on, many of His disciples turned back, no longer accompanied Him. So Jesus asked the Twelve, "Do you want to leave too?* (John 6:66).

Double posts adjusted the rosters as I rode it out, filled in the multiple log services, running from one to the next, but DOC never minded how much could do! Their game strategy stretched the limit and no option. High-alert locked it in fear among my fellow officers to manage the five units, totaling about 5000 inmates, as DOC staffing became more distressing, and I still hung on.

Briefing had another announcement. Sick time benefits lost its preapprovals, which also eliminating any overtime for free once pay froze. I stayed on since nothing had anything to look forward to continue or quit, as our new recruits completely closed from the academy.

If the rosters imposed fear on the token officers working so sparsely, the inmates had to watch their own backs to take over and self-manage their own lives. My friends, my trusting team, silently walked off the job in disgrace. But to go where? I got in too deep, as if bad was ever bad before, but I never stopped to listen for the radio traffic, as if something was wrong to be quiet too long to stay in contact, or at least within reach.

My presence wasn't always visible anymore, and the inmates clung upon their hope which their incarceration was conveniently shortened, or anything to say. The initial tenure to achieve my goal was my sentence... as if it was reward! My career also meant how I'd survive the duration of the inmates, too. The immediate lifestyle was the moment facing my future career, since the academy was irrelevant and another badge was left behind.

I kept my shift commander in his view. He didn't have a quick reaction, frozen through his opened door, and nothing had to say. I had to rely on His power. But what if I would've been the next one against my will?

Unshaken (Psm 16:9), *victoriously* (1Cor 15:57), *His Shepherd in guidance. God will wipe away every tear from their eye* (Rev 7:17). *Run with perseverance the race marked out for them* (Heb 12:1). *Be steadfast, immovable, always abounding in the work of the Lord, knowing that in the Lord your labor is not in vain* (1 Cor 15:58). *Do not be frightened or dismayed for God is with you wherever you go* (Joshua 1:9). Whew...Amen. I needed that!

Still more coverage fell unattended. The manned towers at the corners of the outer perimeters were temporarily traded throughout the shifts as needed. There was a two-officer transport team between the units, who became the sole drivers. Even our upper ranks were pending away from their promotions from any advancing. Just one supervisor was leaned on among our menial chores. The acting supervisors bounced throughout the assigned shifts, who'd reached out to fill in, including their leadership. The amount of work was accomplished in a rush, except the well-done job destroyed the diehard employees, as if they were set up for the fall, and morale plummeted that further affected the inmates.

The inmates had no real backup for their safety and protection by the CO's management. Any kind of power of authority was lost. Unemployment ratings were hidden from the public, while I felt relieved from anyone to know. I was ostracized from my loved ones, and I didn't have anyone to explain why.

At any moment, I could've crossed the wrong inmate, as if I didn't care. Nobody could've been able to protect anyone else in prison. In some cases, the violent inmates seemed to step aside to unite across those boundaries for that grey area, who also over-reached to help. Occasionally a few inmates threw up his hands, but sometimes a few blows used their own language with the fists that made another point.

Then, the books had another issue. Vacation hours were impos-sible to be assigned in for approval. Time away from work was probably more needed than ever, but there was no coverage autho-rized any more annual leave. Policy was only 240 hours of the total benefit of the same year, but there was no room to carry it over into the next year. I had to forfeit beyond the full accrued hours.

Sometimes I looked upon the inmates who landed in prison under the same mindset to allow more wiggle room. The bound-aries eventually blurred, and DOC's accuracy could've easily been interpreted differently for a slight tilt either way.

Our Occupational Health Department required a doctor's note that made it difficult to be cleared back for duty. It was insulting to approve sick time for its absence. I had to have a validated note... to ask if it was okay? The proof of the CO's visiting doctor's appoint-ment or an urgent care visit demanded an additional expense, besides enough proof for the pass. The undue hardship was more like a pun-ishment, but how much worse was bad anyway?

The year's end grew near, and the holiday celebrations played out the results. Our dedicated officers couldn't be with their family and friends, away from work without the original three-times-and-you're-out penalties, when DOC found another cut. They lifted the ceiling for the hours on the books... like a bonus and bittersweet victory. There was no reason to be punished twice: first by missing out on the festivities from work, and secondly to be denied holiday pay remained on the books... to stay on the job.

It wondered what else I could possibly do the right thing to do it in the first place. I'd think how I numb I felt, "Go ahead, hit me. Since I'm already beaten up, one more blow couldn't make it hurt any more". The state took away every tidbit of hope one thing or another, as if a crumb of survival was enough to linger on. After a while, I was too busy bouncing one job to the next, as if I knew DOC would come up with something else. The state needed to pay down the fiscal debt. The accrued hours appeared to pay it off in one chunk, which limited down the taxes with everything left and cleaned off the books, when time off was no longer available to the COs at all.

I'd turned around with the remaining handful who came in on a daily basis, like when the back door sucked out the dead air silence inside, as I held my breath. It felt like a vacuum couldn't hardly catch my breath, closed into a casket and paralyzing fear that spread across the officers forward, until *"We know that the law is not meant for a righteous person, but for the lawless…which was entrusted to me."* (1Tim 1:9,11) when I began from the start. I had the calling, just like those five neophyte officers who I looked on how they also stood petrified throughout OJT week for the choice one way or the other, before my mind was made up. They were about to fold; except I was not the other babes in the woods. *The Lord is my rock and my fortress and my deliverer, my God, my rock, in whom I take refuge, my shield, and the horn of my salvation, my stronghold* (Psm 18:2).

Occasional pizza helped its encouragement, who readily reached out a slice or two, accepting the gracious thanks, as I expected to hear more than his cooperation for another favor. And I was right.

"This is it folks." Our supervisor waited all sitting down with the first bite, as if we were called attention during briefing. "Complex is well aware of the numbers." His diaphragm bellowed into his paperwork to be heard across his desk.

I ate it slowly and cautiously swallowing, as if the die-hards were fed of every word to follow. The former kick-starters were well weeded out, who used to provoke the inmates making them squirm at the brink, but we officers were the solid few behind.

"I'm going to have the housing officers take two buildings today." He raised his eyebrows to look across the room, somewhat ashamed to look us in the eye, but there was no response. "That will allow each side to have an extra yard officer to cover by another float." His creative audience nodded. "Does anyone have anything?" He waited for its input.

"I heard someone talking about the state selling off a complex to be privatized? Did anyone else hear anything about that?" The voice came from the back, since there was no one talking over anyone in that room.

"I heard that too," Sgt. Wallis was well aware of the whispers already leaked down to administration. "but I don't think that will ever happen." He cowardly looked up at the officers under his command. "Go ahead and relieve shift," he insisted with nothing more to say.

When fights broke out in the runs, none of us knew about it. Everything was back in order by the time the COs came around for another hurried security check. The inmates policed themselves, and the injuries were not discovered until the next day at morning meds before chow. The victimized inmate took its own punish, denying any treatment, in fear of another beating.

DOC maintained a low profile but it the media spilled into the public. Like the secrets of the family who leaked out, as if DOC also kept it from anyone tipped out, until a juicy one splashed the headlines that could never be hidden beyond the prisons. *Conduct yourselves honorably, where they speak against you as those who do what is evil, they will, by observing your good works, glorify God* (1 Peter 5:12).

My family would take care of 'it' inside. *Always do my best to have a clear conscious toward God and men* (Acts 24:17), when something always seemed to probe to hear about the good girls or boys which also monitored it kept under hat, the silent treatment denying the black-sheep, or the ugly reputations that inflicted enough two-face lies to accept the consequences. Negative reinforcement exerted the disciplinary rules, like the families who sought out their grapevine connections to maintain a low secretive profile, with just enough fear and doubt.

The feelers were sent out in high alert, like a tempted advertisement to attract the sweet smiles, regardless. *At the same time, they also learn to be idle, going from house to house; they are not only idle, but are also gossips they shouldn't say* (1 Tim 5:13). Pecking order reigned in its control, while the government constrained the additional by-laws, too.

The public or private sectors contested any claim, until there was a war to win over for the courts system, as if something had to give. I kept down, weakened away from the challenging power, like before I worked the job in prison, too.

A lot of the rehabilitation programs were cancelled and the three hot meals were trimmed back, just like the family budget that didn't divulge the expenses in comparison. DOC was in control at hand, just like my large family's chores that fit, according to the size or ages of each one. *Trust in the Lord with all your heart, and do not lean on your own understanding* (Proverbs 3:5).

The inmates allowed just one hot meal and wrap up two sack lunches for bologna or peanut butter sandwiches that trimmed down the grocery bill of the family, too. Although, grown inmates were still young men in their twenties treating the same to the all. They wanted more to eat, but the food allotments met the caloric standards for the prisons on a survival mode. *If in spite of these things you do not accept My disciplines, you will be delivered into enemy hands. They will bring back your bread in rationed amounts, so that you will eat, and not be satisfied* (Lv 26:25,26).

Sometimes the officers ordered a meal to eat at our posts by the kitchen crews. They made around with that same flat-bed wagon to deliver each staffing shift accordingly. The brave officers took a chance on the meals that had been specifically prepared by inmates, who delivered each one working around the yard. *Go on your way and whatever city or house ye enter, first say peace be with you and if you are received, eat and drink such things as are set before you.* (Luke 10:3-8). What's the difference? The same food that was packaged for anyone, except its was rumored who spat in our trays before it was carefully plastic wrapped, but I received that particular tray which was specifically handed to me. I picked out what I took, and I purposely left the tray on the table in the dayroom. But my food was gladly taken the others as planned. I left the leftovers polished off. I knew, and so did the inmates who prepared the untainted tray that passed on after I was finished.

I should've been fine, except that day! There was a meal by a hamburger patty in a bun, potato salad, and beans with a few sliced pickles, and a cookie or slice of cake on the side that didn't look too bad. Although, I only had the hamburger cut in half. I took it at room temperature, thinking nothing like it always was that way, and I was actually impressed with the delicious patty.

No sooner had I hardly finished, I got violently sick, doubling up in gut wrenching pain. I ran off and immediately threw up my meal. Top or bottom, it didn't matter, until I realized how little real meat was in that soy-burger. I was severely allergic to soy, which was under any number of names under the same thing. Otherwise, I ate the food good enough for the inmates, and I routinely ordered a meal without any concern of the processed foods shipped into the kitchen daily clearly marked: **"Not for human consumption"**, with no expiration date to deter me. *The one who eats everything must not treat with contempt the one who does not, and the one who does not eat everything must not judge the one who does, for God has accepted them* (Rom 14:3).

Besides the thousands of hungry criminals in prison, there was another issue rippled aside outside the state prison where I worked. There was another prison built in the far corner of the state. The formal counts were repeated about six hours apart, except they had a few incarcerated inmates who lost track of the private prison. The public media spread like wildfire, as if the state prisons scrambled behind the scenes who dodged the worse 'black eye' on them.

The private prison didn't clear their counts, as if it got too redundant or easily filled in the numbers on paper by the ghost officers several hours after the escape. Plenty of time should've been proactive by every letter and jot by every timely report once their numbers matched, face to ID. The assumed protocols should've been strictly established with the officer's movement... or the lack thereof.

Two criminals got out because no one was manning the towers, just like our state prison corners. They were helped by a civilian just drove into their unchecked perimeter checks, possibly lied, or ignored the routines. *Then the LORD spoke to Moses, saying, "When a person sins and acts unfaithfully against the LORD, and deceives his companion in regard to a deposit or a security entrusted to him, or through robbery, or if he has extorted from his companion, or has found what was lost and lied about it and sworn falsely, so that he sins in regard to any one of the things a man may do; then it shall be, when he sins and becomes guilty, that he shall restore what he took by robbery or what he got by extortion, or the deposit which was entrusted to him or the lost thing which he found, or anything about which he swore falsely; he shall make restitution for it in full and add to it one-fifth more. He shall give it to the one to whom it belongs on the day he presents his guilt offering"* (Lv 6: 1-5). And, it made the undeniable headlines in the newspaper, too.

How much of the State's DOC was afraid of their own guilt? It was had two inmates just waiting, like my life anticipated it every day's trip-wire. It could've been any other pawn, where I took the chances that finally snapped. Who was more guilt? The state or private prisons played both sides, like it had two teams in competition and the challenges amped up just as bad as the other. Every budgeting squeeze turned up one notch at a time, as if it was an all or nothing move for the next turn. But there never was a match, when it blamed the politics with some other excuse.

The private prisons were diverted to cover or protect the damages done, but the public media gladly used it as another distraction for the other side. DOC nervously bought up some time, coming up with something fast, but the truth was about to expose its extent who wanted the answers.

Two inmates escaped with the driver. They hid out in the woods; except an old couple was camping who killed them. But something big sounded good for DOC, who talked up and distracted the future improvements ready for a back-up plan.

DOC's prisons made his COs overwork, which was an understatement, but who would know? My family spared my own low-profile from anyone to know about me, or the career. *But the Lord is faithful; he will strengthen you and guard you from evil* (Thes 3:3).

There I was, surrounded by the inmates on the open yard, and a sole target under a panic rush. One remaining CO filled six posts that maximized its demands (after nine weeks of training at the academy) overnight. The state opened the overtime hours, and suddenly every shift urgently increased the staff on the rosters to stay over, as if sixteen mandated hours had no limit, flying high on auto-pilot.

Our shifts doubled over, twice as hard and twice as long... like a finely-tuned engine on the job. Five-hour energy shots, no-doze, or caffeine (OTC) pills threw around like candy for everyone (that I knew about). Our supervisors' goal came back like a thing of the past that had never mattered how it compound the staff, or at least on paper. Everyone gave it their all, and some COs even slept over in their car's back seat in the parking lot, who never left any more than a nap. They used DOC's facilities, so it would run safe and smoothly.

The state's bottom line raised its debt like a stuck pig that came so closely bled out, to revive it. It was a dangerous compromise to challenge the budget operating in the red, which was initially ignored, by a necessary evil. A political cartoon snickered at the situation, illustrating their democratic sows' laying belly up with its tits exposed. After all, it was just an off and accurate vision, since words weren't needed.

"The state didn't have enough money to pay us." The shift commander could barely come up at briefing. I laughed inside, blowing off the idea of working for free. *Food gained by fraud is sweet to a man, but afterwards his mouth is full of gravel* (Prov 20:17), but it was true! The overtime hours dropped off, but we adjusted; shrugged and kept working. How could the prisons operate, as if sleep deprivation affected their sound judgement? "Naw, that couldn't be true." I blew it off. Surely it must've been misunderstood, or just another rumor without an ounce of truth.

I had every reason to believe the right thing to do, but the governmental system was unsettling with all of the bureaucratic mumbo jumbo. Somehow, I had to trust behind all of the government agencies to rise above the commonwealth's problems. There was no reason to swindle out of our paychecks, unless the underlying problem could be exposed to the light, and believed that they'd deal with it somehow. *For rulers are not a terror to good conduct, but to bad. Would you have no fear of the one who is in authority? Then do what is good, and you will receive his approval"* (Romans 13:3). I leaned on His Word, focusing on the job, as I expected the state's quick-fix problems, but crunch time pressed on all the more.

The rising debt had no cap, like no floor or ceiling without anything to bounce from it. There were no boundaries or limitations without any concern over the chaos. The general public was just the same with their credit cards spiraling out of control, too. While the academy pressed on, the open positions couldn't fill the supporting staff, yet.

I believed in a euphoric drunkenness. I felt infallible. I demanded a selfish drive as I secretly excelled against fear, as if I lost a sense of responsibility. I was fixated, focused to run the prison of criminals before me. *Then Saul and all the people who were with him rallied and came to the battle, and behold, every man's sword was against his fellow, and there was very great confusion* (1Sam 14:20), as if integrity and personal safety didn't mix to hold it together any longer.

DOC developed another pay category for Comp Time (comprehensive time) to keep tabs on the extra hours to be paid at the end of the fiscal year and catch up, later. It wouldn't have any effect! I spent less, hording my earnings at work, since I was too tired to go shopping anyways. For a while, we all chomped at the bit for better pay, but the public sector or private companies announced our record-breaking cutbacks. For what was bad by then, was rock bottom.

No one could've possibly assumed their eminent closing-down firms, which couldn't even absorb the mergers to survive that. I tuned in the news, watching the buy-outs plummet, when the housing bubble burst! The stock market took a nose dive, and I saw money to buy cheap. Nothing ever could've hung on much longer, but it did. Sooner or later, something had to go back up again! Cost-of-living raises fell on deaf ears. The media reported skyrocketing unemployment rates all throughout the country, except for me.

I kept my nose down and stayed to myself. Since no one cared to know how I was doing, when I clammed up too. Who wouldn't believe me anyways?

Financially, I didn't have to face a spouse or children at home. I took a day off of a few personal chores like the laundry and food, lucky enough to feel the pressure alone. It was all about me, but some of my fellow officers returned to work more drained. Their 'better half' screamed "enough" and about to break up, who didn't have another team at home.

I wouldn't dare feed my love ones with the news, or whether I cared to share its consequences who would just rub my nose in the worse career choice again. I smiled, wanting to be the absentee adult of someone to talk to... among my fellow officers. The inmates seemed to feel the same, but not that. I operated a survival mode just like any other void of my family, which was merely my chance to exist in another social life of prison. But I *did* have a relationship!

The Bible transcriptions reworded the messages, as I researched the answers that never got old. I was addicted, craved of His advice. I relaxed, comfortable in His guidance through the worldly life next to God. *For I am persuaded that not even death or life, angels or rulers, things present and things to come, hostile powers, height or depth, or any created thing will have the power to separate us from the love of God that is in Jesus Christ our Lord* (Romans 8:38-39). How did I remember so readily, etched in my heart?

DOC's policies supported my decisions that defended His Word from its doubt and confusion automatically. The academy encouraged to believe right from wrong, listening my gut, until I understood it deeper in my heart, as if I always knew the basic principles and no one else's responsibility over me. I bought into what I owned. I built up my self-esteem in a clean conscious with an upright example, since I shouldn't have expected anything less, before.

I listened throughout our briefings, who'd lost their tempers against the authorities when the DOC stepped in relentlessly. "Push one more time and..." but tongues bit down hard again. *Remind them to be submissive to rulers and authorities, to obey, to be ready for every good work, to slander no one, to avoid fighting, and be kind, always showing gentleness to all people* (Titus 3:1-2). DOC stepped in to protect our health by limited three extra shifts (or a total of three days of sixteen-hour shifts) each week. At least one day had to take off every week.

I lived almost a stone's throw away from work. I was in bed before most other drivers were home, but sleep didn't always come easily. I finally nodded out, and then it was time, answering the alarm clock on schedule. I pushed too long through pure will, as if I merely went through the motions. Some even slurred their speech like a drunk with an uncharacteristic gait, straggling on the job, who barely functioned for a quick response any more. There were times when I lost the ability to recognize the limit of the next shift, begging a few more bodies to stay over one more shift to continue, until safety needed to intervene management for the good of all.

Weeks went by, months passed, and my only social contacts had diminished to anyone in the world, befriending a 'like' with another stranger's chat on Facebook. The extra money about the career was irrelevant, when I set the reserves aside, like my life treaded water at work to stay afloat, when I was cut free. I had no one to answer to, or another sabotage behind my back, as if we all needed His help through the rough times more than anything else.

"What do you want?" That thought nudged His attention. I saw the bills paid off once my divorce fee balances due or my car payment had been sent out by the final slip torn out. That bumped my income ahead after the monthly payments out of debt, and I beamed for a moment! My credit card balance reconsidered its limit, as I also redistributed Christmas expenses. A handsome folded bonus dropped into the red pan jiggling next to Santa's costume before it was spent through the store's front doors, instead of the family traditional packages. "Money doesn't mean a thing until it's spent." I taught my kids to practice of what I preached, whether it made a difference to the one who most the mattered.

"What do you want?" That question urged again, more adamant with every paycheck, but I had nothing to say. *God called out to the man and said to him* (Gen 3:9); *"So then faith cometh by hearing, and hearing by the word of God"* (Rom 14:3). I already knew where that came from.

Some COs talked about traveling, and some talked about making extravagant purchases that could be afforded with the padded earnings, but that didn't pertain to me.

"Don't get too used to the overtime," our shift commander warned, but that only pressed on all the more. "The state just notified us of a cost-of-living freeze." There would be no raises that year, and again, none of us seemed to pay any attention. We had more important things on our minds, like surviving another sixteen-hour work day to do it again. Besides, it felt safer when no one else had to know beyond my paycheck-to-paycheck lifestyle to build back.

My fellow officers couldn't hold it back, but they had the impossible sacrifices to support within their family's joint effort. For what was once impossible, was celebrated to be achieved together.

I had seen that, as if nothing would ever last too long. My family had to keep-up-with-the-Jones's era in my childhood, which skipped over me into the next entitlement generation, like I could control it anyways. I held my tongue to stay out of it. I had no opinion to feed the fight which seemed so petty. Their competition made it look good, rubbing it in or showing off, but they'd never be happy. I'd gladly step back, letting them fight over the next leg-up. *Ill-gotten gains do not profit anyone* (Prov 10:2). Something I had to show for it was always useful, as if I let them, but I'd never earn anything for granted. I eventually hid my things, afraid of being found out, or destroyed of what couldn't be mine. DOC's payments accomplished what they owned, who were so happy to show their things! And, I cheered along with them… but not me.

"Make hay while the sun shines", borrowed the memories my dad left behind. I believed in my supervisor, when I heed the warning, against from getting used to a raised standard of living, as I learned to pace the extra monies, hoarded or finally repurchased to a new normal, as if I couldn't possibly slide back of what I owned. I kept my head down to focus on work and sleep, since whatever money I made, went into the stocks to build back up, too.

There was no time to spend, as I got comfortable enough with myself. And then, I remembered the story in the Bible that also used its example compared with me. Was anything like the farmer's bountiful harvest in Luke chapter twelve? He had so much that he built another barn to store his abundance, and then lost his life the next day.

I shook it off, quickly justified all the harder on the job. Anything else seemed irresponsible. I didn't see any reason to change my lifestyle. I increased my earnings to climb out of my credit score, which I recovered from my ex's CPA's perfectly timed disaster, in comparison with the lowly CO's come back in pride. *But godliness with contentment is great gain* (1Tim 6:6).

Or, was I turned into another Scrooge, who sat in the dark to eat a bowl of soup? *People whose hope is in money are never satisfied; they live uneasy and restless lives* (Ecc 5:10). He had plenty of money to enjoy his meal served at a table underneath a darkened chandelier to harbor his money and use below the expense its electricity. But didn't I know how I'd bask in the glory of owning something special? Or, was afraid I'd fall back on an accident or emergency? It even felt good, holding onto something with a very little bit of guilt inside.

Things were bound to change, just like the final summer trips ended. I was anxious to reunite every year. I believed that I'd find the bonds back home, as if the route was no cause for concern. I entertained my little niece in the back seat of the car, except there was another ride to the folks' house that never had been arranged for me. *The seed that fell among thorns stands for those who hear, but as they go on their way they are choked by life's worries, riches and pleasures, and they do not mature* (Luke 8:14).

The old farm house was sold, when I should've known about the new house I'd moved near the high school. But how could I had been prepared? My empty drawers shared in a bedroom with another sister. A few dangling hangers defined my space in the far corner... of the closet, but I didn't have anything looked after my things. *You must not act deceptively or lie to one another. You must not oppress your neighbor, or put a stumbling block in fear* (Lev

19:11,12,13,14). The only things I thought were safe, had no one else of what I owned.

An inmate grew closer to finish their sentence release date that they carried nothing more than a banker's box of possessions, who left the rest behind. They all valued everything, until it was no longer needed who gently handed it off. I looked away. Their things just disappeared, which also outgrown or passed it forward, as I respected it with the big difference of the inmates. The inmate had the pleasure of turning over their storage space to clear out the property department or what was stored underneath their bed gifted out that was rewarding to an inmate. But it was just like when I'd been moved out, except my valuables were not handed out or where it went, when I carried all I had inside a brown paper bag.

I couldn't bare that level of despair, lost all over again. It was all there, just in my mind. I revisited my memories for another look. There was no one bothering me, or mourn of what no longer existed anymore, since I also let go and didn't get hurt about my loved ones who I couldn't count on anyone else to protect me. *But, if anyone does not provide for his own, that is his own household, he denied the faith and is worse than an unbeliever* (1Tim 5:8).

I scanned one Bible to the other, as if there had to be something else. I expected to interpret a double message to make it fit, but I kept coming back to the same answer. My Higher Power was a separate entity, knowing His own personality and all of His emotions, when I got mad, too.

I wanted my billfold full of my classmates' school pictures since childhood. I owned my first Brownie camera with the negatives developed of my pictures. I loved my little green Singer sewing machine that cranked, sewing anywhere I made my doll clothes from fabric scraps left over of the scraps my ma's clothes altered the church donation. I had my artwork, and the letters we corresponded with my cousin. What I wanted had been bulldozed into the pit. For as much as I'd been dubbed the crybaby of the family, was not even a whimper over the ashes.

I wanted to stroll my children, or the walker scooting around the house which I was denied his expense. Bob had me carry my children at my hip, or where I follow behind the dish towels with their first steps. He was a spendthrift, as if he had enough money to afford my needs, instead. He was the head of the house, and I was a submissive wife. *So they may encourage the young women to love their husbands you love their children* (Tit 2:4).

When I was a single mother, a stressed when I divvied up my earnings to supply my children into the teens, while I'd teetered dangerously thin for my height, feeding them first. *Shepherd God's flock among you according to God's will, not for the money but eagerly, not lording it over those entrusted to you, but being examples to the flock* (1Pet 5:4). For almost a decade, I'd sacrificed to their needs.

I gave in, surrendered to trust Rick's promises, who sounded more like a car salesman for a good deal to make a close on my second marriage. *By justice a king brings stability to a land, but a man who takes bribe overthrows it* (Pro 29:4), as if I didn't catch on fast enough and I repeated the same cycle just like before. My belongings moved in, when my step-son destroyed my saved things who shredded with my scissors, while I turned over my paychecks to manage our joint earnings after there was nothing saved at the end.

Of what was mine didn't belong to anyone else, unless I was generously handed out with a gift. I grew selfish, as if no one could take or destroy my things any more, thinking it was the last time I'd rebuild for no one but me. It got tiring and I got too old, knowing all about competition, affluence, and the accomplishments, who I enjoyed to boasted all around my co-workers, but I had nothing to share in return.

I brewed. "What do you want?" felt like a cruel and teasing joke! "What kind of question is that?" I grew indignant. "What does any of that matter anymore?" I yelled it right back, feeling so egged on... by God.

But God was all I had left! He was that last thread holding me together. God guided me over the years by reading His Word. I'd studied and mulled over the Bible translations and believed, abided by His rules or commandments. I understood of what He said. Except there was a difference between His spiritual desires and the wants of the earthly desires.

I carried His presence, when I kept Him to myself. *No one is able to snatch them out of the Father's hand* (John 10: 29). It was like my secret who no one else could rob me of His existence, which I refused to argue against it. He was that one constant. He knew me by name. But I got afraid. What if I did answer Him, and didn't get it?

Nobody just puts it out there by God. It wasn't like I wasn't used to the word: "no." But why now? *So it is a sin for the person who knows what is good and doesn't do it* (James 4:17). That inner voice was my sole ally in my darkest thoughts, but was God challenging me?

"NO!" I refused God. *Or do you think that I cannot call on My Father, and He will provide Me at once with more than twelve legions of angels? How then, would the Scriptures be fulfilled that say it must happen that way?* (Matt 26:53-54).

I had the advice to settle a lot of my unresolved issues of my past toward peace, but forgiveness was too big for that. *Fathers, do not exasperate your children, so they won't become discouraged* (Col 5:21). I lived enough abuse, as if persecutions were expected to suffer. I grew defensive, but then *God is an honest judge. He is angry with the wicked every day* (Psm 7:11). I held my tongue, and cried silently myself.

I couldn't spell it out any better to imagine my wildest desires, beyond the security I leaned on my savings account. I had to relent. That was the last straw!

"Wasn't it just vanity?" I fumbled, tripping the words in my mind, still searching His verses, as I bowed to trust my heart and soul before Him. *I saw that all labor and skillful work is due to a man's jealousy of his friend. This too is futile and a pursuit of the wind* (Ecc 4:4). There was nothing there for me to run away or toward anything else, which was nothing to prove against it. I turned my back on Him.

There was nothing else I could do. Didn't I already have the desires of my heart in His hands? But it felt wrong. It felt so brazen, and honestly ashamed. How could God want *for* me? I was His servant! I already had everything I wanted. I liked to behave as a CO, meek in this badge when I was surrounded by criminals. I thought I was comfortable, passionate in my chosen career, when I prayed of His Spirit to intervene.

CHAPTER 16

Wake me up, Lord

*T*he rosters were filling up, when DOC redistributed the remaining few to be moved out of the graveyard shift. I'd been switched over to the second shift, where I was paired up in the same open yard. The routines were easily accommodating either side of the buildings, where I encouraged the newest officers to introduce the inmate searches, like it used to be.

I'd grown accustom to work alone, until there were more than twice the number of officers on probation. I showed them through the posts to be the seasoned officer, where my partner stood to guard my back, and then we took turns on the other side switching places. I began, crawling all the way around the inmates' space, started under the bed and mattress, and unfolded clothing, or opened recycled pill jars to find anything that didn't belong. We were methodically examining through everything, which was reported back if needed.

The selected time and place shouldn't have been any surprise by the inmate choices. DOC designated their specific searches, handed out on our way out after briefing, like we got everyone's secret notes that were only allowed to go through the inmate's living area, and overlook anything beyond one bunk.

I scanned my initial overview, who followed along, but no one really saw much more than the surface, until I arrived and let anyone watch me aside, who seemed to be just as curious to see me on my knees. It was just the job, but an ounce of respect didn't need to infuriate the inmate's things, unless there was something for a closer look. And for the most part, the inmates didn't really care who'd hover over my partner's shoulders, who protected my back.

A lot of the inmates left my search unattended, but I couldn't completely relax. I gave my partner the dual watch, by mimicking the search on the other side with respect for the inmate's property, too. Easy peezy, and the safety checks were done!

That was... unless an inmate instigated trouble. Then it was more about the location and its property that amped up some concern. That's when I suspected the worse beyond the usual amount, condition, or smell, until I was sure I passed the inspection to recommend its cleaning. And then, somethings found another problem. I'd been left wide opened and available to get hurt, when alone plus one was enough.

My work style could've been easily misconstrued, until I'd slow it down by a red flag. I'd cautiously reassess, and sometimes I'd have another CO or supervisor's set of eyes, before I'd examine it closely during my poker face with something off. Noxious contraband easily dismissed that slap on the wrist, where I checked out any other form of tobacco, sugar, talc power, or when an undeniable piece of fermenting fruit discarded its seeded batch of hooch, as if my look and his expressions confirmed the message with a pass.

Personalities affected every officer, and some of them were more anxiously tore in, who began each search with an 'accuse first' style. DOC never turned anyone down, who defended a second person's decision to agree, or who rushed over through the motions as necessary. Whatever was really trusted, supported right or wrong of the final call. But the initial hint of suspicion was my discretion, knowing just how bad was bad, like I 'nipped it in the bud' before the threats weighed more heavily, but my searches held it all exposed, one way or the other. *Don't participate in the fruitless works of darkness, but instead, expose them. For it is shameful even to mention what is done by them in secret* (Eph 5:11-12).

I especially remembered how I felt at the scan and tables in the lobby, as if any other officer went in to completely expose it wide open for all to see, who wouldn't just believe me. I wished it could've been more respectful, just like the limited belongings I had before. It was always my choice of what I wanted; except of what I owned. I had no choice. I had to be wagered out to decide what could stay or go, lost to another's decision, with no stand or claim regardless. Or, did I own of what was good enough, who allowed me to keep anything else, instead? *You are not of the world because I chose you out of the world, therefore, the world hates you* (John 15:19).

It was my turn to examined the belongings of what they had, as if the officers and inmates went through everything, except the inspections couldn't change or argue against policy. Either way, ownership fought one over the other. *Do not be mismatched with unbelievers* (2COR 6:14).

Jealousy also festered rage, visibly tempted on a routinely basis in prison, but I had no power who took their personal pleasure on the outside I was too scared when I understood about compliance. I experience a lot less violence in prison and a lot more finesse on the outside. I survived a bone crushing bash that forced me into a spineless coward, bending against the stand. How did they take advantage, when there was no honor, bowed down into a weakling in submission? *But, as for you and your servants, I know that you do not yet fear the Lord God* (Exodus 9:30).

DOC didn't exactly put the academy in practice. I was shocked during the training. It must've been enough to get my attention in class. It must've been exaggerating its abuse in the videos. I squeezed my eyes closed, like if it was time and undeniably seen before me. An overview was shown, and at that time I couldn't hardly absorb anything beyond the surface, until I unearthed the buried truth spilt wide open. I finally realized how threatening I was affected my loved ones, who didn't want me there! They didn't want me to see, where I had to move out from the most familiar and comfortable shift in the dark through the night.

I should've been prepared, but imprisonment became more important than the routine job. I inched my way to through the career. It took years that it finally broke wide opened, like the wedge had to be pounded, split by the final (mental) blow. A search through the belongings of the criminal's space had been mandated to touch and see everything, and an awakening far more than a sense of curiosity.

It was not an underhanded plan of another agenda in prison, when I discovered thorough planted ideas, suggestions, through a deepened brainwash. I was hired to manage the criminals in DOC, but my loved ones were unmanageable to deal... with me behind the badge.

I was ordered to accept the specific arrangements by the rosters, since the prison came back in full staff that enhanced and safely to relive out every criminal area, based according to it should be, which validated the undeniable training to follow though the right examples, when I reestablishing the good habits using Break the Cycle that reflected our prison programs. And in exchange of the hope of the inmates, where I regained it in a hundred-fold of my rehabilitation, too.

Whether the court system was sworn in for the truth by my juried peer and loved ones, since imprisonment was the same thing. I wanted to disprove against every charge. I wanted to see of what I wanted, or of what I'd been allowed to survive, when I wanted more.

Inmates' recidivism didn't always happen to reverse bad behaviors. Another sentence was reinstated, or another stay was repeated in prison facing incarceration, again. Their beliefs were embedded so deeply, so hidden, and impossible beyond any way out of the hold. But, wasn't I just like that, too?

Every inmate started out like anybody else who established their character since birth. One thing after another unfolded that affected its influences. Early development stemmed off, just like anyone else made a mistake who reacted badly toward another direction. Most of their early development couldn't think beyond the options, who impulsively lashed out or relied on another's advice, who embraced the stronger opinions. It was safe who trusted the decisions for him, who couldn't formulate his own decisions.

An inmate's beginning had to unravel each snag, as if early development couldn't go any further, until assuring support had to go back to the beginning and relearn it all over again, but the pre-wired messages couldn't easily erase the past. Their minds were made up, already groomed, and automatically brainwashed in a whim. Of what was owned, denied to believe the horrible criminal acts... the one same people in prison, since I refused to read over each criminal history.

My same questions spent more time about the crimes of their sentences, when I focused more about another place to start over... anywhere else, as if I faced my sentence toward retirement, facing another beginning... somewhere else. My family had a joined decision, a consensus since I'd been kicked to the curb, or George in the SO unit, too.

The final judgements were the results affected every inmate in imprisonment. The only difference between the sworn job of the officer and the inmate defined that line in the sand defined the boundaries, where I made the decision to choose a side, when I reinterpreted a self-imposed detachment that got it backwards. The one place I gravitated to heal.

That grey area had a quiet place to reflection. The same ominous grey prison built solidly grounded, who also began in a sole cell, who were graduated forward into the mix of the open yard. And, I graduated each step, where the inmates were very good at reading people, too. They were manipulative people, where I could finally see the significance at the academy, and it was time where my own demeanor gave it away, face to face.

I heard, and I listened but I didn't get it right away. I didn't play along who twisted or distort the impossible, until I put rehabilitation in practice, as if imprisonment still existed on the outside. It took nine weeks of training in the right direction, but I smiled. I also studied the community college at the bulletin board: You Are Here! which was always at the beginning.

I saw how imprisonment impacted every inmate, knowing why I lived away for my own reasons. *No one realizing that the righteous one is swept away, from the presence of evil* (Isaiah 57:1), which was no different, automatically weeded out my co-workers at the beginning. *But, your iniquities have built barriers between you and the Lord* (Isaiah 59:2).

COs and inmates met face-to-face imprisonment, when saw nothing less than pity. The sentence couldn't be cancelled out to make amends with a profound apology. Was I pathetic who endured every hurtful name, finger pointing to be mocked against me? when I felt sorry for them, including my family. I had to notice how I fought through my own problems, as if I could never regain or reach out, before. *You were just like one of them. Do not gloat over your brother in the day of calamity* (Ob 1: 11-12). I took the blame, knowing I was cheated from my most valuable things, since I refused to fight over my belongings anyways.

The inmates didn't look back in the bus once the sentences were completed, knowing I wasn't done. The radio was no longer playing in my car, when I sang through my prayers in and out every day, examining my improvements or the lack thereof, as I studied the written words of righteousness and the law. *God will bring this about in His own time* (1Tim 6:15).

I followed the example in the Bible, like a baby had to mature, Who showed me... how. *I gave you milk to drink, not solid food because you were not ready for it* (1Cor 3:2). I wanted a better diet when teeth needed meat, as if I was too anxious to bite in! Or when it felt I never saw a smorgasbord spread out like that didn't appeal, and I slowed down for just 'a taste' before I'd take too much on my plate. It was like I'd been served by its assorted situation and character change thrown all at once.

I stepped up hungry. I began with the application for that career, but I was being checked out of me first. I passed through the medical exams including the UA sample that proved against any hint of illegal drugs. The process could've been stopped at any time, as if there was a five-course meal that didn't fit for me, but I was invited in! My financial and lifelong history continued, who dug in, checking out even deeper to expose and find anything against me, but I was sparkly clean.

The ninth chapter in the Book of John must've been like milk that wasn't good enough anymore. I imagined how the innocent and gullible children were bottle fed in front of the tv or pacified at the computer screens that could've ruined their eyes. But it could've been their early development toward vision impairment that denied its proper growth.

Adulthood moved on, who left home and into the world, but the inmates accepted their sentences that never dawned me. I missed about the wool pulled over my eyes, stumbling through the layers that still remained, as I barely got through a hidden glimpse.

They all got scars! But I had every scar validating its undeniable proof among the inmates. They already saw the battle scars, who couldn't show off any more than my baldness that reflected inside, too. They clammed up, speechless during their bad behaviors, who wouldn't share the stories in my presence, but they were all able to survive the way it healed. I was also outcasted, kept away from the pristine, as if I belonged in either side of the walls! I saw how one looked down and out of sight, except there I'd been corralled with the unavoidable sentences, and I was a CO.

We were all divided up, lived within our well-defined community, where the general public designate its safety... but I wanted to reenter prison every day. *Those who war against you will become absolutely nothing. For I, Yahweh your God, hold you right hand and say to you: Do not fear, I will help you* (Isaiah 41:12-13).

They were annoyed who took offense with me around, when I felt bad with just 'that look', except where I dawned my presence among the inmates in prison. Since I couldn't see my hair (or the lack of) what I saw in the mirror, I could only interpret the other expressions, regardless.

So, it was my turn, surprised and didn't understand why. I was caught off guard and too embarrassed, when my physical therapist explained why I didn't need an apology by a stimulated a laugh response:

My index finger rested into her hand. She gently stretched and pulled it in one smooth motion, as I trusted her curl reaching my limits. My stitches were just removed and laid open out of the brace. My therapist measured my finger which support her thumb fitted under its bend. She knew that she'd make it hurt, but I couldn't have known how I'd react that caused an excruciating pain that triggered out an uncontrollable laugh, instead! It was explained by a defense mechanism that took over its specific gland in my brain that released a 'feel good' hormone, which helped me tolerate it.

My therapist remained blameless as I returned with every appointment, which was preapproved by the doctor. My physical therapist was already trained, knowing exactly how the doctor's order followed through, who was easily excused. I didn't get mad at her, when I extended its additional exercises between the appointments that expedited its healing. Just four weeks later, my surgeon returned to see that it was 'on target', and he was pleased to see the recovery to continue on my own.

Ma preapproved just like the doctor, who'd follow through my sisters' orders; except they got angry at me. She expected to inflict pain, except the bullying laughter was far from a 'feel good' hormone release. They got the wrong idea to toughen me up that backfired. I was expected to be hurt and I didn't laugh or any 'feel good' response to heal... which was all backwards. There were no apologies when I was victimized, who wasn't going to assume any part of the responsibility.

The top dogs were edified for being mean. Their presence might as well have gotten an immediate applause who strutted through a wide berth for them to pass; except I grew all the more sensitive, recognizing the fine nuances and subtle deceits.

Sometimes the COs carried a sense of fear, as if that would keep the inmates in line by the kick-starters during my shift, but it never had anyone admit how any inmate had been pushed to the edge, but I learned how *not* to be. I could see myself looking through their cell fronts, trapped and impossible to run or hide, and for just once I puffed up my own self-gratification. *Do not rejoice over me, my enemy!* (Micah 7:8). I tried it on but it didn't fit, when I didn't have to flex authority like that again.

Saint Paul's story of the Bible impacted how rough and vicious he mistreated Christ's followers, until God struck him to his knees blinded and abandoned between the towns. His army fled, who scattered at every direction to save themselves. He needed to be taken along to Damascus for help, who others stepped up to guide him, instead! *I now send you to them to open their eyes* (Acts 26:18). Paul followed them to help his way, where his scales were meant to be fallen from his eyes for a whole 'nother view of life.

Did I come to believe that I could read with the 4.0 GPA? Or was ma just that angry at me for excelling. She was furious! That would've ruined her plan. The Bibles offered more than an element of hope of the love who'd possibly accept my apology. It hurt my ma, but I couldn't relent, seeing how my life didn't belong in her hands, and I made the change for His help, instead.

The message in my heart remained, but I was so frustrated, like a jigsaw pieces flew into the air and start all over, when I also knew that it would never go back the way it was. *When I became a man, I put aside childish things. For now we see indistinctly as in a mirror, but then face to face. Now I know in part, but then I will fully, as then I am fully known* (1Cor 13:11-12). For a while, I felt like nothing fit like before, when I stopped to force two pieces together. I wanted to go back to what was familiar, exactly the way it was, until I returned to His written Word that was easier to believe, steadfast, and undeniably true. Understanding through His wisdom eliminated all of that confusion, just like Jesus who went away to a quiet space to pray the Father. And there I focused on Him, where time was not an issue.

Thoughts resurfaced, remembering how my husband asked to meet with him. He wanted to discuss some very important matters pertaining to our divorce. Bob still needed to cover a few things, but I was afraid that it would carry over our marriage that should've been over. I felt trapped in a corner, when I offered a public place to keep up his appearance and away from my children's audience on display.

The Ground Round restaurant (which was its poetic choice of the 'meet market') had the bar stools set up ahead of me, as if a compliment crowed his choice above all others, while I trusted him to behave. He controlled his voice low enough to preserve our privacy, but then he didn't want to discuss anything. He threw a few mixed messages, when the rest finally looked in the other direction. Couldn't anybody see? I sheepishly shrank, when I finally whispered back.

"Do you know how you kept putting me down?" I quivered in my voice. I paused for a moment, determined to be contained in a lowly bend closer in his ear only. "I understand why you had to do that now." My heart was in my throat that was hard to talk without releasing that floodgate of tears.

"Yeah." He admitted it. He might've as well have unfolded his peacock tail among the remaining lonely men, who were perfectly spaced along the length of the bar, and oh how he loved it.

"You had to do that," I said just as matter-of-factly as possible, while his chest rose so proudly who didn't even try to deny it. I reached my toe down from the bar stool and then to the floor, still distracted in the sport's bar across who were just curious enough or a browbeaten glance, watching to steal a moment away for himself. Or whether I'd been cut free for a moment to touch up my lipstick from a smudge left behind, but I didn't. I swept my breath almost blown in his hair. "That was the only way you could make yourself equal to me" I said, once I had both feet solid on the floor.

I was both angry and scared, knowing that I could've infuriated him, but it took about a second later when it sunk in, but was already too far away to say anything else. I left him alone, but the few other men witnessed his true colors. He had company, who followed their eyes taking off, feeling safer around a hand full of some other men enjoying his beer. I was afraid that Bob could've lunge back at me, as I glanced back who saw my keys ready for the locked doors to get away.

Down deep, I knew! It was just like the parable of the seeds that sprouted quickly from the heat of the rock that died shortly afterwards, unable to take root. It was a nugget of truth, and still, I wasn't ready to accept or quickly excuse his retaliation, taunting me.

Consciously or subconsciously, "People who love you just wouldn't do that!" argued back and forth, as I tried to justify against my inner conflicts in his hold that escalated into ridicule. I was convinced to marry the man who stood before the world, vowed to the rest of my life, until I realized that he wasn't fighting for me. I thought I deserved to be laughed at for another choice, who was chronically disappointed in me. Bob made a spectacle of me, until our divorce was my gift to free him.

Our family should've enjoyed a lifetime bond, but he had no other replacement for another spouse, when Bob embrace all three of my beautiful pride and joy forever. He continued life as he knew it, but he kept same firm separated to himself that compounded the already established financial plans, while I plowed on somehow.

"Hi ma." I called to talk to my dad. I thought he agreed to change the headlight, since I had a warning ticket on my car, but I didn't think that I was out of line to count on him to help me. Didn't he fix one sister's lawn mower, or when he mounted a ceiling fan for another?

"What do you want him for?" My ma was reluctant to put him on the phone. I figured that she might have taken offense, asking too quickly for him or when she already knew why I wanted to talk to him. "He was going to change a headlight on my car but he didn't show up."

"You already had your man. Don't come after mine. He has enough to do around here. Can't you take it to a garage?" She saw me like we were in competition. I was dumbfounded, a single mother and no other man around. Surely, I had to have misunderstood! Did I step on her toes, who'd deny his promise?

"Can I talk to him?" I needed to have him tell me. He knew when and how I'd left my car unlocked in the employee parking lot all day for the right model car with the right light bulb. I wasn't mad, but that took the chance to be left unattended, too?

"Here, it's Marion." I heard it in the background, where daddy was already there.

"Hi, Daddy. What happened? I bought the replacement bulb from the auto-part store and I left it on the front seat just like you told me." I felt bad like he was cornered. I knew that he was going to have to face Ma again, once it would hand it back for her to hang it up.

"Well, you have a foreign car and I don't have any metric tools." I accepted his excuse even though it didn't feel right. Besides, what did I know? It could be true. Although, if it were me and someone would've taken care of it for me, I would've made the purchase of that tool to do what anything he'd need. *But let your communication be, Yea, yea, Nay, nay for whatsoever is more than these cometh of evil* (Matt 5:37). I shouldn't have trusted it at all, but I'd still believed and had been mistaken. So, with plenty of time after dinner, I left my three little ones behind, safely arranged with enough homework, or something aside with its popcorn and tv, when I'd be right back

"Here's your metric tool." The young mechanic at my dealership showed his screwdriver to me. He was barely able to look up by the time I'd finished my story. The mechanic was glad to help me pull up without an appointment after I was relieved who filled in, as if my dad's tools were only meant for domestic cars.

Did I have to be so ashamed, shown just how gullible I was purposely hurt? Was I expected to make that public display through my ignorance, caught off guard beyond the loved ones of the family? Was the bond of my daddy forced apart, while I kept coming back for another chance to fight against denial? Was the victimized mind established at fault? How long went on, and wouldn't see it?

"How much do I owe you?" I asked cordially, when he crushed the box from the replacement bulb tossed it at the trash can, who put some speed behind it. He stepped up my desperate need, which was less than the two-week warning to be removed from the driver's license point against me.

"It's on me," he said, graciously wiping down the chrome with a shop rag as he polished both headlights with his job well done... for me! I thanked him a kindly handshake, and I drove right off to the police station to expunge my road ticket. I'd been pulled over by a burnt-out headlight, but there were no questions and nothing to discuss.

It bothered me when she said, "Now you have no reason to come over," she twisted the same knife still stuck in my back after daddy's funeral, too. And, I still took a step back in private to heal alone. That just must've been a slip, when it didn't make sense. I kept blowing that off, too. She must've been mourning, forgiving anything set off, as if she didn't know what she was saying.

Ma intentionally kept me from knowing how sick daddy actually was, every time he was in town for another chemo treatment, and she didn't want me around him or any of 'the rest'. There was not one of my sisters, neglected to inform or update his condition to me the whole time. *Many seek a ruler's favor, but a man receives justice from the Lord* (Prov 29:26). Ma was always the top matriarch of the household, who hen pecked my dad until his final moments. Then she'd do anything for him, but I couldn't mean to cause any trouble from my sisters' through their body language, when they literally turned my back at his coffin. Secrecy equalized all innocents of blame? But I hid it. I was hurt and I got right the message, shrugged off but each wound still left each scar, with every accumulating reminder.

I flipped through the pages of my notebook which I kept in my backpack, when I stopped in to remember the first time I where I was sent away. The summers were always someone who'd take me in of the more distant relatives, but my loved ones weren't really family anyways. They treated me like guests who 'twisted the arm' against my will. Yet, nothing kept me from George, instead. He was humble and kindly, who I introduced myself in and never turned away.

He lived in the cars at the salvage dump, except ma called him a bum. His only crime was a kiss goodbye at the end of our play date, which was the day Janet tattled who ruined his life, and ma didn't like me from that point forward. He was sued who got rid of him, but worse... I hurt ma's embarrassment.

Molestation or even a touch of affection was labeled indecency, and a fine of restitution was meant to be satisfied. My family had been awarded with a toboggan, who called me a chicken when I refused to use it in trade. It included a whole box of chocolates, but ma did that for anyone else. I had two choices to hurt me one way or the other, when I denied to eat another eczema flare-up, but she also made me hand it out to the rest of my family with the perfect "one less mouth to feed" excuse.

I walked about a mile down the road in bare feet where we played, and nobody else cared of whom or when I ran to visit him. It was no secret, and I played outside all day long. There were no rules, and George was always there to spend time together. Life was good... until the day changed!

I was too young and before preschool age, until daddy reprimanded ma! I saw. I heard it, and I knew that she would never forget... as if her restitution couldn't meet the punishment rolled down to me. But daddy comforted me, instead. She wore the burden, as if I was the most convenient one... to thin down the load.

That was when daddy tied up my time, and coincidently took me to the barbershop... for a boy's disguise. He got his hair cut and I got mine cut, too. We were buddies to discredit my gut feelings for having another name for his boy, who kept rubbing my hair on the top of my head and the tee shirts were no longer used... to reduce the summer laundry... for ma. But there was nothing going back or recuperate what was sold out to discuss or ever see him anymore. That was private! It was kept behind closed doors. There was nothing to say, but I remembered my childhood that shouldn't have hurt through its secrecy, and hiding wasn't allowed to heal.

Life confused right from wrong, unavailable to sort out the benefits of the doubts, who were the worst in people. Of what might have been, or of what should've been, wasn't going to be settled.

"Enough, God! I get it!" I couldn't bear it any more.

I had the things happened from the very people who were supposed to love me! What about: "if you got family, you've got everything"? who I got more respect from the inmates in prison! I grew up vulnerable, and totally dependent at the mercy with an apology always handy on my lips, woebegone and pathetic, and unable to conform, when I'd been taught how I shouldn't "rock the boat" to survival. "What good am I?" I asked my Lord in sarcasm. "And, where were YOU?" I threw all that talk about love in the Bible right back at Him. There was so much anger in me, but He did not treat me in kind. I was comforted in His arms, holding me together as I fell apart.

As long as I could accept blame, I thought I could control things better. I searched beyond the front focus through a snapshot, hanging onto what I could trust, as if the SO yard of the criminal perpetrators couldn't have been happier, *and a man's enemies will be the members of his household* (Matt 10:36). I wasn't a CO facilitator of ill-intent, who could've been vulnerable like me, and yet I did nothing to deserve the treatment I got from the very people I should've expected more.

"Abba, how did the truth set me free? I was betrayed by the very people who should've loved me. Where do I go from here?" My heart swung from depression to anger. Too many years of abuse brought out the surface that was penned up inside. "Why did you bring me to see all this here?" I sat with my Lord where I looked all around. "But now I'm surrounded by inmates' looking after their safety. How does that make any sense?"

I had my melt downs actively seeking out of my God, like I had no one else to hear me. But then I needed to study His reactions, and the feelings He had towards the "stiff-necked Israelites." They nagged Him constantly, until He got so fed up that the whole generation was denied to see the Promised Land. He'd been bickering, constantly pushed too far. Even God could not tolerate His unlimited grace, as if He cut off their second chances.

I read about the awesome wonders He did for them. He wanted to appease His people, who didn't appreciate of what He'd done for His special people. But they made Him angry, hurt over and over again of forgiveness right there in the Bible! He wanted them to give Him credit, where credit and some sincere gratitude was due, returning some heartfelt thanks that just wasn't going to happen, either.

When He had come to the end of His rope, He turned to the Gentiles, where I worked toward peace of the inmates. The family were my special people, who should never had been meant to join a prison of sinners. And even Jesus was run out of town, who had to know about the virgin birth, where I was bashed by the very loved ones I'd grown up with. I was humbled, afraid to grasp by the severity I compared with God. Maybe I was way out of the league, but who else would've been any better able to understand what went wrong?

I was dressed in distinction of the uniform in the state prison to maintain order among known criminals. And there I was, putting myself out there, visibly noticed who had to know that I was different. That line in the sand was Moses decision, when he came down from the mount, asked the tribes to choose God or the idols. How ridiculous. Earthly made statues preferred of what they created, who bowed to worship... art?

The prison's security officer to inmate ratio never did quite recuperate back of the rosters. The academy pumped out hundreds of recruits every month in a never-ending stream, yet the staffing numbers remained low. *You in sheep's clothing, but inwardly are ravaging wolves* (Matt 7:8). People like me were scarcely made it for retirement. *"Enter by the narrow gate which few will find. Easy and wide is the gate to destruction where many will go."* His words supported the call where I belonged. *So you'll recognize them by their fruit* (Matt 7:20).

I was one within the crowd, as if I always was singled out. I was an overcomer that always had its exceptions. I was determined against odds, awkwardly adamant to find out whatever it took. The drive was overwhelming to find the answers... that finally stopped the chase of my loved ones.

"Did I do this? Was that my fault? What's wrong with me? Who did that to me?" That lump swelled, choking up the very real rejections that still lingered too deeply rooted of the hold. "But, I'm still mad." I addressed my Lord right there and then.

"Let me deal with them." God answered, and I left it in His hands.

If God is for us who is against us? (Rom 8:31), when His words spoke on cue. *Who can separate us from the love of God?* (Rom 8:35); *Things present or things to come, hostile powers, height or depth, or any other created thing will have the power to separate us from the love God that is in Christ Jesus our Lord!* (Rom 8:38-39).

Whoever coined the phrase: "Sticks and stone may break my bones but words will never harm me" lied! My words had the most powerful weapon, how I conducted to meet my daily test. It caused them to step back, as I stood solid where no one could argue against me.

"You can't make me do jack!" Inmate Hollman sprung from his bed and lunged up at me. His earphones turned all the way up, who raised over his voice throughout the run. There were so many other music styles; except he competed to drown out all others. He was quick to intimidate me in place, like the rest of the inmates, or he was looking for trouble to display his independent power over anyone else, but especially when he offered the CO's chance to walk away. I took the later.

"It's late. Turn it down or listen to it tomorrow." I faced an abrasive and obstinate inmate, with little to no regard for the other inmates. Some blankets draped his neighboring bunks to enjoy his music, but that music was far from his private space.

"Say please." Inmate Hollman wouldn't give in the DOC directives, changing the game entirely, but I didn't want to waste my time and wouldn't play (games).

"No, I'm not going to say 'please'. It was enough that I had to tell you what you already know." I gave him that 'don't be ridiculous' look, extended another and additional message included under my breath with respect of the inmates' waiting to the reactions, which I spared his embarrassment by a tongue lashing.

"Or what?" He leaned into me, literally snarling his countenance above my slight stature, as if his size was going to scare me. I might as well be dead, since I wouldn't miss anyone that amped up with a touch of attitude. Another CO would just let the inmates make the first blows for the emergency responses instead, but why would I back down? I'd been hit long enough, conditioned getting right back up for more.

"Or what nothing," I said as if he was being silly, trying to play it down to the level it deserved. "You know better than that." I shook him off and I continued to down, deeper into the run with my back, as I hoped he'd agree with me.

He could've crawled up behind me, threatening to the corner against the back wall with no escape, but he didn't. I left him behind to process. Any other options were always available to handle it differently, while I had thirty to fifty other men focused on the rest of the room. Inmate Hollman knew that he was in the wrong, but the general population might've flared up in a temper tantrum, where I'd removed myself without a second thought on the outside. I detached, unplugged, where I deescalating the dispute in the prison runs. It was an act of respect that also reminded who's the CO, while it empowered his choice to behave.

By the time I passed his bunk on the way out, his tape player was turned off, but no body had to know how hard my heart pounded. I sat through a slow exhale at my service log, recording the time of my walk, and nothing else. I conducted high alert for the potential confrontations, but how bad could've been that bad, before? I took a few moments to reduce my stress level, reentering later, while I prayed throughout the day.

DOC stayed 'on call' for the support of the department as I stocked up any other response from riding too suspicious about some other ulterior motives. Some inmates came up and tried to tease a warm shoulder, concern, or flattery with a fraternizing invitation to join in some company. But my loner status had become obvious to the inmates, turned down easily, when I didn't care to mingle.

Sometime COs tied up the phones to embrace their company throughout the shift that carried on, as if the inmates were deaf to the world, while I kept it to myself. I didn't need to spill the chance of being overheard. I kept enough distance from anything exposed beyond the issues on the job, while CO friendships spread through both sides. They'd talk, giving away their personal details, like a local parade merely sat down to enjoy the prison's spectating ticket… which was out of my control. I kept an open ear and eye, while I stayed totally content with His thoughts.

Misused talk only needed a suggestion when the rumors took a change to pull me involved regardless. My lack of interest in their sexual overtures opened the questions that exploded. Sometimes it felt like the inmates would tag-team with one over another that bombarded me of so many ways, before they would bait me with their problems, and then ask me what I would've done for them. Cute, clever, but silly, going away empty handed. Those who tried, gave it up long after their enthusiasm let it stay at bay.

The longer I worked, the easier I could handle the inmates, until my sergeant sniffed out his nightly rounds, and saying "no" wasn't so easy turned down so quietly. Who was I going to call? Who would even believe me? Except for the night Sgt. Chavez entered my control room for my service log to be signed off, who also checked out how good I smelled.

"No, I don't, unless my you're talking about my deodorant," I mused, slithering away as if I offered him my space at the writing counter, to get the message.

"You know, I was really excited to hear about your transfer to work here." He advanced towards me, when I transferred back in the grave shift. He was my regular supervisor when I stepped back, further defining my personal space about anybody including the inmates, where the supervisor was well-trained to know body language that wasn't hardly subtle. The only exit I had for the control room, where he pinned me against the wall with his fat girth who fully pressed against me in full view. The inmates could've seen how easily he'd squatted down who gripped the back of my thighs... for the world to see among the SOs. I fell off balance and forward into his arms. With just one quick movement, I found myself wrapped around his neck like a rag doll, who carried me into the bathroom no bigger than a broom closet.

"Put me down, what's wrong with you?" I fought him off as he chuckled, but I wasn't hardly alone... or quiet! He thought it was funny, lowered onto the sink, as I tried to wiggle away from him. But that was my ranking Shift Commander?

"Didn't you ever wonder why the grout is always broken away from the wall?" He continued, as if having sex on the bathroom sinks was commonplace.

I wasn't the whistleblower. I could've said something, but the inmates reported it the following day. I didn't finger out his improper and unprofessional act, but sexual harassment's investigation weighed in with yet another CO, who reassigned their 'manager' to another unit.

I'd been warned and never forget and 'never tell'! But I created enough about the self-defense moves that included my mouth. I woke them up who knew better than Sgt. Chavez who was so brazen to keep it to himself behind closed doors in prison, and the inmates didn't keep it a secret who didn't turn their backs. There was that fine line always dismissed to deny anything, except when that blur caused confusion. I'd been used as the underdog in compliance between the right and the wrongs before. *Speak up, judge righteously and defend the cause of the oppressed and needy* (Pro 31:9) and secrets by itself compromised it to continue... where the inmates stepped up to break the chain.

My confidence grew. I redeveloping trust through His shield, since I was wide open and vulnerable, embedded to live its depression and anxiety. *When I kept silent, my bones became brittle from my groaning all day long. For day and night Your hand was heavy on me; my strength was drained as in the summer heat. Then, I acknowledge my sin to You, and took away the guilt of my sin* (Psalms 32:2,5-8,9); *The one who conceals his sins will not prosper* (Pro 28:13).

Then, 'The fear of the Lord' didn't scare me, when I wondered about His disappointment in me. *Don't you know that friendship with the world is hostility toward God?* (James 4:4). There was a connection, as if I was always there, bonded with Him... like a good girl, until bravery really needed its prayers for strength and protection. *Pray constantly* (1Thess 5:16). And, every day I asked Him to guide me with every encounter. *So that God may be all in all* (1 Cor 15:28).

I buckled down, pumping out the double shifts, as if I uplifted my co-workers that spilled the sense of pride, like another wave of doubles always wanted. It was well deserved to be the generous daddies of the families, and then once again was asked: "What do you want?" My eyes bugged out! I didn't expect to actually hear that question... which was directed at me from across the briefing room.

It was that one thing that couldn't be ignored. His subtle messages in the privacy of my mind had been vocalized by my co-workers... to get through to me. I swirled around by a few officers standing at the door in the back of the briefing room, who waited, stopped and intently focused for an answer! I was accustomed to sat by myself, who've were overhear of any number of conversations going on within earshot, when my God wouldn't take "no" for an answer. I sheepishly got up, thinking something up to join them.

Jacob wrestled with the angel of God, and God was impressed. But was God impressed with me? Could I possibly be a loser in the eyes of so many love ones, with a pleasant thing in the eyes of my Lord at the same time? I truly did wrestle, fighting with God to withhold my answer? Was my resistance the same thing? I just couldn't answer Him. I refused to be like the Pharisees, who'd needed a sign. Wouldn't that say mean that I didn't trust Him? But I had to start over so many times before, and I was getting tired. What was I fighting for? And, what did I want?

"Don't tell me: 'nothing'. Nobody works that hard without a plan." CO Kirtdouglas spoke a little louder and the rest of the people in the briefing room stopped to look up, as I walked across the room with a smirk on my face thinking, "No one will believe me." I hung my head a bit, wondering what could to say? I didn't have an answer. I didn't have a clue. I was just taking advantage of the overtime so that I wouldn't regret it later.

"Come on, Pruitt. It's not like you're going to live in that shithole (my apartment) for the rest of your life!" It was alright who'd been able to tease me, living nearby in town of work when a prison town had nothing else goes on, or another feeble excuse by driving less saved its money.

"Yeah, what's up with that, Pruitt?" Suddenly the whole room wanted my answer. "Are you saving up for a down payment on a home?" Although my personal business was carried close to my chest, my nomadic existence couldn't go unnoticed.

"Well, if I'd ever buy a house, I'd have one that could be built just for me." I blurted out without thinking.

I restored too many houses. I purchase one run-downed house for another home to be resold on a nice profit to get ahead. Those were the days when I'd mixed enough cement to restore from the bottom of the foundation, remodeling floor plan hanging its drywall sheets, or caulked the glass panes back into the broken windows, like it never happened with each turnover.

"If I'm going to own a house again, I want it to be the first one living in it, before anyone else's hand-me-downs." I must have had an incredible imagination that made everyone laugh. "Really! When I retire, I want to live out life to stay in the best years of my home." I continued whether anyone was listening anymore, when we all took a seat with our supervisor's wave inside.

"I could see myself in the mountains," I thought to myself as I walked all the way across left field, toward my post. The inmates were locked down for the day, who would miss the full moon, trading a soft steel blue glow with the final show of the starlit skies above its great wide expanse... from the prison.

When I was a kid, I could spend the day, squatting in the muck of the little creek at the farm. The cool waters passed over my bare feet, when I wandered along the swimming critters of my secret place that extended underneath the railroad arches on time for the trains. The babbling waters seemed like it was the only thing I could hear, drowning out the sounds tripped over the river stones, which flickered through the wood's canopy above. That's when I'd stare, conjoining the tiny other creatures as if we were one. Nature became my personal world into my peaceful place, when taking it one step further was no reason not to.

I tried to imagine beyond the world in the mountains, like I was invisible in sync there too. And, I wondered whether I could belong into the serenity of life in the mountains, instead.

I learned how to think by a biofeedback technique, imagining that managed against the typical systemic disruption against my health. It deliberately transported mind over matter with another option. It tolerated against the immediate risks that avoided any (unnatural) chemicals or drugs without general anesthesia, well trained to finish my inguinal hernia repair. The room, assistance, and all necessary equipment was completely overseeing every step, when the stats were alerted that interrupted surgery. The concerns grew urgent, when the medical team raised the red flag. My surgeon couldn't trust or believe the decision, who was about to put me under.

"How did you do that?" They gave me one more chance, after I stole away to a wonderful place spiritually, while I left the work of my doctor to continue.

"I took a ride over a full harvest, and I used every sense in a full bloom meadow with the breeze waving over the fields for as long as needed." I tried to explain my safe place from any hint of concerns, which reduced my heartrate and blood pressure for the medical procedure with a nod from disturbing me.

But even that was not so unusual by every other inmate who also detached, lost in a good book. That level of concentration zoned out, to escape and survive it through another day. Either way, I found great pleasure to be left alone, just like the inmates stole away around the commotion as necessary, where they were allowed enough time… to continue.

With nothing more than the back side of scratch paper, pencil, eraser and a six-inch scale when I started to sketch its floor plan, imagining what I'd want with my well-earned savings' reward. I gazed about the life in the mountains that I pictured my home, which expanded into its fresh produce, putting up preserves beyond an earth cellar, pantry, or the entire kitchen wall of shelves behind a sliding barn door, and for just a moment it was all mine. I could use my own carpentering tools, where I'd store a corner booth table in the kitchen for the seasonal supplies underneath, but a garage work bench could've created an endless of wood working projects, forever throughout retirement!

The farmhouse décor included a fine-tuned three-ring binder for my magazine snips specifically collected into more ideas. Possibilitizing (my own created word) offered some new innovative ideas, as if a time-card on the job would make retirement boring, planning a more kindly lifestyle aging, but the hands-on skills over the years seemed so right to reopen the doors still left available for another time.

Nothing stressed the idea living in the mountains, as if there was no sense of right or wrong to enjoy the freedom with no one judging me. In my mind anything was possible. "Oh God! I am so thankful!" I whispered as I began to realize how many gifts flowed through my mind with ease. "I could really do this!"

I thought about senior-friend sports like horse-shoes and a shuffleboard behind the house. A social spot under the pergola could be outgrown into a mister and fan, after the spigot could reroute the sun-controlled ceiling mesh under the fresh vegetables sprout at table height. Its scraps could turn into organic soil underneath its staging compose, where the community would also swap out foods and ideas at the local flea market.

Although it felt good to wonder, I had nothing to show for it. Years passed since I still wore the same clothes, wore from the same resale stores, and the same uniforms. I kept up my old car, where I still lived in the same apartment, taking great pleasure watching my credit score rise. I'd become quite content for the answer that felt more like a break or spiritual vacation.

Until the day I literally took off, I went out and drove around to explore the small mining towns in the mountains to consider the cost of its land. How much was it worth? I googled townships and their populations, altitude, mean income, and crime statistics before the main street felt more like the days in Mayberry with the one lone police car roaming the streets. Sidewalks filled the children running home from their schools, and other towns looked more like ghost towns with the elderly poor barely holding on… one 'weekend' at a time.

I dreamed, careful to avoid anyone else's opinion, as if I wouldn't allow my secret 'burst my bubble', except I spilled over into some cordial chit chat. I thought it was safe, but I'd been overheard among the loved ones. I got a bit too friendly where shared about a twenty-acre parcel during my son's wedding reception. It should've been nothing more than a kindly social spot, when a brief moment was enough to run with it. I let my guard down. It shouldn't have affected anyone else, who fed off my ideas... to destroyed the dream.

There, across the room and between the dance floor was my family singing the theme song to The Beverly Hillbilly's sitcom, stomping around as if they were clumsily balancing around with the shotguns over their shoulders, mocking me during a mountaineer lifestyle, who acted it out like a comic strip. My secret took off like wildfire that swept across the reception room within moments.

I was dressed so elegant in the mother-of-the groom style, graciously introducing myself to the attending guests. Friends and associates of my son's in-laws reached out to greet them, as I fought back the tears of embarrassment from the jeers before I completed the circle, back at my side of the family.

I tried to detach, acting like nothing was wrong. I continued to cover my way around the ballroom, as if the tables had been laid claim around my mother and sisters, but their antics ended abruptly, knowing just how long I'd grow near which spread quickly without a word to say. It should've been a blast to celebrate at a festive wedding, but they were characteristically unkind, when I was inexcusably shameful all across the room.

Nothing would change, except my intolerance. It could've been differently. I behaved, invited to be part of some playful social time, but I was publicly humiliated. They robbed my joy, which should've been focused on my son's wedding day.

But why would anyone need to do that? By what I'd heard about the most honest: "as you would have them do onto you", did not apply my family, who set against their typical protocols with another set of policies. The more incensed I got, the more brazen they became. It didn't matter that I wouldn't and couldn't do that to anyone, including the inmates in prison where I got a far cry more than their respect. By the time the band played the last dance, my family was gone ahead of me, and I went home alone.

"Abba?" I called out to the one constant in my life. "Abba? Can you help me?" I fell to my knees (spiritually speaking). Humbled. I reached out to Him with my eyes welled, finally able to let go of all the pain I saved for my drive home. I felt stripped naked, violated, and impossibly reversible mark against me. "I am so sorry, God!" I was misused with the intent to hurt me, but He had already seen it. Was I supposed to keep from anything said?

"I want to live in the mountains," I began, sorry for shutting Him out, when He'd asked what I wanted from the beginning, but I'd been more afraid of their ridicule, afraid of being stolen away or left destroyed, or rejected of what I had, which didn't belong to them anyways.

"I want to create a peaceful place to retire in." I had only a dream, which should've been my wildest desires. "I want to live out my life as a blessing to You (who should've been happy in my lives… and didn't)." I finally broke down, bawling uncontrollably. I felt like I'd just been kicked in the chest, more than the rug pulled out from under. I was meant to get that final blow, struck right to my heart, for a wake-up call to get it real.

"I am not someone who needs much, just a place of my own, where I can be free to love life," I continued in prayer. Who'd ever cared to compete with the Jones's or own the latest styles of the times? I wasn't in competition, regardless anyone else raise above or measure up anything less… to strive for more?

"It's just that I gave everything away." I brought back to tears, realizing the consequences by another. "But God, I'm not sorry for that." There was no fooling God. "I would do it all over again if I had to, because I'm not sure where I went wrong," I admitted. Was I generous, forfeited to their desires to make them happy, borrowed and never returned, destroyed, or something taken from me? Either way, I'd recover. I pacified their needs ahead of me, but not like that. Generosity backfired! "But I don't want to live destitute for the rest of my life for it." I let my tears run down my face all the way home, all over again. "Abba, if it is your will, please help me. In Jesus' name I pray."

I collapsed shortly after I made it home. My rescue pet purred on my lap, until I fell asleep in my recliner and finally crawled into bed. It took a lot of energy that drained me out through the tears, and slept through the following day. When I awoke, I checked my phone. There were no messages, and I knew that nobody was going to call me. I checked the rosters' schedule about a few more days left off, but the family reunions among the travelers for the wedding was over.

"Sir, it's Officer Pruitt." I called into the complex's shift commander. "I'm from graves and I'm calling to see if I could cut my vacation short and come in to work today." I asked to be filled in. I had less stress going to work than the rest of the vacation time off, which was already blocked off that was wasting my time with family.

"What the hell, Pruitt?" I was greeted in the lobby on my way in to work.

"Yeah, yeah, yeah." My hand went up, asking them to drop it, with enough who understood.

I'd had my eyes opened, since I could no longer live in denial. Of what happened at the wedding reception during the finest pinnacle of the moment didn't trigger in laughter, who laughed at me. That impulsive gland interjected a healthy jolt... when the joke's on me.

CHAPTER 17

Just a Little Longer

The academy explained the most simplistic terms in plain English, which made it the greatest impression about a simple story a long time ago, as if there was something important. So, I listened to pay attention:

In just a moment I pictured a father and son. One was fully grown, tall and strong, but I knew he was the father who walked hand in hand. The little boy wasn't paired up equally, where one looked up and the other looked down upon his son, but I knew how delightfully content they continued along. The morning routine began fresh every day, growing together who talked about any situation, no matter how simple or difficult were satisfied.

I didn't worry about its finer details, which reminded me, seeing the similarities that might as well had been another parable in the Bible, as if He'd taken my hand. I welcomed His response, "Come". He had something for me, as if He never left me (from his hand or) out of sight.

There was a bird landed onto the uppermost branch on the top of a tree, and I looked up at the same thing. The branch was too thin, hardly capable to withstanding the weight of the bird as it bent lowly, bouncing up and down. But that bird was huge! That bird didn't belong! It must've been in trouble, which was hung on so tightly, until it flew off.

I didn't picture it, I saw it! The day couldn't have been more routine to the grocery store, where the bird perched on the top most high twig in the tree. I felt the stress. The little fella transferred his fear of the bird in peril, when I realized the pull, anxiously calling on his daddy, and I understood. I could've expected my Father's situations to rescue one of God's creatures; except He had something to show me. He wanted me to be still and patiently watch, Who didn't want me to intervene.

I took in with a deep breath, as if God lowered down on one knee at my level, reassured to pay attention. I knew the story, as if I wouldn't fret to see how the same bird saw about the strength of the twig or the confidence to fly off that would never fall to the ground… in God's perfect timing, talking to me.

Two days couldn't hardly have enough time to fully recuperate, as if I'd put in the workweek behind me, for the next weekend. But if there was one thing I missed, God wanted something and He didn't let up. The story missed the whole story about the little boy and his father that did not quite sink in, and the following weekend came in a dream. I relaxed under the gentle breeze by the floor fan at the foot of my bed:

A fantastic array of the most vibrant colored flood lights aimed right at me. It felt like I was the center of attention, unchallenged and deserving, and it was wonderful!

I twisted and turned around in bed, but I couldn't avoid the admiring the lights of every direction. I enjoyed the view, like it was the greatest fireworks during the show, except the lights began, as if my eyes adjusted to notice how their shapes changed as curiosity grew. Some of the lights were defined by the elongated on geometric shapes into its crisp points, as if it swelled and adjoined together, perfectly choreographing into a gorgeous design before me.

In my mind I tried to tap against a stained-glass window, but the illuminated collage wasn't hardened which flowed like liquid cloth. I giggled, knowing how awesome a quilt must've waved in the wind on a clothes line, as emotions grew more intense.

I was easily entertained, as I simply sat back to enjoy. Of all my apprehensions or concerns were securely wrapped into my warm and cozy blankets in the dream. I was free to stretch or roll around, unlike that nightmare with that spec of light like anything before. The past gaslighting fear was gone, when the night arrived with the present, since I took on another day. And then, a wisp of air seemed like it puffed at my face. I jumped up in bed that carried the dream when I awoke, and I took flight!

I sat straight up in bed which was still fresh in my mind, where I was rejuvenated and ready to take on the world, but it wasn't merely a nice dream. It might've taken years in the cocoon, when the transformation was done, as if no walls could contain me anymore. It was time to rise, and fly!

Like the inmates who had to wait out the last night before their release date, I was ready to be released as well. Rehabilitation in prison was real. It happened to set me free, where I was ready to spend the remaining sentence, to finish my work.

The night shift was just a small reprieve, like a pliable limb, where I'd regroup. I regained my bearings that I'd already covered, where I wasn't afraid to explore the uncovered territory to spread my wings. It was time to exercise my belief system. I was satisfied, since I surpassed the tests through my principles, which I defend of what I knew to be true among a sea of men, or anyone else who didn't have to agree.

"Is there a specific form for a shift change?" I knew that I had to ask for it. The other forms were readily available that withheld anything dangling its 'carrot' who might leave. I waited for the printer warming up, as Sgt. Murry fumbled through the right key down the hall.

"We're going to miss you," Sgt. Murray said, knowing when the time was up as each officer systematically slipped away. "Is there a problem?"

"No, No! I'm fine." I had no good excuse to explain. "I just think I'm ready to deal with the inmates while they're awake." I added with a slight nod of the head for the day time shifts.

"I think so, too." He slowed finished with that final key, exaggerating to hit 'enter' on the (archaic) computer keyboard with a satisfying grant to pass forward. "You can pick it up." He said with that hawk-eye look, telling me to return his key set right away.

The approved transfer didn't take too long, since I'd bounced around to absorb the extra shifts accommodating the orders, until it was my turn to put in 0600 to 1400 hour shift to stay. Temporarily worked to fill in every ounce of energy, as if I jumped with each order as needed, when I wanted to settle in with the team. DOC monitored it toward exhaustion, limiting just one or two double shifts each week, since it felt more like glutton of punishment who showed up without any training.

I was introduced through orientation week with the team, where I walked around the yard of soccer, soft-ball, volleyball and basketball games in full swing during the day, since I realized where I'd tread softly to avoid the inmates' during recreation time. But I smirked to myself, graciously bowed its wide berth, as if the stakes were much higher in a house full of women, tiptoeing through a PMS alert. "No wonder daddy spent so much time in the garage!" I commiserated the moment, but I'd be rich for every dime I heard: "I meant to do that", when I knew it was impossible to take anything back, or when the daggers embedded the fear of god glare... forever.

The atmosphere inside of the open yard was a lot like the last day of school had the weekend. Whatever the courses, programs, job duties, appointments, or scheduled for inmates were also wrapped up of the second shift of officers, and all Saturday and Sundays.

The shutter gate rolled down, including the sport equipment at the window, who dispensed all sorts of the supplies in line of inmates, awaiting their turn on either side of the yards. I did was watch, but I couldn't hardly catch it all. But play time ran off their energy, where I'd accept the post through recess, albeit full of criminals. The inmates of all ages were considered to be dependents of the state at that level of culpability, where I was held responsible with the end results.

A flooded a sea of orange sparkled in the sunshine over my chest, which it drew attention for all to see, as if I ever needed God's protection more than ever. My communication skills were weak, and my confidence gave away the recited redirectives to the inmates, which choked it up in my throat. I faced a far cry from the innocent youngsters, as if I had to learn it quick, exercising my authority over any of them, regardless.

Back in the day, where the elementary school allowed the parking lot, which was well defined for the children. The school staff borrowed out the volunteers' rules clearly left the far corner of the blacktop pavement within a chain linking fence for the children to play, and they'd have time outside after lunches. However, a rogue ball that happened to roll into the road from time to time, when detention also expired an adult's patience, too tired, or distracted from the responsibility for a while.

Either way, I couldn't ignore the COs and inmates who complied… for the most part. Money wasn't the issue on the job, and nobody challenged the parent in a fine and kindly finesse, while I kept a few mental notes on the inmates among the commotion, where I felt defensive among the savvy manipulation in prison, as if I was fresh meat.

It seemed awkward and even petty to tell a young man to get a shirt on, before leaving the bunk area to be dressed in the runs before he'd play darts in the dayroom. It was also a little ridiculous, when I had to turn an inmate right around in his boxers headed out the laundry room, as if those little infractions were hardly worth writing a ticket about, which started small.

On the first day's shift in lockdowns during my probation, they tested to see of what they could've fooled it out of me. They acted out to see how crazy I'd get about their overt defiance, but whatever I said or did, was witnessed by all.

Then, the questions followed: Why? How come? What if? Don't you think …? Challenges were conveniently set up when the next inmate was timed to pick my brain, as if that could wear me down. Any attempt could've cut it some slack, excusing it into compliance, but it was all too familiar. I understood how the victim pattern was impossible to backpaddle, brainwashed, as if they'd love me!

The constant barrage bombarded the invitation, "Come on!" of the terrible twos or the high-spirited teens and on, except I was ready to face the swarming inmates ready to pounce (by the tigers over my shoulders). I had to be redefining, adjusting at every turn, but the inmates were that quick. Before I even opened my mouth, every approach got my body language spoke first.

The team from the basketball court or self-righteous zealots also played me, who were impossible to prove one against the other, which cancelled it out like a truce, which was never their blame. Any side in a simple game of poker accumulated the debts, when the games were no longer a fight in survival. Thinking it would just forgive and forget, knowing that the risks were bound to face the results.

I had to keep it simply spelled out. I made the decision for the inmates, when I wield the boundaries accordingly. Especially, when the inmates didn't like the officers too rigid. I was suckered in a power play, who tag-teamed albeit one at a time. I'd been pressured until I'd break, which I slipped that tainted my reputation, but that would be reminded and never forgiven. Any insignificant lapse got more clever, but any deviant in prison worked on either side of the walls just the same. The most rudimental piece of truth came to terms, when I'd reassess each nitpicking call, who'd love to strip away any sense of power, as if was especially threatened by a woman... except me.

Like the woman in the Bible, when her mere pittance sacrificed at the altar. In her poverty she gave it all she had, as if I jumped in with both feet. And in comparison, the wealthy man donated lavishly out of his abundance, who relatively assumed more to show off. *"They devour widows' houses and say long prayers for show. These will receive harsher punishment"* (Mark 12:40), when I realized how God's prayers were done for man.

The inmates wore in orange with the exception of their white socks and underwear. And to be honest, it was hard to distinguish one inmate from the other, but tattoos individuality spread beyond the underground industry. Skin art was highly discouraged, but its distinction spread wild in prison. They flourished it like a crazy fad, knowing some things should've been prevented.

Initially, tattoos determined to advertise a mark of allegiance or an accomplishment, but that quickly changed as they covered every inch of their bodies with black ink. Their body language wore a flesh billboard with those specific signs, which snuck a massage in between its camouflage. "What kind of job would I get with a criminal background looking like that anyways?" was a common response. But art was enough of an excuse, when I confiscated their contrabands to limit its equipment, as if I knew that it was only a setback and it started all over again. I couldn't stop them, but it was hard to argue against the controversial tattoo, since my bald head covered the original rose bud, where I dawned it in full bloom.

Anything stood out, who realize that I was no differently. The inmates were bound to studied each other, but I knew their admiring artwork, but I came out. It made the general public too afraid or unable to accept it so oddly, until I went bald in the general public, too. In a lot of ways, it created space for that brave one. They couldn't know but they'd try, who looked up in a smile. I won over the winner that broke the ice! Either way, I set things straight on both sides of the wall, making light talk as if I was the lucky one who never had a bad hair day.

It didn't matter after a while, as if it was nothing at all, except where I kept the watch on the inmates. Once they relaxed to get used to me, my presence inadvertently added its pressure on the inmates who couldn't ignore me. I was unique, all in the same uniforms, except a tattooed, bald headed, and female CO... of the 'the eagle watch'.

They'd reconsider my presence of the plans, wagering or trade among each other. They'd debate, deciphering anything valuable at all, or not at all. It didn't matter to me. The inmates always had another day, and opportunities could wait. Except I didn't give them the opportunity, and let them wonder. I kept my thoughts to myself, well-conditioned before prison.

I was well aware of the underhanded jealousies that was irrelevant at work. They wore orange, I wore brown, period. Whatever I owned or whatever they were limited to was hardly materialistic possessions anymore. The things that stood out was the character that leveled the playing field, checking each other out and even tested the wits, but we were all nervous, skeptical, and finally earning that sense of respect across the board.

So, when I walked into their territory, their home, their space, or anywhere else knew their place, they just needed to know where I stood, and visa/versa:

"Why did you let all those guys go without a ticket but you put my bunkie on report for doing the same thing?" Inmate Austin was indignant, quick to soapbox the spiel.

"What are you talking about?" I learned to understand by asking questions first, which also bought me some time to collect my thoughts.

A shared bunk bed only had one inmate, who's bunkie was missing 'out of place' during formal count. I made the ticket to make it stick, which I meant LOP punishment. All of the inmates stood between their bunks, which were readily recognize to confirm each one. It was expected. It was no surprise by every formal count again and again. They should've cooperated with every time crunch, and all of their sheets were always needed to be finished state-wide within the hour, but I didn't waste the whole hour somewhere within the time I'd start out. Formal counts had been prepared. All of the worksheets were passed down, and handed back out on time, as ordered, but nobody wanted to hear about an unaccounted excuse.

"All those guys delayed formal count and I got a ticket. Explain that!" Inmate Austin stood perfectly still, when I checked off each mark that time forward. He was exactly where I saw him in formal count, since I didn't have a problem, but he stewed. I had the next time where I recorded Inmates Austin and Washington at the double bunks. Each inmate was jotted down, accounted, and clearly handed in, except when he was clearly missing! We had to see and confirm each person all the time, all together as usual. And, there was nothing retroactive, which was appropriate, and it fit.

"That was a different situation." I backpedaled to remember who couldn't finish his shower which was a few weeks ago, when another inmate got the slight and verbal 'slap on the wrist', instead.

"How's that any different? They interrupted formal count and you just stood there and waited for everyone to take their places." Inmate Austin voice just got all the louder as the entire run went silent. The inmates gasped. They watched how I'd respond, who remained perfectly still for the count.

He failed to realize was how many times I'd announce: "stand by for count", making sure everyone heard it. I usually allowed about a full minute to take their places, as if it my grace period allow that far, who blatantly didn't care. I heard that the water was left on, who must've let it continue running. I didn't look inside the shower stall, since I urged him along to hurry up, but it was nothing like a delay. He had no intention to cut his shower short. He wanted to take all the time he wanted, who intentionally missed to show up for count.

"If you think I did something wrong, write me up. I'll be more than happy to print out my name and badge number down for you, and then you can have my sergeant explain it to me. Otherwise, we can take this up later, because right now you're interrupting count." I reiterated another challenge, disregarding the moment during count.

"So, you're putting me on report?" Inmate Austin was agitated, as if he thought I had him take up the issue right there and then, giving it the importance what he thought it deserved, instead. He wanted to take advantage of a perfect setting for a grandstanding stance during the captive audience.

"No, I didn't put you on report. I'm trying to tell you that I need to finish count and that I'm willing to pick this up later because I have to move along." I was curt and insensitive to his implications, and the entire run watched out of harm's way. Inmate Austin rallied the others, but they refused to be uninvolved, like if he'd gang up and puff up the verbally 'muscle' on the edge, who further pressed my apology to expunged his undue claim, and then, he glared to wait for my turn.

There was nothing worse than an unwinnable trap, to hand it over to my supervisor to take up the challenge. I called in my count into the officer working in the Receiving Department, and then, I called my sergeant.

"Hey Sergeant Morris, it's Pruitt. Are you the shift commander? I have a situation and I can take it up with Sgt. Malone if you're too busy." One or the other supervisor was always classified as the shift commander, but it was never too clear as to which one wore which hat.

"Well I am but go ahead, I'm good. What's going on?"

"About a month ago I put Inmate Austin on report, who was 'out of place' during formal count. He was in the shower and even though a few inmates told him to hurry up, I waited about five

331

minutes before starting my count, and he did not finish his shower, until I was already done. Today I called "stand by for count" like always. Some days everyone takes it longer than others. I waited to know when an inmate was finished at the urinal or another one ran through with his towel, before I hollered the final announcement in place. Except this time, Inmate Austin stopped me at his bunk to argue during count, as if I didn't treat them all alike."

"Is he black?" Sgt. Malone asked his race right away. Either way, he baited me along the inmates to witness any potential racial bias. There was none, nor was there going to be any other blame throughout the many ancestors of the world, where originating any roots of his color didn't matter to me. Every double bunk matched up the same races housed down the runs. Inmate Austin and Washington were paired up.

"Yes, sir." I answered his question when I went right back to continue about Inmate Austin, trying to instigate trouble. "I told him that I would talk to him later, but he's still mad. The situations' not the same, but discussing it in the middle of count was not the right time or place, and I told him that." My supervisor was on the same page with me. The issue was not an issue to be taken up during count, but the issue still remained.

"Okay, I'll come down there." Sgt. Morris already knew that he'd be right up. That was not something I'd run up very often at all. I thought I'd take care of just about anything I'd manage well enough on my own, as if I'd surely take it all on my own, and away from the typical whiner. I always had a hard time, and some-things were too big for me. I could've. I just didn't want to open it all up again, when a supervisor's fall back was there for my support, instead.

I wasn't worried about my supervisors, but I still fought the old phrases beaten down. I still felt incompetent to be looked down upon me, but I was wrong. I leaned on my supervisor, as if he waited, glad to take it off my hands who would be there to help me.

I'd reached out to where I wasn't afraid to admit my weaknesses, when I realized that wasn't my fault. In fact, the results were going to be anxious, and for once, made life easier. sooner! I got the help and how I could deal, as if the neglect, rejection, and jealousy was the exact opposite of the family.

No sooner when I happened to meet the neighboring buildings passing along the mail bags, but neither Inmate Austin nor Washington turned to look at me with supervisors, trying to assess the situation for its unbiased presence, aside. *Finally, brothers and sisters, whatever is true, whatever is noble, whatever is right, whatever is pure, whatever is lovely, whatever is admirable. If anything is excellent or praiseworthy, think about such things* (Phil 4:8). That didn't mean I didn't sweat it. I did. Even doing everything right could've been turned out badly with their underhanded attempts to discredit me.

And then, on my next security check, Inmate Clark, an older black inmate, smiled back at me and said, "Don't worry. You're a good person." That helped, but it also brought up a few more questions.

We all lived through the generation of all peoples. Desegregation intended all man treated equally, which mandated DOC through the changes on the laws that rippled all down the line, just like if all people had to struggle through for a better place in the world.

My family roots arrived illegally. The family hid out to prove himself more than the country after the wars. Prussia lived under the thumb of every kingship, regardless where that country no longer existed. Governments accepted any specific birthrights that should've put an end to it, which clashed traditions. The Polish comments bashed them down by their nasty blows who bit their tongues. They kept their nose down who were a strong-bone built and honest people who did what they knew, stigmatized the lower and poor farming integrity.

National origins couldn't stop laughing through the worse insensitive jokes, which shot out any off-color comments, including blue eyed 'toe-heads' with every blond joke, too. We'd hoped, and sometimes we just had to hang our heads, which should've been a relief against the bullying laws, but resentments hid behind a snicker or two.

Change vacillated who mutated it back and forward, who cut it some slack to adjust the law, which also protected it under the 'don't tell' rule. It worked and together it was allowed closed doors, until I signed up to manage the plethora convictions housed all together in prison.

Then Jesus began by telling them: "Watch out that no one deceives you. Many will come in My name, saying, 'I am He' and they will deceive many. When you hear of wars and rumors of wars, don't be alarmed; these things must take place, but the end is not yet. But you, be on your guard! (Mark 13:5,9).

No retroactive laws got a pass that drew the line for a new starting point forward, as if prior crimes didn't count. At least the laws were written down to stop their behaviors, when common sense fell back and resurface, as if nothing happened before.

Inmate Clark experienced in direct contrary between before and after, as if the boxes were always expected to check their races, but the bunks were arranged to pair up, nonetheless. He struggled to fight for the same aspirations, who watched the upcoming generation still slipping back of what they knew. *For I will take you from the nations and gather you from all the countries. I will give you a new heart and put a new spirit within you; I will remove your heart of stone* (Ezekiel 36:24,26).

Altering behavior wasn't that easily to accomplish. *God, create a clean heart for me and renew a steadfast spirit within me. Then I will teach the rebellious Your ways* (Psalm 51:10,13), when I was no longer ashamed to ask the supervisor's help, reaching out to crave peace. *"Lord, how many times could any brother sin against me and forgive him?" Then the master of that slave had compassion, released him, and forgave his loan* (Matt 18:21,26).

The fear of an inmate's policy breach, resolved my Lord's strength and shield on the job. *So it is a sin for the person who knows to do what is good and doesn't do it. The righteous man; he does not resist you* (James 4:17, 5:6).

Day shift offered the time when I unpeeled away the nonsense aside. The cluttering games were easily there too many times, too old to carry the load. It had enough to manage my responsibility, while I guided anyone else's ability, too. I was misused to be the victim, who preferred to keep me back home. But they were mad, when it wasn't my job to fix the problem... on either side of the prisons. *Fear them who are able to destroy your flesh and soul* (Matt 12:28). Sin was sin, no matter how many times remained the same results.

Just as I also try to please all people in all things, not seeking my own profit, but the profit of many. As I also imitate Christ (1Cor 10:33 11:1). *For you were called to this, because Christ also suffered for you, leaving you an example, so that you should follow in His steps. He did not revile in return; when His suffering, He did not threaten, but entrusted Himself* (1Pet 2:21,23).

Stopping abuse during DOC policies were one step closer to relate the Bible, like if it put another way I could read the same things about fear, panic, or threating force, where it all fell in place. *But, perceiving their malice, Jesus said, "Why are you testing Me, hypocrites?* (Matt22:18). My loved ones caused every ounce of stress that I withstood against anything who accused me to be the coward. *Now when, you sin like this against the brothers and wound their weak conscience, you were sinned against Christ* (1Cor 8:12), but their insults were also against my Lord!

The prison sentences held the inmates according to every risk level, as if I'd move down the lockdowns with every graduation day, right out of the academy, where I took the greatest risk level at the bottom. I would never have asked for that assignment to jump through the hoops of probation. It was an all-or-nothing career before any other transfers, but one step at a time, and I was no longer alone to process them all through imprisonment, too.

What if I faced the jury of my peers, except they turned around who made them panic? What if I'd tell? What if I was tricked, and I wasn't the guilty one? What if I walked in to face them all together? And what if my abusers were too ashamed, who never looked back... as if I was always held down (under the thumb or within the walls), when I no longer needed the chase: to run after my loved ones' affection that wasn't there. I was meant to be locked down. I was separated, as if I turned myself in, like an abrupt and violent tackle stopped me in the wrong direction. Did they know and I didn't?

I read the Bible. I had it written in my heart, *I will put My laws into their minds and write them on their hearts* (Heb 8:10), until it was time to apply the truth I knew. The Lord struck Saul, as if he'd been slammed to the ground in an abrupt stop, just like when I felt that demanding jolt that pulled me down by my throat in the Main Control, where I'd been held up in light duty hours... where I was safe inside the cocoon before I could fly.

Saul had been held back, so lost, severely vulnerable and afraid, who were helped by the most unlikely men. God's presence consumed Saul around His light. What changed him? What changed his mind, who never ran back to his army? *So they took him by the hand and lead him to Damascus* (Acts 9:8) for a different path. But, *heard from many people about this man, how much harm he had done* (Acts 9:13). Who could've listened? *He tried to associate with the disciples but they were afraid of him* (Acts 9:26). Were my loved ones afraid of the inmates... in reverse?

Inmates were fully aware exactly where they belonged, as if the sentences ended and cut free, who weren't innocent. Recidivism was going to allow the inmates to resume and continue their wrongdoing, or who fed into their wrongdoing to support it for themselves. But what changed, and what didn't change?

I watched how many congregated together or sparely roamed alone within the recreation yard. I connected when I purposely made eye contact form one to another. It was the good balance of the inmates spread around the yard including the housing units down each run, until something seemed off. *The day of your watchmen, the day of your punishment, is coming: at this time their panic is here* (Mc 7:4). I glued my eyes on an inmate, and I wouldn't look away. *Then my enemy will see, and she will be covered with shame* (Mc 7:10).

I called over an inmate, who grew too eager except he couldn't wiggle away. He didn't want to explain, but I couldn't miss it. He reacted as if I pestered him, who wanted to dismiss me, even forgiving and waving me off, which created it more curious. I wondered whether he was the culprit or mule, when the other inmates crowded around to put enough pressure on me to let it slid.

"What do you mean?" Inmate Hernandez picked an argument. His defiant attitude made a turn, as if I upset him. He accused me to be the issue, as if I was being blamed... 'rocking the boat'.

I finally had to stop him. "What's all that?" No one should've been in the wrong housing unit. Inmate Hernandez couldn't walk away, who broke up and disappeared instead of supporting him in the wrongdoing. They left him standing alone, loaded down with his arms full of the store goods.

"You're crazy, lady!" He tried to turn it right around, as if he had to preserve his delivery... of the contraband.

The State Prisons reorganized DOC by changing the ninety-day rotation of the staff, which was helpful to become more familiar with the same inmates in my care, who was easily spotted out of an inmate who didn't belong from another building.

"No one stops off this stuff around here." Inmate Hernandez was flustered, when he was afraid to face the disciplinary violation in front of me, as if I was made to believe that no other COs allowed business as usual.

"Look, it goes like this." I stepped outside my control room to stand toe to toe that didn't scare me away. His purchases were right in front of me during open recreation, to dismiss it like it was all right to excuse him, without a thought to ask or check it out. "Everybody speeds, but would you flip off the cop with the radar gun as you pass by?" I gave him that 'help me out here' look, when the dispersed crowd honed in to hear my example. "You know and I know that this goes on all of the time." I acknowledged the items to share the inmates' property, as if it could pay off the debts at the end of the month's slim pickings. It would've met a sweet snack with a promise to be reimbursed, as if their inventory could've been replenished later. "But what are you saying to me when you do it right in my face?"

I had to look to see inside his tube of toothpaste, which was unsealed inside the box. I couldn't trust it. A cell phone had been passed through the bag of chips that was smuggled into the kitchen deliveries. When favors, gifts, or sacrifices were blindly passed, weren't innocent by another intent for the hold? That debt was never meant to hurt the mule, who was easily forgiven, which was never meant to swindle out of the promises that never belonged.

I volunteered to help and monitor in elementary recess time, where I watched the recreation yard to protect the inmates, like before. The inmates played cards to pass the time, when the gamblers had to settle the score, who could've been paid off a mule's stipend, too. But there was always another opportunity, and some got better than others, until I described my examples that seemed to get the inmates listening with every scenario described through the stories that helped to understand.

Every day I drove where I prayed to the Father of His work. I prayed for His guidance and wisdom. I prayed for His power to endure His strength. And I prayed, when peace fulfilled every encounter of thanksgiving. In a nutshell, I prayed to be edified in His presence, where I'd been removed of the holds through me.

It just so happened that I was rereading the Book of John, one day. I must've read and reread it several times, and still, something always stood out to understand all the more. *If you belonged to the world, it would love you as its own. "As it is, you do not belong to the world, but I have chosen you out of the world. That is why the world hates you"* (John 15:19). *Everyone who does evil hates the light, and will not come into the light for fear that their deeds will be exposed* (John 3:20).

I gladly exposed what I knew, as if it all fit, including the rules of the prison. *So then let us pursue what makes for peace and for mutual upbuilding* (Rom 14:19). They will resist and expect it, but don't judge them. *He will repay each one according to his works, but wrath and indignation to those who are self-seeking and disobey the truth* (Rom 2:6,8). After that, leave it be. *"Vengeance belongs to Me, I will repay"* (Heb 10:30). While the passion of my career grew, I had to pass it along, unstoppable, for more.

CHAPTER 18

A step of Faith

I should've had the Book of John memorized, when I just couldn't get over Thomas' reaction with the news of Christ's visit with the rest of His disciples after His crucifixion. Thomas had to have been so wrought of grief. He could hardly think straight or even remember what Jesus said just days before He'd died the shock on the cross!

Why wasn't he happy to hear about Jesus' risen? They must've taken him by the shoulders to shake some sense into any one of them. They argued in that room, who'd attested to it! So, I had to put myself in his shoes and how I visualized Saint Thomas spinning out of control just days after the death of His beloved and closest friend!

I didn't have to replay back every word verbatim, since no one in the world translated English that didn't sound like Jesus' walking and talking in the day. It was written to be told in so many ways from another version, but His Word's message remained, unchanged:

At first, Thomas must've been looking over his shoulder. He was so fearful, as he finally made it all through town, lurking around a low profile, darting one corner to another, hopefully making it there. That back room of Jesus' followers avoided the Sadducees and Pharisees to find their fellow Christians all together to comfort one another, who must've been huddled in fear. Thomas got all the more anxious, as if he'd hush them down! They were over-heard from a lot of loud mourning and bawling who closed in. He must've been freaking out, afraid even more. He thought they'd be in a secret place, but they were impossible to be silenced. What if the upcoming slaughter rushed all the faster toward the back door?

Why did I have to know hear this? What hit me? What com-pelled that example in the Bible, unless God had something for me to look at it again.?

He flung through that door, and didn't understand. Everyone was overjoyed, as if they were celebrating a party! It was a roar and wild commotion coming from that room, but they weren't mourning over the death of their Lord, Teacher, and Master. Thomas had to wonder! The dead body of Jesus when Thomas arrived delirious, knowing how angry Thomas must've bucked! It must've the grand surprise and cruelest trick of the Book! What an emotional over-load that must have been, when I remembered another example of the same thing.

Why did Jesus show Himself to the other disciples before Thomas got there? If Thomas thought that he was someone special to Jesus before, he probably wondered what everybody else were all involved... and not him! Imagine that knee-jerk reaction. He was excluded, as if it was thrown right back in his face, indignant at those who couldn't believe what happened!

I heard the news of the greatest news that must've lost it, except they'd continued to laugh, but that was something else than God's murder. That had to be the unimaginable amount of pain held off and expect the explanation, later, like when I wasn't restored to join in and be happy... after I was told?

Jesus' followers carried on, who couldn't be stopped. And Thomas would've been overjoyed, except he was pissed, and so furious! How wrong could anyone of them to be talked down to relax... after the fact? Maybe Thomas was disappointed or sad, but what's more, they were glad about Jesus' visit who missed him. Did the followers were meant to be there first. Did they have Jesus... without Thomas' initial appearance?

Thomas thought it should've waited for it. What's worse, he had to touch the wounds of His dead body and expected Jesus to come back with the proof. And still, Thomas ranted, who remained overjoyed, regardless. Nobody cared how upset he was. As Jesus actually visited that room who'd been gathered, there was a lot more than just the chosen twelve left behind. That room was full which made it worse than the elite few!

There was nothing said to hurt them back to see Him come back, as if Thomas wasn't that special, like a backpaddling afterthought. He panicked all through town who finally took the most treacherous detour to make it there for all his Christ's brethren, but how did they all get there first? Was that the absolute worse gaslight who went nuts? Thomas felt worse than excluded, he felt rejected.

Saint John needed to remain in the Bible of the story. It was written down on their scriptures passed down forever, since I couldn't just dismiss some nice ideas to help identify what meant to know.

Thomas was there about Jesus' raising from the dead. They walked and talked about His own resurrection who forget what He discussed it ahead of time. Jesus made a point of them all to listen, which was a reminder saved in the scripts. Jesus wanted to know His ability, His proof to defeat death, and Thomas knew in his heart of heart that it was all true.

The Bible shared Lazarus' story through the examples, which it further impacted the preview of Thee event. Jesus had His followers to pay attention, when Jesus showed Lazarus's eminent death and relived. He wanted them to recall, when His resurrection wasn't just a fluke about Lazarus, and how the examples came together.

His followers got unnerved. Some listened and some fell away. His expectations couldn't accept that much, lost hope, and they started to let go of the faith. Jesus was unbelievable, Who spelled out His plan left behind, except some of them must've talked behind their backs, nudged to debunk every whisper. Or they were too embarrassed to admit they were wrong?

But Jesus didn't appear to be worried. He let the people believe what they wanted to believe, regardless. He was to be there, in the right time and place, even though He even made sure that Lazarus was undoubtedly dead, even deteriorated, since he was already bound up inside the cave behind the rock... as if that wasn't enough. After four days was that important to let Lazarus rot and it must've stunk, and even that, Lazarus was wrapped up and unable to take one step with another, arrived out of the cave who couldn't walk out... yet. But Lazarus came! He used him for the example, which was also a head's up. Jesus wanted to be expected, to experience, and learn to understand and believe what He said.

I hung onto every Word. Unless, something was blocked out or had too much to take in. Maybe Thomas was so troubled and too overwhelmed by the death of the cross! But it could've been a million excuses. Thomas was mad to be cheated out who stirred up the fight... in defense.

I attended school throughout my life. I had been through enough reasons to pass my education, as if I knew that I was smart enough. But I had to pick up a few more college courses, years after I'd grown. I'd returned for more, as if Jesus had to come back the second visit after all the others. I had to go back, for the proof. I went back the second semester. There was a history to prove my ability. My progress did not debunk the truth, when I returned as a senior student just once again, and I surpassed regardless.

I remaining among the classmates, but Ma lashed out in disbelief! Why was it so important to keep me from knowing? Did Thomas miss out to be told... after the fact? But the examples related in the present time:

I deserved to be praised! I should've boasted through every accomplishment, but too many examples came together. It was the grand gaslight in the event by the Matriarch. It was the Mother's Day of all days, which was slammed shut to keep from hearing about it anymore; except the Words remained on my heart for all to hear.

I felt sorry for Thomas, but that was no pity party! How many times have I said, "I'll believe it when I see it"? I couldn't believe, floundered and full of doubt, which was misplaced, to destroy the hope and faith, toward distrust. Hearsay is one thing, but it was staged, talked about it ahead of time in too many ways. And finally, I had enough, knowing anything written down couldn't have been altered. I wrote of what I knew in my notebook, DOC policies remained to refer it to defend anything off at work, or the Lord God Himself would stay unchangeable, when I had to trust its proof:

I expected to spend the family in honor of my ma, which was planned to be saved with just the highlights. That day, I arrived when I detected something off. Something felt suspicious, like I was the odd-man-out. I came in as the last one, when all my sisters were gathered together at my mother's house to celebrate Mother's Day with another surprise!

Before anyone else, I'd been told that my daughter was pregnant with my first grandchild. I knew about their age ticking down which also involved her husband was sterile before they were married, and they invested the day's technology for a vial from another country to conceive my child without sex for her husband's 'blessings', but it was no secret. It was believable. But, shouldn't I have been the one to it know first? Or, was I supposed relive every example, to eat the crumbs of their wedding cake in the last line again? But why did I have to be singled out... again?

Why did I have to hear it over the phone, at my mother's house, in their presence, to watch my reaction? It felt like the knife that was always transplanted in my back was there for a good twist. I had the phone to be handed over to me. Or, was daddy overhearing who denied his promise with another mechanic?

My daughter wasn't there. I didn't make eye contact, face to face, or the pride to hug each other. I was merely passed over to take the phone! My welling eyes lied through my tears of joy. Their concocted plan felt so wrong, while I swallowed hard to stuff it down!

I should've deserved that special piece of news before everybody else. Maybe it could've been over lunch or during an intimate walk on that path through the park that should've been a better way to share the new little miracle was held out for me, as if the fact didn't really matter to me whether she was pregnant. And it didn't matter whether Thomas' feelings got hurt or not. Belief or faith wasn't anything to argue against the facts. Jesus' was alive!

Of course, I took it personally. Of course, I was hurt, and I understood Thomas who thought Jesus was his best friend. He was offended and got defensive. Didn't he feel slighted? Was he jealous? Did he feel kicked in the chest aside everyone else around him? I was incensed, as if I didn't get enough of the examples, forgiving seven times seventy-seven, which repeated the same things from the Bible, when I got! But then God had an explanation to make sure that there was no other reason to bring it up anymore:

Jesus knew what was going through Thomas' mind, who returned to meet amends. Jesus had Thomas stand out of all to see. That meant more than anything by Jesus, Who made Thomas touch His wounds, and "disbelieve no more"! But that was enough that much behind it when it was time to save it for the real issue. Of all the people who came to see His resurrection, He came back for Thomas, but that was no small refutation, who immediately recompensing Thomas' fragile ego, aside. That was a big deal! Thomas was that important, and I believed that Jesus would've returned to be restored by Jesus, including all His disciples. Saint Thomas had something better.

I had to stop for a moment and absorb the kind of passion Jesus held something beyond the early Christians who embraced everyone together. And then God said to me: "You're that important, too."

"That doesn't make sense, Abba." My heart jumped. My heart pounded, afraid of that I might've been displeasing with God. Was I incensed? I pulled for Thomas, but He was pulling for me?

There was never a time in my life when I'd doubted His existence. My mind raced to validate my belief of a strong and unshakable faith, as if it was the grand cleansing of all sins. Was I too stubborn to admit something else I missed?

"You have not answered Me. Why?" I knew exactly what He was talking about.

He was right. I must've evaded His question, when I knew exactly what He meant. That wasn't able to avoid everything to Him. I was so open that I didn't even worry about His call to work in the prisons. If I didn't think that I had the ability to manage the housed criminals. *God is our refuge and strength, a helper who is always found in times of trouble* (Ps 46:1), since He always interceded the consequences regardless, which was always His will.

I was careful to give Him the glory by thanking Him in all things for His credit. I laid down His hands, who belonged to Him. I made mistakes or any of my painful experiences, when I knew that He enhanced my performance, to learn it on the job, which I passed forward to apply what I knew, especially in prison.

I literally counted on Him time and time again, as if I could do no wrong and He was always a winner. Submission to His will that made it easy to rely on Him, with the very reason I took a leap of faith for the courage, because I believed in Him.

I threw out all of the notebooks of my memoirs that purged room for His Word to accommodate everything healing my body, which was also refreshed in my soul. He took the most unlikely results, Who turned my experiences into use that encouraged anyone, flowing through my most trusted love… from God.

I had nothing to hide or ashamed from anyone. I had a new beginning, as if imprisonment had no walls in the perfect rank or category, which was just as importantly assigned on the wrong side.

"Watch out and beware of the yeast of the Pharisees and Sadducees" (Matt 16:6).

Yet, He proved them wrong. I believed my loved ones, until God's wisdom was impossible to argue against the truth. *"For God is not a God of confusion, but of peace"* (1Cor 14:33), as I developed empathy for the inmates, regardless of their decisions who'd owned up the consequences. *Remember and do not forget how you provoked the Lord your God in the wilderness. You have been rebelling against the Lord from the day you left the land* (Dt 9:7), since the boundaries were easily satisfied between the uniforms or them in color orange than any family reunion back home, but who would know? It was safer to stay closer to work with the well-defined officers and inmates, where the kindly smiles couldn't tell them apart.

DOC had been sorted out the categories, accordingly. And either way, I claimed my place, where every post was exactly where I'd satisfy DOC's rosters, but sometimes I'd make a crisp about-face. I'd feel a panic in a quick turn to look for the hold hovering over me, once I no longer needed a set of eyes in the back of my head. It was my Lord above all, instead.

I had all the time and space in prison, as if the full tenure was enough, since I'd referred every order or policy which expanded its addendum through for the answers in the Bible. Of all the experiences I'd collected, also evolved through His guidance and wisdom. Although I didn't feel empowered, when I believed on Him. I was His tool, as if I welcomed His permission. I was fully capable of His will, as if I couldn't do 'it' wrong. I submitted His use, but never taken advantage against my decision to construct and expanded His mercy to join a new beginning of the inmates, too.

No change was automatic when rehabilitation took a dual effort. Mistakes still happened, but especially the time when open yard recreation was cut short:

I couldn't know why, but the order urgently announced over the speakers, and I obeyed. I could've found out why later, but at that time, I had a job to stop the inmates to be turned in every assigned bunk. They all complied, and in a few seconds every housing unit had them immediately headed to their specific buildings, who came all at the same time, while the dayroom inside had to be folded up, too.

I scanned them headed, who all rushed for the doors. The board games or any other activities at the tables, while I checked a clear path toward the runs, but I'd instinctually made sure anything on the floor. I cared more about anyone tripped on the floor than anything distracted by Inmate Harris finishing to wrap it up in the dayroom. He hurried, but he dropped his comb that slid out to the middle of the room. An inmate could've caused one inmate to slip on the comb to fall or strain a muscle, when the inmates began to pour in.

"What?" Inmate Harris asked in a shrilly voice, but I disregarded it. There were always a lot of disappointments expected to end rec time that carried over in the dayrooms. "Did you just kick my comb to the side with your boot?" when he had that look on his face that made it clear. He was outraged, showing me the amount of disrespect toward his personal property. That comb was just like the same combs were all handed out during picture-days in grade school, but its value in prison was worth the world to everything.

"Oh, yeah. It fell too far into the path of the inmates who were coming in." It was a quick reflex. I explained how his comb was a safety hazard for the inmates coming through, returning it closer to him, not more than a few feet with a slight reach back at his table. It was flicked aside, as if it wasn't a single thought, or a non-issue impulse reaction. I had safety in mind, but that wasn't it.

It wasn't uncommon to see two inmates braiding each other's hair into cornrows, which was truly a time-consuming labor of love for each other, but I misinterpreted Inmate Harris' reaction to be a bit exaggerated. Even though I didn't laugh at him or tell him to get over it, I definitely did something. That hit nerve, and it was up to me to resolve that issue before it could've spilled over and taken out on someone else.

Inmate Harris sucked it up and went directly to his bunk, but he was raw where he'd stew. I couldn't just dismiss it, but I couldn't ask him to explain "what's the matter?" as if it should've been obvious. I wronged him but an apology wasn't going to be enough.

I examined how I'd feel. Maybe I was just too sensitive, but someone got hurt, and how bad? I tried to think how I'd feel, something related that happened before. Did I do something to him, or what was something done to me? Was he upset because the hair doo wasn't done, but I couldn't help that? Was he mad who sent 'home' with the other fellow inmate? Was he laughed back in the other building, who arrived unfinished to retaliate, too? I scanned my mind for another example. When the yard was cleared of all of the inmates inside, I wouldn't ignore him, knowing that it was about me!

"Hey Harris." I went up to him, which was only a few beds into the run, but he acted as if I didn't exist. He laid on his back looking straight up at the ceiling in his upper bunk and he refused to turn in either way. He was unable hide, knowing I was there. He wanted to let loose, controlling every bit of his self-discipline, fighting to resist my appearance. I didn't mean to hurt him, while he controlled onto that edge of rage, while I took the risk. He wanted to hurt me back, but his answer proved how I offended him, trying to shut me out-of-sight and out-of-mind. I needed to make amends, while I continued to put myself in harm's way to help resolve our differences, as if it would just go away.

"When I used my boot to flick your comb to the side, I was only thinking about someone stepping on it and falling. All I wanted to do, was clearing the path for the inmates who were coming, and I didn't give your feelings a second thought." I continued, talking only loud enough for him to hear me, and just safe enough from anything too close with a perfect blow to get it even. Fortunately, the room was busy and no one really paid any attention. "I'm sorry," I said and waited for a moment. He was right. An apology couldn't cover it, and I had to help him heal.

"I wasn't thinking. I never thought about how you would've felt when I kicked your comb to the side." I admitted what I did. *Revive Your work in these days; make it known in these days. In Your wrath remember mercy!* (Hab 3:2). "Do you want to know about how I know what you're feeling?" I looked at him intently. His face was still tight, and his lips remained pursed, but there was no place to go.

"Once my husband was in the basement, I picked up the dishes and washed the kitchen floor," I must've been babbling nonsense, but I paused with a slight glance in between, "since I washed it on my knees that I always felt good about it at the end of the day."

I could've been like a pesky fly that wouldn't go away, but I had him to listen as if it was important. "I always used a rag and bucket, because I thought that it did a better job than a sponge mop, and I didn't need to rush through it." Inmate Harris must've known that I'd eventually leave. "I crawling backwards towards the basement door, when I was just about done and ready to leave the kitchen floor to dry."

His eyes sort of rolled to the other direction, but I ignored his intrusion, and his body language was loud and clear. I continued regardless, who completely rolled over to show his back, but I let him. I didn't need to search out his face to the other side. "Then, my husband comes upstairs from the basement family room." I could tell that my feelings were showing, too. He sensed an offensive reaction… for the comparison.

"He wanted a coffee refill, and he stepped right over me in the doorway!" I had to stop because the rage in me started to brew as if it was yesterday, and my husband blew me off. I should've just let it go, and get over it. But it never forgot how I felt, and it was time to share that same way. "My husband just stepped over me! He straddled over me on all fours, as if it was nothing!" I took a deep breath, as if I still penned up all that anger, when I exhaled like if we slowly blow it out together. He had to know that I had issues to work it out together.

"He didn't ask how long the floor would've taken to dry, or even think to excuse himself, or a chance to get up!" I continued to rant, like if nothing happened. It wasn't it enough who'd walk all over me, who also acted out how he treated me! I remembered how I quickly ducked to let him pass... from that kick in the head. "I felt like I was no more than some stupid dog in his way." Inmate Harris turned to look at me as I regained my composure. "See, I get it." His eyes softened. "I shouldn't have kicked anything aside, including your comb, either. I should've stood next to the comb when I saw it dropped on the floor. I could've said 'excuse me', or anyone would've been safe enough to go around me, so that you could've given it a moment to pick it up."

I said it in all sincerity knowing the difference, when my husband wouldn't even apologize. He felt justified and blew me off... by no amends. Inmate Harris' smiled in a gentle thanks by a slight nod. It wasn't the issue about my husband's foot prints left on my cleaned floor, even though that would've only taken a few minutes to dry beautifully. I was incensed in the way he took care of his own wants. And, I could've taken a moment which was deserving with enough respect, to explain of what I'd passed on to someone else.

A lot of COs didn't like apologizing to the inmates, but by using a similar comparison involved each other. Owning up to my mistakes with a simple apology was the right thing to do, yet so many people considered it with some sort of weakness, which I saw it by an invaluable management tool to use my stories that impacted every opportunity to help in both ways. Because of what they missed out on some, was truly an effective tool of rehabilitation enforced or reinforced behaviors, while I improved for both sides... to grow.

Inmate Harris changed more respectful with every chance I applied of every wrong. I was no longer ashamed when I freely exposed every opportunity with its deeper understanding, as if my old wounds couldn't be forgotten, which edified it all the more. I had nothing to throw out, bury, or deny what I owned, when my excess baggage upgraded to another level, into my grand cache. "How to" or "what if" answers were free, readily available on the job against abuse.

It didn't matter if he wore orange or brown, where sub-human treatment in prison didn't belong as the dog to obey, either. No matter how insignificant it may have seemed at the time, helping both of us grew the right direction. I saw in others what I could see in their eyes in return, where we all carried around enough baggage, however anyone could learn how to reapply their unresolved issues to light, when those "Don't tell" lies came out like an avalanche... in prison.

And on the opposite side, I was the perpetrator every time I harmed another. I satisfied my need to take care of the many, as if I'd be okay by the majority, when I didn't care about a cheesy comb. I prioritized to protect the crowd of inmates. It was my decision, regardless of the one. I wasn't prepared to concoct a scheme, through my ignorance, but I was guilty nonetheless.

It could've been something small, which was on me, but what did I cause Inmate Harris to lose anything? What did I cost him? until I knew that I hurt him. If 'sin is sin' was true, and one person was impacted on another, which one was more important: him or me? Was he the inmate or the CO's responsibility to deal? The pain was just as real, but which one was more important, or more valuable?

I remembered how happy I welcomed two of my sisters on a trip who came along, wasn't my gift to them my delight, too? They were so very impressed. They chose out their postcards, pamphlets, and souvenirs. Of course, I was flattered, when I thought I did a good thing! Didn't they enjoy every minute? Souvenirs honed toward their specific tokens to remind them through the memories.

But, did I make the mistake? Did I do something wrong, when I paid off anything they wanted. Their choices were on separate piles, but it didn't end or anyone in line when I covered it all at the register, on my bill.

Was Alison more valuable than Janet? Did I do something wrong, and they got mad at me? I didn't take favors, one over the other, and I didn't give them the amount I'd pay upfront that soured. Did I hurt anyone, slipping out a quick apology to figure it out later, knowing neither of them were going to resolve it. Their memories were ruined, like that grand finale for the worse. I prayed, since I couldn't ask Him to find the Bible when all I saw was, *Do not be anxious about anything, but in everything by prayer and supplication with thanksgiving let your requests be made known to God* (Php 4:6). And, my reputation changed all throughout the prison tenure, as I gained respect by the inmates, regardless of their crimes, except for those few impossible inmates.

Who would've thought that my freedom would be found inside of a prison, unless that was the reason why I wasn't going to be supported in law enforcement? My loved one hated me in that career. They were afraid to be exposed, as if I didn't have the ability to withstand, regardless. I endured their consequences, squarely landed in my lap, until I understood of how I'd **not** to be! The final parody left me process both sides, which I'd checked it out in the Bible! But, how could I possibly ask Him for any earthly things, since I had been so richly rewarded already!

"No, God." It didn't feel right of even a little more respectful with God. I could've taken care of myself, all on my own, knowing our sufficiency was from God! *Not on men's wisdom but on God's power* (1Cor 2:5). How could I tell God more than I wanted?

Peter must've felt the same way when that sheet was lowered from the heavens, filled with all the crawling creatures on earth to help himself, which God had specifically forbidden man to consume. *Then a voice said to Him, "Get up, Peter, kill and eat." "No Lord!"*

Peter said. "For I have never eaten anything common and ritually unclean!" This happened three times. (1Cor 10:13,14,15). Surely, God refused me three times to know better. Was He testing me?

Peter's understanding was limited, just like mine. *"What I'm doing you don't understand now, but afterward you will know,"* (John 13:7). God was talking about the Gentiles and Peter who were thought about food, and I didn't understand it either. *Trust in the Lord with all your heart, and do not rely on your own understanding* (Proverbs 3:5).

My time on the job demanded constant attention to sort out the decisions all around, as I could decipher the radios once I became familiar on the routine day. But on the outside of work, I had no other life imprisoned exactly where: You are Here!

Time passed and I continued to push myself to continue in as many double shifts, even though I started feeling a little older. I did as much as I could, carefully focused to avoid myself in trouble. *A greedy person provokes conflict, but whoever trusts in the Lord will prosper* (Pr 28:25). Could I assume God would've fulfill my desires, materially? I fought with the enjoyable things of this world, but I wanted my treasures in heaven; I'd argued inside.

An officer fell asleep on the job too many times, who had to pay the penalty, and his excuse was used it to be a perfect example for the rest to get the message, too. Their complaints spread, albeit the water-fountain gossip, throughout the job. DOC base pay was in the lower end of middle-class wages in comparison with the entire Nation of the States. It wasn't what we deserved, but that was acceptable to cover the overtime hours life standards. It was the amount we all agreed to the extra work, so we couldn't say a thing. *Don't wear yourself out to get rich; stop giving your attention to it* (Proverbs 23:4), when my energy waned.

I looked over in my supervisor's calendar for some time to make an extended break, when I found New Mexico, a barren state, as if there was a reason why they'd fence in Area 51, while I inquired the realtor for the excursion. I took in a number of directions, as if I could smell out a shady salesman when they were easily sorted out, while I was "just looking". I grew familiar with the altitude and its effect on temperatures, elevated oxygen and air pressure baking about something accommodating in the mountains or not.

By the time I left my apartment, I rolled out of my sleepy prison town under a full moon, while it shown its great earth through the stillness of the night. I drove the lightest traffic, but even the refreshing air especially embraced its majestic view all around. Foreign lands could've been sacred territory, picturesque on the front of a Christmas card. I drank it down, as the speeds of 75 MPH posted speed limit felt like I was sitting still, as the world unfolded through its glorious beauty.

I admired the mesmerizing silhouettes against backdrop of the sky, as the desert floor illuminated below through the night. And then, the changing of the guard took it at dawn, when the sun rose the wide rolling hills from the horizon, like night time pulled aside the velvet curtains that split opened for the day like the scene of act two, as if the orchestra played in my mind along the song of my heart that also lifted away the moody darkness quickly melted before me. The Land of Enchantment couldn't possibly take in what I was encouraged in even further!

I didn't just unwind and relax back in any location that pulled me in and never leave. It was amazing! The cool fifty-degree temperature dotted their blossoms adorning the seasonal shrubs, splattering the landscape among the cacti, as the map and the realtor landmarks were easily found, for another cup of road tar coffee... as needed.

I was too ignorant or innocent, when Catholicism lead to pray to the specific saints. I obeyed or where I played along as if I was supposed to communicate with dead people, but I knew better. Good ol' Saint Nick or Santa was miracle overnight, when I went right to the Big Man Upstairs.

And I was banned upstairs, where I was happy to keep away from a watch over me, where I always believed His presence. "Was that wrong?" I talked with God as I could feel His nod in a smile than anyone else would know. I'd be mocked or even crazy since the beginning, Who understood. I didn't have the Word from the Bible, or any other significance of the translations, which was enough to reach me. Did God look down on me when I'd be so vulnerable on the 'wrong side'? *And the Lord said to Satan, "Behold, all that he has is in your hand. Only against him do not stretch out your hand,"* (Job 1:12).

We talked Who comforted me as I grew, when I applied His wisdom behind righteousness who lived incarceration, as if I got all the practice I needed. I studied God's feelings in my gut, but I knew for too long how I'd fooled Him. I tolerated the secrets, like the "Don't tell" silence didn't exist. *What use is a carved idol after its craftsman carves it? It is only a cast image, a teacher of lies. For the one who crafts its shape trusts in it, and makes idols that cannot speak* (Hab 2:18), but deceit affected it with just enough doubt, until I'd been well beyond faith, where I surpassed: knowing! His words were rooted into the higher authority, originated by man's household... and I moved on, directly to God, Himself.

Vacation time spent by too fast, and I was back on the road. I sang my prayers to the Father, as I sat back on my car's cruise control to be carried back to my little apartment, but I couldn't stop thinking about my life in the mountains. "Abba, can you please help me make this happen for me?" I let my dream surface.

"What do you want?" That same phrase rang out so quickly, so clearly.

"I want to live in the mountains," I answered, spirit to Spirit.

"Be specific." He moved the conversation for more. "I want details," He added.

I couldn't be talked out, since it shook my confidence from day one, but I couldn't argue against it. I was afraid to be called crazy, laughed off right away, but it remained because I didn't care to convince anyone else, when God reminded me once again... on cue:

I had to ask my gynecologist who inadvertently explained during my pregnancy. I played with my baby... in her belly, who understood and believable the responses, like when the alarm clocks went off, or when a cozy massage urged a foot or head move away from that long stretch inside. We already communicated who couldn't see each other, but I also understood about another being. God elicited the expected responses, too. I didn't need my baby's proof before her birth, and I also carried Him; His entity inside! I was very aware of my presence, communicated with me, too.

"I don't want much." I swallowed hard. I'd grown too humble, feeling like if asking might've sounded sinful. Surely, He had to have known my needs, but having a house built in the mountains was between the need or want, as I baulked to answer, again.

What if I told God about anything I wanted, and I didn't get it? How many times could I've shrugged my shoulders with the excuse that 'it wasn't His will'? Would that affect my faith? Would that had been the last straw, built-up before the final fall? I liked the relationship I had with God, and I didn't want to take the chance of being disappointment, or did I let Him down? I doubted His miraculous outcome through for me. There were so many times over the years when I prayed for Him to step in, and He didn't. Somehow it didn't seem right to put myself out there again. There were some things you just don't pray for, and those old recordings inside of my brain resurfaced all at once.

I'd begged to overcome the scars. I thought I was specific. I prayed to be transformed into a wholesome love, passing forward in His encouraged passion for more, and still I felt kicked down when I found weakness. Was His timing perfect? *Rejoice in our afflictions, because we know that affliction produces endurance, endurance produces proven character, and proven character produces hope* (Romans 5:3-4), and the Bible's Word remained unchangeable to believe. None possibly ignored. I relaxed to rely on Him as I endured my strength, Who took over my battles against the people who purposely hurt me. I stepped aside to let them deal with God, instead. Some people called it Karma, but that's not giving Him the glory He deserved. *For God's wrath is revealed from heaven against all godlessness and unrighteousness of people who by their unrighteousness suppress the truth* (Romans 1:18).

"You saw that, didn't you?" I knew how God felt the wrongs, and how it affected my Father! I hung my head. The thought was prosperous, and too uncomfortable to ask anything other than I deserved. Why? I had been robbed from what I'd aspired toward, as if my desires were turned to rubbles. I resigned to reduce to the basic creature comforts, as I'd adjusted to be trimmed down, minimized from anything else. *Every house is built by someone, but the One who built everything is God* (Heb 3:4).

There was an awesome awareness with God's attention on me. I still struggled, Who didn't quit on me. He was steadfast and patient, nudging: "Go head, tell me." Free to remove the fear of something wrong that calmed me.

My head raised up: "But God, me?" I wanted to hang my head and about to bawl as if the Father should've had enough time on someone else. And I remembered, as if Jesus' apostles needed to be told how to pray: *"Our Father"* (Matthew 6:9), and I almost gasped.

I saw some gorgeous places, and how wonderful the soft night air seemed to stroke the side of my face with the window down. "I want as much privacy as possible." I finally whispered as I checked to see my wig on the passenger's seat. "I don't want a house on the top to look down. Of all things, why do people look for the highest homes at their roofs?" It was like no one could feel better down the road, as if their neighbors didn't settle any better lots? "I don't want to live among pine tree line of the mountains, since I wanted my view for miles all around my back yard. A few trees would be okay," I babbled, until it vacillated back and forth.

I realized how privacy used to mean detachment that felt backwards. "No body likes you" was intended to destroy the bonds, since I couldn't run after the loved ones' approval. I obeyed to stay away, or at least obedient in place, but I wasn't grounded for a punishment. I thought I did the right thing to do, but it was wrong. I was confused, begging every explanation, when every situation, event, or crime let it slide that impaired my mental and physical development.

I tried to please just about anybody around, and especially happy to be useful, as if I was worthy and important, even for a little while. I savored every moment and I let my loved ones taking full advantage of me, but then helping was over. I was emotionally burned that destroyed their trust to be scolded, and still, maybe they'd be back to wait but it grew longer in between, or ruin another opportunity to need me or even ask for another time. I sacrificed, until "tell me everything" took over in the wrong hands. I backed off as if I'd be robbed, when God gave me the understanding: *The Lord is a jealous and avenging God* (Nahum 1:2). I knew how it kept it familiar, since I took the risks... but who would I tell about trust to God?

"My idea of living off the grid included complete independence from the power lines. That would've marred the open wilderness in the view, or the solar panels that cluttered the houses to support its electricity." I realized passing down one pole after another along the highways. "I think I'd want to be wired underground to connect the internet and cable television that would also eliminate the satellite dishes, too. That would've compromised the dead areas in the hills with another tower stuck up like a sore thumb. Stormy lightening weather attracted every earth strike out in the opened area, asked for trouble." I let go the simple pleasures to imagine it a bit farfetched. I laughed in the thought as if it could actually happen. "With God, all things are possible," giggling inside, filled with delight, but He listened...as if I put my wish list with the wildest dream come true.

I knew that I'd be priced out of the picture with the expense underground, run all the way to a place in the mountains. I'd never work enough overtime to pay for it, much less a house built with my custom design, but I laid it all out there anyway.

I said it as easily as if I was sitting alongside a good friend. "I'd like to be able to hike all around my land as I get older, so the mountain shouldn't be too steep. And, I'd need good soil to do some gardening, and I could plant an orchard of tropical fruits, too. I picked out the best pecans trees, pomegranates, apricots and avocadoes trees!" I fanaticized to let every thought flow with no hesitation... with my God. It wasn't pompous, and I knew that He just wanted me to go nut. For the first time, I did imagine a dream... for me! "Then I could see myself riding a quad with a trailer behind me, bartering my produce for local honey, candles, or cheeses with my neighbors," when all limitations were removed as God cheered me on.

God smiled over me. "And, a well already dug!" I added a sense of urgency. I had been shown several plots with an avid water supply, but there were some other lots, besides.

"There has to be a road leading to the property." I remembered when once piece of land was only marked by a spray-painted stick in the middle of nowhere. The adjoining realtor trips were an aspired moment, knowing it wasn't hardly developed or even validated with another glance that would never quite meet my bet. "And a driveway, although that would not be a deal breaker if it was missing." I continued, but I had my Captive Audience, still listing all of the things that would've been a perfect lot for me to describe my retirement.

"There's a lot of dust in the air down here," I continued again after I returned to the car with a cup of road tar from the overnight's coffee pot, which was kept hot for too long at the last truck stop, when a warning sign was blinking 'low-visibility' down the road. "It's not just because of the strong winds either. The bare land and vehicles driving on the side dirt road left a cloud of dust more than a half mile behind it," I said as I saw a pickup truck crossed through the rural fields. "I don't want bare land, but I don't want so many rocks that I can't walk barefoot to hang my clothes to dry outside, either. Maybe I could live at the end of the road?" I gave into every little detail without guilt or shame as I returned home.

The closer I came to the end of my trip, the more frivolous it got. Then, as if I needed even more eye-candy by a mountainside cliff aglow, with the striations of mineral deposits tipped upward, like if it was pointing to the sky. "Thank you, Abba!" I whispered, and moments later, I turned onto my exit... and my trip was over.

CHAPTER 19

It's the Ticket

I was still high when I returned to work, finally looking forward to the mountains, when I had to focus on the job. But it was one step forward and two steps back, when Sgt. Dominguez pulled the rug out from under us, again.

"Think outside of the box," Our shift commander got our attention, when I rolled my eyes wondering what else DOC came up at briefing. "Don't rely on the Disciplinary Department. There's a lot you can do other than writing up every ticket." I couldn't believe it. The Disciplinary Sergeant was the perfect place to send them weed out the other thousand inmates aside.

Where was our support, our back-up? DOC pulled back to manage it better of our own, and the option no longer was allowed to lean on the Disciplinary Department. It had nicely impacted LOP through an inmate's television taken away for a few weeks, but even the inmates worked around that. One run of the double bunks moved over the inmates' support who pull them through, too. That wasn't hardly a punishment for that 'problem child', like when their children acted up to be grounded by their parents when the bed rooms' siblings shared their support in return.

We'd been pushed at wit's end. We had to think twice about the inundated load, as if I'd been taking advantage of the Sergeant's issues instead, but DOC had the worse timing where Inmate Steele was particularly selected in my rotation. There was no break which every day I met up to go toe to toe through the whole 90 days. He drove me nuts and so childish like when he'd sneak up, just as I'd sit down in the control room, who'd scream within a few feet before my face, like a Jack-in-the-box surprise... on my expense. I rode out that last nerve, but one more time hardly recovered, when it started to build up.

Inmate Steele was placed in the yard shortly after he arrived his new residence to the lower assigned bunk by himself, like a wild colt or young buck of piss and vinegar. There was no getting away from him, or any other inmates in the same run. I fell for it. "He was in prison for the perfect place" I thought, strong enough to tolerate him, but I forgave it too many times, as if at any time I would just blow and lose control with another grand surprise for him, but I knew better.

I watched him. I studied him, when I notice that he actually was alone, and no one rallied behind him. Most of the time an inmate would've given it up, assuming he'd wear down enough pulled in prison, but then it was announced in briefing that it was all on me, and the rest of the inmates in the run were pretty fed up, too.

DOC was designed to stabilize the inmates' behaviors just like the abuse on the streets. I learned it, but then the academy was more like a review of what I already knew. It was still familiar that was nothing more than a hamster wheel who could never jump off. Inmate Steele got real good of what he knew; except he grew stronger through the repeats, as if he preferred to exercise and endure above anyone else.

Impaired cognition established a spattering handful of inmates easily spotted out. They were separated apart from feeding off each other, or anyone around who gave him a wide berth from coming in too close, but the open yard wasn't hardly isolating. Quite the contrary, the 'gated community' was handed out throughout DOC's medium risk yard, who minimized the challenge to be sucked in, or hired to step in between 'the umpire', as if the aggressors were just the easy part.

It wasn't uncommon to see an inmate easily identified by a deformed head from a gunshot wound, curved scars, or their paralyzing nerves that couldn't be changed. They were all compartmentalized, who carried their specific stories that simply healed that way. Missing or blind eyes included any number of reasons who'd been disfiguring, and so on. And one particular inmate wore an eye patch for bed that couldn't be closed, but there were a lot of other scars well beyond the obvious.

Inmates teetered on the edge of another seizure who survived one right after another, or they'd recovered from their last one before release, but Inmate Steele needed another category all of his own. No one, except the medical staff, knew the true nature of an inmate's mental dysfunctions, emotional instability, or physical abnormal treatments. That much was confidential, but I watched to figure as much as I could on my own. The general majority shared among the other body language to share among my fellow COs, as if it was read between the 'secret codes' where we ran in for help, which included an alert calling the medical staff by a red flag through my best guess.

I came in bald, but I also wore my visible mark throughout the prison from the beginning. I owned an unnatural stand-out scar of proof, when no one could deny the battles and the war that was never meant to win. Did that include me or beg enough space away? But that didn't affect me in the prisons, where the consequences remained, nonetheless. I wasn't the guilty one to wear the shame, but I'd been damaged by their wrongs, instead. *But even if you should suffer for righteousness, you are blessed. Do not fear what they fear or be disturbed. However, do this with gentleness and respect, keeping your conscience clear so that when you are accused, those who denounce your Christian life will be put to shame* (1Peter 3:14,16).

"There's a new one." Inmate Steele did a double-take, as if he'd be quick to concoct a new plan around me. He gave it his best effort to see who'd break, but I didn't see my own appearances to hide its embarrassment. The mirror was used once, after I'd forget to look into my reflection's daily reminder, and then I was good to go.

I stood out, but my endurance didn't need anything to boast about the scars. I'd forfeited the accomplishments. I should've showed them all, so proud and anxious to share, except it didn't really matter as I learned to accept it in silence.

The entire game was about all their needs to be cheered on. How great they were... and I filled the part. I especially remember the time when Janet wanted a pat on the back, and I was supposed to act out the heads-up and the deceit of the rules. I was supposed to know about the winner, when I was made to play the part, while I worried about the next retaliation to withhold any form of rejection. It was inevitable, but I'd feel enough pain to endure the threats. I couldn't walk away, who egged on, teased, and taunted for more, but the prize was irrelevant which was kept from my awards.

That day, I must've been pushed to the edge, when I knew that I'd make sure she'd feel it, too. We were just a bunch of kids grouped together and the game who opted out of the last one hung onto the low-volt wiring on the grandparent's farm; except still held on. Janet was meant to be the winner, and I knew just how long and how badly! The cattle were there, far enough from a flimsy single wire around the pastures. Some of the wires were flipped on that redirected the overused grasses to rotate and restore the new growth that disciplined it within the right fields.

Those cows just knew, when I tested out the electrical pain that escalated every moment, but only the best players couldn't hardly withstand very long... which it made it look good for the winner.

On the outside, the winner was burned (in other ways). Janet *had* to be the winner, except I made her earn it… when I knew just how bad she wanted it. Did she endure more pain than me, or did I know how long I'd allow her to be the winner? But nonetheless, I forfeited the win… in silence.

Some of the inmates recounted their moments, "One day I woke up and I had no choice to accept it." I heard it so many times, with another kind of awakening. *"For nothing is concealed that won't be revealed, and nothing hidden that won't be made known and come to the light. Therefore, take care of how you listen. For whoever has, more will be given to him; and whoever does not have, even what he thinks has his will to have taken away from them"* (Luke 8:17-18). Life could change in an instant, or never fast enough.

The iron security door bounced off the brick wall in the day room, which was Inmate Steele's signature, kicking it flown open. No arms were used to announce his presence, and that did it! He hit my last nerve that spiked my blood pressure and I could handle it anymore. Something had to change, but what? How was I going to rein in a wild and unruly inmate with no respect of authority for anyone else?

Inmate Steele was obnoxiously intrusive, overbearing, and self-assured who wore down everyone including the run, but I had to endure the abuse when I knew how long I'd hang on… again? I already knew which one was the winner, but he had to earn it. I already had the capacity to wager it just enough, as if the tickets were well used accordingly. DOC wanted me to weigh out the tickets… sparingly! I refused to relent to the winners instead of the punishments. I was prepared or conditioned but either way, and he was going to win… for my choice!

It was no secret; I admitted it. I'd written my share of tickets. I'd gotten creative with the whole process about their disciplinary reports which were not only writing them to make sure they'd would stick, I also knew how to write them weak on purpose, which were then tossed out for the threat and a deep breath of relief of thanks for a second chance. I knew each LOP that would've been reached the Disciplinary Office, whether I handed it to my sergeant's review first, before it was moved forward.

Sometimes I delayed the paperwork purposely, leaving it half-finished on my writing table as I also used it by an eminent threat, and an effort for any other inmate's intercession bought enough time to reconsider. I had within 24hrs to be completed and handed out if needed. It made all the difference, which was still on the table, whether it didn't need any further. I openly and visually let them all be quite aware about how I gladly tossed it into the trash can. I was heard. I made it a point to deterred or save the consequences. After all, my goal was about behavioral stress in a minimalizing manner of management.

I conducted proper managing, but I was further cut back by the sole CO among the assigned inmates. If I was summoned forward to obey the game of my loved ones, I couldn't get away from the inmates expected to be forced and wound down to the final man standing, like when it was just him and I left... hanging onto the electric wire. The inmates easily bowed out, forfeiting his blustering needs who didn't want to cheer him on, but I was going to make sure he'd know why.

He was a young spit-fire in his early twenties with a cocky attitude. Still, the oath to protect and serve of the inmates remained true. *It is a noble thing not to eat meat, or drink wine, or do anything that makes your brother stumble. Do you have a conviction? Keep it to yourself before God* (Rom 14:21-22). But the inmates also drew that line about Inmate Steele, and it was all on me. *Don't be afraid, but keep on speaking and don't be silent. For I am with you, and no one will lay a hand on you to hurt you, because I have many people in this city* (Acts 18: 9-10).

I needed to be hypervigilant, like flea on shit. *It is able to judge the ideas and thought of the heart. No creature is hidden from Him, but all things are naked and exposed to the eyes of Him to whom we must give an account* (Hebrews 4:12-13), like the advice from God intuitively extended His crucifixion about Thomas, which removed all doubt. *They stirred up persecution against Paul and Barnabas and expelled them from their district. But they shook the dust off their feet against them. And the disciples were filled with joy and the Holy Spirit* (Luke 13:50,51,52).

It was all there. The answers were right in front of me. That was why I was so driven to write anything and everything down, going back and adding every detail. *Some things will make sense later* (John 16:12), as I walked in through with His faith.

The Book of Ecclesiastes had nothing new by the time my warnings had been pushed to the limits. It could've caused them on a path back to a single or double cell, extending his time in the lockdowns, but who was I kidding? The lockdowns were full, and if I knew that, so did the inmates. The Disciplinary Department's had to limit of the number of tickets, and another cycle had nothing changed.

"You need to put those earphones on, or at least turn them down," I said it as gently as I could, after I discovered where the noise was coming. Inmate Steele was one of the final few inmates when I'd marked off each count sheet without delay.

"You've got to be shittin' me, lady!" He squirmed around uncomfortably with his reply. (Although, I didn't care to repeat his words verbatim.)

"I can hear it all throughout the run. That's not right. Turn it down," I said it again more firmly, heading to the next run on the other side. It wasn't like he couldn't understand another language, or gutter talk, meant to shake me up. *Shun profanity for it leads to ungodliness.* (1Tim 2:6). *Hold fast the pattern of sound words* (2 Tim 1:13).

"You don't know what the hell you're talking about. Look around. No body wears 'em." His defiance was duly noted, but I didn't have time to argue with him.

"They don't have the sound turned all the way up, either." The volume of his Koss earphones could be heard throughout the run, which was meant to be heard to themselves.

Inmate Steele encouraged the inmates of the run to be joined along to be stacked against me, but the inmates didn't want to be involved, as if I'd be stripped of my authority to be left helpless, when Inmate Steele either liked the attention, or just didn't care. He was disappointed, when he was abandoned with sole inmate, when I realized how the other inmates were reacting in the same room. If I wouldn't have been able to manage him, the rest of the inmates would've been the rest of the inmates' chance, as if they secretly cheered on for my hope.

Inmate Steele misread me, and maybe the accused of DOC was in disbelief of the norm, like he was the one assigned to that run, who could prove its purpose in the prison life. Whether he was afraid among the mid-level yard for the lowest risk level of the violent criminals, he had to behave just as fearless.

His sense of arrogance clouded his perception, when I opened the match-of-wits against me. He was the self-assigned champion, and I had to show his fellow-criminals the stronger or the better decisions. Surely, I must've been an easy lay-down, who was given it a pass, blown-off with his permission to move along. Except, it was more than just about him and I anymore. There was the rest of the run with the bigger issue. Still, I had my priorities during formal count, who communicate their eyes on me. I had them wait, but they knew it was about to draw closer to finish the count report, first things first.

"Where's it say that 'I have to wear 'em'? Get out of here. You don't know nuthin'." He shouted to get the last word in, dropping his final rude expletives between every other word.

I tabulated my reports back to the Yard Office to stop everything, until it's cleared again to continue. I let him believe that he'd won the debate, by the same non-active response answer. There was no contest, who probably hoped for something done right there and then, but I couldn't. I was 'under the gun' to stay on schedule like before, while they weren't going anywhere, with enough set of eyes for the watch.

"Can you read?" I returned to the foot of his bunk about fifteen minutes later with my book at the post orders. I didn't know if he could read, with no intention to embarrass the possible lack of his reading skills. "Never mind, I'll read it," I said in a voice low enough to be heard shared only between the two of us. But his body language was nothing private or subtle. He popped up from the lower bunk who quickly stood in a bit too close to me, apart with anything inadvertently bumped in, while I stayed exactly where I remained very calm and still. I put myself in harm's way, as my boundaries were clearly specified from any touching that also limited it with one opened page. I read the policy with my finger pointing every word, who had the option to follow along, which was undeniably spelled out of the violation against his excessive noise and its proper use of the audio equipment.

"Well, lookie there. She got one!" He said loud enough for the whole run, as if his big mouth compensated his small stature. I knew the wrong "big man in a small cell" choice, but there was no question about it. He suffered from a really bad case of the Napoleon Syndrome.

Inmate Steele stood all of about four-feet-ten-inches tall, lean, and well ribbed, full of energy demanding a wide clearance, like a collision-like cartoon in a Tasmanian Devil spin, which was an unbridled chaos at any direction. Everyone had to be careful, who were especially lived within the housed inmates, ready and in high alert. *Seek to lead a quiet life, to mind your own business and to work your own hands as we command you, so that you may walk properly in the presence of outsiders, and not be dependent on anyone* (1Thes 4:11-12).

I knew the inmates had to count on me to do something, but what? *Trust in the Lord with all your heart, and do not rely on your own understanding; think about Him in all your ways, and He will guide you on the right paths* (Proverbs 3:5-6). Putting him on report didn't do anything. He was on LOP to impose on another inmate's cooperation, who'd just picked it up later. Inmate Steele liked angry energy. He was intrusive and enjoyed breaking up the monotony of a once peaceful run.

Tolerance wasn't working. Ignoring him only made me bite my tongue and go home with a killing headache, when I realized how he wouldn't listen how good I really was. "Inmate Steele doesn't think that I know what I'm doing!" I thought, who had no idea how generous I'd been. He was so combative, when I allowing his extra freedoms to look the other way against policy. I'd worked DOC, whether I was a seasoned officer or not, but he chose how easily I got fooled, which was really my gift. What if I'd show him just how thoroughly he'd find out!

Inmate Steele attended the orientation classes, just like any other inmates, as if he'd been transferred all over again. The state prisons were built to absorb and take in the extra inmates who were sorted out among the five other risk levels. They'd had to be removed from the private prisons, when they rioted and destroyed their private-ly-run facility made it unsafe. DOC moved over to accommodate him without question. Although it was a bit premature, it was not my call. Inmate Steele had his own rule book, and should've known when he'd stepped out of line, unless he thought that *I* didn't know the rules.

How many homes absorbed away from my family, when I was placed somewhere else every summer? Was Inmate Steele afraid to fit in? I'd been farmed out without any questions. I had to adjust the fine nuances of the various family rules, too. I was just another dependent, to live aside perfect strangers, which was all too familiar, all over again.

Managing peace swapped out authority, like when the severe heat of the desert summer cut in some slack, but Inmate Steele couldn't' have known my discretion. He couldn't have read my reputation, who refused to bully me or anyone else, when I put him on the defense in the same shoes... for a truce.

Within an hour, recreation reopened for the inmates to roam around outside of the run. Formal count announced to be cleared, when I held them all up for a second. I needed them to be stopped for a quick security check first. The run cordially complied. It was my turn, as if it was a head's up, and I was in charge! But no one asked, as if it was a relief who understood: "Let's play!"

"What are those clothes doing over there?" I brought Inmate Steele to his attention, away from his borrowed tv, like the hired babysitter.

"What?" He gave me that "you again?" look.

"What's with those clothes?" I pointed to a mass of crumpled clothing shoved between the iron bar at the head of his bed and concrete wall.

"That's my dirty clothes." He shook his head, after a quick look of disgust at me.

"Then they belong in your laundry bag stored underneath your bed." I was quick to point out his first policy violation, which had no effect on his pompous demeanor. No response.

"Steele!" I called out a few minutes later. "Get a shirt on!" I made him jump, which was publicly broadcasted in front of his peers.

Finally! I didn't expect the rest of the run to pick up the lead for his defense, who didn't. I reentered the run of the one side, as I casually passed by a few other inmates without a shirt on, without a word to anyone else. This was just between me and the kid, and the message was received. He was on his own. Although I was winging it, the other inmates throughout the run seemed to step aside as if to say "have at it", with their permission to do whatever I could. I didn't have a real plan yet, but I was determined. *He is able to deal gently with those who are ignorant and are going astray, since he is also subject to weakness. Because of this, he must make a sin offering or himself as well as for the people* (Hebrews 5:2-3). My goal was going to be met by the end of the day, who would find out just how important I deserved the same respect.

"Steele!" My diaphragm bellowed above the noise in the dayroom, unashamed and unshaken for him, specifically. Everyone stopped to turn to check all their IDs from another housing unit. "Where's your ID?" Commanding compliance was the most petty call, when details resounded policy to be advertised for all. A few inmates turned to look away, unable to contain themselves. They didn't want to be caught by Inmate Steele when his bubble popped, embarrassed for the first time.

"Are you blind?" His indignation was evident, as he exaggerated to show his card which he purposely clipped the hem at his sleeve.

"It belongs on the front of your shirt. Clip it to your chest." I was beyond curt as my eyes didn't so much as blink eye contact to drive it home. I was overreaching by all accounts, but he didn't know it.

"Steele!" I was unwavering while I gained an immediate audience throughout the time, throughout open recreation. "You're out of place," I called him out of the laundry room when he clearly didn't belong there, and I amped up to match his energy, when I whisked out from my control room and strutting directly to him, toe to toe. "Are you a laundry porter?" I stood firm, steadfast, and unaffected by his attempt to force me off balance. As his face and head grew red, my eye brows rose as if to say: "Well?"

Inmates have a code-of-conduct among themselves to defend one over another, especially when one of their own is perceived to be unfairly treated by an officer, but no one came to his aid.

"Steele!" I called him out again as he bounced the iron security door banging against the dayroom wall with his infamous karate kick, announcing his arrival into freedom from the congested dorm.

"What!" He shouted back at me.

"Do that again and you're going down for intentional abuse of a security device." I shouted right back. "There's a handle. Use it!" My mom voice kicked in beautifully.

"Steele!" I called him out in front of a group of inmates down the run a few moments later, but he chose not to acknowledge me. "Give me that shirt," I said when I came to a gradual stop behind him, demanding his torn shirt immediately removed, holding my hand out.

"What is WRONG with you Lady?" His bravado did not affect me, regardless of his flexed and dancing chested muscles forfeiting his remodeled shirt.

"Destruction of state property." I referred to the sleeves missing from his orange tee shirt. "Get another shirt on," I insisted while other inmates scattered. I was making a few of them nervous by pushing Inmate Steele to the edge, and no one knew what to expect, either. He was a short fuse on an old keg of dynamite and no one dared to disturb him, but that was wrong. Boy, did I know about wrong!

For just a few moments I thought about how I was putting myself in harm's way, and that a few of the inmates might be thinking about taking a stand to protect me in case Inmate Steele was going to raise a hand against me. I didn't want that. Defending me could get them beaten up later, for defending an officer instead of a fellow inmate, and I knew better than to let that happen. *Be strong and courageous; don't be terrified or afraid of them. For it is the Lord your God who goes with you; He will not leave you or forsake you* (Deuteronomy 31:6). Even if he did try to strike me, I was ready to use a few moves of my own training in defense. I had to expect a turn for the worse at any time. He was singled out, when no one cleared out after a while. The area stayed around at the sound of Inmate Steele's name called out again and again, but a full room of inmates was a form of survival.

This is where I should talk about how I leaned on the Lord in fear for my life, but the truth was, God was not on my mind. I had my talk with Him every day on my way into work, and then I just paid attention to the things at hand. Most people seem to think that everything said to God was done in prayer. To me, prayer was when you fold your hands with your head down while on your knees, with a definite "Amen" at the end, before getting back on your feet. It makes for a good picture, but it wasn't my reality. I needed more of an immediate access to Him without all the pageantry aside.

I had His presence, and I addressed Him at any time. There was no sign of the cross or anything to elude our connection for that specific moment in time. It wasn't an on or off kind of thing. At the end of my shift on my drive home, I gave Him all the thanks, like a spiritual high-five for a job well done, and in between there, I just relaxed in His care. *For the Lord will never forsake you* (1Sam 12:22). There was just no other way to explain the miracles I witnessed. When we talked, I sang my song of submission to do His will with His guidance and protection, but that was not idle words. I counted on Him, like I trusted to withhold with each promise. *He hears my prayers* (Ps 55:17). I didn't have to check in and tell Him when I just plugged in. *This is what the Lord says; that is what you are thinking, and I know the thoughts that arise in your mind* (Ezekiel 11:5). He knew, because He was always with me.

By the time the inmates returned to their housing units when the yard closed, I had eleven violations logged into my pocket notebook against Inmate Steele. He got the message. This officer was no fish!

"Hi Sarg. I spent the last two hours logging in eleven Disciplinary Violations against Inmate Steele with every response. How would you like me to handle this?" I called my supervisor after the fact, but I didn't allow him to answer. "I'm about to write up a report for his permanent file to describe his behavior housed inside a level-three yard." I knew exactly what that meant, and my supervisor knew exactly what would happen on the rest of an inmate's stay.

I was still hot under the collar. I'd been fuming when I called the supervisor and I dropped it in his lap. The administration's paper-pushers couldn't have had a clue about the amount of the disciplinary reports, which were supposed to be cut back by the CO front lines of the inmates. DOC should've been aware of how many other Disciplinary Violations were already overlooked, before I was told that I was expected to be restricted even further.

I didn't hold back. I spewed it all out about how I singled out Inmate Steele's issues, who affected the remaining inmates directly under my care. I wanted to tell my supervisor about how nice the inmates could've had it under my watch, until I was robbed from an important tool of management for something else. I blurted out to disclose everything, including my mistakes. A lot of the policies were wagered the hot and humid condition in the runs, and how I'd cut in some slack, which wasn't about misconduct. I already had any number of options which I'd negotiated into each peaceful resolution, except for Inmate Steele. I spilled my soul. I had him to appreciate the situation, but Inmate Steele was unable to be satisfied. He grew even more demanding, when he got the wrong idea to believe that I was too lenient. I'd reached that limit, when I exposed the flip side, as if I had met the match, and then, I was too nervous to continue. I worried and accepted the blame I caused, when I groped out for help.

I laid it out to show my supervisor for the next step. *He must do honest work with his own hands, so that he has something to share with anyone in need* (Eph 4:28). I didn't deny a thing when I refused to apologize, who flippantly thumbed his nose at authority. I deserved some gratitude, and all the while, my supervisor just listened. I needed to put an end to Inmate Steele's boisterous behavior, and my unconventional 'old school style' management didn't seem to shake Sgt. Borton.

Unbeknown to me, Inmate Stiles was a common name throughout the frustrations among my supervisors who rotated my post's reassignment, which was specifically saved for me of the job. DOC had already been familiar with his situation. Inmate Steele had a lot of problems, who were passed throughout any number of the other COs' history.

"Send him up here," Sgt. Borton said, when I was eager to be lifted from my load and onto him.

"Steele!" I called into the run, which was a safe distance heard though my control room, and I watched him fidget. He was looking all over his bunk, wondering what else he could possibly be doing wrong, again. It took almost a minute later before he stepped up to my fenced in area where I waited. The stony glare was just close enough to continue in a more civil tone. "The Sergeant wants to talk to you. He's in the yard office. You better hurry up because formal count starts in twenty minutes," I added, indicating that any delay would be another policy breach, 'so consider the serious consequences', which was understood.

The claims were filed against me from the start, when I remembered how I had to explain myself. *Do not repay anyone evil with evil. Try to do what is honorable in everyone's eyes* (Romans 12:17). The options of my discretions were within limits. But Inmate Steele got out of hand! Did I feed him to cut it some slack and let him adjust, when enough was enough and I pulled back? Did I offend Steele when I went too far? Did he know when 'no' was disregarding my boundaries, or did he help himself, regardless of what didn't belong to him? I owned my own efforts, but who robbed me, realizing just how much remained too familiar, weakened physically and mentally?

Just because I honored my moral stand, the rules and policies were mostly about the boundaries, and its consequences. *For government is God's servant for your good* (Romans 13:4). Compassion was more important to maintain fairness, when defensiveness wasn't necessary any longer. Coercing drama created or distorted the truths of the most innocent and basic root at the beginning that added the slightest hint of doubt, and the entire issue had to be a fabricate lie. It was no good anymore, when imprisonment was fused as one, until I had everything there to sort out seen or hidden.

Inmate Steele was proudly puffed up and fully callous all by himself, but Inmate Steele's behaviors weren't that differently, who could explain it with my supervisor. I couldn't make any affect any more, who could argue against what I did or say. I was no longer going toe to toe. Inmate Steele had an undeniable change to convince and turn him around, but all the other inmates were meant to see what I couldn't handle anymore.

Did I over react? I treated him, just like he treated that overly harsh and equally loud mouth for the match. I took the most disrespectful on the chin and let him feel what he did to me, and then, I threw it back in the face of DOC's rules to ask another option. Dropping paper was limiting with that last straw for DOC's good look, when I failed the situation.

I saw how my family were in the same situation under DOC: I was there when sat among my fellow COs during briefing when my Shift Commander wanted more from me. Their inundated reports needed another manner of discipline. And in contrast, hearsay never had anything written down, which twisted me around that worked by my family's LOP call to disprove it otherwise, but it worked as I held out the hope to never quit on my loved ones. So then, why were my voiced examples effective in prison? Except, nothing was proved in secrecy. The "Don't tell" rule robbed me from any authority, until I couldn't keep it quiet. Who could've disputed against everyone around every word and deed, who could've said of the same things before? Wouldn't that have proved of what to believe, when the misconstrued whispers seeded the element of doubt, which was undeniably false?

I'd been able to use what I knew through every example that reinforced discipline to grow instead of LOP, when the reverse didn't deserve each punishment during my rearing without a hearing. I sucked up its consequences that satisfied one, but the lessons saved and built it up inside to know better... later.

I learned what not to do, when the 'right thing to do' repeated most favorably... that didn't work. Sgt. Borton had what I missed, until Inmate Steele faced my supervisor's hearing alone, and no one else would cover or protected him. And, I got it too! I'd been fed to believe of the exact opposites about the prison and imprisonment. I'd been mistreated of my own loss of privilege, to be unjustly harmed: victimized of the abuse around the criminals.

If I remembered all the examples to learn from each experience of my past, I was facing an example to learn by Inmate Steele at one end that also compared it with my supervisor's ability to step up where I was not alone. Inmate Steele and I weren't done to walk away, to stew, pout, or lick my wounds... who'd intercede!

Confusion was nicely used by 'filling in the blanks', as if the rules were ever 'written between the line', but I never knew. Maybe I was a bit too naïve, gravitated to disbelieve the worse. I fell for anything, or I just couldn't believe to be snowed, deliberately fooled by real loved ones, who denied what I had. How much had been taken so horribly wrong? I had no one to persuade against what couldn't be right, when I let them be allowed from my wants. But what could I own? For how long? The taking was my habit lose.

I gave up. I quit and I had to let them continue of their choosing's, regardless. *So I gave them over to their stubborn hearts to follow their own plans* (Psalm 81:13). Even God threw his hands up, and let the Israelites believe their own delusions. Some things just were not capable to argue against them, and not me? And, my disheartening loved ones were not an issue, when Sgt. Borton was there to be resolved... for the asking. Wasn't I supposed to be resolved, before DOC?

I was exhausted in a losing battle, when I grasping at straws. *Refrain from anger and give up your rage. It can only bring harm* (Psalm 37:8). Knowing policy gave me the edge, but a lawful foundation had a starting point. Policies had all my attention on one specific inmate, while I ignored the other's violation. There was one, and not the others rebut. I didn't wince, with a bold face "right here" dare look. He saw it. I didn't have to hide or coerce their cover... or me. I wasn't equally treated, and so did the rest all around, but I wasn't ashamed about the possible double standards. I had Inmate Steele realize about flexible acceptance, when the comparisons had the differences on the job.

Of what I tolerated was ineffective. My examples were ignored. His guidance was weak in a soft word. Of 'you know nuthin' was argumentative, and the rules of policy were shallow, until I experienced him that I needed, as my supervisor had a point driven home

I took the wind out of Inmate Steele's sails from one of the most unruly street thugs returned humble in compliant after a very short meeting who faced my supervisor. But even more, the inmates of the run waited to watch his results, too. I searched my conscious to be nothing underhanded, but we all anticipated the impact... about me, until we all seemed to look up with his first step through the door of the dayroom that automatically spread a long sigh of relief.

Maybe he communicated his boundaries to be seen, heard, or acted out with his small stature, but the more he'd behaved to be the proclaimed 'King of the Hill' didn't want it anymore. His façade was all a cloak of lies with a selfish shield of protection, which I stripped him to be seen for what he was.

It was just my turn to be called in face to face with my supervisors during probation. I stood exactly on that oval rug across his desk, with two witnesses at either side of the closed door behind me. I trembled in high alert, where I endured the most challenging changes, too.

Inmate Steele wouldn't dare swing a blow to get even. Did I want to hurt him? He was caught off guard that left him fume. He couldn't fight back left so vulnerable... in fear. And didn't selfish protection and secrecy fit in the same sentences about my loved ones, who purposely ignored a point made, to leave me wonder? Was camouflage important? Was a tattoo or scar that wasn't possibly removed? Was there a partner or stooge? I saw one who was picked up for the other, as if the dirty laundry needed another change to 'get redressed', when hand-me-downs of the finest Sunday best all look so fine… camouflaged on the outside. I envied Inmate Steele, like the gated community of the whole. What's the difference? Truly, they were all in orange… for a look inside.

Did he get in my way, or was he mad when I sought him out? Was I hunting him out, or was it all about his attention who robbed his all-important presence? "Here, if you're that important, let me get that flood light to be turned in his direction!" I had to do something. It was too exhausting to be that demanding every day, when there were hundreds of the other inmates away from my job. Let them watch, but in the parody, he hated to manage that he singled me out, instead. But wasn't that sounding like the 'victim'? Surely, I didn't need to compete with him! But did I need someone else stepped up of the next thing better, too? God?

Inmate Steele appeared to be gung-ho aggressive, when I looked more like the mealy mouse victim who was in the exact opposite. I just didn't want to play, and he set up every opportunity to whoop the next guy, as if I'd keep hoping it would change over time. And for the most part, was good at everyone avoiding him who wasn't making buddies. He didn't trust anyone to forge a common bond, as if he was better off, more importantly alone, too. Although, there was a few decisions to pick:

Sgt. Borton had the meeting when Inmate Steele hung his head, walking through the empty yard to hurry back to take in place for count again. He sweated to face any shift supervisor for a titled-ranking sergeant, or any other shift commander, who just happened the one I'd singled out, as if I was the lucky one who specifically chose my help.

Bucking horns to step up for the piss contest wasn't my style. I'd experienced enough as if another example started from scratch, but my supervisor already reviewed the portfolios, which I imitated to grow in return. *I exhort the elders among you: Shepherd God's flock among you, not overseeing out of compulsion but freely, according to God's will; not for the money but eagerly; not by lording it over those entrusted to you, but being examples to the flock* (1Peter 5:1-3).

I finally drove home, glad to unwind in the opposite direction, to think about the ride in the mountains, instead. The laptop was already opened, when I must've walked away from it, but the window came back up all by itself. I sat down to surf through some redeveloped land, when a low battery warning popped up undenounced to me, as if I couldn't shut it off.

I closed the windows, when my email had a number of its attachments already there. Who wouldn't welcome another look at a dream? The typical laptop was used to distract something else to think about. What else was there? Thoughts of my ride back from New Mexico popped up, as if was if it never happened not more than a week ago. Whatever stress was relieved by that long and glorious drive home, all came back like before; except I plugged in the battery to charge it up, while I'd unwind fresh and clean in my jammies.

Finally snuggled on the recliner welcomed the colorful shades of the glowing dawn never changed after another double shift. Mindlessly, I used to entertain a few easy computer games to zone out for a while, but marketing had been working in full speed ahead of my real estate search.

A single look was no mistake! Developed mountain land split a wide-open range by forty acre lots on the market, for me? The first lots of the most pristine choices were taken ahead of the best, except a buyer changed his mind for the retirement land in Colorado. The asking price was the seller's investment. He wanted a quick sale from the original listed price. It was just a picture, but it was too good to be true! My sleepy realtor sat up about details on the phone, inquiring about the high grasslands in the rolling mountains, when I committed to meet a viewing.

"Can we meet for coffee?" I asked my realtor, who seemed to be caught off guard.

"Where are you?" He seemed confused about an appointment, calculating the time and miles on the road.

"Oh, I love the nighttime drive, it's so quiet and peaceful in the night shifts schedule, so I could be timed for morning coffee." I explained but it seemed more overwhelming about the shift changes than our meeting at dawn.

I woke up and refreshed by late evening, planning a six or seven-hour drive, which was just one place to find it, mapped out on the private roads, when I was ready, and good to go!

My car ran like a charm as I headed toward the early rays of dawn, turning northward in the perfect time away from the bright sun, at the eighteen-mile marker posted at the highway, where I counted down each one. I was sure I'd find it, but the excitement grew which also accelerated, barely watching out for the upcoming traffic. I was reliving the dream, as if every minute unfolded what I imagined. Yet, my ride was peaceful, and I remained wide open, where we met at the side of the shoulder.

"Hello, Charles?" I greeted my realtor parked in the opposite direction.

"Follow behind less than a half mile up the road side." He called out who'd turn around the state highway, but it was impossible for me to watch the hairpin road signs ahead. My heart raced to heed of the road's speed and hidden turns, but oh the view! It was fabulously gorgeous, and inside I giggle uncontrollably. I couldn't barely keep a straight face. I was drawn in, invited just a little further to see it for myself, which I slowed it down by his tail lights to extend his safety... and his back bumper.

He was a salesman, but his footwork was already done. I was already taken. Giving Him "thanks" acknowledged everything laid before me. How could I possibly expect God to believe what I saw? It was in every other direction, where I wasn't even interested to see anything else. I already knew. It was already there!

Six miles was well scraped and culverted into nature's path as he sparsely pointed his arm from the window, later talking about the local HOA specifications to both restrict and show off each piece of paradise. The electric poles did not exist where the green boxes marked each drive way, which the blue poles capped a well on each lot, too. He talked like a salesman, but I couldn't listen. I didn't need to be told what I had on the list! … for a closing offer.

CHAPTER 20

Trust what you Believe

I sowed the 'seeds' of thought that held my head high for all to see. "It's a cover-up." I explained. "I am no rose bud where I'm now in full bloom."

I laughed long with my curious few, who seemed to appreciate the change from the something sweet and fragile, like my lined pots sprouted from seed that finally matured, as if I reaped the benefits of everything I owned... tended on my kitchen ceil. *Let the lowly be exalted* (James 1:9). When, nothing more was needed to be said.

The following day informed our unit to be been locked down. There were two inmate-on-inmate fights at each side of the yard for the hospital. That meant, the remaining inmates were on my watch, who'd been confined inside all day. I greeted them by name with my initial security checks, as guys and fellas passed along their bunks. That's what they were to me, although I never forgot them to belong in the state prison units.

Most of the time, I walked down the center isles where I allowed all the space possible through another quick check for anything unusual. I kept my service log current, and it wasn't uncommon for me to stay inside the runs, while I talked to one or two inmates along the way, too. I spent a few moments as I picked up one thing, a concern of another, or I might've stopped to admire the progress of a hand-crafted item, which I genuinely appreciated their talents. However, that day I also detected to listen of something else more intently. The emotional climate was uneasy down each run.

Most of the time there wasn't much I could do anything differently. They just wanted to be told, or heard by one or another. *For where envy and selfish ambition exists, there is disorder and every kind of evil, without favoritism and hypocrisy. And the fruit of righteousness is sown in peace by those who cultivate peace* (James 3:16-17). A lot of the officers went in and got out as soon as they could, and rightfully so. But many times, we were warned and recommended to have a fellow officer paired up, to watch our backs. No one had to ask, when we assumed the orders. DOC felt it was more important to leave one side of the housing unit's control room posts together. The near fully staffing rosters were like before, but no one had to know whether I doubled up to fill the rosters, when I still carried over the previous shifts, too.

It was the job anyone took my back, when I relied more than anyone else on God, Himself. I took whatever I got on the job as if my fellow officers dismissed it, blowing off warnings, while I suspected even more. I didn't complain who wouldn't dare whine with a brave face, but I didn't feel the same way. I remained the sole officer anyways, as if the inmates were locked in, abandoned safe enough, but I walked in with every check. The restless inmates could've had its factors to be concerned. DOC didn't explain the details, but I felt a well-received warning, who established my well-known inmates kept inside. The boundaries were understood, while I knew my responsibility. *They think it strange that you do not run with them, speaking evil of you* (1Peter 4:4).

Shortly after we were dismissed from briefing to be posted-up into the next day, felt like I held onto the a hundred at their reigns with a whip kept handy at the hip to cooperate all together.

A handful were allowed outside of the runs to maintain the yard. That in itself was hopeful to trust a the few specific inmates more than happy, like when the refreshed water jugs and its wind-blown trash collected the day as usual, but they couldn't ignore any simply measure of control. The protocols had a slow and methodical exercise, which allowed the inmates to be turned out, who I held back each specific building for chow; except my runs were fed dead last. It wasn't rocket science to figure out, but I also understood about the inmates stressing behind an anxiety fix. He was craving a cigarette.

"Do you know how to blend in?" I tempted Inmate Sayers, as if I dangled his carrot just within reach who waited so long, but I should've thought before speaking. How could I take it back? I swallowed hard, asking His mercy to fill in my shortcomings, or bless the inmates' in His grace, when I saw compassion in their eyes.

Inmate tobacco and paper rolls didn't have a hint by any sense of smoking inside. Inmate Sayers insisted that he'd be right back, with a promise. I bled for them when I was proud who remained inside, as I peeked out to watch one building after another folding out accordingly. I walked away to reassess another slight breach against policy, but Inmate Sayers wondered 'if only', and what he could do? I could've just said a flat "no". He patiently waited, but an hour would've been the last building; except for those few inmates still working outside.

He didn't just jump up and assume I'd be handy to make things all better. Another group were timed apart each run by the other housing buildings who passed by, but even the whiff in the air was evident. That urge took hold, when even I knew how long fifteen minutes felt more like hours. He saw one inmate firing up at the electric lighters who strolled by with that final drag once they returned to their runs. No body pushed, or stepped in front of the other, when some didn't need to eat at all.

How nice it must've been who finally broke their fast, but Inmate Sayers' had been fixated through the elongated and narrow window at his bunk, and he just had to ask. As long as they'd move, there was no rush unless their cigarettes seemed to flaunt back or look so pleased, which was even a few times around the yard's designating path before they came back to their runs.

"Don't stand in front of my building and come right back in when you're done." I started to spell out my rules. Did I learn about manipulation? It wasn't their turnout for chow yet, when I started to plan it out together. I wouldn't see let them stand in front of our building, which would've been announced over the loud speakers all though the yard that validated the inmates who didn't belong. The COs were supposed to stay on top of things, as I'd avoid a red flag, explaining it to my supervisor, later.

I'd bent the rules when a little wiggle could've allowed, as if there were no secrets in prison, and anyone could've barters to swap out a skew message to be passed along… as if locking down in the medium and lowest risk level of the hardened criminals followed protocol, who walked all over the yard. DOC was the one in charge, like when I had to clean my plate that was bound to flare up throughout the night, unless a sibling could've allowed it to be scraped off in the dog bowl to take it out myself, and nobody would interfere DOC… to stay out of the way.

"Don't go all out at one time! Stager yourselves. I don't care how many of you need a smoke, just please let me know you're back before you leave for the next one." And, not one inmate caused me any trouble. "I'll pat you down in the dayroom." I knew how embarrassing I'd also find everything to see that there was nothing of my searches. "I'll pat you all over again before you back in."

But what if I missed something? There were any number of anything else. What would I know? I could've been passing by any number of questions I'd like to know, when I noticed one inmate quickly bowed out which would have been another problem, whether they weren't smokers at all. Either way, I was satisfied. I let things slide, well before I belonged in prison. I'd been played to be the stooge, the fool, and the sacrificial victim. "My bad", I thought. As long as their needs were met, I knew how they'd appreciate the thanks, as I oddly gained more respect by the inmates, who protected me from getting any trouble, instead.

It wasn't uncommon when I monitored the inmates' movement to treated them fairly. The blame affected all inmate and officer where it earned trust across the board. I expected to stand out, knowing I was different, but I didn't have to take sides, either. Who would judge over me?

I worked within the rules while I kept from being compromised. There were some inmates who wanted to get to know me, but not that 'familiar', allowing frivolous chat, but I no further. Still it remained when some inmates longed to hear a female voice, knowing how things couldn't change that didn't really matter, but more to the point, they existed to recognize my space. And any amount of "I'm sorry" couldn't buy any room back in the fold... or my loved ones, to embrace 'the right thing to do'.

After a while I began to believe like I could fill any job. I'd been transferred and level-crossed to another post to accommodate any risk throughout the prisons to manage to stayed on the more unpredictable and unstable inmates of the lockdowns. I satisfied any number of well-versed positions, but compliancy became a factor to be mixed up, as I followed the orders.

The staffing rosters were filled throughout the complex, but the openings still welcomed the turnovers, as if DOC shook out the remaining officers to be grandfathered in the original benefits. The four classes stayed in the academy, when the satellite locations went home every night to ramp up too many COs were still coming in, where I'd plug in anywhere.

It was my job and I knew I'd survive to detest the thought, when I prayed to be spared. I hoped that I'd win some compassion in return, but the pounding stairs overused my knees, when the water just came back to work through it any worse. Maybe I was from a good stock in the genes, who'd avoided too many other fellow officers who struggled through their repair surgeries and other medical conditions, which required them some time off to heal, but that was never quite worker's compensation, as if the state budget weighted out each approval.

Surely the regular officers could've let me be to slide under the wire to sit during the suicide watches, but that would've been selfish. I sucked up to make it through my poor aging body, as I milked out every penny against the limited ankle movements for the knees. I was too far along, and too late to quit., but the passion of my career gave it my all, regardless. The best thing I could hope for was surviving every day safe and healthy, while I counted it down of own sentence toward retirement.

"Put her on transports." Lt. Gilbert promoted over the years who worked together up from CO, until he critiqued Sgt. Sommers to override my assumed post.

"Wait a minute!" I blurted it out, when he slapped his hand over the bag of key sets laid out on the head table for someone else's post that I needed to put it down. I forgot how anxious he'd climbed up the rank, but we were no longer equals. My upcoming and rising supervisor stepped aside, who immediately stepped down, and I was certainly the grunt left behind. Lt. Gilbert had a sly gloat. "I don't have a clue what that means." I said in a panic, but had to bite my tongue quickly. I had to pay attention to make it come across more respectfully.

In a darker thought, I worried. Did he intent to push my limits to disprove the fall? I might've lost the chance of the pension pay forever, forced over the edge to prematurely quit and just walk off the job. Was it just business? Or, was I an esteemed CO, seasoned and filled of the passion on the career, and all used up? Did that decision mean more money, resuming the state expense, instead?

It wasn't much more than a week earlier, when I came a little too close of insubordination. It was all about confidence, or the lack of it. Did he have to be knocked down a few notches, sucking up the orders to obey in my place? Maybe I remembered how I was singled out, and maybe I didn't want to pay that much attention to get serious at all. Or, maybe it was ridiculously frivolous, although some things were never in the policies.

There was never an issue of all the distinguished uniforms' selections in my closets, which wore like iron. We all did, as if the starch was worn more comfortably of the years, except Captain Joetage surpassed her new bars... for all to see!

And, for some grand idea passed through our uniforms. All throughout the COs needed to be inspected by each presentation in perfect (formal) Class A dress code. My size didn't change, much. I wore the other duties accordingly, but someone passed it through the Complex, which encompasses all five units. There was nothing discussed or even a simple head's up who were urgently complied. Every one of us had to parade for her to see it for herself. I couldn't tell if I misunderstood, or whether it was funny. I wanted to laugh. It seemed so preposterous. Who would expect me to come to work in 'Sunday best' attire?

A ten or twenty pounds could've made them into a laughing stock! Their high-dress uniform was an exorbitant expense by my fellow officers, but for what? It must've been something else bothering her. But even if it was needed I, or any other CO, had to be caught where the uniform store took some time to alter which was impossible to meet at that very minute, albeit all size and sale tags, aside. I no longer smiled, and I got mad that didn't sit well with my coworkers either, but all they did was grumble underneath their breaths.

I tried to argue against the order at briefing, but the 'rules are rules' before I stomped back in with the tie and all, but then I had to work the entire day on the job. I begged to come in to work on my day off, just so that I didn't have to work among the inmate's routine. Nothing. I offered when I could've run to my lieutenant's office on a day off, but she had the final call and no private approvals. I had to be on display in front of my colleagues! The day was my turn, but the uniform was a disgrace to me. Was it that insignificant? Or, was it about empowering authority?

Was it all about control... for the display to have everyone see exactly dressed accordingly? Somethings just didn't belong in the inmate field. I was supposed to come to work and no one could argue against the ranked officers. I was made to resume my post, where I also had to conduct the daily cell searches on the floor on my knees! My usual work clothes were designed to discourage the inmates against my hour-glass figure. Did I have to show the inmates' viewing, too?

I felt dishonored by the uniform, which was demeaning for the inmates who understood the parity, showing how little it mattered, when the Class A uniform fit it for the same job. What a fool I was. I'd been meticulously saved to be meant for only the most sacred uniforms of each purpose. It could've been worn for the court appearances, funerals or awards ceremonies.

And I remembered how important I had to change out of my school clothes, and into play clothes, once I came home. Every day at school, I had the same outfit to be worn my school clothes before laundry day, regardless of how dirty or clean when I had no choice. It was backwards! The play clothes were my work clothes! Didn't DOC have a choice... for show? And some of my fellow COs went well above and beyond their pressed and dry-cleaned uniforms. Didn't anybody see something off?

It wasn't any more important than my Captain's accomplishment, or her in competition. "Just let her win." I thought but I grasped how wrong that was. She argued against some consideration or its repercussions when I had nothing left, and I kept my mouth shut at that point. "I'm the lieutenant now!" Her final word sent shrills up my spine. "Just do what you're told," was what I heard. I obeyed the stand, regardless. *Submit to every human authority whether to the*

Emperor as the supreme authority or government as sent out by him to punish those who do what is evil and praise those who do what is good (1Peter 2:13). *Obey your leaders* (Heb13:17). She looked down her nose at me, visibly raising her chin in rank.

There was never meant to have a debate. I gave in, but picking my battles didn't involve just the inmates' firsthand experiences in kind, just like when I relented them for a smoke, but I'd exhausted all efforts. "My bad," I shrugged. The inmates seemed to appreciate the differences, who also recognized right from wrong. What was that message, when those things weren't allowed to understand? *Don't be afraid. Stand firm and see the Lord's salvation He will provide for you today* (Exodus 14:13).

"She's a senior officer. There's no reason she can't do this," I overheard Lt. Gilbert's undertone, who'd turned to my supervisor darted back. He was stripped powerless to say anything. *For our battle is not against flesh and blood, but against the rules, against the authorities* (Ephesians 6:12).

"Sir, I've never done transports." I said humbly, remembering that sink-or-swim mentality: "Well, you won't be able to say that anymore after today." They didn't have to say it. It was a spontaneous response echoed in jest back in the days when I actually was a fish.

"Don't tell me you never did transports in all the time you've worked here." Lt. Gilbert took a stronger stand to dismiss any excuse to reconsider.

"I did a lot of hospital transports in my first year, but nothing like that." I explained how I cut short my experience when I transferred right out of probation. I felt the first time like if I just went along with a mere guarding officer aside. I jumped at the chance, like I dropped to join in its post for a nice break, which I knew it was nothing more than an extra body or an extra uniform according to policy. I played that look of confidence, where my partner filled in, well enough for the public eye presence. That was when CO Gilbert was making his way up, except he acted like he was facing for the next captain advance, fitting his ego and no contest aside.

"Do I need to run to Complex to get a vehicle?" I didn't know which cargo van was issued to another unit. "Do I need a weapon or is chase enough? Who is going with me?" I'd always had a partner on every transport in the past, when I was nervous and hoped that he could fill me in on the duties of the job, but he didn't say anything to offer help. *No harm will come to you. For who has stood in the council of the Lord to see and hear His word? Who has paid attention to His word and obeyed?* (Jeremiah 23:17-18).

"I'll need to pick up a stab vest." I realized how my stab vest was left at home, since I was borrowed out from the open yard, but he ignored a need to show any concern. "Is he waiting in the Health Unit...or does Receiving have him in a dry cell? How many are there?"

Transports Department didn't contain the details. I rattled on, but his mind was made up to shut me out. I didn't know where to go, what to do, or anything, stressing to the point of getting angry, but I knew I had to stay respectful.

"Do you want me to wait until I have to bring him back? Where is he going?" DOC had contracts who'd fill in several local hospitals and urgent care facilities, but he couldn't have met the connections to transfer between the inmates from the lockdown unit?

"Are the escape flyers ready or do you want me to start out in the records room to get everything ready?" I could feel myself clenching my teeth. "Are they going to be strip-searched for me or am I allowed to do that now?" The thought of asking naked men to squat and cough, closely looking their butt cheeks apart, and holding up their sack of jewels would've been another first. I cringed when I realized how much worse it had been for the grown men, trying to hold onto as much pride and decency they could. Or was I evolved to separate body and mind, yet? I didn't give up easily as the questions continuously poured out of me. Surely there had to be someone better than me. And then, I finally stood at the front of the table, silent.

Sgt. Gallo put all of his focus into the advice of Lt. Gilbert, hovering over his shoulder who took all the corrections. My lieutenant uncovered his postings to hold them off, pending the additional security staff who'd drift in behind me. Usually the first cross-level stragglers, when I rushed there for the best dibs, as if the final opening deserved to take what was left, but it didn't matter that day. It was all mine without resistance. *For it brings favor, if mindful of God's will, someone endures grief from suffering unjustly* (1Peter 2:19-23).

"Go find Corbet." Lt. Gilbert gave me that eye piercing glare for just a second, demanding me to carry on. *I will instruct you and teach you in the way you should go; I will guide you with My eye* (Psalms 32:8). My pleading was not going to make any difference. It was going to be a trial-by-fire kind of day.

"Male or female sir?" I begged for something, anything, but I got nothing. Lowering my head into raised shoulders, I made my way out the door.

"Just go out to the court yard and holler Corbet." Lt. Gilbert called out to me just before I turned the corner into the corridor, still careful to make me figure it out on my own. "Man, he just got worse!" I grumbled to myself as I remembered how full-of-himself he was back when I was brand new all over again. "That's just stupid! Why insist that everyone has to reinvent the wheel? Why not share what you know!" I shook it off, preparing myself for a needy, 'stinkin' fish'. I had to clean up that attitude and bounce to the next one to help me.

"Anyone know who Corbet is?" I arrived just in time. Most of the officers were drawing that last burn of their cigarettes around the picnic table in the courtyard, about ready to go to their assigned posts.

"She's probably in the yard office." One of the officers threw an arm in the direction of a door clearly marked *Yard Office* that used to be a Supplies Room ajar from the automatic lock on the inside.

"Corbet?" I poked halfway into the door. "I'm a cross-level from Cook Unit and I was posted on Transports." I waited for her to look up. "Ma'am, I have no clue was that means." I pleaded for some support. "The lieutenant told me to talk to you." It wasn't that I didn't want to do the job. I just didn't like to feel inept and vulnerable.

"Why the hell did he post you on Transports?" Her angst actually appreciated it in return. She was expressing exactly how I felt. As soon as she put her work aside, I stepped back and cleared the way. "Wait here," she said, immediately stomped across the courtyard, where I left the supervisors in their briefing room.

My heart pounded as I tried to act nonchalant, abandoned in the courtyard filled with the lingering aroma of the still-smoldering butts pail, tripping that desire for just one long drag. For just a moment I understood how the inmates would've scouted in the trash.

"Actually, you're posted in the kitchen."

I jumped out of that nicotine hold to shake it off. She didn't waste time, or mince words, quick to correct me when she returned, and I didn't blame her for being curt. The yard dog expected my supervisors to chase her down. She could've fumed, but she addressed it who resolved right there and then, knowing her a precious commodity of self-control directed to the right person on the job. "Just the facts, ma'am" was the right attitude to just feed what I needed, but I also pressed her patience, coming in without a plan to add her stress load.

"Go to Main Control. They'll give you the key sets you'll need. Take the van and bring back the kitchen workers from West Unit. They'll know what to do. When they're done, you'll be taking them home and you'll be picking up the night crew around 1900 hours." She was not happy but at least she did not take it out on me.

"Do I need to take my car to Complex?" I didn't know whether DOC's fleet was kept at the Complex as needed, or whether the transport van carried over to the prior shift drivers.

"We have a few vans parked next to administration. One of the key sets will have a chit with a license plate number on it." I nodded, remembering the different lock-boxes lined the wall of Main Control.

"Who's coming with me?" I always took transports with a partner, weapons, restraints and chase because graves transports were typically used for the medical ER visits.

"You'll be doing this alone. West Unit is a low-level yard. You won't have anything to worry about." I probably had that look of panic across my face which she read very well.

"Where's West Unit?" I was getting frustrated. I didn't even know DOC about West Unit outside of my Complex. I wanted to move along but I didn't know anything! I felt so stupid, taking directions like if I was brand new again, but every single question was thoughtfully answered. She understood. She remembered how hard it felt.

"You'll do fine. You just need to make sure they don't go anywhere or do anything they shouldn't be doing." I was nervous on strange grounds full of fear and anxiety of another risk level unit before, but CO Corbet built me up with the self-assurance and confidence which I badly needed. With that, I was on my way.

I found my vehicle, a twelve-passenger cargo van, and when I sat in the driver's seat, I had to laugh. I stretched my neck all around. There was no way I was going to be able to back that thing out of its parking spot! Then, I noticed tire tread marks beyond the paved parking lot. "I can do this." I pumped myself up, repeating the directions to myself as I almost bounced through the ruts and back onto the paved perimeter path, hanging onto the steering wheel while I landed back into the seat. I glanced the perimeter gate rolling closed behind me, knowing the camera screens timed their eyes on me.

His alarm lights were secured, through the rear window to watch. "Check!" I said to myself.

The officer at a traffic control booth made sure my escape flyers were resting on the passenger seat in order, and in a moment, I was driving down the road to a neighboring prison complex. The entire trip was all of about ten miles towards town, as I repeated the directions to myself, as if every marker at the road sides welcomed a new destination. I was told to watch out for it, when my two-way radio cut out. My heart stopped. I was out of range. Of all the questions I had, there always seemed to be something else left out, too late.

I headed for another prison to pick up four inmates, with no radio or cell phone, no restraints, and no weapons of imprisonment controls. I was alone without so much as a partner, or chase vehicle following behind me. Dwarfed behind, I steered a caged vehicle with no ability to contact anyone until I reached the 'back door'. Whatever I was told was all I had to go on. I had no choice. Orders were orders. *Lean on the power of God, not the wisdom of man* (1 COR 2:3-5).

Oh, there's more! My route took across the stretch of the back-roads when I noticed the gas gauge was less than an eighth of a tank. Pangs of fear spiked where there was no room for error… with the inmates in tow!

I had to count on their sally port just like any other gate entrance behind the prison, but I was wrong, again. There was nothing but a locked gate facing a public road. There was no double-gated sally port, in fact, there wasn't even an officer assigned at the entrance! *That* was what she meant when she told me to press the button on the squawk box to pick up the inmates. I announced my arrival, and then, I waited. Everything was planned, and the routine was as usual.

I was parked in the driveway and wondered if they'd let me drive out for gas, but I knew that a transport wouldn't tempt an escape. Do they even have gas inside, against DOC? I had no wallet and didn't come into work with any money anyways. Fifteen minutes passed, twenty minutes later, and I had to make the decision. Could I leave it running to use the air conditioner and take the chance on empty? What if I could've been stranded on the side of the road with four inmates in the back? Imagine the engine killed, baked behind ninety-five degrees of the late August days of summer.

I prayed. I actually prayed as if God Himself had enough gas to let the engine run! I was no good suffering from heat exhaustion and then, a half an hour later, where the side door of my van slid open for the four inmates to have a seat without any help, since they were not restrained with any cuffs. I nonchalantly fingered my key set and I promptly locked them inside, while two other sets hung from my belt clip. Having access to that many keys seemed to give me a sense of importance, as if "I meant it that way". I did my best to play the part, while I forced to fake it for survival sake. In hindsight, the inmates were good at reading people, seeing how hard I'd regain that sense of confidence once it was lost.

I overheard the inmates talking to 'floor that thing', as if I was the ol' grandma teased in return to watch out of everyone safely, when I arrived. The lockdown's crash barrier was quite differently through the double 'no man's perimeter', slowing stopped for the search, which would be more thorough on the way out.

"Hey there, Moreno," felt so good to see a fellow officer and friend from a few years back. "Lt. Gilbert put me in charge of Transports, so I brought four inmates from West Unit to work in the kitchen. Do you want them taken to Receiving?" I remembered that there was a strip shack next to that door, but mostly I was buying time to look around and find my bearings. "Who do I pick up next?"

"Oh, you won't have another trip until seven o'clock of so." I thought I'd be driving the whole time. "You'll be following these guys around while they do their work. Then you'll take 'em home and pick up the night crew before the next formal count." He had no idea how good it felt to hear the next part of my job from him so

I didn't have to hunt down Officer Corbet for more, blow-by-blow instructions.

"Hey!" I made a quick about-face before reaching the steering wheel to lift myself back into the van. "I'm almost out of gas."

"No, you're not. That gauge never worked. There's plenty in there." He laughed at me as if he'd seen that panic in someone else doing transports before.

"Great," I said with a double meaning and I rode the van behind CO Moreno to the back door of the kitchen tarmac.

All four inmates went right to work, as if I trusted them to do what they were hired to do. I expected to get played, and I was right, but I also allowed it. They got away, using lockdown's supplies, until they also tested to see what was ever enough… and I even told them for the milk and cookies! I just didn't realize that the cookies disappeared from the food trays prepared for the officers.

Taking the four inmates back to West Unit was easy. I knew where it was and what to expect. I returned with my empty cargo van that started all over again, but picking up the next challenge was not all cut-and-dried. I was sent to every inmate at any risk level. I climbed into vehicles to operate any one of them. I validated every piece of DOC's equipment, right down the last bullet to make sure nothing was hidden aimed at me… at any level. And when I accepted every post, I went home feeling completed, after I missed a few things, nonetheless.

There was no shame in not knowing something, and who would judge? We were all leaning on each other, as if knowing growing pain was expected that wasn't bad. Someone would catch me, where sacrifice encourages and bring out the best in the other. Even if I wouldn't have asked, my partner would not have allowed us to be put in harm's way. The consequences would've been too harsh, too severe and uncalled for. It didn't matter what level of security an inmate was classified, as if the inmates were the only opportunists. DOC policies had that leg up, but there was a stronger gut feeling.

The perimeter vehicle arrived with an officer carrying a 9mm pistol, loaded and hot on his hip, where the loaded shotgun rested on the passenger's side floor, never fired or expected to use it. I sat in my caged van with an inmate penned inside the sally port, but I had enough coverage. The paper trail and cameras manned my DOC family with my back, and I was no longer scared. The outer perimeter gate rolled opened as chase backed away to allow me to drive out in front of him. Our new addition would not be treated as a lower risk inmate until he was issued a bunk to be housed by the lowest level unit a violent criminal could hope for.

I also swapped out for the kitchen crew who were stripped out and ready for the ride to the maximum-security unit, who followed the menus to serve the others still remained in isolation. Their shackles weren't needed, but the chase vehicle followed closely behind. I was the job and nobody complained, but I knew and so did they! All twelve inmates had to methodically climb that vehicle, and I didn't say a thing, as I drove off with the packed vehicle... for another day.

Whoever said, "rules are more like guidelines" couldn't have said it better. The only time policies really seemed to matter when something went wrong and the policies were used to point the finger. That phrase, "thrown under the bus," kept most of us in line. There was always someone to take the blame. Other than learning how to suck it up and take one for the team, the best defense was to do the right thing in the best way possible. In fact, doing the right thing took a lot of strength, to take pride... for the team! *Since we have died to what held us, so that we may serve in the new way of the Spirit, and not in the old letter of the law* (Romans 7:6). *So then, with my mind I myself am a slave to the law of God, but with my flesh, to the law of sin* (Romans 7:25).

I did not quit the career in DOC because I struggled and it was just too much. Quite the contrary, I wasn't weeded out of the loved-ones to look the other way like an imprisoned victim... for the calling away from the hold. *For My yoke is easy, and My burden is light* (Matt 11:30). Distrust was used by every threat. I lived on high alert in fear behind every lie, but simple honesty dissolved away the undeniable facts. *Therefore, don't be afraid of them since there is nothing covered that won't be uncovered and nothing hidden that won't be made known* (Matt 10:26), but I'd habitually excused to forgive where there was nothing to argue to make the stand. *There is no justification that we can give as a reason for this disorderly gathering* (Acts 19: 40).

I felt every blow, which was against God's will. I couldn't have been more wrong, who couldn't convince away from the career, where I saw through the fog to keep me from knowing what I couldn't be denied from me, when the word 'shunned' twisted it around to make it feel better.

It was so hard to understand. I thought was expected to behave subservient, when others took all the glory. I watched my loved ones rise to the top, as if I'd cheer and celebrate them to lean on me, but it was not anything noble. Loyal support robbed my joy through their abuse, when I joined the incarcerated prison to show the examples which I had them about right and wrongs who couldn't get away… face to face of the missing criminals.

I thought that God meant to call the holy sacrifices, but that was before I read the Bible for myself. *The Angel of the Lord encamps around those who fear Him, and rescues them. Taste and see that the Lord is good, who takes refuge in Him* (Psalm 34:7-8,9), until it really was my turn, wearing my rightfully crowned glory, and openly exposed His example to live in my care. *The Lord is near. Don't worry about anything, let your requests be known to God* (Philippians 4:6). I was signed up to begin at the academy, but I vowed to God through Christ's persecutions, to get up and walk!

CHAPTER 21

Move light!

$\mathcal{A}$ week had come and gone as family time filled my work. All around the people slipped by. The priorities settled in each DOC team who balanced in the community, where I'd imagine the greatest aspirations, *dwell on these things* (Php 4:8). I stood aside to see the bustles all around where I enjoyed their own agendas, when I'd step a true emergency or whether I'd run up as needed. It could've been the adults who watched over the children, or the sounds of an ambulance that quickly pulled over, when I'd never impose on others.

Every extravagance had my wildest desires. *No one will snatch them out of My hand* (John 10:28). It was no harm/no foul, until I got serious... to get real. *If they serve Him obediently, they will end their days in prosperity and their years in happiness* (Job 36:11). What could it had been the most elaborate riches, hope against hope? How could I believe above and beyond my ability, when I finally laid down my all? *Therefore, I will most gladly boast all the more about my weaknesses, so that Christ's power may reside in me* (2Cor 12:9) for a miracle!

I looked over my income and savings, optimistically pushing toward a respectful life in the golden ages, but the comparison in the mountains looked bleak, when I asked, "What do You think" and I waited His reply.

It would require a huge commitment, knowing that I could change my mind and let it go within the forty-eight hours of the law. But God? I'd surrendered all of my financial means all through my entire life that had too many false starts before. *Woe to him who dishonestly makes wealth for his house to place his nest on high, to escape from the reach of disaster!* (Habakkuk 2:9). His words would spit in my face by turning down God, when immediately I fell in ashamed. The word 'if' was conditional in the Bible, and His promises never changed, when the worry was the insult I deserved. My trust in God had been proven of His love when I rebuked all fear in His name!

Humble yourselves, therefore, under the mighty hand of God, so that He may exalt you at the proper time, casting all your care on Him, because He cares about you (1Peter 5:6). I swallowed hard. *I want you to insist on these things, so that those who have believed God might be careful to devote themselves to good works* (Titus 3:8).

It was always hard when I sat on the fence. *For God is not the author of confusion* (1Cor 14:33). What chance did I have? I must've been ecstatic for God, when I been cut down which would've helped myself to be set up toward failure. *Reject divisive men after the first and second admonition* (Titus 3:10) I couldn't make the stand, which was taken away... against God! Did I make the decision, or did God? I was afraid to go from there, who wouldn't believe in me.

Resentment fueled my anger. I would cringe. I was right back to behave, to heal and recover later, knowing my loved ones couldn't own up or amend an apology. "Why should I forgive them anymore?" I cried out to my Father. It felt like the gossip wildfires couldn't be put out with a spoon, which was bound to grow out of hand. It was too big for me, and I'd just get hurt, knowing there was nothing able to deal. I granted forgiveness, except second chances evolved into another title, who'd go from the victim to the code-pendent, with no desire to reconcile.

There was no other way to put it. I was locked into imprison-ment. Unless I had to enter DOC's career, when I understood why they tried so hard to talk me out of going 'there'! I couldn't be kept from the law enforce career, and I went anyways, who'd watch me fail and finally kicked to the curb, nonetheless. Was I that bad? Did I ruin our family bond? But how could I manage the inmates to maintain its peace and not my family? Was walking away, toward what I'd wanted, who didn't want me to have?

Even the lockdowns understood isolation, knowing God came there with me. Except everything transparent in prison, nobody would talk to me about what they believed. Were they hiding... from me? But even a knee jerk reaction was glad to discuss among each other... formulating another opinion, but not me.

I worried to build the house in the mountains' retirement, who wouldn't expect me to get what I would lose. Their unholy secrets seeded the threats under fear that would never end, and the prisons were closely controlled to complete their sentences. How far could I hide from the sins, knowing the blessings weren't meant for me? I admitted or carried the blame, nonetheless.

"Thinking big was irrational," I prayed His mercy to bear with me. I wallowed in my tears to accept the facts. I faced my lim-ited means. I should have resorted for less than I deserved, as if it was my fate. Every paycheck had been turned over, surrendered to my spouses, my families, my loved ones freely. They believed to expect what I entrusted, which I rationalized the needs of my children on the cusp of poverty, because of me. My results had the opposite of greed, when I just ran out who got mad and turned their backs of its usefulness.

Anything substantial had nothing left to reclaim in return. Gracious submission was simply relinquished by my sacrifices.

They should've been appreciative, who stripped me powerlessness. *They will exploit you in their greed with deceptive words* (2 Peter 2:3). My innate beliefs, morals, and sound decisions evolved through their mockery. I was exploited who couldn't come together, except anything else but God.

"What was that glorious drive home all about?" I complained, afraid that I would be found out, who'd degrade it with another example of failure. *You must not follow a crowd in wrongdoing, for favoritism* (Exodus 23:2,3). Although, I tried to act like it didn't matter as if sarcastic martyrdom spelled across my chest.

God doesn't work like that! "Get behind me Satan!" I directed my anger where it belonged. *"Get behind Me, Satan! You are an offense to Me because you're not thinking about God's concerns, but man's."* (Matthew 16:23), using another memory:

I came in with a full bed sized quilt spread over the living room floor, when I called ma in to see what I did. I wanted to show it off, which was strictly made from the samples left behind the fabric lines in my quilt shop. My fabric couldn't throw them away and years later, I spent its swatches worked into my artistic skill. But, "What do you do, wasting all that time with your life?" as I wrapped it up. I had nothing to say.

In the next visit, my ma had her guest bed for me to come and see. Ma worked together with Janet to purchase its yardage from my competitor's store, who finished it in a weekend. Did I do something wrong?

Concerning my help to prosper, rose above with His courage. I stepped forward to believe wisely again. *Let those who want my vindication shout for joy and be glad; let them continuously say, "The Lord be exalted. He takes pleasure in His servant's wellbeing." And, my tongue will proclaim Your righteousness, Your praises all day long* (Psalms 35:27). If I believed in His Word, I had to believe everything I read to be true! Amen means, that's that. I laughed, satisfied inside as I wiped the tears from my face.

"Are you done?" God was ready. "Come!"

But I had one more thing. "When I 'come', did I turn my back knowing what's behind me?" And then I understood. I faced Him in one direction that was limiting, while Thee Omniscient Lord was all around. What I missed, humbly laid down my all before Him, when He added. Asking for ALL SIN was not my all, which was only a portion! I couldn't respond. I had to think about that. There was sin all around... full of the accused felons in the prisons?

I opened the internet on my laptop. My steaming brew settled down for a look at the forty-acre plots in the foot hills of New Mexico, and the land responded that offered almost 50% less than the neighbors. They must've been jealous! *You will weep and lament while the world rejoices but your sorrow will turn to joy which no one will take from you* (John 16:20). The first picks' took one of the finest locations who counter-offered, as if it was saved for me?

I couldn't resist, when I accepted the salesman's appointment. I was compelled, knowing His hand urged me to hurry.

"What do you trust? Don't think about it. Do it!" My soul was connected when I understood. *"Lord God, how can I know that I will possess it?"* (Genesis 5:8). I jittered, like I couldn't sit down for even a second. I was all fired up, anxious, and full of energy. There was no need to hesitate, when I shed away all doubt. *Don't worry about how you should defend yourselves or what you should say* (Luke 12:11). I was called by and for my Lord, simply submitted in God's assurance. I was filled in pure joy, Who extended my permission, asking of me! *Take delight in the Lord, and He will give you your heart's desires* (Psalm 37:4).

It was like everything drowned out the trumpets, strong but not loud. It was like His invitation was on one knee Who spread for His arms wide opened, as I ran in full speed in His embrace! Holy elation overflowed that couldn't be contained! It was ready... prepared for and by God, NOW!

It was no coincidence! What I found online was no accident. Every fiber of my body had the undeniable power of God through me. *So that you will have success in everything you do, and that you will carry out His promise that He made to me* (1Kings 2:3,4). I was a selected, a personal miracle, and living testimony!

Nothing could stop me, knowing it wasn't my decision... of His will! A gas station and a cup of coffee didn't have anything to pack, and I took off. My car hummed without so much as a hint of trouble, Who never lost sight in completely assuring of the entire drive. I rushed, screaming inside to hurry up and open His gifts... locked onto His free-flowing smile upon me.

I understood the word *ask* throughout the stories of Jesus' walk on Earth, and in so many ways. I tilted my head of the scenery at the driving wheel, which was just as natural to see through His eyes. I didn't need to be told where I'd look, just like I was able to touch out and connect without dialog for His understanding!

Each verse in my heart scanned to know, when God the Father wanted my commitment. He wanted me to come, boldly and without doubt, of the same Savior and Lord Jesus Christ and *'ASK'*! There was no time and any more questions, **to believe it!**

"Abba, I want this," I whispered as tears even flooded down my face. *Until now, you have asked for nothing. Ask that your joy may be full* (John 16:24). I finally realized a love I craved so desperately.

How many times since I held out, when He was always right there for someone else. I stretched out to appease my loved ones, who came short. Trying it another time, lured in by another empty promise that was never meant to be. The love I offered was cruelly rejected too often, instead. I truly was so blinded, where I completely missed each pearl's worth.

My emotions fluctuated all throughout the trip, and how I'd broken His heart. Empathy felt each sin of what was always promised in the first place. Those double messages, misguided, or subtly twisted each poke, when I recoiled like an injured animal licking every wound, but I'd been hurting my Lord! I did that to Him! I sought out and chased after my loved ones, but I completely missed out on Him, instead.

"I am so sorry," I whispered my heartfelt remorse. Yet surprisingly, He was not mad at me at all! I was relieved, and happiness was in store for me. Then, I was reminded.

"Hey... get that list!" That day dream was more than an exercise to expand my aspirations... for real. The prodigal son squandered all of his inheritance for his father's sacrifices... and I was greeted back with opened arms. He cried in his relief, and I cried who knew each tear, Who was gladly back home, when I too crawled back emptyhanded.

And then there was the story about two debtors who were forgiven when they owed it, and Jesus asked *which one, then, loved him more? "I suppose the one who was forgiven much."* Simon replied. '*You have answered correctly*; (Luke 7:42-43). It was never His will to have me hurt or feel the pain, but He was there to fix things for the good every time. *All things will work together for the good for those who love the Lord* (Rom 8:11).

Everything written in my notebooks, used my examples for something good! There was nothing to be ashamed of. There was no one to be angry anymore. There was nothing left but gratitude! EVERYTHING that happened *to* me, happened *for* His results. *And, not only that, but we also rejoice in our afflictions, because we know that affliction produce endurance, endurance produces proven character, and proven character produces hope* (Romans 5:3-4).

I never was going to make sense out of anything, until I read the Bible like a good Friend, Who was always explained for me. I came into the world of flesh born into the family, as people grew who extended into another family. *I chose you before I formed you in the womb; I set you apart before you were born* (Jr 1:5), when God took over, as if the spoon gently weaned onto meat. I finally cut my teeth, as if I was fed to be satisfied in Father's basic principles: *Who consider it a pleasure, delighting in their deceptions as they feast with you!* (2 Peter 2:13,14). *The Lord knows how to rescue the godly from the trials and keep the righteous under punishment until the day of judgement* (2 Peter 2:9). I couldn't worry once how differently I struggled. *My yoke is easy, My burden is light* (Matt 11:30). I was never going to fit... against my better judgement.

At the academy I was told: "If you want to know the future, look into the past. If you want to change the future, don't repeat the past," as I asked myself how I could use the prisons' training grounds on a job, where I could break the cycle. *For it would have been better not to have known right from wrong, than having known and returned from the holy command delivered to him* (2 Peter 2:21).

People were contained by the prisons, who were just like me. I lived, who were banned by the gangs, cliques, or family to be somewhere else. Some spent a short stay in jail that amped up in the maximum security... but by whom? Each risk level accommodated to fit any name, stripes, or label at either side. *Associate with anyone who claims to be a believer who is sexually immoral or greed, an idolater or verbal abusive, drunker or swindler. What business is it of mine to judge, but God judges outsiders.* (1Cor 5:10-12). I saw the inmates preying on each other, who couldn't notice how crafty and clever they secretly envied one over another, and it was the same things on either side of the wall.

But I lived a guarantee to be cut free, when I counted down the final release date. Retirement was time, and I was about to close the decision. I envisioned to cut loose. I thought about the imprisoning restrains of walls and chains that kept an eye on the inmates, like freedom set me free in the mountains to wait just a little longer, and my wings were almost ready in my cocoon before flight!

The deed on the land was handed to me... to build a new beginning. It felt like the final sprint couldn't end fast enough toward the end of the race. It felt like I could stop burning the candle at both ends, when I wanted to slow down and spend the rest of my life... during recess.

I played to sketch my floor plan, with and extra sliding door for its easy access through a short cut to the bathroom. Another outside door could plan a future gazebo from my sewing room, too. I reviewed the HOA's limitations that included the landscape for its fence from the wildlife, where New Mexico water approved each homeowner to be limited with one acre that satisfied every tree, bush, and garden accepted on my list.

I hired the architect professionals supporting its structure, when the copies were reviewed to meet the bank and general builders within the budget. The State inspectors monitored the licenses with each project forward, one step at a time, and papers signed off the plan.

I paid the décor fans and its fixtures aside, as I opened the home loan account for each receipt to pace the costs, including mileage and labor. If there was anything overlooked or discussed its wiggle room, but I knew I had the laws on my side, too.

I had it registered, but it was written down, word for word and impossible to misconstrued, while I relaxed back to watch it unfold. *The untaught and unstable twist them to their own destruction, as they also do with the rest of the Scriptures. Since you know this in advance, be on your guard, so that you are not led away by the error of lawless people, but grow in the grace and knowledge of our Lord and Savior Jesus Christ* (2 Peter 3:16,17,18), as I counted on His final decision.

Every day on the job was one day closer to live the life I deserved. I thought about how happy I'd have, and nothing to waste. I'd fill my time to enjoy every moment that would never end, to create and share. I'd replenish company on their way out, or meet the local flea markets to make some more of God's good blessings, as I'd keep some old habits!

I changed, as if a commitment was signed over to God. Total submission cut free from it to worry on the building crews on the job, knowing the promises established more than a hand shake... in His hands. He was in control, knowing the consequences remained true to believe beyond my ability, and excuse a little wiggle room to understand. My sins throughout my little white lies were ignored but not like Sunday mass missed it for a mortal sin to require Penance. The weight was taken off of my shoulders, and even my mood had been lifted higher than I imagined. "God is so good" couldn't slip out with every situation!

"What about the rest?" God asked.

"But I gave you my all, my trust, and my love. What else could it be?"

"What about ALL sin?" God's Word was no mistake.

I searched through my conscience. I looked back to think about anything I did against Him. I couldn't imagine how many conventional booths recited its confession in the Catholic religion, since I stopped in to visit confession or its expected sign of the cross. Was I just going through the motions, a living fake?

"No, my child." I felt His gentle touch. If I did something, I'd surely apologize to make up and take away any shame that I might've caused. "I want all of the sins caused against you, too." I had it all out there, nothing hidden, and nothing held out from Him either! *If we deliberately sin after receiving the knowledge of the truth, there no longer remains a sacrifice for sins, but a terrifying expectation of judgement* (Heb 10:26). *Vengeance belongs to Me, I will repay* (Heb 10:30). All of the criminals in the prison involved everybody that included all sin in His hands.

Jesus washed Simon Peter's feet, when the rest of the story help me to understood why he wanted to be completely cleaned from head to toe (John Chapter 13).

I learned of His teachings which I understood how I used my experiences, and some would never listen. *But if you will not listen to it, my soul will sob in secret for such pride* (Jer 13:17); except I broke the cycle, and that someone was me. I was the biggest cry-baby, when I turned around... the inmates.

"Are you 'Ms. or Mrs.?" It was a fair question.

"They call me CO." It was a fair answer.